The Future of
U.S. Retailing

THE FUTURE OF U.S. RETAILING

An Agenda
for the 21st Century

Edited by
ROBERT A. PETERSON

Prepared under the auspices of the IC² Institute

QUORUM BOOKS
New York • Westport, Connecticut • London

Library of Congress Cataloging-in-Publication Data

The Future of U.S. retailing : an agenda for the 21st century / edited
   by Robert A. Peterson.
      p.   cm.
      ''Prepared under the auspices of the IC² Institute.''
      Includes bibliographical references and index.
      ISBN 0-89930-679-9 (alk. paper)
      1. Retail trade—United States—Forecasting.   I. Peterson, Robert
   A.   II. IC² Institute.
   HF5429.3.F88   1992
   381'.1'0973—dc20   91-24432

British Library Cataloguing in Publication Data is available.

Library of Congress Catalog Card Number: 91-24432
ISBN: 0-89930-679-9

First published in 1992

Quorum Books, One Madison Avenue, New York, NY 10010
An imprint of Greenwood Publishing Group, Inc.

Printed in the United States of America

The paper used in this book complies with the
Permanent Paper Standard issued by the National
Information Standards Organization (Z39.48-1984).

10 9 8 7 6 5 4 3 2

Contents

Tables and Figures

TABLES

FIGURES

Preface

The Future of U.S. Retailing resulted from a unique symposium held on the campus of The University of Texas at Austin in November 1990. The uniqueness of the symposium was exhibited in four distinct ways: mission, participant composition, approach, and sponsorship.

Ostensibly, the mission of the symposium and this book was to develop a series of informed speculations about the nature and structure of retailing in the year 2000. What types of retailers will exist in the next century? How many retailers will there be? What will be the relationship between retailing and society? In particular, how will society influence the nature and structure of retailing, and how will retailing influence the nature and structure of society (a concept perhaps alien to some but not really far-fetched)?

More subtly, however, the purpose of the symposium and book was to provide an agenda for retailing leadership not only into the next millennium, but in the present decade as well. Leadership can only be achieved by possessing and successfully executing a vision. But a vision, by definition, is a normative view of the future—how things "should be" at some point in time, whether near or distant—and such a vision can be achieved only by peering into the future, constructing alternative scenarios of the future, considering present options, and carrying out those requisite activities that will ensure that the vision will "come true." This book provides a framework or foundation for simultaneously developing scenarios of the future and present-day options for retailing leadership.

The recipe underlying the symposium was simple. Identify individuals who collectively could circumscribe present retailing knowledge, yet provide insights into retailing in the future. Provide a conducive environment and format for these individuals to efficiently transfer and communicate their knowledge of retailing. Coalesce these individuals for intensive, uninterrupted, no-holds-barred interaction. Mix these three ingredients together and *voilà*—an agenda for retailing leadership in the year 2000. Although this recipe was conceptually simple, it was operationally challenging.

Because retailing was broadly defined to include all entities selling to consumers, it was necessary that a broad spectrum of individuals be represented to ensure a full complement of retailing perspectives and retail knowledge. This required the identification of both leading retailing practitioners and academicians conversant in retailing theory and practice. The goal was to bring together a group of experts—experts in the operations and strategies of retailing and experts in areas influencing retailing. Each was expected to bring to the symposium a unique perspective on retailing and the forces impacting retailing.

Once appropriate individuals were identified, it was then necessary to convince them to give up time that might be dedicated to other pressing matters, to attend and actively participate in the symposium. Not only were these individuals asked to take time from their schedules to attend the symposium; they were also asked to prepare for it by reading background materials designed to stimulate their thinking about the topics to be addressed. Luckily, the symposium was able to attract an outstanding, indeed, "awesome" array of "thought leaders."

The symposium itself consisted of three major activities. First, six plenary sessions were held. In each session, one or more academics presented background material on a particular topic of relevance to the symposium. These topics focused on trends taking place in six distinct areas:

- Consumer behavior
- Technology
- Traditional retailing
- Direct marketing
- Direct selling
- Multiple-channel distribution

Following each presentation, a distinguished practitioner provided a commentary. In certain instances, these commentaries corroborated the presentation. In other instances, they provided a different perspective. Together, the presentations and commentaries served to focus attention on "drivers" of retailing in the future.

All symposium participants, presenters and nonpresenters alike, interacted in one of five discussion groups. These groups convened after each plenary session to discuss the implications of the information provided in the session and construct a working agenda of predictions regarding retailing in the future.

The third major activity was coalescing the group agendas into a single, composite agenda. The final session of the symposium consisted of having a representative of each discussion group present the group's agenda to the remaining participants along with a justification for the agenda. Individual agendas were then discussed and integrated.

The symposium represented the first time a high-level group of educators and practitioners had been constituted with the purpose of predicting the future of retailing. The presenters included such distinguished practitioners as David V. Evans (vice president of J. C. Penney), James Preston (chairman of Avon), and Richard C. Bartlett (president of Mary Kay Cosmetics), outstanding academicians such as Stanley Hollander (recipient of the 1991 Academy of Marketing Science Outstanding Educator Award), Gary Frazier (chairman of the Marketing Department at the University of Southern California), and Dale Achabal (director of the Retail Management Institute at Santa Clara University). Nonpresenter symposium participants included executives such as Erick Laine (chairman of Alcas Corporation) and Morris Meyer of the University of Alabama (and coauthor of the best-selling retailing textbook).

Another characteristic that made the symposium unique was its sponsorship. The symposium was cosponsored by the Direct Selling Education Foundation and the IC^2 Institute at The University of Texas at Austin. In addition, it was held in conjunction with the American Marketing Association and the Academy of Marketing Science. This sponsorship represents a mix of "the real world" and "the ivory tower." Never before have these organizations, each representing different constituencies, worked together. Indeed, despite the commonality of retailing, virtually none of the educators, executives, and representatives from these various organizations had met before. Hence, an added benefit of the symposium was the networking that occurred as well as the interpersonal relationships that developed.

For a variety of reasons, the symposium was unique. Indeed, because of its uniqueness and timeliness, it is not likely to be duplicated. Because of a variety of circumstances, not the least of which was the immediacy of the next millennium, it is not likely that a brain trust of this magnitude devoted to retailing will be constituted again in this century.

Although it is impossible to capture completely the essence of the symposium—even videotaping the sessions failed to convey adequately the excitement and exchanges that occurred—this book attempts to communicate that essence. It contains eight chapters. The first chapter provides a context, not only for the remaining chapters, but for the general topic of predicting phenomena likely to occur in retailing. The next six chapters consist of the background materials (white papers) presented at the symposium as well as the commentaries on them. The final chapter attempts to synthesize both the symposium and the previous chapters; much of what is contained in the chapter is drawn from group discussions and interactions apart from the formal session presentations. The chapter concludes with two hundred eighty-two questions or possible options a retailer must consider as it plans for leadership in the future.

Like the symposium, the book is unique and operates at two levels. At one level, it exists as a conceptual transcript of the symposium. At a higher level, it consists of material that is instructive for improving the day-to-day operations of a retailing entity and of insights, comments, and opinions that provoke in-depth strategic thinking—thinking that should focus on both the essentials of retailing and the implications of retailing. The book should not be glossed over lightly as a novel or skimmed as if it were a dry academic tome. Rather, it should be read at least twice, the first time for breadth, the second for depth. Indeed, an astute thinker may well decide to read the last chapter first to enhance knowledge attainment.

As with any endeavor, appreciation and thanks are due to a number of organizations and individuals. The symposium would not have taken place without the guidance and support of the Direct Selling Education Foundation. In particular, the assistance of Marlene Futterman, executive director of the Direct Selling Education Foundation, was especially critical to the success of the symposium. Further, the current and past chairmen of the foundation, Jerry Heffel (president of the Southwestern Corporation) and Robert King (president of Consumer Marketing, Inc.), respectively, facilitated the entire event through their confidence in both the symposium concept and its execution. Appreciation is also expressed to Drs. George Kozmetsky and Raymond Smilor (director and executive director, respectively, of the IC² Institute) for their participation and support; Jeffrey Heilbrunn (president of the American Marketing Association); and Dr. John T. Menzer (president of the Academy of Marketing Science). Thanks also are expressed to the respective staffs of the Direct Selling Education Foundation, the IC² Institute, and the RGK Foundation. Finally, without the diligence and assistance of Galen Bollinger, Linda Teague, and Pam Nelson, this book would never have been completed. To all the above— organizations and individuals alike—I express my heartfelt thanks.

The Future of
U.S. Retailing

1

A Context for Retailing Predictions

Robert A. Peterson

It is appropriate to begin *The Future of U.S. Retailing: An Agenda for the 21st Century* with the following quotation: "At no time in this twentieth century has the dynamic and changing character of retail distribution been more in evidence than is the case today. This character of American distribution is a composite result of a high-level economy, an economy which by any comparative standards is relatively free, and an economy in which distribution is highly competitive." What makes this statement interesting is that it is thirty-five years old (McNair 1958, p. 1), even though virtually every retailing analyst, manager, and observer today would agree it concisely and accurately reflects the current economic and competitive situation in the industry. Moreover, the statement will most likely apply at any time in the future, regardless of the nature and structure of retailing. Retailing is, always has been, and no doubt always will be evolving, challenging, and competitive.

Given that retailing is continuously in flux or, perhaps more appropriately, is continually undergoing transformation, the goal of this book is to provide a framework for anticipating and capitalizing on the changes that will occur in and to retailing by the year 2000. Why this particular date? Partly convenience. The year 2000 is a transition year that marks the beginning of the next millennium. More predictions and forecasts (the two are used interchangeably here) have probably been made about this year than any other. (Orwellian 1984 comes in a distant second in terms of interest.) Entire books—Bellamy's (1888) *Looking Backward, 2000-1887,* Kahn and Wiener's (1967) *The Year 2000*, and Naisbitt and Aburdene's (1990) *Mega-Trends 2000,* for example—have focused on what the world will be like in the year 2000.

Simultaneously, the year 2000 is a logical focus at this point in time. It is far enough in the future to be "interesting" and allow speculations, yet close enough to allow informed judgments. By focusing on what retailing will be like at the end of the century, future-oriented individuals can begin to plan for it now by establishing a vision, creating and testing concepts, and monitoring trends likely to facilitate or hinder achievement of corporate objectives.

The goal of this chapter is not to provide a compendium of forecasting or prediction techniques. As literally hundreds, perhaps even thousands, of procedures, approaches, and techniques are used in futures research, it would be futile to attempt to systematically catalog them in a single document. Moreover, doing so is not necessary for the present purpose. Besides, numerous books do a much better job of describing the various procedures, approaches, and techniques than could be done here. Nor is the goal to provide a vision of the future or even to set forth a comprehensive set of predictions. Such a task is best left to other, more qualified and knowledgeable individuals.

Rather, the intent of this introductory chapter is to provide a general context for the two focal points of the book—predictions and retailing—and for the substantive material contained in the remainder of the book, especially the retailing agenda set forth in the final chapter. Providing such a context should facilitate the integration and interpretation of the various facts, opinions, and speculations presented in the book so that the end result—a decision framework that can be used to achieve retailing leadership—will be useful to anyone (retailers as well as nonretailers) preparing for retailing in the remainder of the decade.

Because its goal is so broad, the chapter will meander a bit as it moves from topic to topic. The next section consists of a comment on futures research. Subsequently, several general trends that have been predicted to influence retailing are briefly described, along with specific trends in retailing. The chapter concludes with some thoughts on the future of retailing.

A COMMENT ON FUTURES RESEARCH

Predicting the future is both an avocation and a vocation, an art and a science. Prognosticators range from soothsayers who predict the future by charting the stars or reading the entrails of a goat or sheep to econometric forecasters who use computer-based models with more than ten thousand equations.

Not only is predicting the future a popular activity, but the individuals who predict the future are often themselves very popular, sometimes achieving celebrity status. Nostradamus, perhaps the most famous prognosticator of all, is more widely read today than ever before. Clairvoyants such as Jeanne Dixon have millions of avid followers. Clients of Faith Popcorn pay six-figure retainers for her pearls of wisdom. Nearly six million copies of *Future Shock* (Toffler 1970) and *Mega-Trends* (Naisbitt 1981) have been sold, and *The American Forecaster Almanac* (Long 1990) is in its eighth annual edition.

Prediction Characteristics

Predictions consist of two primary elements—the occurrence of an event (a qualitative element) and the timing of the event's occurrence (a quantitative element). They range from "sure things" (Wallechinsky, Wallace, and Wallace 1981) and "surprise-free" (Kahn and Wiener 1967) to "highly implausible." Exemplifying the former is the Wallechinsky, Wallace and Wallace (1981, p. 468) "prediction" that in the year 2000 a U.S. presidential election will be held. Exemplifying the latter is their prediction (p. 468) that by the year 2000 "an interplanetary ship brings back to earth an alien virus that kills a tenth of the world's population." Together the two examples illustrate a third, often implicit, element of a prediction: the likelihood of occurrence or probability that the prediction will come true. Inspection of a large number of predictions reveals that they frequently omit the timing element and nearly always omit the occurrence likelihood element.

A Cautionary Note

Despite the obvious need to predict future events and in spite of the potential value and popularity of forecasting, the accuracy of futures research is less than stellar. Examination of hundreds of forecasts reveals several rather curious insights:

- Many forecasts are too broad to be practically useful. Most are hedged through the use of terms such as "could," "may," "likely," or "probably," and are stated in such a manner as to be non-falsifiable.
- Predictions oftentimes appear to be normative, more "subjective" than "objective."
- The majority of predictions turn out to be incorrect. Predictions are more likely to be correct for an event's occurrence than for its timing.

Demographic trends and changes are among the easiest to monitor and project forward. Given known birthrates, death rates, immigration rates, and the like, it is a fairly straightforward task to predict the demographic composition of society at a future point in time. The existence of a trend, though, is obviously no guarantee that it will continue unabated. In a 1965 article in *Look* magazine, Gross (1965) wrote that "15 years ago, the median age was 30.2 years. Today, it is 27.8 years. Fifteen years from now it will be 25.5 years" (p. 21). In 1980, however, the median age of Americans was actually 30 years, and it has been increasing every year (in 1990 it was 32.5). What Gross failed to realize was that the "baby boom" was over. Almost inexplicably, Americans stopped having children, virtually overnight, and the birthrate plummeted.

The most provocative predictions—the most widely quoted and disseminated—tend not to be subject to empirical testing. Consider what is perhaps the most famous prediction of Nostradamus (Cheetham 1973, p. 33): "The great man will be struck down in the day by a thunderbolt. An evil deed, foretold by the bearer of a petition. According to the prediction another falls at night time. Conflict at Reims, London, and pestilence in Tuscany." According to Cheetham (1973), this remarkable prediction refers to the assassinations of President John F. Kennedy and his brother, Robert Kennedy. Unfortunately, Nostradamus's predictions were so broad that the same prediction has also been "successfully" (retrospectively) applied to different events (Armstrong and Armstrong 1983).

Or consider the technological innovations that Kahn and Wiener (1967) deemed "very likely" to exist by the year 2000. Prediction 54 (p. 53) is that there will be "automated grocery and department stores." What does this prediction mean? Does it mean there will be completely automated stores such that customers input their orders via computer and robots fill, ship, and deliver the order? Or does it mean stores will be using scanning devices at checkout counters? At this point in time, the prediction is either completely right, completely wrong, or both right and wrong!

Predictions must be viewed with extreme caution even though they may appear to be specific enough to be useful. In fact, placing a value on a prediction (i.e., assessing its validity and reliability) requires assessing the potential motives and personal characteristics of the predictor. Not only do predictions appear to be influenced by fleeting factors such as mood, hope, and fear; they also seem to be influenced by the basic optimism or pessimism of the predictor. Bertrand Russell's (1924) book of predictions, *Icarus or the Future of Science,* is very disheartening because it reflects his essentially pessimistic nature.

Oftentimes, predictions seem to reflect the purpose for which they were derived. Klopfenstein (1989) analyzed twenty-nine forecasts of the home video market. He reported that "not surprisingly the audience to which the report is directed had some bearing on its content. Few studies were pessimistic . . . many of the reports . . . painted a very rosy picture of the home video market. An optimistic bias in such reports seems almost inherent" (p. 23).

In a scathing review of two futures-oriented books, Parrish (1986) attempted to point out the bias present in much futures research. He concluded his review by noting that "although futurism has no rational basis, its practitioners are mainly gullible of selling hope. . . . Lincoln Steffens wrote the real epitaph for futurism back in 1931 after visiting the Soviet Union: 'I have been over into the future and it works' " (p. 80). Although a bit harsh, Parrish's points need serious consideration by anyone attempting to employ futures research.

Even so, a few predictions seem to be unerring and even unnerving. In 1915, Charles P. Steinmetz (Martino 1978) predicted the existence of electrical automobiles, temperature-controlled homes (electrical heating and air-conditioning), wireless telephones (cellular telephones), and cooking by electricity on the kitchen table (microwave ovens) by 1999. However, even Steinmetz blundered in some of his predictions, and close scrutiny (albeit retrospectively) reveals that the vast majority of predictions do not come to pass. Errors of both commission (predicting events that do not occur) and omission (failing to predict events that occur) are commonplace. Of the two error types, errors of commission are probably less defensible than errors of omission. Some prediction errors are classic. In the 1950s, UNIVAC, despite extensive and vigorous research, estimated that by the year 2000, only one thousand computers would be sold. By 1986, more than one hundred million computers had been sold.

Ashley (1988) studied the forecasts of twelve well-known private and governmental forecasting organizations with respect to their success in predicting such macroeconomic variables as the GNP and the unemployment rate. He concluded that "most of these forecasts are so inadequate that the forecast MSE (mean square error) exceeds the variance of the variable being forecast. . . . Put another way: most of these forecasts are so inadequate that simple extrapolation of historical trends is superior for forecasts more than a couple of quarters ahead" (p. 363). Similarly, following an analysis of predictions culled from the news media, Scarupa (1990) concluded that "as predicted, the nation's most famous psychics failed to accurately forecast 1990 news events—and in most cases, they were just plain wrong" (p. A4). This conclusion was echoed by Crossen (1990), who stated that "much of what today's visionaries are seeing will prove utterly and amazingly wrong" (p. A1).

Consider the fifteen predictions compiled by Wallechinsky, Wallace, and Wallace (1981, pp. 465-466) for 1990, shown in Table 1.1. Of these predictions, the last is perhaps the most intriguing: "The Soviet Union's communist government is overthrown by a social democratic faction working inside the party." It is intriguing in that it was essentially correct (liberally interpreting the term "overthrown"). Most likely it will be the one prediction remembered of the fifteen, consequently enhancing the status not only of the book but also of the particular individual who made it.

Table 1.1. Some Predictions for 1990

- Spanish joins English as an official language in the U.S.
- Areas of Texas and California split off to form new states.
- Vegetarians outnumber meat-eaters in the U.S.
- Most large corporations provide paid educational sabbaticals.
- Control of outer space shifts from civil to military authority in the U.S. NASA gives way to the U.S. Department of Defense.
- A male astronaut in outer space shoots and kills a crewmate in an argument over a woman.
- All school buildings vanish as students receive their education from portable communications-linked appliances which are cast on pieces of semiconductor silicon.
- Every automobile is equipped with microcomputer, sensor, and control actuator for self-operation by voice command. Also, every auto is equipped with collision-avoidance electronic gadgetry.
- Wrist telephones are popular.
- Daily body checkups by computer provide ample warning of any impending illness.
- In the past 10 years, heart disease has decreased 37% due to improved diet and exercise.
- Diabetics have pumps implanted in their bodies to feed them insulin automatically as they require it.
- Artificial eyesight is invented for blind people.
- Chemicals are produced that arrest senility in the aged.
- The Soviet Union's communist government is overthrown by a social democratic faction working inside the party.

Source: Wallechinsky, Wallace, and Wallace (1981), *The Book of Predictions*, New York: William Morrow and Company, pp. 465-466.

The example illustrates a difficulty in evaluating predictions. When is a prediction correct? In this instance the event did occur. It was correctly predicted, even though the timing was off. (But was it close enough in time to be considered correct?) Most of the other predictions ("vegetarians outnumber meat-eaters in the U.S.," "a male astronaut in outer space shoots and kills a crewmate in an argument over a woman," "areas of Texas and California split off to form new states")—those that proved to be wrong—

tend to be overlooked and forgotten. The key to success for prognosticators would seem to be to make many predictions, ignore those that do not prove to be correct, and publicize extensively those that are, or at least can be justified as being, correct (see Batra 1985).

Benefits of Futures Research

On average the track record of futures researchers is not very good. Why then do their forecasts continue to be used? The answer seems to be multifold. First, many users appear to apply predictions creatively and seem to possess selective memories. They seize upon predictions they agree with and discard those they do not. The predictions of Nostradamus seem to be used more to prove a point or to justify an individual's action than to plan for the future. In other words, they are used more in looking backward (retrodiction) than in looking forward (prediction).

It is important to note in passing that "prophecies" (especially predictions due to divine revelations) do not allow for the operation of free will. Anyone believing literally in prophecies is accepting the natural consequence that all futures are immutable, preordained, and not subject to change. In brief, it seems that a common use of predictions is to reinforce presently held beliefs rather than to look into the future.

There are other, more defensible reasons for attempting to forecast the future. By trying to look into the future, one is actually taking the first step to creating it through present activities, behaviors, and decisions. Hence, by attempting to predict the future, a firm can be prepared to take advantage of events that will positively impact it while simultaneously addressing proactively, not reactively, those events likely to negatively impact it.

Sophisticated decision makers are really not interested in precise point-estimates of future events (either the occurrence of the event itself or the timing of the event). Instead, forecasting is used to develop comprehensive sets of "alternative futures" or scenarios (hypothetical events constructed to focus attention on causal processes and decision points). Given such a use, forecasting is valuable in that it forces one to explicitly identify key variables (controllable and uncontrollable, dependent and independent), issues that need to be analyzed, and trends that need to be monitored. Further, and perhaps more important, it forces the forecaster to explicitly set forth the assumptions underlying the forecast. Studies have indicated that assumptions used in futures research are often vague and unrealistic and at times internally inconsistent. By having to set forth assumptions that are subject to review and possible criticism, the forecaster is more likely to think through the entire forecasting process carefully. Doing so ultimately produces "better" forecasts.

Finally, the forecasting process fosters creativity in the planning process and allows a forecaster or decision maker to study the implications of the forecast. It is these implications that are important for decision making. Stated simply, the value of futures research lies in the means, not in the end results.

BUSINESS AND SOCIETAL PREDICTIONS

As noted previously, the goal of this chapter is to provide a context for anticipating, assessing, and capitalizing on changes likely to affect retailing or take place in retailing. Toward this end it is instructive to review some of the trends that have been predicted to impact business and society. Tables 1.2 to 1.4 contain a sampling of the predictions that have received publicity in the past few years. These specific predictions were selected in part because they reflect different emphases and in part because they are based on different research approaches. For example, the predictions in Table 1.2 were derived from survey research, whereas those in Table 1.3 were derived from systematic content analyses of print media.

It is useful to compare the various lists of predictions for their similarities and differences. The extent to which the lists contain common predictions suggests consistency and may increase a user's confidence in them. However, commonality might also suggest a bandwagon effect. In any case, no predictions should be accepted uncritically, nor should they be dismissed without due consideration. Rather, they should be carefully analyzed, synthesized, and integrated into a comprehensive whole if possible. Collectively the trends presented in the tables serve as a starting point or foundation for both predicting and assessing changes likely to occur in retailing.

Consider, for instance, just one trend predicted in Table 1.2: the growth of antibusiness attitudes. Is this in fact a long-term trend? What does it portend for retailing? What is the evidence for it? With regard to the last question, Peterson, Albaum, and Kozmetsky (1990) have documented what may signal a decrease in favorable attitudes toward capitalism in the 1990s. As capitalism is the foundation of the American business system, their research may well corroborate the predicted antibusiness attitudinal trend. However, as they point out, their evidence is somewhat equivocal: Does it suggest the beginning of a significant trend, or does it simply reflect a reaction to the financial debacles in the savings and loan industry, Wall Street excesses, and the mergers and leveraged buyouts in retailing? At this point both the existence of the trend and its implications are unclear. Even so, retailers with foresight will closely monitor the public's attitudes for their potential implications.

Table 1.2. Thirty-one Major Trends Shaping the Future of American Business

- Increasing importance of time
- Component life-styles
- Demand for convenience
- Dramatic growth of home shopping
- Shopping habits of the genders to converge
- Escalation of the home entertainment boom
- Market segmentation in physical fitness activities
- Return to fashion
- Spread of the diversified diet
- Declining use of alcohol
- Growth in bottled-water usage
- Bifurcation of markets
- Increasing importance of product and service quality
- Increased importance of visual dimension in advertising
- VCRs improve image of television
- Media market fragmentation
- Increased emphasis on family
- More employment benefits for two-income households
- Heightened telecommuting
- Entrepreneurship among older Americans
- Conservation among younger Americans
- Growth of antibusiness attitudes
- Personalization of large business
- Perceived irrelevancy of unions
- Growing environmentalism
- Negative attitudes about nuclear energy
- Increase in government regulations
- Increase in budget deficit
- Decrease in defense spending
- Elimination of tax breaks for wealthy

Source: The Roper Organization, *The Public Pulse*, Volume 2, November 1, 1988.

The Baby-Boom Generation

One of the most widely studied phenomena in the futures arena is the baby-boom generation. The baby-boom generation consists of Americans born between 1946 and 1964. According to Russell (1987), seventeen million more individuals were born in this period than would have been born if tradition had been followed. In other words, during this time period, a "bubble" appeared in the birthrate. Russell posits one hundred consequences (predictors or propositions) of the baby boom. These consequences relate to baby-boom families, children of baby boomers, work, money, the home, business, beliefs, retirement, and aging. Many of these consequences are discussed in this book. Some of Russell's consequences are corroborated, others refuted. Consider the following retailing-related consequences (predictions), principally fueled by secondary data analysis (p. 22):

- The baby boom will create a new industry that sells experiences.
- Baby boomers will do a lot of their shopping by mail.
- The buying habits of the baby boom will hurt the nation's shopping malls.

As each of these consequences is obviously important to retailing, each is considered in detail at various points in this book.

Table 1.3. Naisbitt's Megatrends

Megatrends, 1982
- Industrial society to information society
- Forced technology to high tech/high touch
- National economy to world economy
- Short term to long term
- Centralization to decentralization
- Institutional help to self-help
- Representative democracy to participatory democracy
- Hierarchies to networking
- North to south
- Either/or to multiple option

Millennial Megatrends
- The booming global economy of the 1990s
- A renaissance in the arts
- The emergence of free-market socialism
- Global life-styles and cultural nationalism
- The privatization of the welfare state
- The rise of the Pacific Rim
- The decade of women in leadership
- The age of biology
- The religious revival of the new millennium
- The triumph of the individual

Source: Naisbitt (1982), *Megatrends,* New York: Warner Books; Naisbitt and Aburdene (1990), *Megatrends 2000,* New York: William Morrow and Company.

Table 1.4. Key Trends of the 1990s

Blockbuster Trends

- The world will be more competitive than ever before in the history of modern economic society.
- The increasing "globalization of the corporation" will lead to a few giant transnational corporations surviving a major corporate shakeout and dominating key industries.
- Employee empowerment, through various forms of employee involvement and participation, will pace the revolution in the way work is organized.
- A number of emerging revolutionary technologies will boost productivity substantially and transform entire industries.
- Global warming—the "greenhouse effect"—will be the number one environmental issue and will lead to calls for, and possibly implementation of, radical changes by consumers and business.

Good News Trends

- Productivity growth will increase.
- Personal savings will increase.
- The Federal Reserve will be vigilant in pursuing price stability.
- Inflation will be lower.
- The business cycle will be smoother.
- Employees will have more of a say about their jobs.
- Employees will have more job flexibility to balance family and work.
- Revolutionary new technologies will boost the nation's productivity.
- New technologies will transform the factory floor and boost productivity for many companies.

Bad News Trends

- The budget deficit will remain a serious problem.
- Japan will be more competitive and powerful than ever.
- Europe will be a much tougher competitor.
- Trade tensions will rise.
- The Third World debt problem may explode.
- America's foreign debt will grow astronomically.
- A fundamental mismatch will exist between jobs and workers.
- Health-care costs for corporations and government will skyrocket. The high cost of capital for U.S. companies will continue to hurt American competitiveness.
- Short-term speculation will continue taking precedence over long-term investment.
- An oil crisis will become a serious threat.

Source: *Economic Upheaval: 60 Key Trends of the 1990s Reshaping Your World.* Washington, D.C.: Nathan Associates, Inc., 1990.

The primary message of Russell is that demographic changes lead to predictable changes in behavior and attitudes. Human beings progress through a cycle, behaving in a certain fashion as a function of their age (i.e., the family life cycle), and these behaviors in turn have predictable consequences for business. The greater the extent to which these age-behavior linkages hold, the easier it is to predict changes likely to occur in retailing.

PREDICTING THE FUTURE OF RETAILING

No one would deny that predicting the future is challenging. It is especially challenging when the events to be predicted are in the distant future and/or are "people-related" as opposed to "phenomena-related." As Kahn and Wiener (1967, p. 13) point out, "almost any day has some chance of bringing up some new crisis or unexpected event that becomes an historical turning-point, diverting current tendencies so that expectations for the distant future must shift." Mahajan and Wind (1989) talk about market discontinuities: "A market discontinuity is a shift in any of the market forces or their interrelationships that cannot be predicted by a continuation of historical trends and that if it occurs can dramatically affect the performance of a firm or industry" (p. 187).

Retailing Prediction Roadblocks

Predicting the future of retailing is difficult not only because of its general instability and market discontinuities but also for reasons somewhat unique to the field. In particular, there are four major reasons that it is so difficult to predict accurately what retailing will be like in the future: definitional issues, the dynamic nature of retailing, environmental forces, and a lack of theory. Each of these is briefly discussed.

Definitional Issues. One reason it is so difficult to make accurate predictions about retailing is that there is no clear consensus as to what actually constitutes retailing. A leading retailing textbook (Mason and Mayer 1990) does not even include a definition. Consider the following three definitions:

- The activities involved in selling goods or services directly to people for their own use (Nisberg 1988, p. 242)
- The activity of purchasing for resale to a customer (Rosenberg 1983, p. 433)

- Selling merchandise for personal or household consumption and rendering services incidental to the sale of the goods (*Standard Industrial Classification Manual* 1987, p. 313)

At first blush, one would think that the differences between the definitions are of no consequence. However, a broad definition of a retailer as any entity that sells products or services to consumers means that certain forms of business are included that would not be included under a more narrow definition. An obvious definitional consequence is that the dollar volume ascribed to retailing changes dramatically as a function of the definition.

For example, consider direct selling. Direct selling is a form of retailing since firms sell (by definition) directly to consumers. Even so, direct selling is not covered in most retailing textbooks, nor is it considered by most retailing analysts or observers as being a part of the industry. Rather, it is treated separately from or simply as an adjunct to the industry, or it is ignored. If direct selling were included in retailing, the question would arise of what firms should be treated as direct sellers.

According to the Direct Selling Association, sales in the direct selling industry totalled about $10 billion in the United States in 1990. However, the Direct Selling Association explicitly excludes insurance firms, firms that sell household improvements (e.g., siding), and the like from both membership in the association and its dollar estimates of industry size. Including them would dramatically increase retail sales attributed to direct selling.

Furthermore, it is not clear how direct marketing firms—those independent firms selling through catalogs, telemarketing, television shopping shows, and the like—are treated. Many retailing textbooks do not consider direct marketing to be a part of retailing, and the Census Bureau does not report sales figures for all types of direct marketing firms.

The point of this discussion is that until agreement exists on the boundaries of retailing, predictions about it will be greatly hindered and will be subject to numerous qualifications and contingencies. Although the definitional issue is often overlooked, it is no less real than those discussed next.

Dynamic Nature of Retailing. A second reason it is so difficult to predict the future of retailing accurately is that it is so dynamic. Retailing institutions are constantly evolving and changing. New retailing concepts and approaches are continually being introduced, tested, discarded or modified, and tested again. No one predicted the dramatic and swift structural changes in retailing in the mid- and late-1980s, especially those involving department stores, shopping malls, and traditional discount stores.

Consider Bates' (1977) prediction that there would be a "new fundamentalism" in retailing in the 1980s, with a "major effort being made to improve the internal operations of existing businesses" (p. 39). Yet within the timeframe of his predictions, the industry witnessed several financial debacles, including those of Campeau, Hooker, and Ames. Most of the problems came about because of questionable financial practices. Fundamentalism was forgotten. Eighteen months after Ames Department Stores purchased the Zayre chain and became the fourth-largest discount retailer in the country, it declared bankruptcy. The reverberations of the widely discussed retailing spin-offs, mergers, and acquisitions of the 1980s will no doubt continue for years. Even Sears, once retailing's "star," appears to be in trouble and may not survive the decade (at least in its present form). In February 1991, Sears began eliminating more than thirty thousand jobs in an effort to streamline operations and remain a viable competitor.

Likewise, virtually no one predicted the success of video specialty stores. At the end of the 1970s, only a handful of video stores existed. In 1981, 5.5 million prerecorded video cassettes were sold; by 1989, the number had risen to more than 200 million. The revenues of the largest ten video retailers exceeded $1.2 billion in 1989, and sales continue to grow exponentially ("Home Video" 1990, pp. 25-26).

Environmental Forces. A third reason it is difficult to predict the future of retailing is that everything that affects society—demographic changes, technological changes, political changes, economic changes, environmental changes, whatever—will affect retailing. The effects may occur slowly or rapidly and may be direct or indirect. Regardless of timing and directness, ultimately anything that influences society will also influence the nature and form of retailing. Like retailing itself, society is continually changing.

Unless one is "all-knowing," it is difficult to derive accurate predictions about the future of retailing. Many of the changes and trends in society may well have unanticipated consequences for retailing, consequences that are neither straightforward nor obvious (forecasters have always had difficulty with nonlinear projections and second- or higher-order consequences). Consider three trends observed in education: the steady increase in the percentage of high school graduates attending college, the simultaneous decrease in average SAT (Scholastic Aptitude Test) scores, and the doubling of the number of foreign students enrolling in U.S. colleges and universities. According to the *1990 Statistical Abstract of the United States*, the percentage of high school graduates attending college increased from 52 percent in 1970 to 58 percent in 1980. Simultaneously, the average SAT score decreased from 948 in 1970 to 904 in 1988. These trends have conflicting implications for retailing (and society) and illustrate the difficulty of forecasting its future.

Lack of Theory. A fourth major reason that it is difficult to make informed predictions about retailing is that no comprehensive theory exists to guide the predictions. Without a comprehensive theory, there is no basis either for hypothesizing, a priori, certain trends or changes or for explaining them, a posteriori. However, several "middle-range theories" (concepts) have been proffered over time in attempts to address the evolution of retailing institutions. Three of these theoretical contributions are the "wheel of retailing" (McNair 1957), the "retail accordion" (Hollander 1966), and the "retail life cycle" (Davidson, Bates, and Bass 1976).

The wheel of retailing is perhaps the most widely used concept for explaining the evolution of retail institutions. It essentially posits that new institutional forms begin as low-cost, low-price operations that subsequently tradeup to become high-cost, high-price operations. These forms then become vulnerable to the next turn of the wheel when a new low-cost, low-price institution emerges, and so on. The retail accordion concept posits that there is an evolutionary cycle alternately dominated first by institutions selling a wide variety of products and then by institutions selling a limited variety of products, followed by a wide variety, and so forth (i.e., a general-specific-general merchandising cycle). The retail life cycle concept essentially states that new forms of retailing pass through the same stages that a product does—birth, growth, maturity, and perhaps decline. The three "theories" are essentially one-facet concepts that share the characteristics of being cycle-based and more useful descriptively than analytically or predictively. Each seems to work in certain situations but not in others. The wheel of retailing especially has been given close scrutiny and has both backers and detractors (e.g., Brown 1989, Hollander 1966, May 1989).

What is needed is a comprehensive theory that would prove useful in predicting the evolution of (many) retailing institutions. Although Brown (1988, 1990) has attempted to develop such a theory by combining notions from the retail life cycle, retail accordion, and wheel of retailing concepts, and Etgar (1986) has set forth an evolutionary model based on ecological concepts, at this time no comprehensive theory exists. Until one is developed, predictions will probably be limited to those based on inferences, empirical deductions, and analogies.

Other Reasons. In addition to these four major reasons, many others too numerous to name make predicting the future of retailing difficult. For example, consider two trends in American management. One is the trend toward more centralized decision-making, fostered by advances in computer networking and communications. Simultaneously, though, there is a trend toward "bottom-down" management, wherein hierarchical organizations are being replaced by matrix organizations whose decision-making authority is being moved from higher to lower levels of the organization. Because these trends are conceptually conflicting (although it is possible they could coexist in a firm), their ultimate impact individually or jointly makes predictions about retailing more difficult.

This section should not be interpreted as criticizing either the usefulness or accuracy of retailing predictions. The intent is simply to point out (perhaps to rationalize) why it is difficult to predict trends or institutional changes in retailing. As before, the objective is to provide another dimension to the contextual mosaic being presented.

RETAILING PREDICTIONS

Just as the literature is replete with predictions regarding society and business, there is also a plethora of predictions regarding the future of retailing. For whatever reason, predictions about retailing seem to be a favorite topic of forecasters interested in business. For example, in 1977 an entire issue of the *Journal of Retailing* (anchored by Berry and Wilson's "Retailing: The Next Ten Years") was dedicated to the future of retailing, one of the favorite recurring themes in that publication. (See, for instance, Sheth's (1983) thoughtful article, "Emerging Trends for the Retailing Industry.")

Because 1990 signaled the beginning of the last decade of the century, it fostered numerous compilations of retailing predictions. Several of these are reported below to provide a broad spectrum of predictions. Although the various lists of predictions must be recognized for what they are— simply illustrations—an attempt was made to obtain predictions from relatively disparate sources.

Johnson (1990), in *Discount Merchandiser,* predicted:

- There will be a general trend toward fewer stores, larger stores, and higher-volume stores with lower margins.
- One-stop shopping will increase in importance.
- Stores that find a niche and department stores will continue to prosper.
- Customers will continue to demand service.
- Retailers and their suppliers must become socially conscious in ways that have never been done before.
- Retailers must use technology to improve performance.
- Retailers must develop different relationships with their vendors.
- Retailers must focus on the needs of their customers.

In *Catalog Age*, Haggin and Kartomten (1990) predicted that, among other things:

- The catalog business will grow because it is positioned to fulfill customers' needs.
- Every state will collect taxes on catalog sales.
- Global marketing will increase.
- More catalog mailers will co-mail to keep costs down.
- Fax orders will replace mail orders.
- On-line information will markedly improve customer service.
- Guaranteed next-day delivery will become the norm.

Probably the most comprehensive attempt to peer into the future of retailing is contained in a document authored by Hyde, Steidtmann, and Sweeney (1990). This document, titled *Retailing 2000,* characterizes the present state of retailing, describes changes likely to impact retailing, and offers nine predictions about retailing in the year 2000. The predictions focus on:

- Contraction in retailing (with respect to number of organizations and space)
- Increases in non-store shopping
- Emphases being given to relationship merchandising
- The demise of discount department stores
- A decline in retailing innovations
- An increase in one-stop shopping
- A flattening of the management hierarchy
- Increasing social consciousness
- Retailer-supplier alliances

Finally, Mason and Meyer (1990, p. 30-33) predicted:

- A proliferation of specialty stores
- Continued development of very large stores
- Increasing importance of convenience
- Increasing importance of home shopping
- The emergence of power centers (open-air theme centers)
- The integration of factory outlet stores into mainstream retailing
- The growth of integrated retailing (i.e., sharing of physical facilities)
- Continued development of mega-malls
- More consolidations and mergers
- More retailers becoming developers and more developers acquiring retailers
- Greater acceptance of technology
- Increasing foreign investment in U.S. retailing
- Intensifying competition among discount stores

- Continuation of broad-ranging trends (e.g., more private brands, continuation of retail polarization, multichannel distribution)
- Increased focus on consumers rather than suppliers

As might be expected, there is more consistency among retailing-related predictions than among societal or business predictions. Unfortunately, since forecasters focusing on retailing seldom document or provide the sources of their predictions, it is difficult to determine the forecaster's logic or to investigate whether there is a bandwagon effect.

THOUGHTS ON THE FUTURE OF RETAILING

In one sense, all predictions represent risky endeavors because, at some point, someone will question whether the predictions are right or wrong. Perhaps that is why futurists like to predict far into the future—to ensure they will not be present to suffer the consequences (e.g., shame) of incorrect forecasts. (By doing so they will obviously miss any accolades for their correct predictions; however, as previously noted, their chances of making incorrect predictions are much greater than their chances of making correct predictions.) This is also why futurists tend to hedge their predictions wherever possible, either presenting them in very general terms or protecting themselves with appropriate adjectives.

While the preceding paragraph may be a bit facetious, it points out the greatest weakness of evaluating predictions—the focus on whether a prediction is correct or incorrect. A more appropriate criterion on which to judge predictions is whether they cause one to think about the future. In particular, the ultimate usefulness of a forecast or prediction is the extent to which it leads one to ask questions—questions about the predictions themselves, obviously, but in addition and more important, questions about the assumptions underlying the predictions, questions regarding the implications of the predictions, and questions about the relevance or importance of the predictions and whether they mean anything to anybody. For this reason, scenario analysis has become popular. Think of it this way: predictions are made to be proven incorrect. Consequently, whether they are correct or incorrect should not be the sole criterion upon which they are evaluated.

At its essence, this book is about predicting changes—changes in retailing and changes impacting retailing; obvious changes and changes that are not so obvious; dramatic, revolutionary changes and gradual, evolutionary changes. By correctly anticipating the future, it is possible to gain an edge on the competition. Hence, managers are literally forced to be continually thinking about the future.

As Savitt (1989, p. 326) has so aptly noted, "The challenge for the future is to put the themes of the past into a pattern that will provide the opportunity to confirm or deny their existence and validity." This can sometimes be done by looking forward backward. When planning for the future, managers often tend to be shortsighted when they think about trends and changes likely to affect their industry or their particular firm. Moreover, they sometimes tend to be misled by examples or isolated instances. Perusal of recent media reports reveals that they tend to focus on the same two, three, or four retailers who currently are successful or unsuccessful. Every report on retailing seems to refer to Sam's Club or Wal-Mart, The Limited, Sears, Penney, The Gap, and the like. Often this happens because journalists have a herd mentality. One journalist's mention of a particular company frequently leads to a bandwagon effect and, in essence, copycat reports. Simultaneously, retailers tend to think that what is occurring with respect to competition or environmental pressures is unique to them and/or this particular period in time.

What is needed for successful prediction is a longer-term perspective, a modicum of theory, and substantial retroreflection. In brief, the counterargument to the recurring theme that "retailing is extremely dynamic and at no time has competition been so fierce or at no time have things changed so rapidly" is "nothing changes but the players; the game remains the same." As Edwards (1957, p. 35) correctly noted, "[in retailing] the problems with which we are struggling today bear a striking resemblance to those of yesterday." He illustrates this point by looking at geographical decentralization, product diversification, unorthodox competition, and expense reduction. Although his terminology and the examples he uses are different from those of today—one only need replace such terms as "discount house" with "category killer" or "merchandise specialist"—the fundamental conclusions remain the same.

Moreover, retailers in particular appear to be myopic, focusing only on their narrow areas of expertise, not committing sufficient resources to environmental scanning, and in essence ignoring the lessons of history. While the retailing literature contains numerous references regarding dramatic changes occurring within and to the industry, retailers have generally been slow to react to new trends and innovations. Many of the "startlingly new" innovations actually were a long time in the developmental process.

Three examples selected from different retailing categories illustrate that most "retailing innovations" actually evolved over a period of time. Consider first the example of Toys "R" Us. This company typifies a category killer or merchandise specialist. Indeed, it might even be thought of as *the* category killer prototype. From most reports about Toys "R" Us, one would be led to believe that it was virtually created overnight and that it completely surprised both competitors and industry analysts. Such is hardly the case. Toys "R" Us had its origin in 1928 and slowly evolved over time, arriving at its present format in the mid-1970s. West Edmonton Mall is cited as the megamall that best combines shopping and show biz, with the implication that it was specifically designed as an entertainment center. The fact is that the mall was developed in three distinct phases over a fifteen-year period. Its final configuration appears to be due as much to coincidence as vision. The Price Club is typically cited as one of the pioneers of the warehouse club retailing format. Yet it too evolved over a period of time. The Price Club started as a wholesale operation for member retailers who paid a $25 membership fee. Analogous to Toys "R" Us and the West Edmonton Mall, it did not simply come unannounced, springing full-grown into a competitive organization.

The point of this discussion is twofold. First, by systematically looking backward, it is possible to make enlightened forecasts about the future in general terms; it is also possible to be cognizant of individual innovations.

Some predictions will always be true and in that regard are timeless. For example, Davidson and Rogers' predictions (1981) that there will be

- more internationalization in retailing
- greater attention given to consumerism and environmental issues
- increasing interest in measuring and improving retail productivity

will probably always be in order (and fashionable).

Other predictions never seem to come true. Perhaps the best example relates to technology predictions. Predictions regarding the occurrence of technological innovations have tended to be relatively on target. Although the timing of such predictions has often been off, the introduction of technological phenomena such as video cameras or cellular telephones was predicted with relative accuracy. Such innovations develop from a cumulative knowledge base and hence lend themselves to reasonable extrapolations. Simultaneously, though, forecasts of the diffusion of technological innovations have typically exaggerated their potential acceptability (Schnaars and Berenson 1986).

For decades marketers have predicted the extensive role of teleshopping and the completely automated store. Nearly a quarter of a century ago, Doody and Davidson (1967, p. 5) predicted that storeless shopping by terminal with automated package delivery would be "commonplace sometime in the 70s. The technology necessary for it is already here, and the market conditions that will help create the demand for it are fast materializing." In 1978, McNair and May acknowledged that the Doody and Davidson projection was a bit optimistic. However, they went on to predict that "by early in the 21st century almost all food and other basic household needs will be acquired through the use of in-home television computer systems" (p. 81). Their prediction has been echoed by several other observers (e.g., Rosenberg and Hirschman 1980, English 1985).

At this point in time, however, an objective observer would be hard-pressed to be as optimistic as past forecasters on the future of computer-based shopping. Several attempts at developing home shopping systems have been made in the past decade. None can be termed an unqualified success. Perhaps the most ambitious effort in this area is the joint work of IBM and Sears in developing Prodigy. Even so, in spite of capital expenditures in excess of $500 million and the imprimaturs of two well-known companies, the viability of Prodigy is still in question. After several years in existence, Prodigy is yet to show a profit.

The point of this brief discourse is that, while predictions of the occurrence of technological innovations have been relatively accurate, predictions regarding their acceptance in the marketplace have been less accurate. Many technological innovations do not seem to possess the benefits or advantages consumers value. Perhaps analogous to the diffusion of ATMs, consumers first have to be educated as to the usefulness of an innovation before there will be widespread adoption. Recently Backer Spielvigel Bates ("Media and Measurement. . . Coming Decade" 1991) predicted robots that are capable of directing customers to specific items, demonstrating products, stocking shelves, and even recommending appropriate products for specific need sets by the year 2000. Although the technology is presently available to create such robots, the jury is out as to whether they will be perceived by consumers as adding value to the shopping experience.

Parallel optimism is also seen in those predictions that forecast technology as the "competitive advantage that will determine success or failure in retailing in the 1990s" (Sarkissian 1989, p. 46). It is unlikely technology will provide a long-term sustainable advantage to a firm. Although technology may lead to relatively short-term advantages, because of its very nature—available to everyone, often at similar prices, or easily duplicated—it seems more logical to characterize the possession of technology as a necessary but not sufficient condition for retailing success. Real competitive advantages will go to those firms that can best manage the consequences of technology, not those that merely possess it.

On the Horizon

What should forward-thinking retailers be prepared for in the future? Obviously they cannot be prepared for all possible events. However, retailers should be selective in focusing on those events and phenomena that are likely to have an impact on their firms and business. This requires a creative approach, both with regard to scanning the environment to determine what trends or changes to focus on and then interpreting these trends and changes for the retailer's best advantage. Some events and phenomena are large in scope, whereas others are relatively minor (at least until they explode or get carried from one arena to another). Consider what many would term a minor trend—the increasing appearance of slotting allowances in supermarkets the past few years.

Much has been written about supermarkets increasingly dominating the food distribution channel because of their power to control information. In part because of the increased use of scanning devices and inventory control systems, supermarkets often know more about a manufacturer's products than does the manufacturer itself. One result of this knowledge is the widespread use and enforcement of slotting allowances—money that manufacturers must pay supermarkets merely to gain shelf space for their new products. Supermarkets have found slotting allowances to be easy money no matter what the success of the new products because they are guaranteed a certain return on their shelf space. Because of the success of slotting allowances (at least to supermarkets) and the recent behaviors of some supermarkets and manufacturers, several "scenarios of the future" can be derived:

- Many supermarkets focused their attention on ways to obtain "free money" from manufacturers. Because of their attention to the profits that could be obtained from a variety of promotional devices, it appears that some supermarket chains lost sight of the customer. Chains that lost their customer focus will lose not only market share to competitors but will become vulnerable for takeover in the not-too-distant future.
- Because of supermarkets' growing use of slotting allowances and similar devices, manufacturers will attempt either to band together or to offset individually the increased power of the supermarkets. Most likely this will be done through attempts to gain what Palamountain (1955) has so aptly termed "countervailing power" (or, as they say in physics, for every action there is a reaction). Already the seeds of such behaviors on the part of manufacturers have been sown. Procter and Gamble, for example, has created retail sales teams to better coordinate and integrate (read "control") its relationships with supermarkets.
- Given the success of slotting allowances, there may well be attempts by retailers other than supermarkets to institute such devices. It is easy to visualize the slotting allowance concept being applied by firms dominating particular channels/markets. Indeed, there is already evidence of, for example, category killers applying leverage to manufacturers through "cooperative advertising arrangements" and the like.

Many trends and changes are easy to detect. What is difficult to discern are the implications of the trends and changes. For example, there will be a European Community (EC) in 1992 or 1993 or 1994. The consequences of this internal-market initiative are less well known but will probably (Dawson 1989, p. 30):

- Encourage more product sourcing from within the internal market
- Permit shorter lead times and lower distribution costs, in part because there will be fewer delays at border checkpoints
- Lead to higher product costs as a result of EC directives on packaging and information as well as consumer welfare
- Encourage merger and acquisition activities on an international scale
- Result in larger companies and/or more intercompany alliances

Recently the immigration quota of 550,000 persons per year in the United States was increased to at least 700,000. Virtually all of the new positions will be allocated to professional elites (e.g., scientists and engineers or individuals who can prove they will bring at least a million dollars in investment capital to the United States and create a business employing ten or more Americans). The extra 150,000 individuals are equivalent to creating a new city the size of Pittsfield, Massachusetts; Medford, Oregon; or Lynchburg, Virginia every year. Although these individuals most likely will be diffused throughout the country, the chances are high they will end up in one of the coastal areas. Given the likely ethnic makeup of these individuals, the implications for retailers are numerous and varied.

In other instances trends are more subtle, which makes predicting their impact even more difficult. For several years retailers have been moving to different accounting bases. Almost unnoticed, firms are changing from an emphasis on gross sales and profits to using return on equity and assets to using fully costed approaches to evaluating individual product offerings (e.g., DPP). Such accounting changes, made possible by increasingly sophisticated computer technologies, have the potential to completely upend not only retailing operations, but the processes used to valuate the businesses themselves.

Recently firms of all ilk, retailers and manufacturers included, have been moving in the direction of "relationship marketing," most notably through the use of database techniques made possible by advances in computer and communication technologies. Although the underlying concept is sound, and most experts on the subject are optimistic (see, for instance, chapter 6), the trend is not inevitable. The most ambitious and well-publicized attempt to expand the availability of consumer databases was terminated when consumers vociferously criticized it for invading their privacy (Miller 1991).

At times both trends and consequences are difficult to discern. In such cases, scenarios can be especially valuable. Currently simultaneous trends are taking place in retailers' use of store and private brands: some retailers are moving toward them, whereas others are attempting to eliminate or reduce them. Will one trend dominate the other, or will they continue to coexist? What will be the outcome of the current trend to eliminate middle management? Will it result in reduced operating costs and increase decision making at lower levels in an organization, thus increasing competitiveness; or will it result in an organization's ultimately becoming less competitive because of a lack of experienced upper-level managers? Without vertical management tracks, how will lower-level managers gain the necessary experience to grow into leaders? The current emphasis on "horizontal movement" may either be a boon or bane for developing competent senior managers. The consequences of such trends are as yet unknown. However, by constructing alternative scenarios, decision makers could at least be prepared to confront different possibilities.

Or, consider a trend or tendency that many individuals have observed piecemeal: bifurcation. There appears to be a growing number of "gaps" that have significance for retailers. At an industry level, an increasing discrepancy exists between retailers that are high performers (profit, return on assets, and so on) and those that are marginal performers. At a store level, there is a growing tendency for two types of retailers—full-service, premium-price retailers and limited-service, commodity-price retailers. At the market level, there appears to be income polarization such that a rich-poor gap is emerging. Finally, at the household level, consumers increasingly seem to be seeking value in two distinct ways, either by maximizing quality ("first class") or by minimizing price ("no class"). Whether such trends are short-term or long-term, ephemeral, or inevitable is not at issue. Given their existence and the fact that they are interrelated (and often conflicting), retailers must be open-minded in their thinking and flexible in their operations so they can appropriately position and reposition themselves for competitive leadership.

CONCLUSION

Forecasting the future is a necessary activity for any firm seeking to survive. Heraclitus' conclusion that "nothing is permanent except change" is no less applicable today than when it was first proffered. Even so, to forecast the future today is probably more difficult than it was in his time. Changes in the political and economic infrastructures of the world are intricately interrelated and are occurring at an accelerating pace, and their impacts are being felt nearly instantaneously around the globe. As Forrester (1991, p. 61) asserts, "the challenge to business in the coming decade will be to operate in a world where trends of the past no longer predict the future." In the past two years alone changes have taken place that virtually no one would have predicted ten years, one year, or even six months prior to their occurrence.

In the future, no one retailing strategy will always be correct, and "following the leader" will more likely lead to disaster than success. As Levy (1989) notes, in the future managerial focus must be more external than internal. Technology will increasingly direct retailing strategy and impact the manner in which business is conducted. Bergin's (1990) advice, that to successfully compete in the 1990s, a retailer must:

- invest in technology
- find (and exploit) a niche
- prize its people
- make shopping fun
- know its customers
- be convenient
- know its product offering
- widen its vision

is probably as valid a guide as now exists.

Although following Bergin's advice will not guarantee success, not following it will ensure failure. The key to retailing success is constantly to anticipate the future, then to prepare for it by leveraging the firm's distinctive competency.

2

Retailing in the Year 2000: Quixotic Consumers? Exotic Markets? Neurotic Retailers?

Wilton Thomas Anderson

Although the 1990s have only begun, perhaps the most significant single event shaping retailing in the decade ahead has already occurred, halfway around the world. The Iraqi invasion of Kuwait and the allies response illustrate once again that the world economy is a frighteningly fragile Humpty Dumpty. While all the king's horses and all the king's men may be able to put this Humpty Dumpty back together again, there can no longer be any shadow of a doubt that the economies of all the leading countries of the world are simply yo-yos on the same string, their economic ups and downs tied to the egos and actions of a handful of key players in the game of global petroleum politics. To date, the war in the Mideast has cost consumers worldwide billions at the gas pump, billions more in increased costs of products and services, and more billions in tax allocations to support the allied defense of Saudi Arabia and the economic embargo of Iraq, with no end in sight—all in response to the unanticipated actions of one megalomaniac in the Mideast.

Nearly two decades after the 1973 OPEC oil embargo, the United States and her allies still have no energy policy. Their enemies do. In less than one year in office, Ronald Reagan quickly unraveled the energy conservation, diversification, and self-sufficiency initiatives of Jimmy Carter—while Congress sat idly by, hardly more than a spectator in a drama that would return to haunt the economy again and again. Elevated to office in the afterglow of the bulletproof presidency of the "Great Communicator," George Bush has perpetuated the ostrichlike energy policies of his predecessor, while Congress remains comatose. But Congress, as distinguished historian Barbara W. Tuchman points out in her contemporary classic, *The March of Folly*, is "a body of followers not leaders" (1984, p. 367). Since Congress may be presumed to follow what it senses to be the trend of public opinion, its persistent torpor is evidence that until the Iraqi invasion of Kuwait, the silent majority *was* the majority opinion of indifference to the issue of energy dependence.

Today, the fallout from twenty years of political and public inertia on the issue of energy dependence is that the economic futures of both the East and the West are intertwined in uncertainty. All economic estimates have been rendered abruptly invalid, all financial forecasts suspect, all long-range strategic business planning shelved, all bets off.

The fact is that the 1990s promise unending economic uncertainty (Fierman 1990). Perhaps the 21st century will bring international economic stability—and therefore predictability—but we doubt it. In spite of *glasnost*, *perestroika*, the reunification of Germany, and EC 1992, the fact that Iraq's Saddam Hussein, Libya's Colonel Muammar Khadaffi, Iran's spiritual leader Ayatullah Ali Khamenei and president Ali Akbar Rafsanjani, the late Ayatullah Khameini's handpicked successors; and Yasir Arafat and the PLO have a not-so-hidden agenda of ongoing political, economic, and military agitation and hold so many key cards means one thing: unending economic volatility worldwide. The Medellin drug cartel, Michael Milken and the junk bond junkies, and Charles Keating, Jr., and the thousands of nameless, faceless culprits behind the savings and loan, banking, and impending insurance crises have only added fuel to the fire closer to home.

What does unending economic volatility have to do with retailing in the 1990s? Everything. Business organizations everywhere ultimately take their marching orders from the marketplace. That is, consumption drives production and distribution; demand drives supply. In more personal terms, anything that affects consumers ultimately affects producers and distributors. The recurring reverberations of the volatile price of petroleum will leave consumers in a perpetual state of sticker shock. Unable to plan their purchasing with any confidence, consumers will spread their uncertainty to the supply side of the economic equation like a persistent plague. Producers and distributors who survive will live by their wits, unable to plan for an uncertain future. It is not a pretty picture, and we owe it all to the politicians and political sycophants who failed to put an energy policy in place these past twenty years.

If the only economic certainty is economic uncertainty, how can we forecast the future of retailing for the 1990s? Long threads decipherable in the demographic fabric of the United States, as well as persistent themes in consumer behavior for as long as there have been consumers, are the topics of this paper.

Rather than engaging in idle, unsupportable speculation about changes in consumption behavior, we will focus on what we do know, and can document, about the glacial drift in the demographic composition of the U.S. population, followed by a glimpse of the exotic markets emerging in Europe and Asia. Then we will turn our attention to perhaps the most overlooked facet of consumption behavior—*continuity*, rather than change. Specifically, we will focus on the impetus to consumption, the five fundamental themes that have shaped shopping and consumption for as long as there have been shoppers and consumers: value, convenience, the constant collision of the old with the new, the marriage of shopping and show biz, and self-indulgence.

THE NEW DEMOGRAPHICS

Demographics have been much debunked as market segmentation variables for good reasons. What can you learn about "real" people from a superficial descriptive demographic caricature? The answer is, "A lot!" Unlike speculative behavioral, psychographic, and life-style segmentation that presumes "past behavior is the best predictor of future behavior," all other things held equal, demographic segmentation requires no ceteris parabus. Demographic change occurs with a kind of glacial certainty in the absence of catastrophe; and in the face of global economic uncertainty it may be the only reliable barometer of future consumption behavior.

Rather than burying consumers under a blizzard of demographic data and other debris, we are going to focus on several major emerging markets in the United States—markets that will keep right on growing in spite of world economic uncertainty. Interestingly, these emerging markets are often at odds with conventional interpretations of demographic trends, a contradiction that can be best understood by examining what Deloitte & Touche strategic consultant Brian Kardon (1990b) calls "demographic disparities."

Bigger, but Smaller

The U.S. population passed the 250 million mark in 1990, a gain of more than 23 million or 10 percent over 1980. Between 1990 and 2000 the population will increase another 22 million or 8 percent to more than 270 million consumers. Put in perspective, the population increase for the decades past and current is only slightly smaller than the entire population of Canada!

Although the U.S. market has grown in absolute terms, the 1990s promise smaller targets of opportunity, both in sheer size and in duration. The factors fueling population growth are conspiring to produce what some have termed "the death of the mass market—and mass marketing." Although birthrates continue their downward trend, immigration and longer life expectancy are more than sufficient to make up the difference. The unprecedented emergence of the "gray market" and the rebirth of "ethnic markets" have fractured the mass market—not beyond recognition, but certainly into fragments. *Market fragmentation* is the retailing watchword of the 1990s.

Older, but Younger

Over the past thirty years the medical march against mortality produced breakthroughs against the major causes of death from infectious diseases, especially among children. Over the next thirty years the major medical advances against mortality will be in controlling chronic and degenerative diseases afflicting older people. The war against mortality means one thing: longevity (Exter 1990, p. 32). Large-scale longevity is virtually without precedent in any marketplace worldwide.

Between 1980 and 1990 the median age in the United States increased from 30 to 33, and it keeps right on climbing. Life expectancy reached 78 years in 1990 (Kardon 1990b, p. 3). Today, one in four Americans is aged 50 or older. By 2020 one in three Americans will be 50 or older as baby boomers pass midlife. Even more startling, the American population of people aged 50 or older will increase 74 percent, whereas people under 50 years of age will increase by a mere 1 percent. Most Americans will face more years of adult life *after* their children have grown and left home than years of parenting (Dychtwald and Gable 1990a, p. 65). But these superficial statistics disguise more than they reveal.

As the smaller group of people born during the Depression enter retirement over the next ten years, the number of people in their 60s will decrease. Hence, the prospects for businesses targeting the retirement market are mixed. They face a shrinking market for the 1990s, but the year 2000 should usher in a boom for the retirement industry, including retailers.

The boom markets of the 1990s and beyond are the oldest age groups. Over the next thirty years the most conservative estimates forecast that the number of men in their 60s will increase by 75 percent or 17 million. The number of women in their 60s will increase by 68 percent to 19 million. Together they will nearly equal the current population of the Pacific Coast states. Although the absolute increases are considerably smaller, the percentage increases will accelerate for both men and women in their 70s, 80s, and older (Exter 1990, p. 36).

What does the growing gray market mean for retailers? It is far from clear. The life-styles of large numbers of people in their 60s, 70s, and 80s are unexplored territory, both for the people themselves and for retailers. What does seem certain is that the very concept of age will undergo radical revision as large numbers of people contemplate how to spend ten, twenty, or more years beyond traditional retirement age, health permitting. While the future of medical research is a foggy window, it is almost inconceivable that a society that has historically placed so much emphasis on activity, on work—on *business*—would resign itself to a sedentary life as medical and health sciences push age beyond current limits. The U.S. market may be getting older, but it will act considerably younger than its predecessors.

Incidentally, U.S. retailers will need 22.9 million workers by the year 2000, an increase of 20 percent or 3.8 million workers over the next decade, making retailing the fastest-growing employment sector in the nation, according to the U.S. Bureau of Labor Statistics (Liebeck 1990, p. 125). The shrinking percentage of people in the MTV generation in particular— individuals 16 to 24 years of age—will create severe personnel shortages, forcing retailers to look past young workers to the elderly, the disabled, and the handicapped and to employee prospects who have a limited English-language proficiency.

Melting Pot, but Polyglot

"Give me your tired, your poor, your huddled masses, yearning to breathe free" (Lazarus 1886) had a different meaning a century ago than it has today. Europeans in particular who passed through Ellis Island prior to the turn of the 20th century wanted to live the American Dream to its fullest extent—to become Americans, literally, figuratively, in every way. In one generation much of their ethnicity evaporated.

The Land of Opportunity is no less hypnotic and seductive today, but today's immigrant is different. The Mexican, Filipino, Chinese, Korean, and Vietnamese immigrants who form the vanguard of immigration are proud of their cultural heritage and seek to preserve their ethnic identity. During the 1980s they collectively numbered five hundred thousand legal and two hundred thousand illegal immigrants each year, more than one-fifth of the U.S. population growth, and their numbers are increasing.

Blacks number thirty-one million, a stable 12 percent of the population, up 16 percent over the past decade. Today Hispanics number twenty-one million or 8 percent of the U.S. population, up 44 percent since 1980, although it is essential to note that people of Hispanic cultural origin are comprised of white, black, and other ethnic categories. The largest gains are among people of primarily Asian origin, today numbering nearly nine million, up 65 percent since 1980. Although whites increased by 8 percent or sixteen million to two hundred ten million, their share of the total U.S. population dropped from 86 to 84 percent. These racial and ethnic trends will continue. America is both a melting pot of cultural diversity and a polyglot (Garreau 1981) of ethnic insulation.

What do increasing cultural diversity and ethnic insulation mean for retailing? More market fragmentation. Certainly a number of established retailers are poised to capitalize on the one common denominator that cuts across racial and ethnic diversity—the persistent emphasis on bang-for-the-buck, or *value*. However, currently most retailers are ill equipped to capitalize on the new opportunities promised by market fragmentation because they do not have access to the expertise required to understand the behavioral manifestations of cultural heritage and ethnic identification. The leading retailers of the 1990s will be those that shore up the knowledge gap by recruiting, hiring, training, and promoting people or by employing outside consultants from cultural and ethnic backgrounds corresponding to those market fragments that promise the greatest profit potential.

Nationalism, but Regionalism

The image of the Land of Opportunity has always been accompanied by an asterisk, since access to opportunity has always been unequal among individuals and groups in America. However, opportunity is the one theme that cuts across the cultural diversity and ethnic identification that increasingly characterize the United States. Opportunity is the essence of our sense of nationalism.

Nowhere is the inequality of opportunity more visible today than in regional population figures. Today the South remains solidly in first place with eighty-seven million people, followed by the Midwest with sixty million people and the West with fifty-two million people. The Northeast is the least populous region of the country, with fifty-one million people. However, population growth rates reveal a very different picture.

Over the last decade the South and West captured nearly 90 percent of the national population gain, with the Northeast and the Midwest together accounting for 10 percent. The West grew by 21 percent. California passed the twenty-nine million mark and now has more people than Canada, Australia, and three-quarters of the countries of Europe (Barringer 1990). The South grew by 15 percent. In Florida alone eighteen hundred people move in every day, but only nine hundred leave (Papandrew 1989), pushing the population up to nearly thirteen million. The Northeast lagged considerably behind with a percentage growth rate equal to the national figure of 10 percent. The Midwest grew by a paltry 2 percent, with Ohio and Michigan, two of the most populous states, exhibiting virtually no growth and Iowa losing 3 percent. The death of the American heartland has gone nearly unnoticed.

Slowly but relentlessly the one hundred thirty-nine thousand square miles of the vast and troubled Great Plains, one-fifth of the nation's land mass, is stumbling back in time toward a frontier reborn, where grass will be king, some buffalo may actually roam again, and people will be few and far between (Sidey 1990, pp. 53-54, 56). In the dying American heartland Philip Burgess of the Center for the New West in Denver sees the rebirth of an "archipelago society"—a few small cities sprinkled across great washes of sparsely settled land, with tiny towns at death's door and vast ranches eating up the vacant acres. The few surviving towns will be oases in the American desert, offering sparse services and cultural amenities for the few diehards who remain. The principal beneficiaries of the impending death of the heartland will be the big cities.

Swelling Cities, but Shrinking Suburbs

Ten years ago demographers looked back on a decade of unexpected, unprecedented *non*metropolitan population growth and heralded a new age, a return to basics, a turning back of the clock to a simpler time when people's relationships to each other and their environment mattered more than their career or their materialistic "pile of things," as singer and social-activist Tracy Chapman terms it, or "stuff" as comedian George Carlin describes it. Today, demographers acknowledge that the 1970s were merely a hickcup in the uninterrupted tradition of urban-directed migration and metropolitan population growth that has dominated the country since the Industrial Revolution. With nonmetropolitan areas beset by the farm crisis, employment cutbacks in major industries, and recovery from waves of national recession, people spent the 1980s looking for work. Employment opportunities, more than any other factor, explained population growth (Beale 1988). And employment opportunities were, and are, found in the cities.

The 1980s saw metropolitan areas grow at a rate nearly twice that of nonmetropolitan areas. Indeed, shopping-center developer Alexander Haagen maintains, "the inner cities are literally the only big market left in the American economy" (O'Neill 1990b). The big winners—or big losers, depending on one's point of view—are the big cities. By 1990 Los Angeles-Long Beach eclipsed New York City as the most populous metropolitan area with a population of 8.8 million, an increase in excess of 17 percent. The hottest metropolitan growth areas both literally and figuratively, however, are in the South and the West. Leading the top twenty-five metropolitan statistical areas is Riverside-San Bernardino, which borders the Los Angeles metropolitan area, with a population of 2.3 million, up 45 percent, with Phoenix hot on its heels at 2.2 million people, up 43 percent. Dallas, with 2.6 million people, grew by one-third; whereas Atlanta with 2.8 million, San Diego with 2.4 million, and Houston with 3.5 million, in spite of its lingering economic illness, all grew more than 25 percent. Among the top twenty-five metropolitan areas, only Pittsburgh with 2.1 million (down 6 percent), Detroit with 4.4 million (down 2 percent), and Cleveland with 1.8 million people (down 4 percent), lost population.

What are the hot spots of the 1990s? Four metropolitan areas in Florida are expected to grow by more than half by 2005: Orlando (86 percent), West Palm Beach (75 percent), Fort Lauderdale (64 percent), and Tampa/St. Petersburg (55 percent).   California will add another four: Anaheim/Santa Ana (83 percent), Sacramento (63 percent), San Jose (62 percent), and Oakland (56 percent).   Dallas (60 percent) and Phoenix (52 percent) will make it an even ten metropolitan areas with expected population growth in excess of 50 percent.

During this resurgence of metropolitan growth since 1980, big city problems have followed the flight to the suburbs: crime, congestion, smog, bureaucracy and bankruptcy, and governmental deficits and insolvency. In fact, the urban sprawl around major metropolitan areas has grown so dense that it is all but impossible to tell where the city ends and suburbs begin, blurring the distinction between urban and suburban retailing. This trend will continue, placing an increasing premium on "location, location, location" in spite of the fact that location is no longer the number-one determinant of retail preference (*Monitor* 1990, pp. 27-30).

More Migration, but Less Mobility

One in six Americans—more than the population of New York City, Los Angeles, Chicago, Philadelphia, Detroit, Washington, D.C., Houston, and Boston combined—moves each year, a percentage that has remained remarkably constant since the 1960s (Beale 1989). Many Americans believe that mobility is on the rise because of job dislocations, disillusionment and divorce, and the apparent restlessness of the baby-boom generation (Long 1990, p. 48).   According to experts, deliberate residential relocation decisions have been rendered both desirable and feasible by a quiet conspiracy of factors: rapid transportation, advances in communication and computer technology, rural modernization, and urban concentrations so large, expensive, and anonymous they overwhelm the advantages of city life (Beale 1988). Still others point to the fact that the apparent emerging scatter-pattern of population migration is the result of a reconciliation of employment opportunity with a variety of lifestyle factors—climate, environmental amenities, recreation, and family and friendship ties. The factors fueling increasingly complex mobility patterns are potentially many and may reflect a significant evolution in life-styles and values.

Exactly how often does the average American (whoever she or he is) move? That is a question that defies a precise answer. Householders on average have lived in the same residence five years and nine months, but there are significant differences by age, location, home ownership, and income. Middle-aged householders have lived in their homes more than eight years, whereas those under 25 years of age have occupied their residence under six months. Hence, average length of residence increases with age, peaking at nineteen years for householders 75 years of age or older (Long 1990, pp. 46-48).

Length of residence also varies inversely with degree of urbanization. At one extreme, the median length of residence is slightly more than eight years for nonmetropolitan areas of the South. At the opposite extreme is two and one-half years for large urban areas of the West (Long 1990, pp. 46-48).

Surveys have consistently found that renters move far more often than homeowners. The median length of residence for renters is slightly more than one and one-half years, whereas the median length of residence for homeowners is nine and one-half years. At every age householders at the lowest income levels have occupied their current residence for the shortest period of time.

In spite of the fact that one-sixth of the U.S. population moves every year, there has been a significant decrease in mobility among young adults, possibly because they are living longer with their parents. Rates of interstate migration have also fallen because of the growth of dual-income households and the increasingly exaggerated differences in housing prices among regions of the country. Most people who change addresses move only a short distance—a median of about six miles! Six miles is about the same as the median distance they commute to work—and has not changed in forty years. The symbol of America on the move is not a massive moving van barreling along I-35, but an overloaded pickup truck shuttling back and forth between two apartments (Long 1990, p. 49).

Although most moves are local, the sheer magnitude of the annual migration is impressive. In the face of steady-state rates of growth in domestic population and discretionary income, consumer migration may be the single-most significant source of change in shopping and consumption patterns for the foreseeable future. The implications of consumer migration for urban, suburban, and rural markets have been virtually ignored by retailers.

Along with their possessions, consumer migrants pack up their shopping and consumption protocols when they move. While past behavior is the best predictor of future behavior, past shopping and consumption protocols are reconciled with present market opportunities available in the new community of residence—and a new consumer is born. The magnitude of the adjustment in shopping and consumption protocols necessitated by a change of residence is a function of the compatibility between past and present market environments. Simply put, mainstream migrants—those moving toward more metropolitan areas—face far richer retailing alternatives and take advantage of them. Conversely, counterstream migrants—those moving away from metropolitan areas—face far more restricted retailing alternatives and must downscale their shopping. These are only two of many possible patterns of consumer migration that remain to be explored.

Together, but Alone

Although the number of households grew by 17 percent in the 1980s—significantly faster than the U.S. population—household size shrank from 2.8 to 2.6, down from 3.3 as recently as 1960. Today only 7 percent of U.S. households consist of two married parents and two children. One in four households consists of a person who lives alone, up 26 percent in the last decade.

The fastest-growing household consisted of women with children— and no husband present—up 36 percent since 1980. Among nonfamilies, the fastest growing household consisted of people living with nonrelatives, up 46 percent to 4.5 million. Nonfamily households headed by men grew faster than those headed by women. Retailers have recognized this trend in downscaling their portion options and emphasizing individual, self-indulgent motives rather than family or social consumption motives.

Interestingly, in spite of more single-parent households, traditional values have made a comeback, counterbalancing the promiscuity of the 1970s and the conspicuous consumption of the 1980s. Concern for family, religion, and home are on the rise, fueled by conservatism and concern about the AIDS epidemic following the experimental 1970s and the flamboyant 1980s.

Richer, but Poorer

Although Americans are richer than at any time in U.S. history, the income gap between the rich and poor grew into a chasm in the 1980s. Sales of Rolls Royces reached an all-time high at the same time as the number of homeless did. In the 1990s the rich will get richer as the poor grow poorer (Kardon 1990b, p. 4). The beneficiaries are simultaneously the exclusive specialty retailers and the downscale discounters.

While the national median household income adjusted for inflation increased nearly 3 percent to $30,000 between 1980 and 1990, the distribution of income has been uneven. While the number of householders under age 25 fell 30 percent over the decade, median household income fell as well—by 10 percent. At the opposite extreme, householders aged 65 years and older experienced the greatest economic gains during the 1980s, with a 14 percent increase in real income. These statistics are more ephemeral than real, however, because both groups are more than 40 percentage points below the national household income median. For virtually all other householders, real income adjusted for inflation increased at or near the national median of 3 percent.

These superficial income figures disguise significant regional and metropolitan differences in the cost of living. The cost of living in New England and the Pacific Coast is 12 percent higher than the national average, whereas in the East, West Central, Southwest, and Rocky Mountain regions it is 5 to 10 percent below the national average. The cost of living in the Mid-Atlantic and Southeast regions is 2 percent above the national average.

Differences among regions, however, are not as large as differences between big cities and rural areas (O'Hare 1990). People who live in cities of one million or more estimate an annual cost of living that is 18 percent above the national average, whereas those living in small towns and rural areas estimate a cost of living 20 percent below the national average. Suburbanites say the average annual cost of living is 7 percent above the national average, a figure identical to that reported by central city residents. Overall, metropolitan residents say it takes 33 percent more to live in their community than nonmetropolitan residents must spend. This figure is identical to the disparity in their respective incomes, suggesting that what you *earn* may determine what you think it costs to live. Or, as a colleague of ours put it, "I can be poor at any income level."

What you think it costs to live also depends on who you are (O'Hare 1990). People in the second half of the baby boom—people aged 25 to 34—estimate their annual cost of living to be 11 percent above the national average, whereas younger people and people aged 55 or older estimate their cost of living to be 9 percent below the national average. Curiously, although whites and Hispanics estimate their cost of living to be at the national average, blacks project their cost of living as 5 percent above the national average. The estimated cost of living varies directly with education and with annual family income. People without any college education estimate their cost of living to be at or significantly less than the national average, whereas college graduates place their cost of living 15 percent above the national average. People earning at or below the national average estimate their annual cost of living to be 10 to 15 percent below the national average. People earning more than the national average estimate their annual cost of living to be 5 to 15 percent above the national average, peaking at 26 percent above average for those earning $50,000 or more. Clearly, the cost of living must be taken into account when assessing market potential.

What do current and projected household income patterns mean for retailers in the 1990s? A decade of impending economic volatility is likely to render past real-income gains null and void, leaving the economy in general, and households in particular, teetering on the brink of recession and perpetual budgetary belt-tightening. The picture for the retail industry is not bright, but it is substantially less dim for the downscale discount retailer.

Better Educated, but Less Literate

Americans continue their climb up the educational ladder. Today more than 77 percent of Americans are high school graduates, the highest percentage ever. The educational discrepancy between high school-educated men and women has narrowed to less than 1 percent. One in five Americans has completed at least four years of college, up from one in six a decade ago.

Although these raw figures imply greater consumer capacity for accessing, processing, analyzing, interpreting, and acting on information, several factors point the opposite direction. First, a declining percentage of minorities are graduating from high school or attending college. Second, high school graduation standards and standardized test scores have steadily decayed over the last decade, leaving many high school graduates as functionally illiterate dependents on social welfare programs and drains on the economy. Third, with education comes a "revolution of rising expectations," if not ambition and accompanying ability and achievement, producing generation after generation of chronic underachievers imprisoned by lack of opportunity or initiative. Fourth, essential prerequisites for technical and scientific employment continue to outstrip the throughput of trained talent, rendering science and technology impoverished and noncompetitive in the international marketplace of ideas. Fifth, in spite of limited educational gains, the American educational system lags behind those of other countries, implying that the United States is losing ground to her competitors where it matters most—in the flow of intellectual talent into the economy.

More Employed Women, but Fewer Employed Men

Nearly fifty-five million or 60 percent of all women aged 16 or older are employed outside the home, double the 1960 percentage, and up from 50 percent in 1980. Conversely, the percentage of men aged 16 or older employed outside the home has dropped from 88 to 75 percent or sixty-seven million over the last forty years. These trends are the manifestation of several factors: (1) the rapid increase in single or single-head households, especially households headed by women; (2) the increase in house husbands, reversing the traditional division of parental responsibility within the home; and (3) an increase in the number of individuals working at home using the new computer and communication technologies rather than commuting to and from work. These trends will continue.

THE BOTTOM LINE ON THE NEW DEMOGRAPHICS

The decipherable threads of demographic change in the U.S. market signal growing market fragmentation. Growing market fragmentation does not, however, imply the "death of the mass market," as so many contemporary observers of American retailing have maintained (Hogsett 1990, p. 42; Leventhal 1990, p. 16). The scale and financial momentum of the mass market, as well as the economic viability of emerging "market fragments," can be assessed by arraying consumers along a continuum using some of retailers' favorite words: downscale, midscale, and upscale. These terms evoke widely held stereotypes, only half of which are accurate (Waldrop 1990b, pp. 24-30).

Using the *American Demographics* cutoff criterion of an annual household income of $25,000 or less, almost half of all U.S. households—nearly forty-three million—are downscale (Waldrop 1990b). One-third, or thirty-one million, are midscale with an annual household income of $25,000 to $49,999. Only one-fifth, or nineteen million households, are upscale with an income in excess of $50,000, and fewer than half of these earn more than $66,000. Slightly more than 3 percent or three million households earn more than $100,000 annually (see Table 2.1).

Downscale Consumers

Downscale households have median incomes less than half the national household median. Education is a critical denominator of occupational and economic opportunities, and fewer than 10 percent of downscalers have completed four years of college. Although downscalers are more likely than midscalers or upscalers to be black or Hispanic, minorities comprise a relatively small percentage of the total: 16 percent are black and 9 percent are Hispanic, versus 11 percent and 7 percent of all households.

Downscalers are least likely to live in families. Married couples comprise 37 percent of downscale households, in contrast to 56 percent of all households. Only 57 percent are heads of households, versus 71 percent of all householders. Fewer than 30 percent have children at home compared to more than 40 percent of higher-income households. Nearly 20 percent are female househeads, twice as many as midscalers and five times as many as upscalers.

Downscalers are comprised of the youngest and the oldest householders, with a disproportionate share of householders under age 25 and over 65. The picture of the downscale household is a house divided—between young people who are struggling to be self-supporting and old people who are struggling to survive on a fixed retirement income in the face of insatiable inflation. Imprisoned within insufficient income, the young must settle for the low-priced version of the American Dream. Equally economically constrained, the old face fewer options on all fronts, with far less energy and an overarching need for security.   Their consumption behavior is dictated by need or controlled by insurance, governmental subsidy programs, or logistical lack of access to alternative retailing options outside the neighborhood or community.   Although tight economic constraints should point in the direction of value-oriented, price-sensitive shopping of off-price or discount retailers or category killers, such retailers are often inaccessible to downscalers.   They must settle for the available local options, which are often high-priced, even predatory, retailers.

Table 2.1.   Upscale, Midscale, and Downscale Households

Characteristics	Total	Downscale less than $25,000	Midscale $25,000 to $49,999	Upscale $50,000 and over
Total households (*in thousands*)	92,830	42,569	30,927	19,332
Percent of all households	100.0	45.9	33.3	20.8
Median household income	$27,200	$12,900	$35,500	$66,300
Percent family households	70.9	56.9	79.1	88.7
Percent married-couple households	56.1	36.6	66.9	82.0
Percent female-headed households	11.7	17.5	8.5	4.1
Percent with children under 18	36.1	29.2	41.6	42.7
Percent with one person in household	24.5	39.5	15.4	5.9
Percent with two or three persons in household	49.8	44.2	54.6	54.6
Percent with four or more persons in household	25.7	16.4	30.0	39.5
Median age of householder	49	51	41	42
Percent high school graduates	75.8	61.0	85.1	93.3
Percent with four or more years of college	22.3	9.7	23.7	47.5
Percent Black	11.4	16.4	8.2	5.4
Percent Hispanic	7.1	8.7	6.6	4.4

Source: Adapted from Judith Waldrop (1990), "Up and Down the Income Scale," *American Demographics* (July 30), 30. Reprinted with permission ©*American Demographics*, July 1990, Ithaca, NY.

Midscale Consumers

One-third of all households—31 million—are midscale, with median annual income nearly one-third higher than the national figure. Diversity is their defining characteristic. In many ways they mirror their upscale counterparts, but with less money. Indeed, it can be argued that one of the primary constituencies that comprise the midscale market consists of young families too early in the family life cycle to have climbed the income ladder into the upscale segment. They are just passing through. Other segments of the midscale market are there to stay. The latter include empty nesters, retired pensioners, and single-earner young families.

The correlation between education and income is detectable among midscalers. One in four has completed four or more years of college, twice the percentage of downscalers, but half the percentage of upscalers. Although it is tempting to conclude there is a causal link between education and income, the connection is far from clear. Does upscale or midscale background lead to greater emphasis on income, and on education as a window of opportunity to higher income, and hence lead to higher income? Or does education open opportunities to earn a higher income? Whatever the causal relationship, the correlation between education and income is irrefutable and provides one of the most important windows of opportunity for retailers for the 1990s. Education is not only correlated with income, it is also a barometer of taste and therefore one of the most sensitive denominators of emerging market segments or fragments.

Two-thirds of midscalers are married, twice the percentage of downscalers, but less than upscalers. Nearly 80 percent of midscale households consist of a family, 20 percent more than downscalers. While both midscalers and upscalers cluster in their early 40s, a higher percent of midscalers are under 40 or over 60 than upscalers. The percentage of minority households declines steadily from downscale to midscale to upscale households, but their numbers and proportional representation are growing rapidly and merit close monitoring.

Midscalers are an important mirror of the evolution and maturity of the mass market since they are a crossroads of consumer diversity. On the one hand, their diversity is submerged under the weight of income constraints. They are value-oriented, price-sensitive shoppers because they have no alternative, and abundant retail choices are within the realm of logistical accessibility. Hence off-price and discount retailers and category killers will continue to find viable mass market opportunities among midscalers. On the other hand, because many midscalers are merely passing through—on their way up or down the income pyramid—they represent potentially important developing or dissolving market segments or fragments. Midscalers on their way *up* the income pyramid are guided by their expectations of increasing economic opportunity and their consumption protocols are crystalizing into discernable discrete market opportunities—first splinters of the mass market that may mature into viable market fragments that mature as their discretionary incomes increase. Midscalers on their way *down* the income pyramid carry their established shopping and consumption protocols with them. In the face of ever-tightening income constraints, they constantly reallocate shrinking discretionary dollars among a shortened list of shopping and consumption priorities. Caught in an income vise, they may rank among the most attractive intensely loyal market fragments because their shopping and consumption protocols are the result of deliberate priority decisions.

Upscale Consumers

Upscale consumers have median annual incomes nearly two and one-half times the national figure. While constituting only 20 percent of U.S. households—nineteen million—they outpace their downscale and midscale counterparts in both total absolute and discretionary income. Yet, there is very little real affluence among upscale consumers given the multiple demands on their incomes—children in college, care for aging parents, saving for retirement, and paying others to perform household chores.

Upscalers are clustered in the peak earning years, in their 40s and 50s. Collectively they make an almost irrefutable case that education is a kind of predestination to economic opportunity and income. Half have completed four years or more of college; 20 percent have completed five or more years of college.

While the national divorce rate climbed from 50 percent to 66 percent between 1965 and 1985 (Glenn 1989), upscalers have been largely immune to the disease. Upscalers are predominantly married (80 percent) with children living at home (43 percent). Few are female househeads (4 percent) or single persons living alone (6 percent). It is seldom lonely at the top.

Although fewer than 10 percent of upscale consumers are minorities—half black, half Hispanic—both groups are growing rapidly, far in excess of whites. Coupled with the rapid growth of the Asian population in the United States and the influx of primarily Asian and Hispanic immigrants, upscale minorities are among the most important emerging market segments and fragments.

The markets that emerge among the younger segment of the midscale strata mature into economically viable targets as they climb the income ladder. Yet upscale consumers are no less price sensitive than their downscale and midscale counterparts. These seemingly schizophrenic qualities imply that discounters and category killers must consistently compete for upscalers' dollars on the basis of value-for-the-money, whereas specialty retailers must sharpen their marketing focus to capitalize on the idiosyncrasies of upscale consumers whose discretionary incomes permit self-expression—at a price.

NEW INTERNATIONAL MARKETS: EUROPE AND ASIA

In the face of anemic economic growth and radical economic volatility at home, the most attractive retailing options for the 1990s and beyond may lie across the water in Europe and Asia. Although few domestic retailers are positioned to capitalize on international opportunities, virtually all retailers will be affected by the emergence of the one-world marketplace. As the international borders and barriers come down and the free flow of products goes up, even the smallest mom-and-pop store will be swept up in change.

The New Europe

By 1992 the twelve nations of the European Community or EC—Belgium, Denmark, France, Greece, Ireland, Italy, Luxembourg, Netherlands, Portugal, Spain, United Kingdom, and a newly united Germany—will merge into a united market of 350 million people, diverse in cultural, ethnic, and economic background but united by a common currency and a pent-up appetite for consumer goods and services. Ironically, by reaching over, under, and around the Iron Curtain, capitalist television and radio advertising may have been the decisive factor in bringing down the Berlin Wall (Mount 1990). Open roads, however, by no means imply equal economic opportunities east and west of the Iron Curtain. Foundering in failed economies, Eastern Europe will be slow to join the economic revolution sweeping across Western Europe. Where the wall once stood, an invisible economic barrier now exists; and few Western retailers will venture behind it.

While the U.S. economy inched along ahead of Western Europe at a 3 percent rate of growth through the 1980s, Western Europe's economic growth will likely outpace the projected anemic 1 percent rate of growth of the U.S. economy during the 1990s. The removal of physical, fiscal, and technical barriers in the European Community will create immediate market opportunities for those positioned to capitalize on them. European investment, manufacturing, development, and retailing opportunities in particular are likely to explode. In anticipation of the explosion, total European Community cross-border acquisitions increased by more than 50 percent in 1988 and are increasing at an accelerating rate (Schiro and Skolnik 1990, p. 4). European-based retailers have aggressively moved to forge strategic organizational alliances, both vertically and horizontally, to forestall anticipated competition. European-based retailers have shown their U.S. rivals the weapon. The challenge confronting U.S. retailers is to form strategic alliances and position themselves in the European Community before their European competitors capture unassailable market positions.

To date, U.S. firms have not aggressively targeted European retailers. U.S. investment in Europe increased 20 percent in 1989, but only 2 percent was in the retail sector. Instead, U.S. chains have resorted to entering the European market by opening a series of stores abroad, with notable success. Toys "R" Us, The Gap, and Pizza Hut are cases in point.

Perhaps the most striking aspect of the European Community is the extreme diversity of retailing conventions and practices from country to country and within countries. The progressive economies, such as those of Germany and the United Kingdom, have undergone rapid concentration in retailing. Conversely, less progressive economies, such as Greece and Portugal, and rural areas are still dominated by the independent family shopkeeper. Over the last two decades, however, mass merchandisers such as the hypermarket have emerged throughout the European Community, even in fragmented markets. Their emergence has been accompanied by progressive consumption, closely paralleling that in the United States. Still, long-standing contrasts persist, rooted to deep-seated cultural differences.

Ian Flanagan, CEO of Landauer Associates Inc., a New York City-based real estate consulting firm, puts it this way: "You shop in Europe on two feet. . . . In America, you shop on four wheels." The U.S. shopping environment is dominated by suburban malls. The traditions and conventions of much of Europe are reflected in more rigid shopping and consumption protocols (Papandrew 1990, pp. 101-102). Still there have been major shifts over the last decade: European consumers' disposable income has nearly doubled, with an increasing percentage of women entering the work force. European consumers place great importance on quality family and leisure time, resist infringements on either, and often work at home. European consumers are sensitive to health and environmental issues.

Although the sheer size of the European market has many retailers panting, few U.S. retailers believe they will be able to expand overseas to take advantage of the new international marketing opportunities, smothered as they are under staggering debt loads from leveraged buyouts. Only a small group of U.S. retailers has an international presence: Kmart, Sears, and Woolworth are the three major general mass merchandisers, whereas Toys "R" Us is far ahead of everyone else in establishing an international presence (Kelly 1990, pp. 149, 160).

Profound changes are anticipated in the structure and composition of the European market during the 1990s. Overall the projected pattern is toward fewer shops, larger retail outlets, and greater rationalization of the retail market. Hypermarkets currently account for 10 percent of all sales in the European Community, 13 percent in France, and 19 percent in Germany. France has been far and away the most progressive in experimenting with adapting retail structure to the characteristics of each market.

A curious legacy of generations of tradition and regimentation that lives on in spite of the rapid dismantling of borders and economic barricades also poses the greatest constraint on the potential of the emerging European markets: regulations. European retailers are closely regulated. Unlike other European industries, retailing regulations are imposed by each member nation, rather than the European Community itself. There is no European Community legislation specifically addressing the retail sector, and it is highly unlikely there will be any in the near future.

Retailing standards and practices are deeply entrenched in national culture, an arena in which the European Community conscientiously avoids interference. For example, national planning restrictions prevent hypermarkets from reaching their full market potential by limiting square footage or disallowing permits, even in France where they are well accepted. Hours of operation are also controlled by either national or regional legislation in all member countries. Retailers are open an average of fifty hours per week, but over half of European Community member states do not permit Sunday openings. Liberalization of hours of operation is a very controversial political issue. Since there is no coordinated effort among European Community members to address them, regulatory restrictions on market potential are unlikely to be reduced in the near future. "When in Rome, do as the Romans do" is a universal truism that poses a real limitation on market potential throughout Europe.

The obstacle that overseas expansion poses for U.S. retailers is not an unfamiliar experience. It is a classic market development/diversification dilemma—creating new markets for either existing or new products. Even extensive marketing research is insufficient to unlock the door. Partnerships or other workable relationships with indigenous retailers is indispensable to market penetration. Joint venturing with native European firms also permits U.S. retailers to take advantage of indispensable expertise and established distribution networks.

The New Asia

When Commodore Matthew Calbraith Perry's four "black ships"—symbolic both in color and in traumatic impact—sailed into Tokyo Bay on July 8, 1853, he confronted a society so certain of its cultural superiority that it had turned its back on the world and had lived in self-imposed isolation for over 250 years. Fearing the same contamination by Western culture and technology that had had such shattering impact on China, her long-time model and mentor, Japan had even refused the return of her own shipwrecked fishermen if they had been rescued by foreign vessels.

When Perry issued his infamous ultimatum to "open your *market*, or suffer the consequences" (that is what he actually said), no one could have anticipated that a sleeping giant had been awakened that would turn its self-conscious introspection outward, harnessing the technology of the West to its samurai tradition of being second to none. The words of the Tokugawa Shogun's adviser, Masayoshi Hotta, proved prophetic when Japan emerged as the world's dominant economic power 130 years later (Schlossstein 1984, p. 104):

> Our policy should be to stake everything on the present opportunity, to conclude friendly alliances, to send ships to foreign countries everywhere and conduct trade, to copy the foreigners where they are at their best and so repair our own shortcomings, to foster our national strength and complete our armaments, and so gradually subject the foreigners to our influence until in the end all the countries of the world know the blessings of perfect tranquility and our hegemony is acknowledged throughout the globe.

The rise of Japan was as remarkable as it was rapid. By 1900 Japan's capital industries were the technological equal of the West. By 1938 Japan was among the world's leading industrial and military powers. By Bloody Monday—October 19, 1987, the day the Dow Jones Industrial Average plummeted 25 percent—Japan had won World War III without suffering a single casualty on the battlefield of the international marketplace, eclipsing the United States as the leading industrial, technological, and financial power in the world. Only in military power could the United States challenge Japan's claim to world leadership (Prestowitz 1988, pp. 6-9).

Although Commodore Perry demanded that Japan open her market. . . or else, Japan managed to outthink, outflank, and ultimately outlast its antagonists for 130 years. Japan opened her windows to the West, but not her markets until recently, and then only a crack (Rapport 1990). The death of Emperor Hirohito on January 7, 1989, marked the death of economic isolationism and the birth of market opportunity in Japan. The 1990s will witness an explosion in international business presence, including international retailing, in Japan and throughout the Pacific Rim. By the end of the decade, Pacific Rim economies will be larger in total than that of either the United States or the European Community.

The economies of the Pacific Rim—those of Japan, Singapore, South Korea, Hong Kong, Taiwan, and Malaysia—grew at an accelerating annual rate over the 1980s, cresting at slightly less than 7 percent by 1990, whereas the U.S. economy declined from 3 percent per annum to less than 1 percent today. Collectively, Japan and the not-so-little dragons contribute most of the capital, technology, equipment, and expertise for Asia's developing economies, which provide the other half of the development equation— abundant natural resources and labor. Symbiosis has worked so well that American investments in Asia are currently paying off at an average annual rate of 31 percent in Singapore, 29 percent in Malaysia, 24 percent in Hong Kong, 18 percent in South Korea, and 14 percent in Japan, in contrast to 15 percent for U.S. investment in all foreign countries. Louis Kraar of *Fortune* (1990, p. 12) summed it up this way:

> The greatest danger in Asia for any global competitor would be failure to get there. What company can afford to pass up a market that soon will be larger in total GNP than the European Community? The risks of not tapping its potential are global. If Western companies do not establish a firm position in Asia, competitors from Japan, Taiwan, and Korea will gain more strength at home for even bigger assaults on markets in America and Europe.

The political, economic, and social changes sweeping through Asia, so evident on U.S. television screens halfway around the world, are mixing with the region's traditional values and life-styles and producing unprecedented, unexpected market opportunities. Change is occurring so rapidly—and often abruptly—that only the most intrepid (or foolish) marketing analyst pretends to understand their unfolding impact (Worthy 1990a, p. 51). Asians are undergoing the same revolution of rising expectations that engulfed the U.S. and Western Europe decades ago. The impact for consumer goods manufacturers, distributors, and retailers will be both large and lasting.

Collectively, the Asian side of the Pacific Rim is home to a staggering 1.7 billion people. Although population growth has slowed through most of the component countries, by the year 2010 an additional 400 million people will call the Pacific Rim home. China alone accounts for the lion's share, with an almost unimaginable 1.1 billion people, most of whom are living largely at the level of subsistence. Japan with 130 million people, South Korea with 42 million, Taiwan with 22 million, Malaysia with 18 million, Singapore with 2.7 million, and Hong Kong with 2.4 million—a total of 216 million people—collectively constitute a primary market only 10 percent smaller than the United States but will likely overtake the U.S. population by the year 2000.

Asian family composition is undergoing unprecedented change in two ways (Worthy 1990a). First, women are having fewer children as traditional roles splinter into multiple responsibilities for reasons that are familiar to women in the West—rising levels of education, need for additional household income, and occupational opportunities outside the home. Educational and occupational opportunities, however, have not been accompanied by a widespread acknowledgement of equality between the sexes, but the wheels have finally been set in motion. Second, rising incomes are fracturing an Asian institution, that of the entire extended family living under the same roof. South Korea has seen a downsizing of households from an average of more than five members fifteen years ago to fewer than four members today, a trend that is echoed from Taiwan to Hong Kong to Singapore. While household size shrinks, the sheer number of households continues to explode as a tidal wave of couples aged 20 to 30 establish families. Young family households independent of the extended family may pay less deference to their elders. Affluent Asians may be on the threshold of unprecedented consumer independence.

Although the vast majority of Asians continue to live at a subsistence level, McKinsey & Co. estimates that more than seventy-five million people live in households with annual incomes of $10,000 or more, one third the U.S. median, exclusive of Japan. In a decade that figure is expected to surge to 110 million. Korea and Taiwan have outpaced their counterparts with per capita gross domestic products of $11,000 and $13,000, respectively.

The industrialization and commercialization of Asia are slowly but relentlessly following the same rural-to-urban course that they took a century ago in Europe and the United States. The composition of South Korea's population has shifted from nearly 75 percent rural to nearly 75 percent urban in just thirty years, and the figure will continue to climb to more than 80 percent by the year 2000. Major cities all along the Pacific Rim are expected to grow by as much as 50 percent over the 1990s, straining their already overextended infrastructures—housing, transportation, energy, and the environment—to the breaking point, creating what a United Nations report has termed a "tinderbox situation."

The impetus to industrialization and commercialization is the driving force behind the emerging markets of Asia, as it is throughout the world—the unceasing, accelerating immediacy of information, courtesy of the relentless diffusion of communication technology. Radical communication theorist Marshall McLuhan (1964) coined an apt expression for the emerging one-world market twenty-five years ago: "the global village." If the swelling population of emerging markets of the Pacific Rim is the immovable object, the irresistible force of communication technology is more than sufficient to the task. The impact will likely be a reduction in threshold level of household income required to open windows of market opportunity throughout Asia. If there is a single hypnotic, even addictive feature of the West, it is *materialism*. Once a population is exposed, materialism seems to spread like a virus, and there are few inherent immunities. Even the gray market is expanding for everything from adult diapers to checking and credit card accounts, to continuing education, to recreation and travel—at an exponential rate throughout the Pacific Rim. The same forces that undermined the Iron Curtain are at work on the Bamboo Curtain.

THE IMPETUS TO CONSUMPTION

In attempting to peer into retailing in the next century, Management Horizons, a research subsidiary of Price Waterhouse, chronicled the economic chaos of the 1980s, the "creative destruction" or shakeout of the 1990s, and the anticipated consolidation and downscaling following the year 2000 (Hyde, Steidtmann and Sweeney 1990). During the 1980s, economic turmoil opened the door to retailing innovators who cut the cost out of distribution and drove conventional department stores or discounters to their knees or to bankruptcy court. In their wake came the category killers such as Toys "R" Us, Home Depot, or Office Depot, price clubs such as Sam's Club and Price Club, and power centers such as Franklin Mills in Philadelphia with 1.8 million square feet, the most heavily trafficked mall in the country. More than fifteen million consumers shopped at the latter in 1990 (Sutton 1990, p. 42). Of the top twenty discount department stores in 1980, fewer than half remain in operation today, while the doomed still stick to business as usual.

The seeds of "creative destruction" were sown in the 1980s but will be harvested in the 1990s. As many as 20 percent of the regional shopping centers currently operating in the United States will close by the year 2000 (Turchiano 1990, p. 37). In the meantime retailers continue to rattle around within overstored retail square footage that outstripped both population growth and consumer spending over the past decade. The coming shakeout in retailing has been preordained by a copycat, follow-the-leader mentality, a quiet conspiracy toward "sameness" in retailing—in layout, location, presentation, products, and service.

According to Management Horizons, in contrast to the 1980s, which were marked by "tax reform, political conservatism, and conspicuous consumption," the 1990s will be marked by creative destruction of the old order in retailing fueled by "diversity, democracy, and decentralization" (Hyde, Steidtmann, and Sweeney 1990, pp. 4-5). Diversity in products, in consumers, in employees, and in the environment will demand diversity and dexterity among retailers. Democracy and decentralization, both political and economic, will crescendo in Eastern Europe, in Latin America, and in Asia, turning command and control economies to the free market for economic solutions. By the end of the 1990s more than half of today's retailers will be out of business.

The new millennium will be marked by consolidation and downscaling. Retail sales will become concentrated among fewer, but larger, smarter, and more streamlined companies. Some lines of trade will be virtually owned by four or five major players operating from a portfolio of distinctive store concepts customized to strategically selected target markets. At the same time "storeless shopping" is projected to reach escape velocity, facilitated by at-home interactive shopping technologies with broadcast-quality audio-visual capabilities.

Management Horizons forecasts that the "death of the mass market" will be accompanied by a rebirth of specialty stores with an expanded but tight matrix of merchandise conceived to make a powerful statement to select market targets. Surviving department stores will evolve into "local market relationship merchandisers," an ungainly term but a logical move toward humanizing retailing by moving away from products toward personal services such as food, insurance, travel, legal, catering, and tailoring. In short, retailers in the next millennium will target a larger share of the customer's spending rather than a larger share of the customer pool.

In spite of the changes evident in this portrait of retailing in the 1990s and beyond, there is substantial evidence that the future of retailing will echo the past (Hisey 1990a, pp. 178, 180). Continuity, not change, will characterize consumer behavior in the 1990s. In the following sections we will examine two important issues. First, we will explore the negative but enduring legacy of the concept of consumption itself. Then we will examine the impetus to consumption—five persistent threads through the history of shopping and consumption behavior since the Industrial Revolution that are here to stay: value, convenience, the constant collision of the old with the new, the marriage of shopping and show biz, and self-indulgence.

The Negative Legacy of Consumption

Perhaps the most chronic and crippling handicap confounding consumer forecasting and the science of consumer research today is directly traceable to the origin of the term *consumer* itself. Since entering the consumer research literature through classical economics two centuries ago, the term *consumer* has been cursed by a connotation that the satisfaction of needs *required* destruction, waste, or at a minimum, transformation of resources or the environment (Murray 1933, pp. 801-803). Open any contemporary dictionary and there it is: Consumer n. one that consumes, wastes, squanders, or destroys.

The two to three million year saga of human history has been an uninterrupted orgy of need satisfaction by wasting, squandering, and destroying resources—of feeding off the environment like locusts. Because consumption is, and has always been, synonymous with destruction,

destruction has always been the dubious legacy of consumption. Even the American Indian culture (or any other tribal culture, for that matter) did not escape the destructive legacy of consumption.

While there is a nostalgic myth in American history that Indians lived in perfect harmony with nature, taking only what they needed to survive, the facts point in the opposite direction. The plains Indians in particular were nomadic not simply because they followed wherever the buffalo roamed. They constantly moved because they had to. Indians often killed buffalo for sport far in excess of their subsistence needs, deliberately burned hundreds of square miles of forest and prairie to simplify the process, stripped the land bare of firewood, and stripped the bark off trees to feed their horses in winter, leaving them to die naked on the assumption that there was "plenty more where that came from," or plenty more somewhere else (Connell 1984). They were America's first consumers—wasting, squandering, and destroying resources and their environment from sea to shining sea. The only regions of the country that escaped the assault were those so rich in natural resources they replenished themselves, primarily those along the east and west coasts.

Breaking the vicious cycle of consumption-destruction-consumption-destruction is perhaps the most imposing challenge facing marketing scholars and analysts into the next millennium. To date, attempts to put a different "spin" on a concept so deeply ingrained in human experience as consumption—to convert consumption into a creative, constructive concept—have been faltering at best. During the Viet Nam War era, a wave of social and ecological activism swept across the United States, sweeping primarily the young along in its wake. The "return to nature" movement was more conspicuous than widespread. Conservation, recycling, alternative energy initiatives, self-sufficiency, and organic communes living in homespun harmony with nature took their place alongside other experimental life-styles. But the 1973 oil embargo brought almost everyone back to earth with a resounding thud, and ecology was shelved along with the other antiques of the Age of Aquarius: hair, hippies, bell bottoms, pot, protests, Viet Nam, and veterans. When consumers can no longer afford their appetites, they strip away the nonnecessities and get back to the basics of making a living. Ecology was expendable, one of the first sacrifices to necessity.

Today history is repeating itself in the resurrection of "green" consumers and "green" products. Although we all applaud the revived interest, both green products and green consumers will go the way of their predecessors. Economic urgency is the least common denominator of consumption and has a way of killing off the expendables. The abrupt increase in the cost of living is the immediate, irrefutable impact of the war in the Mideast. Economic volatility will be its long-term legacy. But the fallout from both will be the death of ecology, except where ecology makes sound economic sense, such as recycling aluminum or reforestation, or is mandated by legislation. The Reagan and Bush administrations unmask an ironic, but irrefutable truth: What ecological initiatives one administration puts in place, another can erase with the simple stroke of a pen.

Value

In a survey of more than two hundred fifty thousand shoppers, *Monitor* (1990, pp. 27-30) uncovered compelling evidence that retailing survival and success is far more than a matter of "location, location, location." Listed below are the reasons that consumers shop their favorite stores, along with the percentage of consumers who cited each.

Reason	Percentage
Price	21.6
Selection	18.1
Quality	16.8
Location	14.7
Service	10.4

Although there were variations across the six retail categories surveyed— women's specialty apparel, men's specialty apparel, department stores, discount department stores, grocery stores, home improvement/hardware stores, and TV/VCR stores—and by region of the country, the overall conclusion that emerged from the *Monitor* survey was that consumer loyalty built on a one-legged platform of price, selection, quality, location or service is inherently precarious. Variations abound (O'Neill 1990a, pp. 27-30):

- Location is the most important grocery store selection factor, followed closely by price, but location ranks no higher than third most important for any other category of retailer.
- Grocery retailing is most price sensitive; furniture is least price sensitive.
- Quality is twice as important for department store shoppers as for home improvement/hardware store shoppers.
- Although often cited as a cure-all for consumer disaffection, customer service ranks last in consumer appeal across all retail categories except men's specialty stores. Surprisingly, service ranks higher for grocery stores than for women's specialty stores,

department stores, home improvement/hardware stores, or discount department stores.

Price has displaced "location, location, location" as the number one determinant of consumer preference for places as well as products (O'Neill 1990a, p. 27). The discount store is still "America's favorite place to shop" (*Chain Store Age Executive* 1989b, pp. 17-19), although Management Horizons maintains it is losing its competitive edge to "category killers" because "discount stores no longer represent off-price, but represent *the* price" (Hogsett 1990, pp. 42-43).

The persistent emphasis on price on the part of customers from the top to the bottom of the income spectrum has had a dramatic leveling effect on retailers. The result? Value-oriented retailing. Value-oriented retailers do well because they tap into strong and enduring consumer themes, pushed along by the shifting age distribution of the U.S. population. Patience O'Connor, senior vice president of management and marketing for the Washington, D.C.-based Western Development Corporation, puts it this way: "Baby boomers are aging and the next generation is smaller. Disposable income is not only decreasing, but under intensifying pressure from economic volatility. People know, understand and want high profile labels and brand names but have less disposable income to buy them. They are looking for value, and retailers across the board have responded."

Caught in a margin squeeze, retailers of all types have converged toward a common denominator—value. Says Richard Steinberg, executive vice president of Mall Properties Inc., New York City (Sutton 1990, p. 35), "Off-price seems to have disappeared. Everybody is charging the same price. They have the same sources, so it wasn't long before they started getting the same breaks and the same markups. The [competitive] edge then disappears."

Norman Kranzdorf, president of Conshohocken, Pennsylvania-based The Kranzco Group, concurs: "I don't feel there's any difference anymore between any type of retailer, after you get past the high end" (Sutton 1990, pp. 35-36). Price remains the indispensable ingredient in value-oriented retailing, but maintaining significantly lower prices is becoming harder to do. Today the off-price retailers are being absorbed into power centers.

One of the most significant of the value-oriented retailers is the factory outlet center. Clipping along at a 20 percent growth rate per year, factory outlet retailing poses no significant threat to more mainline mass merchandisers, according to Andy Groveman, senior vice president, Belz Enterprises, Memphis, Tennessee (Sutton 1990, p. 36): "Factory outlet centers will not become the new wave of retailing, or a serious alternative to traditional distribution." We disagree, to this extent: manufacturers will increasingly look for ways to control distribution, and control is the key to survival and competitiveness in the 1990s and beyond, both in the United

States and in Europe and Asia. Gary Geisler, vice president of the Muskegon, Michigan-based Horizon Group Inc., hit the nail on the head: "Manufacturers are looking for another way to get product to market. They look in the mirror, ask themselves who they can trust, and say, 'Myself' " (Sutton 1990, p. 41). Factory outlets are one modest step toward the ultimate solution to the problem of maintaining control from the factory to the customer—strategic organizational alliances.

The ingredients for successful value-oriented retailing are widely known, but it is difficult to find unfilled market opportunities: a location with high visibility on the way to or near a tourist destination, close-in metropolitan population density, critical mass of tenant and product diversity, and massive square footage. As Geisler succinctly puts it, value-oriented retailing is destination retailing: "We're not in the convenience business" (Sutton 1990, p. 45).

Convenience

Geisler is only half right. Virtually every retailer, except the top end specialty store, is in the convenience business. Convenience, in location, in access, in parking, in product selection, in hours of operation, in terms of purchase, and at the cash register, is one of the oldest, most enduring themes in retailing. Department stores and mail-order houses began to dominate retailing in the United States by the 1870s, but by the early 1920s large decentralized shopping centers and supermarkets with parking for thousands of automobiles began to dot the retailing landscape. These innovations reflect a fundamental shift in control over mass-market distribution built around centralized processing and postal communication through the 1910s to decentralization of retail outlets built around the private automobile after the 1920s. Seventy years later, retailing in the United States continues to revolve around the automobile.

Although the automobile was the catalyst that drove retailers out of the central city into the suburbs and eventually into the rural marketplace, the drive toward convenience was fueled by a succession of innovations dating from the mid-1800s (Beniger 1986, pp. 330-343): packaging in containers of fixed sizes and weights (1840s); standardized methods of sorting, grading, weighing and inspecting (early 1850s); fixed prices (1860s); standardized clothing sizes (early 1880s); periodic presentations via catalog (1880s); the buffet-style restaurant (1885) and the cafeteria serving line (1895); fully automated vending machines (1897); standardization through franchising (1911); drive-through auto service station (1913); self-service store layout (1916); preselection like Book-of-the-Month Club (1926); packaging that "sold itself" (late 1920s); "fair trade" enforced price uniformity (1931); and wide selection of competing brands displayed on open shelves (1934).

The idea that retail establishments could be designed to process automobiles brought drive-in stores and restaurants to California in the 1920s, the drive-in motion picture theater to Camden, New Jersey, in 1933, and the drive-in Dairy Queen to Moline, Illinois, in 1939. This idea was married to an innovation coined by John Hartford, son of the founder of A&P, the "cash-and-carry" economy store established in 1912. Hartford intended his term "cash-and-carry" to convey precisely what his stores were *not*: not credit and not delivery. Hartford's innovation proved so popular that he opened an average of one store every three days until 1915 and grew to fifteen thousand stores by the time of the Great Depression.

The marriage of retailing and the automobile peaked with the birth of the supermarkets in the 1920s and ended in divorce a decade later. Supermarkets merged the advantages of department stores, with their extensive product selection, and economy chain stores, with their cash-and-carry value appeal. In 1923 one of the first supermarkets—the Crystal Palace in San Francisco—opened on a former circus ground in a 68,000 square-foot steel-frame building with parking for 4,350 cars. By the mid-1930s the Crystal Palace set sales record of twenty-five tons of sugar in an hour, five freightcar-loads of eggs in a month, and an average of nearly a ton of apples per day for an entire year. Seizing the potential of one-stop shopping, the Crystal Palace quickly expanded to offer liquor, tobacco, and jewelry as well as drugstores, barber and beauty parlors, and a dry cleaner—like the hypermarket of today—and sowed the seeds of its own destruction. While consumers could find almost anything they wanted at a supermarket, they could not get past the logjam at the checkout counter to buy it. The door was left open for the latest in the uninterrupted chain of innovations to facilitate consumer convenience: the convenience store.

The rapid rise of the convenience store was perhaps foreordained by America's love affair with the automobile and the chronic failure of supermarket merchandisers to solve the problem of convenience at the cash register. Today, convenience is big business for more than 69,200 convenience stores employing 498,000 people nationwide, generating in excess of $61.2 billion in sales, $10.1 billion in gross profit, and $1.5 billion in pretax profits per annum (National Association of Convenience Stores 1989). That translates into a per store average of $580,000 in merchandise sales, $600,000 in gasoline sales, and an annual gross profit margin of nearly 33 percent for merchandise, 11 percent for gasoline, and 22 percent overall. Ironically, however, history has a strange way of repeating itself. Today's convenience store is sowing the seeds of its own destruction for precisely the same reason its predecessor left the door open for further retailing innovation.

In an effort to dig deeper into their customers' pockets, convenience stores added prepared foods, and even seating for self-service snacks and meals, and found themselves in direct competition with fast-food retailers. They then added petroleum products and found themselves in direct competition with self-service gas stations. They added check cashing and ATM machines and found themselves in direct competition with a whole host of cash exchange merchants. The net result? An inadvertent traffic jam on the concrete and a logjam at the cash register. The 1990s will likely see convenience stores taking two forks in the road, both in response to one of the most enduring themes in retailing—convenience. The first fork in the road will be a return to basics, to the simple formula for success that got the convenience store off the launching pad in the first place: high-velocity products in high-velocity locations, trimming away the products and services that slow down sales. The second fork is more intriguing in that it streamlines the same simple formula for success and creates a higher level of consumer convenience—the *ultra*convenience store. The key to capitalizing on either fork in the road is to exploit the same controls over distribution developed by older established retailing institutions, with some ingenuity thrown in: centralized management but local market monitoring, regular bulk purchasing, reduction of middlemen, standardization of quality and prices, and state-of-the-art intelligence systems integrating expert systems with computer and communication technology in an instant-response format (Abramson 1989; Pancari and Senn 1989).

Something Old, Something New

Consumers are constantly balancing continuity and change. The evolutionary nature of consumption is perhaps its most undervalued and unexplored facet. There are two important manifestations of the collision of continuity with change that retailers should note. One is the American consumer's insatiable appetite for something new, something different, something "state-of-the-art"—so long as something "new" does not deviate too far from convention. However, nowhere is the collision between continuity and change more evident than among consumer migrants and consumer immigrants.

The evidence of our insatiable appetite for something new is perhaps most visible in the waves of fad and fashion that sweep across the landscape with predictable regularity. Rarely does radical change take hold, except at the fringes of the market, and never for very long. Instead, change is incremental, like one brick in the Great Wall of China. Although the wall may disappear over the hill, it reappears on the next in its uninterrupted march to the horizon with a kind of certainty that makes forecasting possible, if only as far as the eye can see. Like the Great Wall, consumption behavior is characterized by both continuity and change—continuity in the sense that it exhibits an unending, if imperfect, regularity; change in the sense that the ups and downs are seldom so abrupt as to disallow prediction. The best line of sight on the path of future evolution in consumption behavior is the path of past consumption behavior. Hence the themes we identified in this paper—value, convenience, the marriage of shopping and show biz, and self-indulgence—are likely to persist without abrupt interruption or radical alteration, unless the faltering economy starts to fibrillate.

With one in six consumers moving every year and with the accelerating rate of immigration of consumers from exotic lands into insulated ethnic markets, consumer evolution will present one of the greatest challenges to retailers in the next millennium. Mainsteam retailers have responded to consumer migrants by pushing category killers and power centers farther out into the suburban and rural marketplace but are universally ill-equipped to accommodate consumer immigrants. Mainstream retailers have a choice. They can either default on the market opportunities immigrant consumers present, or they can attempt to accommodate their idiosyncrasies. The assimilation of knowledge of consumer differences rooted in cultural diversity will be a slow and painful process given that the U.S. economy is the largest *island* economy in the world, insulated by an accident of geography and its legacy of cultural ethnocentrism. It will require hiring, training, staffing, and managing retail businesses with people who share the same cultural roots as their customers. Above all else, it will require that U.S. retailers adopt the same global perspective on the U.S. market that is essential to successful penetration of European and Asian markets. Few U.S. retailers will successfully make the transition.

The Marriage of Shopping and Show Biz

West Edmonton Mall in Alberta, Canada, represents far more than the largest shopping mall in the world, with 5.2 million square feet containing over eight hundred stores including eleven major department stores, nineteen movie theaters, one hundred ten eating establishments, five amusement areas, and a seemingly endless array of distractions everywhere. It also represents the logical evolution of retailing from products and services to one-stop destinations and entertainment experiences. The marriage of shopping and show biz has been widely hailed as the last great hope of the shopping center (*Chain Store Age Executive* 1989a). In fact, like the constant quest for convenience, the unending pursuit of entertainment experience as an accompaniment to consumption is one of the oldest, most persistent themes throughout the history of consumer behavior.

Passive spectator sports had a long and checkered history throughout the rise and fall of the Roman Empire, often to divert the menacing hordes of Roman unemployed. Up to fifty thousand people watched gladiators fight wild beasts or other gladiators in the vast Colosseum. In the even larger Circus Maximus, two hundred sixty thousand people gathered to watch charioteers race around a perilously tight track. But the Roman counterpart to today's active entertainment-anchor malls cropping up from coast to coast were the public baths. Beginning in the 2nd century B.C., public baths became more and more elaborate, providing not only baths but games, lectures, musical performances, calisthenics, and places to lounge, gossip, shop, and seek entertainment.

The most elaborate bath of all was constructed by the Emperor Caracalla in the 3rd century A.D. A stunning architectural and engineering triumph, it quickly became the center of Roman social life. Sprawling over some thirty-three acres on the outskirts of Rome, the baths were a vast complex of business and entertainment establishments. At the center of everything were the baths themselves—a "frigidarium" (cold bath), several "tepidaria" (warm baths), and a "calidarium" (steam bath). Most bathers passed through them in that order, on their way to or from the bath's other entertainment: two libraries, four gymnasia, a sports stadium laced with decorated grounds with gardens, and colonnaded walks and statuary, all surrounded by hundreds of shops and offices. Seneca, who once resided above a public bath, captured its constantly changing mosaic of sights and sounds in words that make today's central city shopping district or shopping mall seem lifeless (Hadas 1965, pp. 86-88):

> When your strenuous gentleman . . . is exercising himself by flourishing deaden weights; when he is working hard or else pretending to be working hard, I can hear him grunt, and when he releases his imprisoned breath, I can hear him panting in wheezy and high-pitched tones. Or perhaps I notice some lazy fellow, content with a cheap rubdown, and hear the crack of the pummelling hands on his shoulders, varying in sound as the hand is laid on flat or hollow. . . . Add to this the arresting of an occasional roisterer or pickpocket, the racket of the man who always likes to hear his own voice in the bathroom, or the enthusiast who plunges into the swimming tank with unconscionable noise and splashing. . . . Then the cakeseller with his varied cries, the sausagemen, the confectioner, and all the vendors of food hawking their wares, each with his own distinctive intonation.

The Roman baths prove not only that there is nothing new under the sun but also that we constantly rediscover and resurrect the insights of the past. The reason the baths emerged as the center of Roman social life was precisely that they combined all the essential ingredients of social life in one open forum: passive leisure, active recreation, shopping, and gossip and deal-making amid an unending variety of entertainments, including human beings' favorite pastime through the ages—people watching. While the entertainment-anchor malls of today have not gone quite as far, they have taken one giant step down the same path, and their success or failure will be predicated on the same premise. If all essential ingredients of contemporary social life converge in today's entertainment-anchor malls, they too will become the center of contemporary social life. In short, if the new age developers can breath life back into the entertainment malls, they may well recapture the vitality of the Roman baths.

Islands of Self-Indulgence in a Sea of Anonymity

To say that consumption is, and has always been self-indulgent may seem redundant. All consumption is self-indulgent, but few forms of consumption permit total self-indulgence. The constant quest for convenience in consumption is self-indulgent, as is the unending pursuit of entertainment experiences. But by their very nature neither the convenience store nor the entertainment-anchor mall permits complete consumer self-indulgence, the kind of consumer self-indulgence that can come only from customization of products and services to the individual customer's idiosyncrasies.

The rebirth of the boutique represents one logical response to the consumer's unquenchable thirst for self-indulgence. It has been fueled by two forces. Rising discretionary incomes since World War II have permitted a growing spectrum of consumers to pursue self-indulgence. At the same time, consumer idiosyncrasies have been drowned in the sea of anonymity that is the essence of mass merchandising. Many consumers are fed up with retailer indifference, and they can afford to be. This has opened the door for boutiques specializing in consumer indulgence, from Club Med and fat farms to singing telegrams, consulting experts, custom clothiers, and personal bodyguards.

Boutiques represent islands of consumer self-indulgence in a sea of retailer anonymity—small compensation for the indifferent, uncaring hand life dealt each of us in almost every other aspect of our lives, interpersonal and occupational. No price is apparently too high to pay for personalization of attention: $125 for a hair stylist to listen to our complaints about our children or our spouse; $1,500 a day for a fat farm to tell us "fat is okay . . . if you're healthy!" or $5,000 for a Club Med cruise that caters to our every compulsion or whim. Although they will never challenge the retailing dominance of the category killer, the power center, or the entertainment-anchor mall, boutiques have a virtually unlimited future, particularly in services and ideas retailing, because of the degree of customization their personalized format permits. Increasingly the savings the category killer or power center provides is funnelled into self-indulgent consumption.

THE QUIXOTIC CONSUMERS OF THE 21ST CENTURY

Retailers are generally the first to sense significant change in the marketplace; they are like front-line shock troops on a battlefield. Some survive. Some do not. Although all speculation about emerging psychographic and lifestyle segments has been rendered suddenly suspect by the war in the Mideast, there has been no dearth of both empirical and idle speculation on "new" life-styles, "new" markets, and "new" retailing opportunities. Overall, the decipherable threads of demographic, psychographic, and life-style change in the U.S. market signal growing market fragmentation. Growing market fragmentation does not, however, imply the "death of the mass market," as so many contemporary observers of American retailing have maintained (Hogsett 1990, p. 42; Leventhal 1990, p. 16).

One of the most ambitious recent attempts to peer into the future of the mass market is Dychtwald and Gable's *The Shifting American Marketplace* (1990b), which chronicles the consumption consequences of "the age wave"—the aging of the baby boomers. Their portrait of the consumer in the year 2000 envisions a maturing American market dominated by the self-concept, concerns, perspectives, and priorities of middle age. The characteristics of aging baby boomers can be captured in ten snapshots summarized in Table 2.2.

Pete Hisey (1990b, p. 188) of *Discount Store News* sees things differently. Despite the widespread perception of demographic similarities among baby boomers, the days of sweeping trends to hop on may be over. Instead, hundreds of coexisting microtrends will be the rule. Baby boomers, Hisey maintains, don't like to follow the crowd. Often portrayed as the trendiest demographic group in history, that very trendiness has made them both more concerned with fashion and more confident in their individual taste than were their parents or grandparents. Home-centered life-style should be a significant driving force for consumption in the year 2000. This tendency will open the door for small, creative retailers to step into specialty niches. The proliferation of specialty retailers should build margins back into specialty products and services.

Hisey's emphasis on idiosyncratic life-styles is echoed and endorsed by the Cohort Study, a DuPont-sponsored survey of four thousand consumers nationwide conducted by Management Horizons. "More important than gender, income or ethnic origin, are the historical and social events that help shape an age group's values between the ages of seven and 21" (Lettich 1990, pp. 191-192). By the time the consumer has reached age 21, core values have crystalized as a result of parental influence through preadolescence, peer pressure through early adolescence, and "a taste of life" acquired in the experimental years of late adolescence. Thus core values that have crystalized in the context of unique historical and social events provide both the impetus and objective of consumption throughout the consumer's life cycle. What does this mean for retailers? Each consumer group will buy according to a uniquely different set of core values. Table 2.3 describes eight insights from the Cohort Study.

Table 2.2. Characterizing Aging Baby Boomers

Aging baby boomers will:

- Dominate and shape the self-concept, concerns, perspectives, and priorities of the entire consumer marketplace, including self-assessment, responsibilities, family, work, intimacy, and personal relationships.
- Retain many of their cohort characteristics, including their tendency to delay traditional markers of maturity, their diversity, their distrust of authority, their educational attainment, and their entanglement with the media and marketing arms of business.
- Embark upon "cyclic life-styles" and defy the age markets traditionally associated with maturity.
- Seek ways to balance work, family, and recreation.
- Become increasingly concerned with health, wellness, vitality and youth maintenance, and physical abilities.
- Become increasingly indistinguishable by sex.
- Evaluate their consumer choices based on years of consumer experience and product trials, and seek and recognize quality above all else.
- Become increasingly preoccupied with convenience and comfort.
- Look for ways to increase their sense of control over the terms of their life.
- Increasingly be interested in purchasing "experiences" rather than "things."

Source: Adapted from Ken Dychtwald and Greg Gable (1990), *The Shifting American Marketplace*, Emeryville, CA: Age Wave, Inc.

Elsewhere Anderson and Golden (1991, p. 1) have argued that the most persistent problem confronting consumers today is time or, more precisely, too little time, too much to do. Time and information have emerged to eclipse money and materialism as the primary constraints on contemporary life. Allocating increasingly precious time among ever-expanding obligations is an unending, unsolvable problem for almost all consumers. But time is the insatiable adversary of consumers caught in a vise between multiplying domestic and employment responsibilities on the one hand and intensifying financial pressures on the other.

Bill Flately, a principal with retail consultants Kurt Salmon Associates of New York, forecasts a return to basics as the consumer insists on keeping it quick and simple: "The time poverty everyone feels precludes people from shopping together for pleasure. Now they are shopping for necessities" (Lettich 1990, pp. 110, 191). The new pragmatic consumer is a "short-cut shopper" searching for a bargain, a brand, a specialty item, exceptional service, or special destination in a tightly focused retail environment. Short-cut shopping implies an increase in niche stores and shops-within-a-store designed for focused buying. Exceptional service is not limited to upscale specialty store salesperson-to-customer attention. Among off-price retailers, service implies being in stock all the time with items in demand. Short-cut shopping also implies an almost unlimited future for nonstore retailers: telemarketing, direct selling, direct marketing, and mail order. The MTV-Nintendo-computer generation will have little difficulty with absentee shopping.

Table 2.3.   Characterizing the Cohort

- *Depression Babies* (1930-1939) began life with rationing but grew up in relative comfort in the post-World War II period. At or near retirement, their consumption is defined by comfort and conservatism.
- *World War II Babies* (1940-1945) grew up during the boom years following World War II. At the peak of their professional and occupational stature and income today, they are less conservative than their predecessors yet intense bargain hunters.
- *Mature Boomers* (1946-1950) experienced adolescence amid the social and political upheaval of the 1960s but have retreated from the front lines of activism into conservatism while grudgingly losing their grip on youth.
- *Mid-boomers* (1951-1957) are consumed by family obligations and must therefore balance price with quality.
- *Young Boomers* (1958-1964) are self-expressive, self-indulgent, computer-literate consumers, and prime prospects for direct marketing.
- *Mature Busters* (1965-1970) are the MTV Generation, long on external stimulation and excitement-orientation but short on interpersonal communication skills.
- *Young Busters* (1971-1976) are still in their developmental years, experimenting with first cars, clothes, and electronic gadgets.
- *Mature Boomlets* (1977-1982) are highly indulged, relatively affluent adolescents with great influence on family consumption.

Source: Adapted from Jill Lettich, "Consumer of '90s: Smarter and Wiser, But with Less Time" Reprinted by Permission from *Discount Store News,* May 7, 1990 issue. Copyright Lebhar-Friedman, Inc., 425 Park Avenue, New York, NY 10022.

Cheryl Russell (1987), immediate past-editor-in-chief of *American Demographics*, sees significant life-style changes on the consumer horizon:

"Attitudes are moving away from community and more toward individuals. The unit of discussion has gone from family to households in the '80s, and from households to individuals in the '90s" (Leventhal 1990, pp. 16, 18). Russell forecasts further splintering of market fragments into "particle markets"—ironically bound together by a shared sense of individualism (see Table 2.4).

Table 2.4. Twenty-five Particle Markets of the 1990s

Parents
There were more than four million births last year, the highest number since 1964. About 90 percent of Americans have children at some time during their lives. For a huge segment of society, that time is now.

Fathers
As the baby boomlet begins to walk, talk and do homework, fathers will become more important.

The Very Old
The number of people aged 85 and older will continue to grow rapidly in the 1990s, making it the only growth segment among the elderly population.

The Fit
Millions of baby boomers will join in a passionate battle against time, doing everything from running marathons to having plastic surgery.

Hispanics
Hispanics will become this country's largest minority group by 2010, when the Census Bureau projects they will outnumber blacks.

Children
The baby boomlet started in 1977, but it's peaking right now--making children a hot particle market for the 1990s.

Empty Nesters
The family nest is most likely to empty when people are in their 50s. The baby boomers will begin turning 50 in 1996. You can bank on healthy growth in the number of empty nesters toward the end of the decade.

Individuals
In the 1980s, we moved from the family to the household as the primary unit of consumption. In the 1990s, we'll move from the household to the individual.

The Unfit
Beyond age 40, serious health problems become much more common. The number of people with chronic diseases should increase sharply with the aging of the baby boom in the 1990s.

Teenagers
The oldest members of the baby boomlet became teenagers in 1990 when they celebrated their thirteenth birthdays. After a decade of steep decline, the teenage population will grow again.

Grandparents
In just ten years, one-third of all grandparents with grandchildren under the age of 18 will be baby boomers.

Stepfamilies
Families are not a hot market for the 1990s, but stepfamilies are. They now account for 20 percent of married couples with children.

Asians
Asians are the fastest growing minority group in America today, a particle market over eight million strong.

Savers
As college costs loom on the horizon, the baby boom will try desperately to save money. This makes the boomers hot prospects for saving instruments in the 1990s.

Downscale
The pendulum of public concern is swinging back in favor of helping the poor and near poor. We may even see a redefinition of poverty that increases the size of the downscale segment.

Women in Charge
As career-minded baby boom women gain in job experience, the number of women who control the bottom line will grow rapidly.

Entrepreneurs
There are too many baby boomers for the few top spots in America's businesses. The consequence will be a lot of new businesses started by frustrated employees.

Activists
As the baby boomers reach middle-age, the nation's activists will take center stage. If your business is not prepared for attack, the activists could severely damage your company's image.

Upscale
With the baby boom generation entering its peak earning years, the number of affluent households will grow.

Workers
The share of the population in the paid labor force is greater today, at 66 percent, than ever before in our history.

Fun Seekers
Americans now spend more money on entertainment than on clothing. Look for fun-seeking to continue into the 1990s, especially for experiences like Disneyworld.

Vacation-Home Owners
The baby boom generation is about to become prime customers for vacation homes. Look for vacation-home owners to take off in the next few years.

The Middle Class
Americans continue to identify themselves as middle class, no matter how upscale their income.

Students
During this decade, the number of students aged 18 or older will approach, and might even pass, the number of students under 18 for the first time in history.

Housewives
Markets may have fragmented, but traditional markets continue. They've become particle markets like all the rest. We've come full circle from housewives as the mass market of the 1950s to housewives as an important particle market of the 1990s

Source: Adapted from a speech by Cheryl Russell, "Countdown to the 21st Century: 25 Particle Markets for the 1990s." Reprinted with permission © *American Demographics*, 1990. Excerpts cited in Leventhal, Larry (1990), "Retail Reality Is Placing a Wakeup Call," *Home Textiles Today* (July 2), 16, 18.

A CUBE IN A VISE

The American marketplace is and has always been as diverse as the number of people who comprise it. That is, just as individualism is the defining characteristic of American society, idiosyncrasy is the defining characteristic of the American marketplace. Yet it was not until the aftermath of World War II that rising discretionary income reached mass market proportions, the mass market began to fragment, and retailers capitalized on the newly viable economic opportunities with ever-finer market segmentation and positioning, ultimately culminating in the "particle markets" that have been hailed as the future of retailing.

From the retailer's perspective the issue is, and has always been, economic: What are the economics of slicing the mass market into ever-finer segments or particles? Only recently have the economics of market segmentation favored focusing on market fragments, and only for the very few. In spite of the fact that economics currently favors particle markets among a limited number of specialty retailers, the mass market is still bound together by a single thread—value.

In the face of growing market fragmentation, the question of market viability will pose a persistent challenge to retailers. Today's consumer is trapped in a vise. The twin sides of the vise are money pressure, resulting from unending economic volatility, and time pressure, resulting from the multiplying demands of domestic and occupational roles. The pressure from both sides of the vise tends to intensify over the consumer's life cycle as financial, family, and occupational obligations multiply. Although retirement relaxes the time pressure, the money pressure intensifies as retirees try to stretch their fixed income over the ever-inflated cost of living. It is the twin pressures of time and money constraints that squeeze consumers into the cells of the Consumer Cube (see Figure 2.1). The money pressure may be greater at the downscale end of the economic continuum, but time pressure is greater at the top. But, as we have noted, nearly no one is exempt from both.

Values

Borrowing a page from the Cohort Study, one dimension of the Consumer Cube captures the determinant role of values—formed in the historical, social, and economic context in which children mature into independent consumers—in shaping shopping and consumption behavior. Rather than using contemporary terms like "boomers," "busters," and "boomlets" that will grow quickly obsolete with changing social and economic conditions, the values dimension of the Consumer Cube can be characterized along a far more generic and universal continuum, that of stage in the life cycle:

- *Pre-adolescence*, where parental influence predominates.
- *Early adolescence*, where peer pressure predominates.
- *Late adolescence*, where peer pressure is reconciled with personal experimentation.
- *Early adulthood*, where the individual first assumes adult educational and occupational responsibilities.
- *Marriage and family formation*, where occupational responsibilities are reconciled with growing domestic and financial responsibilities.
- *Parenting*, where occupational and domestic responsibilities are kept in precarious balance.
- *Empty nest*, where occupational responsibilities predominate.
- *Retirement*, where time pressures relax, but money pressures intensify.

Figure 2.1.   The Consumer Cube

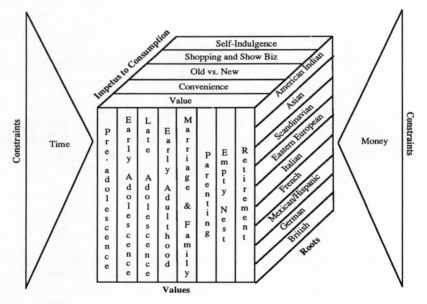

Although individuals can, and often do, hopscotch through the stages in the life cycle in their own arrhythmic way, the historical, social, and economic events that define the first three stages in particular also dominate and shape consumption behavior through successive stages in the life cycle. The simple insight contained in the values dimension of the Consumer Cube is a familiar one: past behavior is the best predictor of future behavior. Specifically, the defining features of the times in which we grow to adulthood play a determinant role in defining and directing our consumption behavior through our lives. Subsequent significant changes in the life cycle—marriage, family formation, parenting, empty nest, retirement—alter established consumption behavior, but seldom beyond recognition.

Roots

A second significant determinant of shopping and consumption behavior is *roots*—the consumer's cultural and ethnic ancestry. There have always been crosscurrents of change at work in American society. One is the current of cultural and ethnic diversity and insulation that is the legacy of polyglot immigration. The other current is the relentless erosion of cultural identity and ethnic insulation from generation to generation toward a melting pot of homogeneous expectations. More than any other factor, the marketplace, with its unending array of material opportunities and possibilities, has been the great leveler, the most common denominator, in American culture.

The significant cultural and ethnic threads through American history are customarily collapsed into four major categories: Asian, black, Hispanic, and white. These terms and the stereotypes they evoke do an injustice to the rich diversity of cultural backgrounds that has been both the strength of American society and her beacon to the world. In fact the United States is, and has always been, a checkerboard of cultural and ethnic identities that remain structurally separate and, for all intents and purposes, separable, despite a decline in overt acknowledgment of differences. Whether we view cultural and ethnic differences as healthy or invidious, we cannot ignore the pluralistic character of American social structure. Accordingly, the roots dimension of the Consumer Cube identifies the major threads of American cultural and ethnic ancestry. Approximate percentages of the U.S. population currently corresponding to ethnic background are presented below for illustrative purposes (acknowledging the fact that many significant ancestral streams of immigration are omitted):

Ethnicity	Percent of Population
British	39
German	19
French	5
Italian	5
Scandinavian	3

Eastern European	5
Afro-American	12
Mexican/Hispanic	8
Asian	3
American Indian	2

Focusing on the general (all cultures) rather than the specific (American culture), there are three significant denominators of the roots dimension of the Consumer Cube. Above all else is the number of generations the individual's family has lived in the host culture. First-generation immigrants, caught in the grip of their cultural and ethnic roots, assimilate slowly occupationally, socially, and in their consumption behavior. Their children and their childrens' children may maintain their cultural and ethnic identification but are typically far less insulated in the cocoon of their cultural roots.

A second significant denominator of the roots dimension is the *discontinuity* between the value system of the culture of origin and the value system of the host culture. Immigrating across the ocean from Australia to the United States may be as effortless as crossing a street since the cultures share similar value systems. Conversely, immigrating across the city in the West Bank in Jerusalem may not only cause culture shock, it may get you killed.

A third, far less important denominator is the contrast between the retailing infrastructure of the culture of origin and that of the culture of destination. Moving from Checotah, Oklahoma, to New York City may cause more market disorientation than moving from Pretoria, South Africa, to London, but far more market disorientation in the case of a black South African immigrating to either destination. The greater the discrepancy in retailing infrastructures, the more difficult the upscaling or downscaling in consumption and shopping behavior. Overall, however, people assimilate shopping and consumption behaviors of the host culture much more rapidly than they assimilate its values.

Impetus to Consumption

The third dimension of the Consumer Cube is the impetus to consumption, comprised of the five consumption themes just identified:

- Value
- Convenience
- The constant collision of the old with the new
- The marriage of shopping and show biz
- Self-indulgence

It could be argued that consumers work their way through the five consumption themes in much the same way Maslow (1954) proposed people work their way up his hierarchy of motivations. Regrettably, it is not that simple. People living on subsistence incomes are often convenience stores' best customers because grocery stores and discounters have fled their neighborhood, frequently tread endless miles around shopping centers because it is cheaper than a movie or baby sitting, and occasionally engage in extravagant self-indulgence.

CONSUMPTION IN THE YEAR 2000

The challenge that market viability presents is both constantly confounding and full of surprising possibilities, like a Rubic's Cube in a vise. A complete analysis of the implications of the three-dimensional Consumer Cube is beyond the scope of this chapter as well as beyond the ability of any consumer analyst or clairvoyant. However, a number of insights emerge from peering into the cube:

- Time pressure intensifies with every stage in the life cycle through parenting, and decreases thereafter.
- Money pressure intensifies with every stage in the life cycle through parenting, decreases at the empty nest stage, and increases again at retirement.

Since time and money pressure follow essentially parallel paths over the consumer's life cycle, a number of implications follow:

- Emphasis on value increases with every stage in the life cycle through parenting, decreases somewhat at the empty nest stage, and increases again at retirement as people are constrained to fixed incomes.
- Emphasis on convenience increases with every stage in the life cycle through parenting, and decreases thereafter.
- Newness dominates oldness through marriage and family formation primarily because of peer pressure, but decreases in importance over the entire life cycle. Oldness dominates newness from the parenting stage on, and increases in importance over the entire life cycle, largely because of a growing appreciation for the importance of enduring value.
- Emphasis on the marriage of shopping and show biz increases with every stage in the life cycle through parenting, and decreases thereafter, primarily because time-constrained consumers are

forced to combine activities (such as housework and baby-sitting, shopping and entertainment) where possible.

• Opportunities for self-indulgence decline with every stage in the life cycle through parenting, and increase thereafter even through retirement, because while money pressure may increase at retirement, the relaxed time pressure is more than sufficient to compensate.

The way cultural and ethnic identity are expressed in consumption is far from clear, primarily because the relationship between them has been the subject of little research. Hence, our insights into the relationship between cultural and ethnic roots and consumption are quite general:

• The meaning and importance of value and convenience will vary little according to the consumer's ethnic and cultural identity.
• The meaning and importance of old versus new, shopping and show biz, and self-indulgence will vary considerably according to the consumer's ethnic and cultural identity.
• As successive generations of consumers are assimilated into the host culture, the meanings of each of the five consumption themes— value, convenience, old versus new, show biz, and self indulgence—will converge with those of the host culture.

Although there are enormous cultural and ethnic differences among the newly emerging markets of Asia and Europe, the preceeding propositions are thought to have general, if not universal, applicability across cultures—with modification. Because each of the five consumption themes discussed in this chapter can be expressed through an almost infinite variety of products and services, exploring their implications for specific products, services, or retail institutions is beyond the scope of the present chapter. Instead, these propositions are food for thought for consumer and retailing analysts for the 1990s.

THE KEY TO FUTURE RETAILER
COMPETITIVENESS: CONTROL

Worldwide economic volatility is the watchword for retailers in the 1990s. Economic instability renders any forecast of the future of the domestic or global marketplace suspect. But three things seem certain for the foreseeable future: increasingly quixotic consumers, increasingly exotic markets, and increasingly neurotic retailers. What's a retailer to do in the face of unending economic uncertainty?

Business was like a game of chess that American executives played as well as any—and won more often than not—as recently as one generation ago. But business, the very nature of business, has changed. The civilized and sophisticated game of chess has given way to ice hockey! Today, American firms of all types are increasingly losing their grip on survival itself. Nowhere is this more evident than in the international arena where Japanese firms routinely rout their Western rivals whereas American executives continue to coast on the momentum of past concepts, principles, and practices.

The challenge to American firms today is no longer the sinister one from the Eastern bloc, but the friendly one from the Far East. American executives continue to assume that Japanese industry has the same consumer-oriented objectives as American and European firms (Prestowitz 1988, pp. 21-23). Faulty policies and strategies based on false assumptions and ignorance continue to fuel the decline of the U.S. economy and standard of living while the Japanese increase their lead on both fronts.

This is not a discussion about the rise of Japan or the fall of American industry in the international marketplace. It is about how American executives are hamstrung by self-imposed handicaps, concepts, principles, and practices that once worked well within the rather civilized confines of their domestic or regional marketplace, but which are crippling in the free-for-all reality of international competition. Most crippling of all is a widespread managerial myopia about the very nature of the relationship between the firm and its environment. Nowhere is the crippling consequence of this managerial myopia more evident than in the contrast between American concepts of management and the Japanese concept of management, a contrast whose roots run to deep-seated cultural differences. Today management in American organizations is viewed essentially as a *re*active process of managing internal organizational resources to *meet un*controllable external environmental forces. In Japan management is viewed as a *pro*active process of *controlling* relationships between the organization and its environment, therefore controlling its survival and competitiveness.

For the retailer with roots in the United States, Europe, and the Pacific Rim present exotic unknowns for which past experience is poor preparation. For those who venture into the emerging markets of Western Europe and the Far East, the awaiting challenges will exceed any the organization has previously faced. Borrowing a page from the history of Asian culture is perhaps the only way to build a mutually beneficial living bridge across the water.

The key to understanding the economies of the Pacific Rim is contained in the principal institution and instrument of organization in Asian culture historically, the extended family or "house." The house, rather than its members, owned property. The household head managed property in the interests of the house, its current members, its generations of ancestors, and its unborn posterity. The house was therefore the keeper of a common culture, and the living link between its past, present, and future.

Families did not own businesses in the Western sense. The house *was* the business, its structure and organization of operations dictated by a single goal, control over the destiny of the house itself by controlling its relationship with its environment. In responsibly managing the business of the house, the household head had to provide for its material, physical, spiritual, educational, and security needs. To provide for these needs, the household head constantly sought to control the sources and flows of material and energy resources and information essential to the survival and prosperity of the house.

The most obvious and effective way to control essential material and energy resources and information was to form mutually beneficial relationships with other houses that controlled them. Reciprocal relationships among houses naturally evolved into intricate webs of strategic alliances, which controlled virtually all the essential material and energy resources and information that determined the destiny of each. Carried to its evolutionary extreme, the unending quest for control resulted in the great houses that have dominated and shaped every chapter of Asian history— interdependent companies in different industries linked by common house origins, ownership, sources of capital and insurance, trading companies, and preferential trade relationships, all of which were supported by a sympathetic government and the press. Today, as in every prior era of Asian history, those houses, or strategic organizational alliances, that have most successfully secured control over their environment dominate and shape virtually every aspect of life: government, business, education, law, science, and technology.

What is the glue that holds the strategic organizational alliances together and makes such extraordinary coordination and control possible? It is the extensive networks of personal relationships merging separate organizations into a single house, where personal obligation and honor override contracts and professional ties.

The lesson to be learned from this brief chronology of Asian history is that the key to business success throughout the Pacific Rim, or Europe, for that matter, is strategic organizational alliances. To put it bluntly, to attempt to compete in the international marketplace without a network of strategic organizational alliances is to go to war unarmed. American firms must either find ways to forge strategic alliances or consign themselves to being scavengers, picking over the pieces left behind by the big leaguers competing for the big stakes in the international arena.

The key to strategic organizational alliances is networks of personal relationships that form the living bridge between the organization and its environment. The U.S. retailer seeking a foothold in Europe or the Pacific

Rim has no alternative but to leave his Western concept of organization at the doorstep along with his shoes and start networking at a personal level. It is never easy, but in Europe or the Far East it is the only alternative.

If strategic organizational alliances are indispensable weapons in winning the international economic war, they are becoming increasingly essential in effectively competing at home. To compete effectively at home as well as abroad today, who you know—and who knows you—is at least as important as what you know or can do. The sun has set on the long day of the Lone Ranger in American business. Today it's team competition, teams that tie separate organizations together in strategic organizational alliances that magnify their competitive impact.

CONCLUSION AND IMPLICATIONS

The critical difference between the concept of organization in the East and the West can be captured by an analogy. Ask almost any American executive to draw a picture of his or her firm, and what will you get? Something that resembles a pyramid. Ask almost any Japanese executive to draw a picture of his or her firm, and what will you get? A spider web, or something similar.

A picture of a pyramid captures the kind of command and control hierarchy of authority and responsibility that has dominated American executives' concept of management since the Industrial Revolution. But a pyramid also creates the illusion of an organizational boundary and, with it, an "us" versus "them" mentality. A picture of a spider web captures the interpersonal network concept of strategic organizational alliances that has dominated Japanese executives' view of management since the Shogunates. No organizational boundary; no "us," no "them," just "we."

When American executives look out the windows of their executive suites they see nameless, faceless, uncontrollable environmental *forces.* Japanese executives see *faces* of people who control critical material and energy resources, information, and communication essential to their organization's survival and competitiveness. There, in a nutshell, is the critical difference. Environmental forces cannot be controlled. Relationships with people can. In fact, Japanese executives across the board are estimated to spend up to two-thirds of their time out of their office cultivating and caring for networks of personal relationships with key people who control essential material or energy resources, information, or communication.

What does this have to do with retailing in the 1990s? In the face of an unending economic uncertainty that has rendered the domestic and international marketplace an unsophisticated and uncivilized hockey game, retailers have only two weapons: (1) a network of strategic organizational alliances that control those aspects of the environment that can be controlled and (2) instant response capabilities to monitor and meet those aspects of the environment that cannot.

The implication of the realization that organizational boundaries are arbitrary is important: control is not, cannot, and should not end with organizational employees and resources. The key to controlling the firm's environment is to build and manage networks of personal relationships—a living bridge between people in the organization and key people in the organizational environment: customers, resource and technology suppliers, liaisons, including the media, regulators, even competitors. A strong implication of this realization is that executives should spend less time in front of their PCs analyzing trends or communicating through memos or letters or over the telephone and more time out of the office communicating. Only by one-on-one communicating through key contacts with key people can executives convert uncontrollable environmental forces into controllable relationships. And to do this, organizations must mirror their market—demographically, ethnically, culturally, and behaviorally.

REMARKS

John C. Beyer

"Retailing in the Year 2000: Quixotic Consumers? Exotic Markets? Neurotic Retailers?" serves well the purpose of establishing a framework for examining retailing at the start of the next century. As an economist who only occasionally steps into the world of retailing (other than as a consumer, of course), Dr. Anderson's treatise was extremely informative, challenging, and useful. It provides the foundation of an economic environment that affects consumer behavior, addresses basic demographic changes that will influence retailing, deals with the fundamentals of consumer behavior, and looks at the effects of the increasing internationalization of the world's economy on retailing.

In my remarks, I am commenting on those areas closest to my field of knowledge and discipline, which is economics, and less so on the specific areas of retailing per se. I am also focusing my comments on differences between Dr. Anderson and myself. By doing so, I do not want to leave the impression that there are only differences in our respective perspectives. In fact, that is far from the case, as many of his observations and conclusions concerning specific likely changes in consumer behavior are similar to mine.

I want to focus my attention on three principal areas. The first concerns the economic environment of retailing, an area where Dr.

Anderson and I diverge rather substantially. The second concerns demographic and related trends that I believe will have a significant impact on retailing. In this subject area the differences between Dr. Anderson and me are more of emphasis than of substance. The third area concerns internationalization and the impact it will have on retailing in the next century. Here there are some similarities in perspective, but there are also some differences.

THE ECONOMIC ENVIRONMENT FOR
RETAILING IN THE YEAR 2000

The economic environment is the real foundation for any assessment of retailing in the future.[1] Without understanding changes in the economic environment, realistic projections of future changes in retailing are difficult. The economic environment determines key parameters for consumers, such as disposable income, the rate of inflation, and interest rates, all directly affecting consumer demand. The economic environment also influences retailers, not just with respect to the demand for the products they are selling, but also in terms of their cost structures as suppliers through the availability and cost of capital, the availability and cost of labor, and so forth. Hence, it is essential to put realistic boundaries around the future economic environment when predicting changes that are likely to occur within retailing itself.

Dr. Anderson and I have substantially different perspectives on the character of the economic environment in the 1990s. Dr. Anderson's perspective is that the economic environment will be "highly volatile" and one "of unending economic uncertainty" with consumers "bouncing like a yo-yo" from year to year.

To what does Dr. Anderson ascribe this extreme volatility? His principal reason is that uncertainty regarding the availability and price of oil will be the cause of a continuing and unending uncertainty within the American economy. In some ways it is understandable that this is a focal point because we are currently in the midst of another "oil crisis," but I think we need to step back and put the current petroleum challenge into proper perspective. First, let me say I could not agree more with Dr. Anderson when he concludes that the present difficulties surrounding Saddam Hussein's annexation of Kuwait has been complicated for Americans by the absence of any meaningful energy policy in the United States during the 1980s. Americans seem to have short memories; it was only several years after the second oil shock in 1979-80 that virtually all serious efforts toward energy conservation and development of alternative energy sources vanished from the horizon.

With the exception of the war with Iraq, the world is able today to deal much more effectively with the oil crisis than it was in 1979-80, and certainly in 1973-74. In saying this, I do not want to minimize the impact of increases in the prices of petroleum products by 40 to 50 percent in the matter of only two or three months. Even so, the United States, Europe, and Japan have been able to go about their business as usual despite the significant increase in oil prices. World supply of, and demand for, petroleum is coming into balance, and demand will likely decline in absolute terms as the higher prices and slowing economies worldwide affect it. Indeed, absent the current recession, an increase in oil prices of the magnitude we have experienced would have had relatively modest impact on consumer behavior and hence on demand and on retailing. Furthermore, our ability in the future to withstand similar types of oil shocks is enhanced by the fact that there has been a fundamental restructuring of the world order. With the closing of the curtain on the Cold War, the United States and the Soviet Union, with Europe and Japan, can act jointly on matters of economic importance, action that would have been totally impossible only two or three years ago.

My comments should not be interpreted to mean I believe there is no uncertainty in the future on the performance of the U.S. economy. That clearly would be foolish. Nor am I saying that potential shocks from oil crises are to be dismissed. Indeed, under certain circumstances they could be quite severe. Rather, what I am saying is that Dr. Anderson has overstated both the extent and frequency of the volatility of the U.S. economy, the extent of uncertainty, and the cause of that uncertainty. I will comment shortly on two other "dark clouds" on the horizon that could have adverse impacts of retailing far more than the effects of another oil shock.

Before doing that, let me take what some would consider to be a risky posture, which is to articulate the proposition that during the 1990s the American economy will be relatively stable. If this proposition proves to be correct, it has significant implications for retailing because it removes uncertainty that otherwise would have to be considered when making basic investment and strategic market decisions. What are some of the reasons for my proposition concerning the relative stability of the American economy in this decade and the beginning of the next century?

First, I believe economic growth in the 1990s will be slightly stronger on average than in the 1980s. Economic growth is basically a product of labor force growth and productivity. In the 1990s labor force growth will be down considerably from the high rate of the 1970s and the still healthy rate of the 1980s. The good news is that productivity will be up by more than enough to offset the decline in new entrants to the labor force. Thus, real economic growth should be relatively strong, a bit stronger on average than it was in the 1980s. Several different econometric estimates show that the real growth rate of the U.S. economy will average between 2.5 and 3.0

percent per year in the 1990s; furthermore, there is a lower probability of wide swings in the economy's performance such as occurred from the 1970s through the early 1980s, going from boom to recession to boom to the 1982 deep recession.

Second, productivity growth will increase, reversing nearly two decades of subpar growth. America's chief economic malady over the past fifteen years has been its miserably slow pace of productivity improvement. Since 1973 the volume of output that American businesses get from a typical hour of labor has increased just 1 percent per year on average. That compares poorly with the 2.7 percent annual productivity increments that were enjoyed over the fifteen years prior to 1970. Significant gains in productivity during the 1990s are likely to come from three sources: demographic shifts, technology, and service industries.

A slower-growing labor force contains the seeds to give productivity a boost. As labor becomes scarcer and more expensive, business is likely to invest more heavily in productivity-enhancing capital. Another demographic shift that could enhance productivity is the aging of the "baby boomer." As workers become more experienced, they typically become more productive. In the technology arena the biggest punch in the productivity growth rate will come if the billions of dollars that U.S. businesses have poured into computers finally pays off. And this is likely to occur. By historical standards computers are still a relatively young technology, having gained widespread use only within the past fifteen or so years. The 1990s should be the period when we turn the corner and realize gigantic productivity gains from the computer revolution. Productivity in services should improve substantially in the 1990s. One reason is that we will reap the benefits of the computer revolution; the rapid expansion of information technology in general is especially suited to the needs of service industries. The service industries are also under mounting pressure to control costs as direct foreign competition intensifies and as U.S. manufacturers seek to control the rising bill for services they purchase.

Third, inflation will be low and relatively stable. For a long period, roughly from the mid-1960s through the early 1980s, inflation was considered a nearly intractable problem. The successful disinflation that took place not only during the 1981-82 recession but also during the ensuing recovery therefore came as a surprise to many observers. Although several factors contributed to the decline in inflation rates, by far the most significant was that the Federal Reserve demonstrated convincingly that it would not accommodate the fiscal deficits of the 1980s but instead would lean against the expansionist thrust of fiscal policy. On balance the disinflationary factors outweigh the inflationary ones, pointing to the 1990s as a period of low and relatively stable inflation. The average rate of inflation for the decade should be in the range of 3.5 to 4.5 percent per year. While the inflation rate will move up and down, it should stay within a fairly narrow range. Three primary factors will be responsible: the continuing vigilance of the Federal Reserve in seeking to achieve price stability, the fact that the 1990s will be an age of global surpluses (there is so much excess capacity in the global economy that competitive pressure will hold down price increases in each country's import competing sectors), and intense international competitiveness, the effects of which will be reaped within the U.S. economy by keeping prices of goods and services lower than they otherwise would be in the United States. There is one major offsetting factor—rising wages—that will make it difficult for the inflation rate to fall below 3 percent. These wage increases will come from increasing tightness in labor markets as the labor force growth drops toward 1 percent a year, compared to a 3 percent annual growth rate around 1980.

Potential Dark Clouds

I mentioned earlier the potential impact of two dark clouds on the horizon. These are the erosion of America's financial institutions and the likely continuing growth in federal government budget deficits. I am somewhat surprised that Dr. Anderson did not place more attention on these two issues because both have potentially significant adverse and direct impacts on retailing. Erosion of financial institutions would have a real impact on consumer confidence, causing consumers to be more risk averse, reducing their expenditures, and clearly affecting demand for goods and services. It most likely would also cause interest rates to be higher and the borrowing for consumption more difficult. The erosion of financial institutions would also affect retailers, since the availability and cost of capital would again have a negative impact on the ability of retailing to respond to changes in the marketplace. A continuing and growing budget deficit would cause similar problems in the sense that it could lead to higher interest rates as the Federal Reserve monetary policy attempts to deal with an impotent fiscal policy. If there are further tax increases (likely over the course of the next decade), disposable income for consumption will be reduced. And that, of course, directly affects retailing.

The savings and loan crisis is the greatest economic debacle that America has experienced. Before our very eyes, in the matter of only a few years, an entire set of institutions has become terminally ill, causing diversion of hundreds of billions of dollars to unproductive assets and affecting adversely the confidence of consumers in financial institutions. But the erosion of financial institutions only begins with the savings and loan segment. It has now infected regional and national banks, including the money center banks. Some financial analysts and economists working within the banking industry genuinely fear that a severe and prolonged economic recession could cause a collapse of the banking system. Whether the problem reaches these proportions or not, the fact is that the changes we are experiencing at the moment and which could become more serious in the immediate years ahead could result in increased consumer anxiety and reduce borrowing for consumption. Whether the United States can come to grips with its infected financial institutions remains to be seen. It is certainly within our grasp to do so if Congress and the responsible regulatory agencies go about their jobs in a serious and determined way. Thus far, the Federal Reserve has taken this matter seriously, which itself is a positive sign. In other words, this crisis can be avoided because we do have some control over the causal events.

It might be surprising to some that I am talking about continuing growth in budget deficits just after Congress and President Bush have spent months forging a deficit reduction plan that totals $500 billion. The reality is that, even with this plan, budget deficits are expected to continue to grow. If, in the early part of the 1990s, economic growth is relatively slow or the current recession is prolonged, the budget deficits will continue to grow. The federal government will have to confront these deficits because the economic consequences of not doing so will be severe. The result of dealing with these budget deficits will cause disposable income to decline from what it otherwise would be.

THE INTERNATIONALIZATION OF THE RETAIL MARKET

Dr. Anderson devotes a good part of his treatise to describing the increased interdependence that is occurring among economies throughout the world and the likely impacts this will have on the United States and on the retailing sector. He also draws some interesting conclusions concerning how changes in management perspective and performance are required if retailing in the United States is to withstand foreign competition and create new opportunities for American retailing in Asia and Europe.

Without doubt, the world is becoming a global economy and becoming one at an increasingly more rapid pace. What are the effects of increased globalization on American retailers? On balance, the effects will be positive, a conclusion that differs to some extent with that reached by Dr. Anderson. First, I believe that American retailers are relatively well prepared to deal effectively with foreign competition in the American marketplace. Just as Dr. Anderson points out the potential difficulties American retailers would encounter in attempting to enter Japanese retailing markets, so it is the other way around. American retailers know America. American retailers also have been in the vanguard of experimentation and use of technology and are experienced in working within a sector that is constantly experiencing change. This environment of change, which is generally accepted as a given within retailing, is a parameter that is by and large absent from the traditional retailing modes of Europe and even more so in Asia. French and German retailers, or even more so Japanese retailers, are not able to move into the American retail market (in the sense that Toyota or Nissan or other manufacturers have been able to move successfully into the U.S. market) because they currently do not have a mode of retailing that can effectively compete in the American economy. There are exceptions to this, some of which occur in specific niches and product categories. But I believe the basic proposition remains true.

It is interesting to note that the entry into American retailing by non-Americans is primarily through the acquisition of existing retailing outlets. Investments by Canadians, the French, Germans, and the English in department stores and specialty retailing (such as clothing) and the Japanese acquisition of Southland Corporation, the owner of the 7-Eleven convenience stores, are examples that have occurred over the last four or five years. What these investments by foreign entities may bring is different modes of management to the retailing environment. But that is quite different from new entrants affecting competition in the United States.

Second, and probably more important, is that American retailers have greater opportunities of penetrating retail markets abroad than do retailers from any other countries. In effect, the United States has a comparative advantage in retailing. The success of American retailers in Europe and Japan indicates that in this sector we bring value to a foreign economy. Japan alone has more than eight thousand U.S. fast-food franchise outlets and over three thousand American-franchised 7-Eleven convenience stores. It may well be that the history of changing consumption patterns in the United States, which Dr. Anderson has thoroughly presented in his paper, is in the process of occurring in Europe and Japan. If that process parallels what has occurred in the United Sates (there is little reason to expect it to be otherwise), American retailers are in a remarkable position to capitalize on rapid growth and change in retailing in Asia and Europe. American retailers can clearly maximize their leverage by establishing strategic organizational alliances, as Dr. Anderson has recommended. It is clearly to the advantage of any American retailer to understand and work with people and businesses that can facilitate the process of change where there is an interaction between the company and the final consumer.

A brief illustration is the remarkably successful experience of Amway in Japan. Amway is a large direct selling company that has grown to be a successful firm in the United States, Canada, and many other countries. But it has added to its accomplishments the fact that it is one of the largest exporters of American goods to Japan. How did that happen? It happened because Amway took its approach to retailing and in effect bypassed traditional distribution channels in Japan to tap the energy and resources of Japanese households. The Amway experience in Japan (and indeed of many American direct selling firms internationally) is an instructive example of the potential comparative advantage American retailing can bring to other parts of the world.

In brief, internationalization is not likely to cause displacement by foreign competitors in the United States. Instead, internationalization will create new opportunities for growth and profits abroad for American retailers.

TWO KEY DEMOGRAPHIC TRENDS

Dr. Anderson provides an excellent demographic framework for assessing retailing in the 21st century. He contrasts the "glacial and certain" change of demographics with the "volatile and uncertain" changes of the economic environment.

I would add emphasis to two demographic trends that are moving faster than at a glacial pace and are having and will continue to have important consequences for retailing. The first is the significant and growing participation of women in the work force. Indeed, over the last two decades the change has been almost revolutionary. By the year 2000 nearly 90 percent of new labor force entrants will be minorities and women. In contrast, white males, long considered the prime working group, will make up less than 10 percent of the twenty million people expected to be added to the labor force by the year 2000. The implications of the increasing participation of women in the work force for retailing are several. Obviously they are valuable additions to a scarce labor pool (especially important for the retail sector, considering the expected growth in job requirements in retailing). At the same time, increased participation reduces time available for purchasing and shopping. More than anything else, the two-wage-earner household has placed a premium on time, which translates into convenience and absentee shopping.

The second trend concerns immigration. Immigration, which brings new talent and youth to an aging population, is one of America's richest resources and potentially a major competitive advantage over Japan and the many European countries that lack our immigration tradition. Principally because of the presence of a large number of immigrants, America in the 1990s will have the youngest population of our major economic rivals. As Dr. Anderson has pointed out, the new immigrants are also changing America's ethnic composition. The vast majority of them come from nations other than Europe, predominantly Asia and Latin America. The proportion of new arrivals from Asia soared from 6 percent in the 1950s to almost 50 percent in the 1980s. Every indicator points to an increase in the number of people who will be immigrating to the United States in the 1990s. This makes American a "world nation" with direct links to virtually every part of the globe.

This demographic trend also has several important implications for retailing. First, increased ethnic composition offers challenges for retailing and provides an incentive for further market segmentation. Second, it is expected that the past experience of new immigrants using retailing as an initial economic building block will be continued, in part because of the low entry cost in retailing and in part because of the immigrants' accustomed use of personal contacts and networks, which Dr. Anderson appropriately considers so important. A third implication, and one which we are only beginning to see now, is that some of the immigrants who have moved into the retailing sector can become important exporters of American retailing back to their original homelands. They acquire the expertise and knowledge of the American retailing system and are able to quickly adapt it and develop the network required to make it successful in their country of origin. This is particularly relevant for franchise-type operations and, hence, I expect we will see many Koreans, Vietnamese, and other Asians in particular moving back with their retailing capabilities to establish important beachheads of retailing in their respective countries.

CONSUMER VALUES

Through his multidimensional consumer cube, Dr. Anderson has explored fully the factors influencing consumer behavior and how consumer behavior is likely to change by the 21st century. I wish to address here only two of those factors: convenience and the impact of health and environmental concerns on consumption.

Changes in demographic characteristics (as noted earlier and more fully by Dr. Anderson) place an increasing value on time and, therefore, an increasing premium on convenience for retailing. Time will become the principal driving force in consumer behavior and in the demand for easily accessible choice information (in an economist's terminology, there will be incentives to minimize transaction costs reflected in time and the availability and accuracy of information). When this premium on time is combined with the revolution and technology of communications, we have probably seen only the tip of the iceberg in absentee shopping. The increasing presence of (and some would argue, ubiquity of) fax machines has already begun to transform consumption patterns. I order deli sandwiches for the Sunday football game, and my wife shops easily and instantaneously from home for a variety of her needs in Hong Kong, Paris, and San Francisco.

Dr. Anderson seems to discount the impact of health and environmental concerns on consumer behavior in the 1990s and beyond, pointing to the experience of the last two decades as being essentially ephemeral. The increasing value placed by American consumers on health and a higher quality of life—with the impact these concerns place on their demand for health services, the cost of those services, and their availability through various delivery mechanisms—is clearly a major subject in and of itself.

I would, however, like to offer several observations on what I perceive to be a permanent change in values regarding the environment and its relationship to consumption. I see the environment having two different impacts on consumer behavior. One is price. The reality of scarce resources will increasingly be translated into higher prices for those resources. This may take the form of higher gasoline prices because of new clean air requirements, or it could take the form of dramatically increased prices for water (prices for the latter may in some regions of the country increase five- or tenfold) and will affect consumer behavior accordingly. The other environmental impact on consumer behavior is reflected in changing values that affect choices by consumers between those retailers who are in tune with their values and those who are not. Admittedly, the signs of a permanent movement in this direction are limited, but they are beginning to appear. A few examples may tell the story. Burger King uses only recyclable packaging, and this example has been followed by a commitment from McDonald's to recyclable packaging material. Star Kist tuna commits a 60-second commercial in prime time to images of dolphins and places a sticker on each can of its products to demonstrate to consumers that it not only is conscious of changing values, but in fact is committing resources to see that the changes are reflected in the product it markets. Other examples can come to mind quite readily. Do these examples reflect fundamental change? I believe they do, and I believe they will cause a change in consumer behavior which by the year 2000 will have fundamental impacts on American retailing.

A FINAL OBSERVATION

Dr. Anderson's treatise has a subtitle with three questions: "Quixotic Consumers? Exotic Markets? Neurotic Retailers?" There may well be validity to positive answers to the first two questions, but I believe retailers in the American economy will not be neurotic or have reason to be.

As an economist, I view the American retailing sector as being highly competitive. This competition reflects itself in a variety of ways. Some of it is in the form of price competition, some in the form of attempting to distinguish markets, and some in the form of major investments in the retailing outlets themselves. Many of these changes are in response to changing consumer behavior and consumption patterns. But as Dr. Anderson points out, the combination of demographic trends and the continuity of consumer behavior (future behavior being influenced by past behavior) provides a road map to retailers that enables some anticipation of change.

Moreover, given the strength of American retailing vis-à-vis foreign competition in the American market, I see one less dimension of competition than does Dr. Anderson. And, in further contrast, to diminish any tendency toward mental instability by retailers is the growing potential for exporting American retailing into Europe and Asia. The changes in American retailing will continue at a fast pace, but the pace is one to which American retailers are accustomed. They are accustomed to competition, and they are accustomed to changes in consumer behavior. This is a healthy environment in which American consumers, investors, and financial institutions can proceed into the 21st century.

NOTE

1. The content of this section draws heavily upon *Economic Upheaval: 60 Key Trends in the 1990's Reshaping Your World,* Washington, D.C.: Nathan Associates, Inc., 1990.

3

Emerging Technology in Retailing: Challenges and Opportunities for the 1990s

Dale Achabal and Shelby McIntyre

INTRODUCTION

The world is in the midst of a continuing technological revolution that is accelerating over time. Retailers face a number of important challenges in the next decade, driven in part by the threats and opportunities that technology spawns. Retailers can apply technology to their own operations to make them more efficient, which will increasingly become a competitive necessity.

Technology is becoming a primary tool for serving the customer, improving decision making, and streamlining the management of the retail enterprise. Towards this end, it is important to keep systems "in sync" with how the business is run today and will be run in the future. As Joe Nagy, former vice president of systems for Macy's, has suggested, "good systems permit a greater fluidity of management." Managers who are adept at analyzing the business can move rapidly up the learning curve because good systems allow them to uncover the nuances of a business in a very short period of time. Successfully responding to the systems challenge will provide an organization with a significant competitive advantage, but it will come only through a deeper understanding of the emerging technologies and changing marketplace.

As a result, MIS should not be left totally in the hands of the computer experts and treated as an administrative cost center, but should become an integral part of the strategic planning process just like merchandise planning, financial planning, and human resources planning. The most significant challenge facing managers preparing to compete in the year 2000 and beyond is to capitalize on the substantial opportunities that come from learning to do things better rather than just doing the same things faster or cheaper (Hammer 1990).

This chapter focuses primarily on the systems side of retailing, which is the key area of technology application in our increasingly information-based economy. Also, the focus is on department stores and specialty stores rather than food and drug retailing.

Strategic Use of Systems

In the past, systems have been used by retailers to "automate the back room." Dramatic improvements have been made in the areas of inventory and receivables management and centralized data capture from far-flung stores. For the most part, these changes have enabled retailers to do the same job faster or at less cost.

Data vs. Information

In the future, certainly more automation of current, back room activities will take place. However, there will be a greater use of systems to initiate new procedures and enable retailers to pursue business strategically.

Retailers will move away from capturing and moving data around the organization to concentrating on converting data into information for managing their operations. The transaction system of a retail establishment is still its backbone. Vast improvements can be made in this sphere, but equally important improvements will also be made on the management decision support side.

Competitive Advantage

The key will be to apply technology in order to gain a sustainable competitive advantage. Only by applying technology in this manner can exceptional profit performance be achieved. Michael Porter, professor at the Harvard Business School, has identified the competitive pressures that come to play in any industry (Porter 1985). Porter reminds us that we face competition not only from the obvious direct competitors in the retail industry, but from suppliers, from possible new entrants, and from substitutes for our services (see Figure 3.1). What follows will reveal the threats to retailers from each of these potential competitors due to developing technologies that can be applied by others as well as by current retailers. The real challenge for retailers is, because the technologies are available to everyone, the mixing and blending of different technologies together into an applications system that constitutes the competitive advantage. The difficulty of developing such applications constitutes the basis for generating sustainable competitive advantage.

Figure 3.1.   Strategic Use of Systems

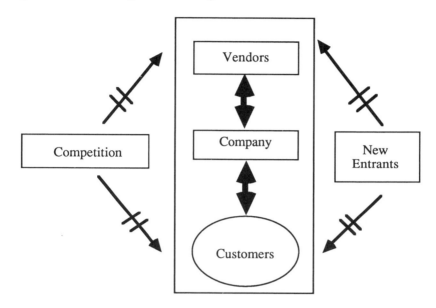

Strategy, Structure, and Systems

It is also important to recognize information systems technology, particularly as it interacts with the strategy and organizational structure of the retail firm. Often executives think of strategy first, their organizational structure second, and their information systems third. This sequential thought process is inappropriate. Retail strategy and organizational structure need to be analyzed simultaneously with the implementation of new information systems. At some point, new strategies and structures are required on the basis of what the information technology can deliver. It is all too easy to improve the information technology of the firm in increments only to find that it does not mesh well with the existing strategy and structure. As a result, these separate components become impediments to successful implementation. Strategy, structure, and systems must be melded together as an integrated whole. (See Figure 3.2 for a conceptualization of this integration.)

Figure 3.2. Conceptual Relationships among Strategy, Structure, and Systems

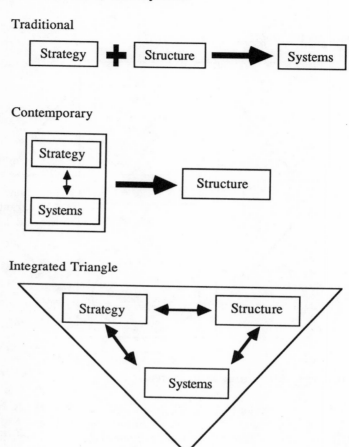

RETAIL TRENDS

It is often said that need is the mother of invention. We believe that the environment of a retailing firm, and particularly the changes and trends in that environment, will foster the adoption of technology and will determine which technologies are implemented and which are not. It is helpful to review a few central trends in three key areas of the retail environment, namely, consumer trends, competitive trends, and resource trends.[1] Each will have a large impact on the application of technology in retailing.

Consumer Trends

The average retail consumer is changing, becoming money-rich, time-poor, and ethnically diverse. Dual income households are the norm—households with more money, but less time to spend it. Commuting times are increasing as people live farther from work and as highway congestion increases.

The graying of America means fewer buyers in the youth segment and significantly more in the senior category. The older segments are not as interested in traditional shopping, and largely gone are the housewives of the past who were dedicated to being the household purchasing agent.

The ethnic diversity of the population is increasing so that more and more segments and targets exist for the retailer. The market is literally fragmenting.

Consumers are more accustomed to information technology and the use of computer displays. A large portion of the population will use computers in school and at work. Consumers are becoming more comfortable with information technology in the form of VCRs, telephone answering machines, TV remote controls, microwave ovens, and programmable security systems (Keller 1990a; Lopez and Carnevale 1990). Vast numbers of households will buy computers and modems as they join the information society (Rothfeder and Lewyn 1990; Siegman 1990). Consumers read less and increasingly expect communication to be in the form of full-motion video because they have become accustomed to the "hot" medium of television (Hirsch 1990; Armstrong 1990b).

Competitive Trends

America has become "over-stored" in many parts of the country. Competition among retailers has become more and more intense with category-killers in almost every merchandise area. Retail-oriented venture capitalists allow new retail start-ups to roll out new formats at break-neck speeds. The retail industry is consolidating rapidly as the larger firms gobble up more of the independents. As retailers consolidate, they must mesh their organizations and their information systems. This trend is preoccupying many retailers in the early 1990s. Retailers are getting bigger, and more of them are taking on a national presence. Advanced retailers are taking over their less adept rivals and using their more sophisticated information systems to rapidly assimilate them into their existing organizations.

Labor Resource Trends

The cheap labor pool that retailers enjoyed in the 1980s will decrease in the 1990s. Fewer, and less educated, candidates will fill out job applications. The cost of retail labor will jump dramatically and training and support needs for the typical retail clerk will increase. Young sales people will be in great demand whereas older, semiretired individuals will be seeking part-time work. Retailers will have to learn to manage a vastly more diverse work force. For example, the number of white males will drop from the current 45 percent to 30 percent of the labor force by the year 2000. People from a variety of ethnic backgrounds will be entering the labor pool in increasing numbers, particularly Spanish-speaking individuals. The labor pool shifts come at the same time that serving the customer is of growing importance. Retailers will have to provide more service but with less labor input.

KEY TECHNOLOGIES

This section will focus on three important general technological areas or spheres: computer technologies, communications technologies, and what we call analytical technologies. The following sections will address the applications for specific components of these technological areas within retailing.

Because so many important technological developments are taking place, we have prepared a glossary that explains the specific terms used and something about each technology. It should be emphasized that it is the synergy among these emerging technologies that will have the most dramatic impact on retailing as opposed to the sole effect of a single breakthrough.

Three Spheres of Technology

Computer Technologies. It is widely accepted that computing power in both the hardware and software areas will continue to improve at an accelerating pace. Parallel processing, even within a single chip, promises to demolish all computer speed barriers and make computing vastly cheaper and faster. Compact disks, optical disks, and electronic image management (EIM) systems promise to vastly expand the amount of information that can be stored to the extent that document images and full-motion video will become cost effective. Paper documents may soon seem to be expensive, slow, and inflexible compared to their electronic counterparts. The continued expansion of local area networks (LANs) and wide area networks (WANs) will provide increased communication and integration among computer systems (Robins 1990).

All of these computer hardware advances are making computer software developments possible (Hammond, 1990). No longer do programmers need to focus heavily on the hardware resources their programs use. For example, the introduction of 4GLs and computer-assisted software engineering (CASE) is allowing easier programming. Thus, the technology of developing software is improving, which has a compounding effect.

Communications Technologies. Communications technologies are improving almost as fast as are computer hardware and software technologies. The move to fiber optics over the next decade will provide a quantum leap in what can be done with communications (Lopez and Carnevale 1990). We will be moving from a copper wire technology that can carry twenty-four voice conversations simultaneously (on what are currently advanced T1-lines) in an analog mode to fiber optic lines that can carry sixteen thousand conversations simultaneously in a digital mode.

It is all too easy to underestimate the vast changes that will take place because of improved communications. For example, fiber optics will allow movies to be "downloaded" over telephone lines to individual homes in minutes, shoppers will be able to "turn through the pages" of full motion hypermedia catalogs on their high-definition televisions, and picture telephones will finally become a reality (Buderi 1990; Depke 1990; Fruendlich 1990; Reilly 1990). Other technologies include digital cellular radio, which will expand the capacity of the radio frequency channels to allow portable telephone communication anywhere. The fax communication protocol provides faster and easier transmission of images, and microwave and satellite communication allow increased efficiency in the transmission of signals. The Yellow Pages will surely go "on-line," and millions of households will be able to comparison shop from home computers. This is not the environment that retailers are currently familiar with, but it is not that far in the future.

Analytic Technologies. Finally, there is the sphere of technologies that revolve around what we term analytic technologies. Basically, this is the area of decision making that has been called the "decision factory." The key to better retail performance is for the retailer to make more, better, and faster decisions. Computers and communications set the stage for the implementation of business "smarts" (Richman 1987). However, these smarts go beyond what computers can do; computers are just workhorses that can get the job of decision making implemented. Behind the scenes are the technologies of neural networks and econometrics used to (1) analyze data and develop causal relationships, (2) develop mathematical programs to allocate resources most efficiently, and (3) allow mathematical modeling, mathematical programming, optimal control, and simulation to tackle difficult and/or highly repetitive decisions.

Humans will never be replaced by computers to make the broad-based decisions, to supply the high-level understanding, to create ever better systems, to inject innovation, to provide creativity, and to execute the crucial personal side of business. But, humans will be freed to deal with these central matters by the automation of low-level decisions. By the mid-1990s vast amounts of inventory and logistics decision making will have been automated by the use of models housed in computer programs. This trend will spread and penetrate many other areas of the organization. This is really an extrapolation of trends that trace their roots back to the development of operations research during World War II.

Customer Need vs. Technology (Existing vs. New)

The application of technology in any organization is a risk. However, not to apply technology carries a risk of its own: the risk of always being behind the most advanced competitors. On the other hand, it is equally possible to apply too much technology and be at what is sometimes called the "bleeding edge" of technological developments, which can prove to be too expensive to be profitable. The objective, of course, is to study the technologies that are emerging and to apply them carefully and at the right time so that they serve to maximize profitability.

A companion issue is the fact that low technological risk is often coupled with low expected payoff, whereas higher risk comes with higher expected payoff. Thus the retail firm must make a decision, perhaps implicitly, as to its appropriate risk/payoff posture.

The appropriate application of technology to retailing is driven by two forces, the force of technology that represents the existing possibilities, and the need or trend that could be addressed by the technology. This viewpoint can be expressed as a matrix (see Figure 3.3). One axis is the customer need that can be an existing need or an emerging need. The other axis is technology, which can also be existing or new.

The matrix illustrates that, at least in the short run, the risk of applying technology increases as a retailer moves from the application of existing technology to existing customer needs. When the retailer is knowledgeable about a given technology, say, bar code reading, then it is a less risky move to apply that known technology to a new area or need, say, applying bar codes to an interstore transfer application, than to use some new technology to accomplish that task.

Figure 3.3. Technology vs. Need

Customer/Need

		Existing	New
Technology/ Possibility	Existing	Little Risk	Moderate Risk
	New	Moderate Risk	High Risk

The retailer could alternatively move from applying existing technology to existing customer needs by applying new technology to serve those same needs. For example, rather than simply allowing credit customers to dial a number and talk to someone about their credit balance, the retailer could provide the ability for a customer with a computer to dial up and view the entire account history on-screen.

Of course, the most risky move would be to apply a new technology to a new customer need. For instance, it may be possible to provide the customer with the capability of doing home shopping by viewing holographic displays of the merchandise (Walash 1990; Ward 1989). This, of course, would entail both the unknowns of the new technology and the unknowns of the needs of the customer for an in-home shopping capability of that type.

The best approach to applying technology typically lies between the two extremes and involves taking a small step in one direction and then in the other direction. However, some of the highest payoff projects in retailing have involved high technological risk that required moving in both directions at once.

APPLICATION AREAS

This section identifies several areas of opportunity for retailers where trends will best be met with the application of new technologies. This section focuses on three key interfaces: the interface between the customer and the retailer, the interface between departments and functions within the retail firm, and the vendor-retailer interface (see Figure 3.4). It is in these three areas that the retailer must develop sustainable competitive advantage, and in them several trends can be identified that will drive the application of new technology.

Figure 3.4.   Key Interfaces Where Technology Will Be Applied

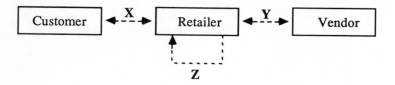

Retailer and Customer Interface (X)

The retailer-customer interface is always important, and as we have identified, the retail customer is changing in many important ways. This section discusses changes that are taking place which will affect the retailer-customer interface and will provide opportunities for application of emerging technologies.

From Segmentation to Relationship Marketing.   Retailers will look beyond the segmentation of customers into groups and will apply technology to track customers as individuals and consequently respond to them on an individual basis. This will require the development of customer tracking systems at the store level, greater integration of purchasing and credit histories, and sales associates supported by intelligent decision support systems.

One key trend in department store and specialty store retailing is a movement beyond segmentation to relationship marketing as a key way of treating customers differently. Relationship marketing is an attempt to establish a relationship with the customer and create a competitive advantage that is sustainable. Relationship marketing means treating customers individually and catering more precisely to their specific needs in a timely fashion. This requires tracking individual customers.

Tracking customers using a bridal registry, a birth registry, a graduation registry, or the like is important in many retail settings. These events in the life of the customer are at the core of what buyer-behavior analysts would call the impetus to "need recognition." Helping consumers by tracking events in their lives, by communicating directly with them at key times, and by treating them differently is the foundation of relationship marketing. Relationship marketing is based on knowing customers individually, not as segments or groups.

Knowing customers individually in the information age means keeping track of customers in a database and recording information about them that can be used to serve them better. Does the customer always buy on sale? Only buy apparel at the store? Shop at the same time each year? Utilize the layaway plan? Buy on a credit card or pay cash? Always buy from the same clerk or department? When is the person's birthday? Did the person just change addresses? These are not segmentation questions. These are questions upon which to base a relationship between the retailer and the individual customer.

Currently, registries are used when the gift recipient comes into the store and makes a list of the things she or he wants to receive. Gift-givers come in, review the list, and decide what they want to buy. Up to this point, the customer and/or the consumer has done all of the work.

Think about what the true relationship could be. If you have a database about the charge customer and you analyze the pattern of buying, it would be possible to provide your sales associates better information, or to send direct marketing pieces to clients based on their past purchases. For example, if customers bought a sofa, you could send a catalog of all furniture; or if they tend to buy a lot of skirts, blouses, and dresses and you are going to have a coat sale, notify them of it. Alternatively, advanced information systems would allow this analysis to be done automatically, labels prepared, and product information mailed directly to the customer. Also, it would be possible to identify those customers who buy on sale and notify them first when goods that they want are discounted. This is currently being approximated in a Nordstrom's environment, where sales associates make telephone calls to those customers who are the most likely to buy specific merchandise.

In the near future, customers will be able to dial up stores via a computer modem, access their own credit accounts, and monitor full information about what they have purchased. They will be able to communicate with the store from home to leave notes for clerks as well as receive messages from the store.

Advanced technology in the form of relational databases, expanded point of sale data capture capability (EPOS), fast mass storage, and software such as knowledge-based systems to manipulate the growing information base will be necessary to accomplish relationship marketing. The new competitive advantage will be the data collected on customers, the relationship that has been built with them, and the speed and richness of the information captured. The database will be a set of tables that keep track not only of the customer but also of the events in the life of the customer. This goes far beyond just information about what they bought. It goes into an event file that tracks key occasions in the life of the customer—the purchase of a new house, the birth of a baby, the spouse going to work, and so forth.

Particularly central to the implementation of relationship marketing will be the use of credit cards, debit cards, and smart cards. Companies such as Verifone are focusing on what might best be termed "transaction automation systems." Such systems will soon expand the use of cards into fast-food outlets, movie theaters, schools, grocery stores, and taxicabs— essentially for any transaction. The key is to check the validity of the card in an instantaneous way. This is being done by satellite broadcasting to update local information about bad cards. But the use of these cards goes much, much further than just checking credit. For instance, in one application, fifty thousand drugstores are hooked up to a system whereby pharmacists can run a magnetic card through a terminal to find how much of a purchase is covered by insurance. The customer then pays only the amount not covered, and the insurance company is informed without the pharmacist and the customer having to fill out forms. In another case, children across the country are utilizing school cafeteria cards that allow them to buy their lunches with credit cards scanned by computers to keep an automatic record of purchases (*San Francisco Chronicle* 1990). Under these programs, parents may also specify what types of food their children may purchase with the card. No more lunches of just cookies! In yet another example, some states and counties are beginning to issue cards to recipients of food stamps, welfare payments, unemployment insurance, and other government benefits. These are just precursors of what will be coming in the future.

Thus, relationship marketing will be a natural application of mass storage technology to store all of the relevant information on large numbers of customers. Relational database technologies will be needed to organize the data in a way that will require the least space, will reduce redundancies, and will provide high flexibility as to how the information might be used (prior to the introduction of relational databases, a hierarchical database structure was used to organize data). Neural network technologies and econometric analysis will be needed to identify relationships in the data such as sale-proneness. Knowledge-based systems will be needed to address the ever-growing mass of information and to carry out a policy such as sending birthday gift certificates to customers who meet certain criteria.

Also, as more and more households become equipped with computers and computer-based mail addresses, it will be possible to send messages to customers via a modem. More customers will be able to buy via computer, which completes the Electronic Data Interchange linkages that began with the retailer-vendor interface.

Obviously, relationship marketing will carry risks as well as opportunities. The risks revolve around the issues of invasion of privacy and possibly the loss of customer goodwill because of "electronic hard-sell." However, counterbalancing these pressures are the ever-decreasing costs of executing relationship marketing and the ever-increasing benefits to customers as retailers become better at managing information to meet their needs. Information and credit risk will continue to be considerations with which to deal.

From Customer Service to Customer Experiences. There is a
need to move beyond customer service into new areas that we will call "customer experiences." For many firms, the current emphasis on customer service is very narrowly defined and does not truly encompass the breadth of opportunities available to the firm to gain a significant competitive advantage in the marketplace.

Traditionally, many organizations have equated the term "customer service" with activities involving a direct personal interface with the customer, such as more sales associates, faster checkout, or gift wrapping. They have often not recognized that the core of customer service is "serving the customer," which really addresses issues such as having the desired assortments, being in-stock, having attractive prices, and having convenient hours of operation.

The growing labor shortage will drive the effort for alternative ways to supply point-of-purchase information to the consumer. Technology can augment the sales associate and also provide the customer with improved access to product information. Even if the customer does not ask for the audiovisual information, the retailer will provide it as a way to cope with the impending labor shortage. And as customers become used to the new technology, they will come to rely on it, as in their acceptance of automatic teller machines (ATMs).

Opportunities exist, via technology, to help consumers buy products in a more efficient or more enjoyable way. Retailers will increasingly have an opportunity to move into new areas that apply technology to what we will call "customer experiences." Many of these "experiences" take place when people are in the store; others do not. For instance, through advanced computer graphics it will be possible for a customer to bring a photograph of a bathroom to a store, have that photograph digitized in a computer, and then to match the sink and vanity with a new model from a pallet of alternatives. It will then be possible for the customer to try out different color schemes, to check the availability of the components that are under consideration, to review delivery time for items that are not currently in stock, and to rotate the view of the room so that it can be "seen" from different perspectives. Holographic presentations, which are essentially three-dimensional representations, would be a natural extension of this approach.

In a similar way, retailers are experimenting with a "magic mirror" concept that allows customers to rapidly "try on" different clothes that are projected over the customer's image in the magic mirror. The customer can try on a particular outfit, change the color, try out different shoes, and experiment with different accessories without ever actually trying on the individual items. Again, the customer could check on availability, price, or care instructions by means of hypertext that could be built into the system.

Other current examples of interactive video applications are in the cosmetic and plastic surgery areas. In cosmetic departments, the customer can touch a screen and see how she will look in different cosmetics and combinations of cosmetics, such as eye shadow and lipstick. Another fledgling development is in plastic surgery. When someone is going to get a "nose job" or a face lift, the surgeon can show them how the proposed work will make them look. The key is to allow different alternatives to be "experienced" by the customer or patient before the actual transaction is completed.

The key technologies underlying good in-store audiovisual presentations will be powerful full-motion video computers that allow hypermedia presentations. Customers can traverse the information in the order they choose and interact with the hypermedia presentation. Many will already have been exposed to this hypertext and hypermedia browsing approach in school or on the job and will be coming to the store fluent in the technology.

Because of possible education-related constraints, one might think that hypermedia would be difficult for some segments of the population. However, hypermedia is so simple that it can be used, after a little practice, even by those who are illiterate or who do not speak English. The key to the simplicity of the hypermedia approach is that it uses a "point and click" mouse interface that can be programmed so as to be intuitively obvious even for young children. It is a medium that actually can be implemented in a way that does not require good language skills.

Consumers will view a listing of what the store offers in a given category. They will be able to browse directly to price information or a store layout map showing in which department the product is available. They will be able to access product information, stock status, product price points, and products on sale or offering a manufacturer's rebate. The customer may even be able to buy directly from the terminal and take delivery at home via United Parcel Service (UPS).

An example of this is the ByVideo system used by Florsheim Shoe to provide customers with a form of electronic retailing. Florsheim uses the ByVideo in-store electronic kiosk to sell shoes. The company manufactures more than seventeen thousand shoes (including all styles, colors, and sizes). However, even the largest Florsheim store can stock only fifty-five hundred individual stock-keeping units (SKUs). One survey found that 30 percent of the shoppers leaving a shoe store without having made a purchase reported the only reason was that they were not successful in finding the exact color, style, or size of shoe that they wanted. The Florsheim electronic kiosk, called the Express Stop, is manufactured by ByVideo. This system is fully capable of making sales transactions with the customer. The shoes are delivered to the home via UPS on a two-day delivery promise.

The time-buying consumer may come to expect such multiple shopping methods to be offered by a firm. Retailers are going to have to provide such technology to regain or retain a modicum of store loyalty in the decade ahead.

Manufacturers will be able to supply a consistent message, and retailers will be able to make appropriate tie-in sales suggestions. Customers will no longer have to find and wait for a knowledgeable sales clerk. Instead, the clerk will be available in the form of an in-store hypertext audiovisual display terminal with an efficient search mechanism that consumers have learned to utilize effectively.

One day it may be the case that customers shop a retailer because they prefer the way the store's software works in comparison to that of competing stores. More likely, general software standards will develop so that consumers can feel immediately at home in any store that has the hypertext audiovisual sales and information service.

To date, some of the fledgling attempts in the interactive video area have not succeeded. One reason is that interactive video system technology has been expensive. The interactive video terminal has cost $8,000 to $10,000 per unit, and the cost of producing a video disk for the system has often exceeded $250,000. These prices will drop dramatically as the technology improves and economies of scale are achieved in production. When these units cost less than $1,000 per terminal and video disks can be produced and updated for $25,000, instead of $250,000, the equation for success will be altered substantially.

An additional opportunity for the retailer to tie in with experience-based shopping will be a data collection capability for the store. When customers see things they like during a "magic mirror" presentation, these preferences can be stored. It will be possible to assess what is consistent across the items selected. Is it color? Is it style? Is it silhouette? This will help retailers make early assessments of trends and the way the merchandise mix is working together for the customer. Never before have retailers had such a rich way to assess the interests of customers in an unobtrusive and natural way.

It will be possible to view even products that the store does not currently carry, products that might be drawn from electronic catalogs provided by manufacturers. It will be possible to do in-store or in-mall intercepts and have customers go through a magic mirror experience, rating the items they view as a way of assessing new products and how those new products would attract different segments of the customer base. In this way, the magic mirror, tied in with a data capture capability, could be the retailers' approach to advanced product testing and trend merchandising.

Even today, J. C. Penney is leading the industry in this direction with its advanced satellite service. Penney can now obtain market research information in two to three days instead of three to four weeks as in the past. Under the Penney satellite system, consumers are brought into one of its testing centers to view the broadcast of a program featuring products or concepts that are being tested. The participants enter their responses via a personal computer, and at the end of the session the data are electronically transmitted to the computer center. Much of the testing is with live broadcasts from Europe and the Far East, and the results are immediately available for planning merchandise mixes and for picking sources. Penney, in addition, sells the research information to manufacturers as a research service (Tahmincioglu 1990a).

From Store-Based to Distance-Based Retailing. Twenty-five million homes now have computers (Siegman 1990). Homes are rapidly being linked by fiber optics that will allow incredible capabilities at home. Customers will be able to achieve full-motion videotex experiences right in their own homes—probably on a high definition television (HDTV) screen that will match the quality of a 35mm slide, but as a full motion display. The Yellow Pages will be fully on-line so that customers can identify the stores closest to their home that have the items they require. Customers will be able to retrieve a map showing the shortest route from home to the retail outlet of their choice. This could provide a new alternative to direct mail and today's catalogs—their electronic counterparts can be delivered to the home via fiber optics. The use of multimedia computers will retain the "hot" medium quality of television with hypertext browsing capability. We all know how adept consumers have become at using the remote control on their television sets.

Distance-based shopping does not need to be tied to a computer in the home. Much of the capability can be provided via fiber optics on home television without the need of a home computer. The computer at the retailer's end of the communication can handle the "smarts" of the two-way communication.

Also, it should be remembered that distance-based retailing need not necessarily take place only at home. Consumers can shop from their place of work, on their cellular telephone, in airport terminals, or even while in-flight. The retailer no longer will be just a fixed store that the customer visits, but rather will become a source of assortment and the age-old utilities of time, place, and possession. Remember that the importance of place is fundamentally concerned with where the customer is located, not where the retailer is located.

New forms of retailing will open up to the distance-based shopper via information services. The potential of this approach has recently been recognized by Sears and IBM, which have entered into a joint venture to offer the Prodigy consumer shopping and retail information service. Among other services, customers can review airline travel schedules and even buy tickets on-line. The system has been tested in a number of cities and was rolled out to a national level in August 1990. This is the beginning of a growing new retail format that meets the shifting environmental realities of the American marketplace.

Compuserve, Telaction, and Prodigy demonstrate the growing vision for distance-based retailing. This potential will grow into reality as two things happen: consumers become accustomed to using technology and households become more equipped to handle it. Just as interstate highways provided the necessary infrastructure for the automobile, fiber optics will enable the formation of an underlying network for distance-based shopping. As that takes place, retailers will have the opportunity to move into the new medium or be left behind as others do.

Innovations have been said to differ with regard to how they will change the potential adopter's behavior. Is the innovation continuous, requiring little or no change on the part of the adopter; dynamically continuous; or is it discontinuous requiring whole new types of behavior for the adopter (Robertson 1970)? Many developments are easing the consumer into a position where distance-based retailing will not be a discontinuous innovation and therefore a difficult one to adopt. Computer experience with mouse-based and hypertext media, remote-controlled "zapping" with the TV, catalog buying, and experience with ATMs are all developing the needed adaptation on the part of potential customers that will make distance-based retailing a natural extension and thereby change it from a discontinuous to a more continuous innovation.

Distance-based shopping will vastly reshape the retail landscape because it may become easier to shop a retailer located in a different city than it is to shop one a couple of miles from home. In the future will it still be the case that the three most important factors in retail success are location, location, and location? As Marshall McLuhan (1967) noted in the 1960s, print is a cold medium whereas TV is a hot medium. Perhaps the TV links of the future will make some form of catalog shopping a truly viable alternative to visiting stores for millions of consumers on many occasions.

In the future, it may be that the most important attribute for retail success will be a national or even worldwide image. Stores such as Bloomingdales or Nieman Marcus may be able to penetrate smaller geographic markets where it is not economically feasible to locate a store. Retailers can serve those smaller and more remote markets via the distance-based shopping medium. The consummation of the sale would then take place via a vastly expanded delivery system along the lines of Federal Express and its growing set of clone-like competitors. Overnight delivery of distance-based retail purchases may be the ultimate target of the small-package industry; it seems like a natural extension for them. These retail developments and distribution systems would provide greater working and shopping flexibility for consumers in the 21st century.

Internal Interfaces (Y)

This section will focus on trends internal to the retail organization that technology will enhance. Four trends will be examined in depth.

From Static Reports to Ad-hoc Queries. Retailers have moved from periodic or static reports printed on paper to on-line computerized reports. At the same time there has been a tremendous proliferation of these reports. In the future, there will be fewer static reports that presume the manager wants to view the operation from only one perspective. Instead, ad-hoc queries will become the standard. Managers will make queries of their decision support system when and how they want to make decisions.

The transaction system is the low-level system that tracks the purchase-by-purchase details of the business. To manage the business, decision makers need to change data about transactions into information. This transition from data to information requires summarizing the data in myriads of ways and allowing for the flexibility to respecify how data are to be summarized. It also requires developing reports that indicate what is going on in the business as a whole.

Historically, paper reports were the only basis for managing the business. The computer turned the paper reports into electronic reports displayed on the CRT screen. But virtually all of today's reports are still prespecified reports that allow the manager to view the operation of the firm only in a predetermined way. This approach has tended to generate a deluge of reports in order to gain some understanding of the underlying relationships among decision variables. What is really needed is the ability to create a new report, on the fly so to speak, that addresses the business decision directly. This is the real transition from data to information.

To accomplish this transition from reports to ad-hoc queries, systems must translate the transaction data into summary files small enough to be stored, maintained, and manipulated in any way desired. Also, data must span a significant historical time horizon, that is, at least several years. Today, it seems that many retail organizations are providing data only on this year and last year. However, decision makers often need more to identify trends and to assess seasonality effects on the business.

Only with ad-hoc query capability and adequate historical data can trends be identified, comparisons made, and management analyses in general be undertaken in a practical and cost-efficient manner. The technology required to provide such a decision support system is relational database technology and computers that are tuned to implement the input-output intensive operations of advanced relational software. Computers that are developed for relational database manipulation will become crucial as more and more decision makers begin to access relational databases simultaneously. As the user base grows in a relational database organization, current large mainframes will suffer significant response-time degradation. Several major retailers have recently been installing hardware known as intelligent-database-machines (IDMs) to combat this response-time problem.

The real significance of relational database technology for the retail firm is that it moves information retrieval to the end user: the buyer, the merchandising manager, and the store management staff. These key decision makers will be able to conduct analyses without contacting the MIS department with requests for coding of new reports. In the relational database environment, the movement will be away from standardized reports and toward ad hoc queries that will directly address the decisions that are being made. Most reports will be "exception reports" generated by the computer to notify retailing decision makers of situations in the business that need attention. The remaining reports will be those that track performance against goals; these will become more and more graphic in nature.

Most important will be the ability of decision makers to make ad hoc queries via terminals to determine individually what they need to know to run the business. How has the test in stores #219 and #312 been doing compared to the base in other stores? Have blue handbags from vendor #17 in the southeast region done better during sales promotions than blue handbags in the central region? Are out-of-stock conditions in the high-priced end of the line more prevalent than in the low-priced end of the line? These are questions that cannot be addressed from standardized reports. They require ad hoc queries. Yet these are the kinds of questions that it takes to make good decisions. The infusion of relational database technology coupled with the hardware necessary to run it effectively will be a key trend during the 1990s. Retail firms will have to grapple with the design of normalized relational data files that work off of databases that are updated on a daily basis from the transactional records of the firm. Someday, the entire operation, including the transactional processing, may go relational, but that will probably not take place in the next decade.

From Data Delivery to Decision Support. Today, retailers are struggling to report what has gone on in the business in the past and what is currently happening. The general state of the art is to deliver to decision makers facts about the past and the present. However, this is not really what managers most need to know. What they really need to know is:

- What will happen in the future (e.g., how will trends extrapolate and interact)?

- What would happen if things were changed (e.g., how many more units would be sold if the markdown were 20 percent instead of 15 percent)?
- What is the best policy to follow (e.g., how often should promotional markdowns be taken on a given item)?

These might be termed, respectively, questions about What will be? What If? and What's Best?

The key to dealing with these questions is to develop causal models that predict sales, that is, models, measurements, and analysis capabilities that can calibrate the effect on sales of different factors, such as price, advertising, display space, and seasonality.

The technologies that can be applied to the "What Will Be" and "What If" questions are the analytic technologies of exponential smoothing, adaptive control, and econometric analysis as well as the artificial intelligence technologies of neural networks and expert systems. The technologies that can be applied to the "What's Best" questions are mathematical programming (e.g., linear programming, dynamic programming, and integer programming) and basic calculus (e.g., maximizing profits under a specified causal model, perhaps with budget and space constraints).

Applying these technologies will require a number of organizational changes. First, firms will need more computer-literate support staff in their buying offices and stores to develop decision-support systems and causal models. Second, decision makers will need to be freed of the more mundane decision problems by the automation of much of what they deal with today. Third, more sophisticated decision makers who have advanced business training will be needed (e.g., MBAs who have an understanding of both systems and models, supported by econometricians and artificial intelligence specialists who can tune, debug, and consult on the use of statistical analysis and pattern recognition approaches to causal modeling). Undoubtedly more help from specialized consultants in the underlying technologies will also be in order. The bottom line for all of this activity will be higher profits from better tactical decisions throughout the merchandising cycle.

From Centralized or Decentralized Decisions to Optimally Located Decisions. At present, retailers think in terms of centralized or decentralized operations and decision making. In the future, information will be centralized and the decisions will be decentralized. Centralized data are best for storage and maintenance. Decentralized decisions are best for marketing, accountability, and motivational reasons. The new generation of systems and networks will allow both goals to be achieved.

In the past there has been much debate among retailers as to how best to handle the issue of centralization. Should most key decisions be made at corporate headquarters, or should they be made at a regional or store level?

In the future, information technology is going to require the centralization of data as part of the movement to systems integration and the use of corporate data dictionaries in conjunction with relational databases. There are strong advantages in centralizing information management because data can be stored with fewer redundancies and with better data integrity if they are put into a single relational structure. Also, data can be safeguarded and backed up on a more systematic basis if centralized. However, the centralization of data does not dictate the centralization of decision making.

Decision making can be decentralized even though data are maintained and organized centrally, because the data and information can be communicated and accessed more readily from remote decision-maker locations than in the past. This will be even more true in the future as fiber optics, WANs, and intelligent database machines (IDMs) allow for faster communication and more simultaneous database query at acceptable speeds. What will happen, then, in the age-old tension between centralization and decentralization? The answer is that the debate and tension will subside as it becomes clearer what decisions should be centralized and what decisions should be decentralized. Also, as information will be accessible from anywhere in the organization, companies will be more fluid and flexible with regard to altering the decision structure over time. This will make the degree of centralization of the decisions less of a long-run strategic choice and more of a fluid or dynamic choice to optimally locate decision making in an organization.

Centralized information offers some advantages to decentralized decision making because local decision makers at the store/market level will have the ability to access corporate-wide information and corporate-level systems. This, in turn, will allow them to determine, for instance, if trends in their store are unique or are being experienced in other stores in their region or even nationwide. They will be able to see if stocks at other stores are in line and whether they can be replenished by appropriate interstore transfers, and the like. The key is making decisions closer to the customer when appropriate and to centralize other decisions to gain efficiencies and greater automation of low-level decisions when that is optimal.

Additionally, local decision making instills local involvement in the decision and therefore local responsibility. This human-nature side of decision making and organizational psychology cannot be overlooked, even with systems capable of making centralized decisions. Local decisions drive local responsibility, which in turn drives local motivation and commitment. All of this ultimately influences local performance.

Therefore, the key is to get the knowledge of the organization closer to the local decision makers so that they can make the best decisions and at the same time achieve that local commitment and responsibility for the decisions. The motivation to centralize decisions really is to coordinate them, to automate them, or to make better quality decisions. The challenge is to allow all of the centralization benefits to be achieved without actually making the decisions centrally. Information systems allow this to take place.

Technology can do a lot of things, but in the final analysis, retailing is a people business and the motivation and commitment of employees is the key. Technology should never be allowed to get in the way of important human factors. Rather, information technology should be used to improve the human factors of the business by automating routine, low-level decisions and achieve a form of job enrichment because it allows employees more time and better support for those functions that only humans can do—functions such as assessing changes in the environment of the firm, providing motivation, instilling creativity into the organization, and treating others in a personal and humane way.

From General Data to Exact Data.   Retailers have been improving their information capture, storage, and retrieval capabilities during the last decade. Supermarkets and mass merchandisers have led the way because they have fewer SKUs than do other retailers. Not everyone understands that at the major department stores inventory and purchase data have not been kept at the lowest SKU level. A supermarket may carry fifteen to twenty thousand SKUs while a department store would require over a million SKUs to track every item down to the lowest SKU (i.e., by color-size-style). This movement toward lowest-level SKUs will accelerate and expand to all of retailing and will spread most dramatically to department and specialty stores. All retailers will join the crusade to achieve lowest-level SKUs, which really requires vendor UPC bar codes on all products, and Electronic Point of Sale (EPOS) terminals capable of capturing the precise and accurate sales information in those bar codes. The confluence of these technologies will allow, for instance, the mainline department stores to bring data integrity levels up from 75 percent to more than 95 percent.[2]

With lowest-level SKUs and acceptable data integrity levels, department and specialty stores will be able to maintain their own model stocks.[3] Maintaining and updating model stocks requires knowing exactly what is sold down to the lowest SKU level and knowing accurately what inventory levels exist by store. As acceptable data integrity is achieved and model stock maintenance is taken over by the retailer during the next decade, retail buyers will be in a position to place fully specified purchase orders (particularly in apparel) that indicate the full detail down to the individual UPC level on purchase orders. Retailers will also be able to order in full detail on a weekly basis to achieve true quick response. Quick response, in turn, will allow better in-stock performance with less inventory. All of these internal advancements are dependent on computer systems and data reporting capabilities of an accurate real-time nature.

Vendor and Retailer Interface (Z)

The third area that technology will impact, besides the customer-retailer interface and the internal operations of the firm, is the vendor-retailer interface. Three trends in this area are discussed.

From Electronic Data Interchange to Quick Response. The movement towards electronic data interchange (EDI) in the department and specialty store segments of the retail industry really began in 1988 with the formation of the Voluntary Inter-industry Communications Standard (VICS) committee. This committee of major retailers and key apparel vendors established the UPC-A bar code and the ANSI X.12 electronic document protocol systems as the standards for retailing.

The setting of these standards, in turn, caused a united movement on the part of retailers to encourage all vendors to mark goods with UPC codes, something that had not been the practice in the apparel area of retailing. In 1988 and 1989, the department and specialty store segments accelerated into the EDI world as more and more vendors and retailers became equipped to handle this approach.

The 1990s will see a rapid implementation of these trends as EDI diffuses to almost all vendor-retailer transactions. Firms are following different strategies for implementing EDI. Some are bringing up all of their vendors on the Electronic Purchase Order (EPO) and then moving to secondary documents such as the Electronic-Acknowledgement-of-Purchase-Order across all vendors. Retailers that follow this strategy generally have a large number of stores and a large number of vendors with centralized purchasing. Other retailers are focusing on a few vendors and are trying to implement all transaction documents, including such things as electronic packing slips, electronic change of order notification, electronic billing, and electronic funds transfer.

The ultimate goal is quicker response (QR) by eliminating the various mailing cycles, lower costs by automating many clerical functions, and the integration of systems. In fact, QR offers the possibility of interorganizational systems integration. For instance, in some cases the receipt of a purchase order at the vendor automatically generates an inventory status check and the return notification of intention-to-ship dates and shipping plans, as well as the automatic generation of warehouse pick lists. Thus, time and paperwork are cut out of the system, clerical errors are eliminated, and buyers are kept abreast of exactly where orders stand in the delivery cycle. All of this allows for quicker response to orders; what were once monthly orders will now be weekly ones. What were once twenty-week lead times will be two-week lead times.

This movement will result in lower inventories in the pipeline while at the same time improving customer service levels. Also, because buyers will be operating closer to the time of final customer purchase, they will be more aware of trends and will stock less undesirable merchandise. This QR movement will collapse the time needed to complete the merchandise cycle, and will improve inventory turns as better customer service levels are achieved with less inventory and fewer clearance markdowns are needed to move end-of-season inventory. The result will be improved profitability to those who lead in this movement (Haber 1988).

So important is the reduction of pipelining in the merchandise cycle that some economists have suggested the past performance of the economy, with fewer and less severe recessions, may have resulted in part because inventory stockpiling does not accelerate the boom-and-bust ordering that used to result from a small change in final retail sales. Now the changes in retail sales cause only about the same magnitude of changes in wholesale ordering. Of course, the same pipelining reduction is taking place across all industries and across all levels in the supply chain from raw materials all the way to retail sales (Magrath 1990).

One key EDI development is the services of third-party networks, with central mainframes that receive communications from all retailers and vendors alike. These are basically middlemen in the communication channels who provide the key service of vastly reducing the number of individual communication links necessary to carry out EDI. In the retail area, AT&T, GE, IBM, and McDonnell Douglas are key players. Third-party network services are expanding continuously, even as prices drop because economies of scale are achieved. Transaction-set verification, electronic catalog maintenance, electronic funds transfer, electronic security, ever-increasing transmission speeds, and a host of other communication services are technological advances taking place in the third-party network area.

As these communication channels improve and become cheaper, the amount of information that will flow over them is tremendous. For example, Levi Strauss manufactures over one hundred thousand SKUs, and Mervyn's Department Stores stock approximately ten thousand of these SKUs, placing weekly orders. Mervyn's will be providing daily sales data on those ten thousand SKUs so Levi can assess trends as early as possible. Consider that there are up to seven documents resulting from each purchase order (e.g., acknowledgement of receipt of order, intention-to-ship, packing slip, acknowledgement of receipt of goods, invoice, payment, etc.). And finally, consider that Mervyn's has fifteen hundred vendors and over six hundred thousand SKUs to contend with in total.

The future will see massive information flows taking place over the third party networks that will be the invisible backbone of the retail operation. It will be these information-based efficiencies and cost reductions in the supply chain that will be necessary to keep the retail store competitive with the home-based shopping capabilities that information technology will also made available.

> *From Slow to Rapid Product Development Cycles.* Not only will EDI be speeding the merchandise ordering cycle, but information technology will vastly improve the product development cycle, which now takes many months. The major trend in this decade will be towards competing in time (Keen 1986). Buyers will be able to communicate around the world with factories that are equipped with computer-driven laser cloth cutting machines that can turn out prototypes in hours and move into production in days. Buyers will be able view and assess new designs in full motion video, often without the need to see samples of the actual goods.

Orders will be placed and goods will be manufactured with advanced technology all over the world, wherever costs are least and capabilities are greatest. More and more goods will be shipped by air, much as The Limited, even today, flies Boeing 747s from the Orient directly to Columbus, Ohio, on a regular basis.

Also, computer manufacturing technology will continue to offer more and more goods in smaller and smaller lots. The absolute necessity to make large orders to get low prices will ease. There will be even more proliferation of product offerings. Thus, the volume of SKUs being tracked by the buyer will increase not only by the movement to lowest SKU level marking, but also because there will be a growing number of SKUs to deal with, even at that lowest level. Retailers that can keep up with these trends without being choked by them will be the ones that prosper.

> *From Vendor Push to Retailer Pull.* A final vendor-retailer interface trend will be a movement away from what might be called vendor push to what might be called retailer pull. In the past, as has been noted before in this discussion, retailers have not had the information systems, the bar-coded goods, and the scanning capability necessary to fully specify purchase orders, at least not in the apparel merchandise areas.

Buyers have had to rely on the vendor to fill in the details of the order. In the past, the buyer might order ten thousand shirts, but the vendor would have a large degree of discretion as to the color and size breakdown. This was the case because the vendor had more information about the movement of the goods and better information about the SKU level designations. Often buyers could not distinguish among the colors of their inventory, and they certainly could not write fast enough to make weekly orders on thousands of line items.

Now, however, and even more so in the future, retailers are taking charge of the situation. They are maintaining their own model stocks by store and increasingly have lowest-level SKU information as well as reasonably high data integrity levels with which to assess store stock levels.

This, coupled with the EDI and electronic ordering systems, is allowing buyers to efficiently place fully specified orders to the vendor. Thus the retailers, at least in the mainline department store segment, are finally taking charge of their destiny and are ordering exactly what they want to carry rather than having to rely on vendors, who were always suspected, at least, of pushing only what they wanted to supply (because of overstock, slow sales, or cancellations by other retailers).

CONCLUSIONS

It is clear that retailers face substantial opportunities and challenges resulting from the dramatic technological advances that are taking place in the information systems area. As this paper has stressed, there are strong consumer, competitive, and resource trends that can best be capitalized on by the use of this new, emerging information technology.

Technology will not be embraced for its own sake, but rather to support key applications. Retailers can organize their thinking about the use of technology by keying in on three interfaces: the retailer-customer interface, the within-firm departmental interfaces, and the retailer-vendor interface. The use of advanced networks within the retail firm will allow it to develop seamless information systems, even out to vendors and customers. This will make possible less middle-management and generally more efficient operations that are at the same time more effective than today.

In particular, to prosper in the next decade, the retail firm must quickly move to full relational database management. Relational database systems will be needed to manage the business but also will come into play in tracking customer behavior data at the transaction level. Retailers must have the ability to deal with customers on an individual basis—moving to what we have called relationship marketing, at least in the department and specialty sectors of the industry. Mass retailers, on the other hand, will be able to match response to products offered and marketing strategies to smaller and more targeted segments. Even the largest firms will adopt localized marketing programs, giving them tremendous use of scale and long-run competitive advantages over smaller firms in the marketplace.

Quick Response and Electronic Data Interchange will be the norm. They will cover virtually all of the transactions and will provide one of the key enabling factors for seamless systems integration between the retail firm and its suppliers.

Massive data storage capacity coupled with data compression techniques and advanced data servers will support real-time access to huge databases. Expert systems and statistical systems (including neural networks) will be used to segment databases, to predict response to marketing efforts, and to send this information upstream to suppliers. Distributed processing will take the pressure off today's overloaded mainframes.

As we move closer to the next millennium, interactive home-based systems that integrate the PC, telephone, and HDTV will provide more alternatives to fixed-location retailing. Consumers will never abandon shopping at stores, but the percentage of the purchases via home-based shopping will increase several-fold. Clearly, retailers that do not plan for and respond to these technological developments will be the dinosaurs of the decade and possibly extinct by the year 2000.

NOTES

1. See, for example, Hyde et al. (1990) and Cox (1989) for a more extensive discussion of many of the trends in this section.

2. "Data Integrity" in this context is interpreted as follows: A data integrity level of 75 percent would mean that if store #129 is supposed to have six of a specific SKU in stock, it would actually have that number in stock with a probability of .75.

3. Model stocks are the color-style-size distribution that should be in stock at each store. These vary by store and over the seasons of the year.

APPENDIX

This appendix contains a listing of different technologies that will have an impact on retailing. Some of the technologies are specific to retailing, but many of them are general and will affect most forms of business including retailing. These more generic technologies are just as important for retailers to track as are the ones specific only to retailing.

The intention of this appendix is to identify various technologies and briefly discuss how they work and the likely future developments that may take place with respect to them. Retailers might think of technologies as a jigsaw puzzle from which they can build a more effective and profitable business. The key is to have a strategy for investigating and integrating the various technologies over time. This is a challenging endeavor, to say the least. However, organizations that succeed will be the ones that will survive into the future, and those that fall behind in the use of technology will likely suffer substantially.

Many of the technologies will likely be familiar. However, it is our belief that most readers will find some entries to be new or to contain information that clarifies what certain technologies are and how they might be used.

4GLs

4GLs refers to Fourth Generation Languages, computer languages operating at a high level and therefore easier to write programs in than previous languages. The first generation of computer languages used binary coding (just 0s and 1s) and was extremely tedious and difficult to use. The second generation of computer languages used machine language, which required the programmer to identify the precise registers in the computer's memory that were to be manipulated. The third generation of computer languages was based on computer code that was designed to be compatible with the human programmer and then translated by the computer into the lower languages. This was done automatically in a "compile" stage by the machine before it would execute the code. Typical of the third generation languages are Fortran (short for "FORmula TRANslator") and COBOL, which is a very English-oriented language extensively used in business programming. Fourth generation languages are still one level higher because they do not require that the programmer know how the data are stored.

Adaptive Control

Adaptive control refers to the use of experimentation over time and across control units (i.e., stores) in order to determine what policies work best. The key idea behind adaptive control is that if an organization executes what it believes to be the optimal policy (say for assortment) in all stores, then it does not allow for experimentation with alternative assortments that are believed to be superior, but which are not known for sure to be superior. Experimentation opens the door for the possibility of discovering better policies. Adaptive control also addresses the issue of what might be the optimal amount of such experimentation given the costs and uncertainties involved.

ANSI X.12

The American Standards Institute (ANSI) has established the X.12 (pronounced X_dot_twelve) transaction set protocol for the specification of documents. The retail industry adopted the ANSI X.12 transaction standards in 1988 and is adopting the different parts of the total X.12 protocol on a document-by-document basis. For instance the electronic purchase order (EPO) transaction set from X.12 has been adopted, as have been the transaction sets for electronic acknowledgement of receipt of order, electronic funds transfer, electronic advanced shipping notice, and electronic packing slip, among others.

Artificial Intelligence

Artificial intelligence (AI) refers to a set of computer approaches to symbolic reasoning that mimics some aspects of the way humans are believed to think. Expert systems is one area of artificial intelligence that relies on a rule-based or "if-then" strategy for problem solving. Neural networks is another area that deals with pattern recognition. Robotics is yet another area commonly treated as falling into the artificial intelligence area.

Automated Shelf Tags

Automated shelf tags refer to shelf tags that are under remote control and usually under computer control. This allows for automated repricing from a central location without the need for clerks to physically change shelf tags throughout the store. Shelf-tag automation would be linked to price look-up tables and point-of-sales (POS) terminals.

Case

Computer-aided software engineering (CASE) refers to tools that are becoming increasingly important for the rapid development and maintenance of computer software. These computer tools are similar in concept to the computer-aided design (CAD) movement in manufacturing. For instance, one CASE tool allows a programmer to lay out a screen display with a mouse and then to have that screen display automatically translated into, say, a computer program.

Causal Modeling

Causal modeling refers to the prediction of sales based on the consideration of various data thought to "cause" sales (such as price, advertising, the weather, etc.). Causal modeling is the key alternative to naive forecasting that relies only on the past history of sales to predict the future. Causal modeling relies on statistical techniques to determine the causal relationship between sales and the factors that are believed to be affecting sales.

CD-Rom

Compact disk-read only memory (CD-ROM) refers to the optical disks that are written and then read by laser beams. These have recently become very prevalent in the storage of digital music. However, the use of this technology for computer data storage has also grown very rapidly.

Cellular Radio

The radio frequency spectrum is fixed and can carry only a finite set of message channels at a given time. This had restricted the use of radio communications substantially and had limited its potential for growth. In the late 1970s, the cellular radio approach was developed wherein the radio signals are used in very local cells so that the same radio frequency can carry different signals in different cells. As the size of the cells gets smaller and smaller, the number of signals that can be carried simultaneously skyrockets. This has allowed the development of car telephones and other forms of portable telephones that utilize the once crowded radio channels.

Decision Support System

Decision support system (DSS) refers to any computer-based system that is designed to assist a human being in making a specific decision, as opposed to just delivering reports or information of a general nature. The term is generally used to identify systems that go beyond just the delivery of information and focus more on systems that evaluate alternatives and make recommendations.

DPP

Direct product profitability (DPP) systems attempt to determine the true profit contribution of a unit of merchandise sold as opposed to relying solely on the unit contribution (sales price less purchase cost) involved.

Econometrics

Econometrics is the use of statistical procedures (particularly multiple regression) to estimate the causal relationship between sales and a set of causal variables that are believed to affect sales. The use of econometrics requires consistent and complete data over several seasons of history.

Electronic Catalog

The electronic catalog concept refers to a national network that would contain information about products. The information could contain basic text information such as UPC code numbers and product specifications, and contain images. All of this information would be retrievable over telephone lines. The electronic catalog could be accessed by both retail buyers and consumers.

Electronic Data Interchange

Electronic data interchange (EDI) is the electronic transmission of basic business documents from computer to computer. The documents must be encoded into a certain form (called "transaction sets") and are typically transmitted via third-party networks. EDI is particularly important for the transmission of large volumes of electronic purchase orders (EPO), which can contain individual quantity specifications from one retailer to one vendor of ten thousand line items per week (e.g., the size-color-style level SKUs of apparel).

Electronic Image Management

Electronic image management (EIM) refers to the organization, storage, and retrieval of electronic images. Some suggest that EIM is going to be one of the strategic economic events of the 1990s, as this technology brings the paperless office closer and closer to reality. In an EIM system, incoming paper documents are scanned by a device similar to a copier, which digitizes an image of the document and sends it to a computer, which burns the data onto an optical laser disk. Pages are referenced according to key words or numbers entered into the computer through keypunching or optical character recognition.

EIM promises to win a lot more users as it sheds 10 to 25 percent of its price during each of the next ten years or so. EIM will replace microfiche and other storage techniques because it makes information accessible in seconds. It will soon be effective for credit card billing and vendor payables.

Electronic Retailing

Electronic retailing refers to the execution of sales to final consumers by electronic means (i.e., by computer). Electronic retailing can be store-based, home-based, or public-access-based.

Store-based electronic retailing is epitomized by Florsheim, which has installed an electronic kiosk in many of its stores through which customers can locate and order a pair of shoes that are later delivered to the individual's home by UPS within two or three days. Home-based electronic retailing is becoming more and more viable since computers penetrate up to 25 percent of American homes today. IBM and Sears recognize this potential and are trying to tap into it with their joint venture called the Prodigy service, which allows consumers to purchase goods and provides other services via dial-up computer. Compuserve is another offering in this category that has been around for some years and continues to expand slowly. Home-based electronic retailing is clearly an area that will offer growing potential as communications devices and computers continue to improve and as they penetrate into more homes.

EPOS

Electronic point of sale (EPOS) terminals are the modern replacement for the cash register. Not only do these terminals carry out the sales transaction, they do much more, depending on the way they are linked into the firm's information systems. Price look-up of bar codes that are laser scanned is a frequent application today. Inventory updating can take place directly from the EPOS system. Some retailers use the EPOS terminals even to handle time and attendance tracking for the sales associates. With the point of sale device becoming a full-fledged computer terminal, the possibilities for its expanded use are limitless.

Exponential Smoothing

Exponential smoothing is a mathematical procedure that allows a partial adjustment each period to new information that is received. The effect of this adjustment mechanism is to weight information from the past in an exponentially decaying fashion so that information further and further back in time is given less and less influence in current predictions. This technology underlies many inventory adjustment systems.

FAX

Fax stands for facsimile and refers to the electronic transmission of images. Although many people think of fax as a machine, it is actually a communication protocol that specifies how the pixels of an image are to be decomposed into bytes in an electronic transmission. Also included is the reciprocal transformation that reconfigures the image at the other end.

Fiber Optics

Fiber optics involves hair-thin fibers of super-clear glass used to direct a laser beam from one location to another. A transmitter containing a tiny laser converts electrical signals that represent human voices, computer data, text, or pictures into modulated light waves—flashes of ones and zeros—for digital transmission. Lasers in fiber optics can transmit at the rate of 1.8 billion bits per second. This is enough capacity to transmit sixteen thousand telephone conversations at once (compared to twenty-four on a twisted pair of telephone wires) or to transmit the entire text of the Encyclopedia Britannica and the Bible around the Earth in less than two seconds.

Most authorities believe that the majority of the current telephone system will be replaced by fiber optics by the year 2015. The underlying determinants for expansion are economic and regulatory. Much will depend on whether there will be enough demand for fiber services to justify speeding up construction of a nationwide fiber-based broadband network, conservatively estimated to cost $250 billion. Meanwhile, telephone companies and cable television firms are battling over the vast potential market. Because so much can be carried on fiber optic lines, telephone companies could use their lines for cable TV. But telephone companies are currently barred from the cable business, and cable companies are working hard to make sure that doesn't change.

Hierarchical Database

Hierarchical database refers to the way data are structured in the records of a computer file. When the database includes pointers from one record to another as a part of the data, it is said to be in a hierarchical structure. The hierarchical data structure is rapidly being supplanted by relational data structures that reduce data to simple tables and exclude any pointers as part of the data (see relational database).

Hypermedia

Hypermedia is a combination of multimedia and hypertext. Multimedia refers to the integrated use of different media such as graphics, images, sound, text, and full motion video. Hypertext refers to information that is organized for interactive browsing (i.e., jumping around in the text). Hypermedia, then, is the use of the hypertext browsing capability, but with a multimedia presentation.

Hypertext

Hypertext allows for specially highlighted words in computer-based text to lead to other passages of text and back, according to the paths designed by the author. This provides the reader of the text with many options for proceeding through it besides the traditional processing, which is sequential from the beginning to the end. For instance, a reader reading about birds might come across mention of the Audubon Society. If the Audubon Society is a hypertext word, the reader could "click" on that word and proceed directly to information about the Audubon Society. Hypertext is also being extended to hypermedia so that the text, graphics, images, motion-video, and sound are all integrated into the hypertext capability. In this case, for instance, the reader (or viewer) could click on the image of a map to see a video tour of the house at that location on the map and then click on an icon and see the county assessor's records on that piece of real estate.

Intelligent Database Machines

Intelligent database machines (IDMs) are specialized computer data storage devices that are tuned to optimize relational database searching. Relational database querying is a very input/output intensive activity. As leading retailers began to implement relational database technology on their mainframes, they often experienced very sluggish response times from the computer when many users simultaneously searched the system. Because the intelligent database machine downloads much of the relational database activity from the mainframe, response time is vastly improved even with scores of users searching simultaneously.

Knowledge-Based Systems

Knowledge-based (KB) systems are a new form of computer programming whose objective is to operate as a consultant to a decision maker. The rules of experts are coded into what is called a knowledge base, and these rules are then used via an interactive dialogue with the user to make recommendations and to offer advice. Expert systems can be based on hundreds of rules and can access databases and interact with other computer programs to bring large amounts of information into the process of advising the decision maker. Expert systems are also important because their simple, English-like rules are easy for programmers and users to understand. In fact, one intent is to have users and/or experts update the rule base rather than programmers.

Local Area Networks

Local area networks (LANs) are the links that tie together microcomputers so that they can utilize common resources and communicate back and forth. This is an important alternative to having everyone in the organization logged into a central mainframe that must then service hundreds of users simultaneously. The LAN allows distributed processing on local microcomputers but also the communication and sharing of computer resources (disk storage, printers, databases). Retailers typically run LANs in conjunction with a mainframe and a centralized database; however, a LAN can be run independently of a mainframe, in which case one of the microcomputers typically acts as a server. One key advantage of a LAN is the centralization of standard software so that it does not need to reside on each of the microcomputers on the system. This eases the maintenance and updating of standard software packages and provides for good backup policies that individual users are often lax about.

Mathematical Programming

Mathematical programming refers to the branch of management science that deals with certain types of optimization. In general, an objective function is defined (i.e., profit is some function of sales and costs). This objective function is to be maximized. Often there are constraints involved, such as that advertising can not be above some level or that selling space is fixed at a certain value.

When the objective function is linear and the constraints are also linear, then linear programming is appropriate. If the objective function is not linear, then nonlinear programming is necessary. If the solution requires a series of decisions over time, then dynamic programming is in order. If the solution must be only certain values, then integer programming may be needed.

Microwave

Microwave refers to a specified bandwidth of the electromagnetic spectrum. Microwave is the carrier for many communications including cellular telephone and satellite transmission. Microwave is constrained to be line-of-sight, which requires frequent relay stations to get over obstacles such as mountains.

Modem

A modem is necessary to translate digital data into a format that can be transmitted over analog telephone lines. The modem modulates the digital information onto a carrier tone (by either amplitude or frequency modulation) and transmits the resulting signal over the analog line. As the modem also demodulates incoming signals by the reverse process, "modem" is really short for demodulator.

Model Stocks

The model stock is a distribution used for predicting what assortment should be carried by a specific store at a specific time and is based on the past sales performance of that store. Each store of a chain has a slightly different demand for the colors, styles, and sizes of the products that are being carried by the chain. These distributions change over time and exhibit seasonal variation. For instance, the size distribution of Levi's 501 jeans will be different in a Macy's store in San Francisco than one in Los Angeles. Also, the size distribution will be longer and narrower during August than in November (because of back-to-school buying in August). Exponential smoothing is often used as the underlying technology for adjusting model stocks.

Multimedia

Multimedia refers to the use of multiple media such as sound, images, motion video, and text to present information. The term was used to describe presentations that utilized many media. However, recently the term has been applied to computer-based information systems that utilize the hypertext approach (see hypertext), which provides a link between items of information that the author of the presentation feels are somehow related. When this link is applied to the mixing of sound, images, motion video, and text, multimedia interactive computer environments result. Another term that is sometimes used for interactive multimedia is hypermedia.

Multi-Echelon Inventory Control Theory

Inventory control theory, in general, addresses the problem of minimizing costs in light of the ordering and holding costs involved with buying merchandise against the forecasted demand for the merchandise. Multi-echelon inventory systems refer to situations where there are several levels of inventory stocking, such as at a warehouse and at several stores. In those cases, the theory determines how much stock should be distributed to the stores versus how much of it should be kept in reserve at the warehouse to minimize the total cost of the system given the uncertainty about how demand will turn out.

Naive Forecasting

Naive forecasting refers to forecasts that are based only on the past observations of the time series being forecast with no reference to other variables or sources of information. Exponential smoothing (see entry) is one common mechanism used to execute naive forecasting. The Box-Jenkins and auto-regressive-moving-average procedures are other, more sophisticated naive forecasting procedures.

Neural Networks

Neural networks is the name of a computer software approach to pattern recognition that is learned over repeated trials or training. The basic strategy of neural networks is to relate the input pattern to a "middle plane" and then to relate the "middle plane" to the output. The hope is that neural networks will improve upon causal modeling so that retailers can better predict sales based on factors such as price, store events, advertising, and so forth.

Optical Disk

Optical disk refers to the writing and reading of information from a disk by means of an optical laser beam. Currently the technology allows for a single write but an almost infinite amount of reading from the disk once it has been loaded with information. The amount of information that can be stored on an optical disk is truly staggering. As mentioned previously, the entire Encyclopedia Britannica and the entire Bible easily fit on one optical disk.

Optimal Control

Optimal control is a branch of mathematics that deals with multiperiod problems. For instance, to maximize the contribution margin over the weeks of the season by varying the retail price would technically be an optimal control problem.

Parallel-processing Computers

Computers have always been constrained to processing one instruction at a time through the logical processor of the computer. Thus, computers execute one instruction at a time, albeit at blinding speeds. Recently, computer technology has been approaching the limits in speed with which instructions can be executed. However, parallel processing is about to smash all of the speed barriers as machines are built that will process more than one instruction at a time (i.e., in parallel). In fact, some computer CPU chips, such as Intel's i486 chip, actually process two instructions per clock cycle even within the same chip. Various organizations are working on massively parallel machines that will lash together sixty-four or more CPU chips, all working simultaneously. This will bring computer speeds that are thousands of times faster than what exists today. The major obstacles to parallel processing are software difficulties in breaking the problem or program down into parts that can effectively be handled in parallel.

Pattern Recognition

Pattern recognition is a topic within artificial intelligence. It is an area that is being addressed by neural networks and parallel-processing computer hardware.

Quick(er) Response

Quick(er) response (QR) is the term that has been applied to signify the minimization of order times for retailers. The term is the retailing equivalent of the manufacturer's "just-in-time" inventory concept. The basic idea is to minimize the amount of goods in the order pipeline and to reduce the time from order to delivery. The purpose is to manufacture goods as close to the time of sale when consumer demand is best known, to avoid manufacturing goods that consumers do not want to buy. This should improve customer service by having the right goods on hand and at the same time improve retail margins by reducing the need for clearance markdowns of goods that consumers do not really want.

Relational Database

Data are often organized in computer files in a hierarchical way so that pointers to other data are imbedded in the records of the files. Such files can be searched efficiently only by using the file pointers originally provided in the data. In addition, application programs written to address the files rely on the pointers provided. When the data are changed in any structural way, all of the application programs must be modified to reflect the change. Relational databases, in contrast, are designed to be independent of the programs that will address them. The data are arranged into many simple tables that represent only the most fundamental data relationships rather than any programming issues. The relational database languages then handle all of the file pointers and cross-indexing, leaving this set of considerations out of the application programs. The key benefits of relational databases are easier maintenance and more flexible searching of the data. The tradeoff is in the speed of access and the amount of computer resources that are needed.

Satellite Communication

Earth-orbiting satellites are placed into stationary (sometimes called synchronous) orbits so that radio signals (usually microwave signals) can be bounced off them. Each satellite has a number of transponders to deal simultaneously with many different transmissions. Satellites are also important for broadcasting in the TV frequencies of the electromagnetic spectrum.

Scanning

Scanning refers to the use of a laser beam and electronic sensors to interpret the information on universal product codes (UPCs), a particular type of bar code. In supermarkets, scanners are embedded in countertops where UPC-labeled grocery products can be exposed and their codes read. In department stores and elsewhere in retailing, hand-held laser guns or wands are commonly used.

Smart Cards

Smart cards refer to plastic credit cards that contain massive amounts of storage capacity. Some even contain computer chips. One early use of these cards was to store the medical history of army personnel.

Systems Integration

Systems integration refers to the ability of different computer-based systems (say, payroll and accounts payable) to work together without the need for human intervention or direction. Organizations with a high degree of systems integration operate with fewer employees and can process information more rapidly. Some systems integration takes place across organizational boundaries, as when vendor warehouse pick-lists are tied directly to electronic purchase orders coming in via electronic data interchange systems.

T1-Lines

T1-tie lines are special high-capacity telephone cables with a communication protocol that takes advantage of the extended capacity. These large digital pipelines are essentially the equivalent of twenty-four voice lines, but they can transmit at an effective rate of 1.544 million bits per second. Specially designed multiplexers are used to send data over T1s. Large corporate networks are typically based on dedicated T1 lines leased from common carriers.

Third-Party Networks

To accomplish electronic data interchange, electronic documents must be sent from the sender to the receiver. If this is done directly, the retailer would have to send messages to each supplier, which would often entail establishing computer links with thousands of organizations. To alleviate this, a wide area network (WAN) is used to access a centralized mainframe to which all orders are sent and from which all orders are received (by retailers and vendors alike). This central computer and its access system is called the "third-party network" because it is provided by companies such as IBM, AT&T, GE, and McDonnell Douglas that are not actual parties to the transactions occurring over their systems.

Trend Merchandising

Trend merchandising refers to the continual adjustment of merchandise assortments in light of shifting demand. The retailer must react to change but must also protect against overreaction and must minimize costs, given the merchandise already under commitment. Many retailers do fairly extensive testing of merchandise in different stores, and the potential exists to raise this practice to the level of a science with sophisticated experimental designs and systems to track and optimize the information gained from such experimentation.

Universal Product Code

Universal product codes (UPCs) are bar codes that contain ten digits; the first five identify the vendor and the second five identify the item. Currently retail goods for sale are encoded with the UPC-A code standard. The codes are issued by the Uniform Code Counsel. These UPCs are read with optical scanners at the point of purchase. Such scanners are counter-based (as in supermarkets) or are imbedded in hand-held wands or guns (as in department stores).

Videotex

Videotex refers to the delivery of text on a computer screen over telephone or other communications lines. Videotex is almost synonymous with information retrieval and is becoming a commercial industry through services such as Compuserve, Dialogue, and Prodigy.

WAN

Wide-area networks (WANs) are networks that operate over telephone lines and typically over long distances. These are frequently interorganizational networks (such as the EDI third-party network mentioned above). However, WANs can be established within organizations that have far-flung locations. For instance, Mrs. Fields Cookies communicates daily with each of 500 wholly-owned stores to collect accounting and operations data over a WAN. WANs can use conventional telephone lines, but often they are implemented over higher capacity lines such as T1 lines that can handle more capacity. Multiplexers can be used to combine voice, data, and image over the same line. WANs will obviously benefit from fiber optic lines that allow for 1.8 billion bits per second.

REMARKS

David V. Evans

Discussing the future of information technology in retailing is daunting because the technology is changing so fast that the word "revolution" is highly appropriate. At no time in my twenty-five years of experience has technological change been more rapid than it is today. Consequently, when we start talking about technology in the 1990s, we are still in fact talking about it in 1990. If you have been following the news reports, you know that some of us retailers have quite a bit of work to do right now without even trying to conceptualize what technology will be like at the end of the century. In brief, our horizons for the moment have perhaps shortened a bit.

One of the things that focused my thinking about this topic is a passage I recently read that stated our job as managers is not to see the future, but to enable it. That being the case, rather than worrying about specific technologies that I might see on the horizon, I would like to briefly describe some of the basic technological changes that are currently occurring and are going to be enabling. (I am still having a little trouble wondering just what it is that we are going to enable. But the most important things for us to enable are the things that we could not do before.)

So, with some credit to Lewis Carroll and the Red Queen for that bit of logic, I would like to comment on several technologies—both "soft" and "hard"—that will allow retailers to do things in the future they could not do before.

DATA CAPTURING

I would first like to discuss how new technologies can help us "capture" or collect data. Data collection in retailing is pretty old hat, although there is a very important technological advance for general merchandise retailers, the availability of low-cost printers to print bar code tickets in small batches. When we print bar code tickets, we do not need to print a million copies of Campbell's tomato soup as would a supermarket.

We really have to do smaller batches of tickets.   Moreover, in general merchandise retailing we have about fifty to one hundred times as many SKUs as supermarkets, so the task is really quite difficult. Even though the underlying technology might get lost, it is very, very important.

Checkout scanning is another way technology has improved data collection in retailing. In particular, laser scanning is the superior way to carry out the checkout function. In either a fixed checkout environment or with a hand held scanner, it is superior—better, faster, cheaper—to all previous means, and all transaction- and product-related data are captured very accurately as a by-product.

A very fundamental and important technology is electronic data interchange (EDI). EDI is going to be the universal way for customers and suppliers to interact with each other. Indeed, EDI is imperative for a global electronic market. The key to successful EDI is ANSI standards.

Technologies accepting handwriting will play an increasingly important role in retailing. Handwriting is the oldest form of data collection and has the advantage that everyone over the age of 6 is able to do it. It is a technology that has come along nicely and will be *the* important technology in the 1990s.

Generically speaking, portability is a technology that will allow us to do our work where and when we want to. This is a basic change in that we traditionally work at a fixed location during specific time periods. Portability will allow us to organize a lot of technology implementations more efficiently and effectively. Good examples of the impact of portability can be found in the way Frito-Lay and Federal Express capture data, although there are many other good applications and there will be even more when we can have a PC in a four-pound box and radio-frequency, cordless terminals.

DATA PROCESSING

Another important technology consists of parallel microprocessor-based systems. The microprocessor is going to bring the economies of the PC and merchant microprocessors to new types of mainframes. Parallel means these inexpensive microprocessors will allow us to solve huge problems very quickly and inexpensively. The first real implementation of this technology was Teradata. Although Teradata's database computers are for specialized applications, in the future we will see many more generalized applications of the same principles.

Relatedly, the Unix operating system is going to become a universal, multiuser, multiprocessor operating system. Huge amounts of R&D are being invested in Unix and these investments should lead to great breakthroughs. In the future we will be able to construct absolutely huge networks of parallel microprocessor-based systems with the basic Unix operating system.

A fundamental breakthrough in disk storage is the array disk, frequently called RAID. What has happened is that the least reliable part of a data processing system has just become the most reliable part, while its speed has increased fourfold even though it is constructed of inexpensive parts.

DATA ANALYSIS

Several technologies have independently improved the ability of a retailer to inexpensively and quickly analyze data at a micro level. Relational data bases have been around for only fifteen years, but they are the fundamentally correct way to store data for future reference and analysis. I think a lot of us, including myself, got off on the wrong foot with punched cards. We started organizing data by what we could fix on a card and its handling constraints and have been wrong ever since (which is why most of the data processing systems in the industry are nonsensical today). Parallel relational databases allow us to take the large relational databases and separate them into chunks that we can then query in parallel (using those processors we talked about) and do large analyses very quickly and cheaply. Teradata does it now, Tandem does it now, and several merchant database houses are working on it. When parallel, relational database technologies will fundamentally change our capabilities to process data.

Intelligent workstations hide a very complex set of systems behind a very easy to use graphical interface. They allow managers to move a lot of the presentation workload from a mainframe computer and have many other capabilities.

Statistical modelling will assume more importance because of the availability of cheap microprocessors. It will be possible to do large statistical analyses faster and more often. J. C. Penney has about 1.7 billion stock-keeping units that it has to track in its seventeen hundred stores. With current technology it is impossible to do a forecast of every SKU every week. But Penney will be able to do it with the "new" statistical analysis packages and hardware. Statistical analysis is going to be more important in the next ten years than it was in the last ten or the ten before that.

Similarly, expert systems will become commonplace. Their major benefit is that complex reasoning can be applied consistently time after time by fairly unskilled workers. Moreover, an expert system can be a sort of staff for a supervisor or trainer. Even though retailers will have a less-skilled workforce, they will be able to bring in an expert system to help them.

Neural networks are an exciting new technology in that they find relationships that exist in data without being encumbered by statistics and hypothesis tests. Some versions can even be operated by clerks.

COMMUNICATIONS

We need to move all the data we have collected and analyzed around without having to worry. This will be done using enablers such as high-frequency communications and wide-area networks as well as local-area networks. Because of such enablers, we no longer have to make the design compromises for time and cost that we had to make before.

A related topic is that of standard communications protocols such as the Open System Interconnect (OSI) standard. The importance of OSI becomes evident when something as simple as the group 3 fax standard is considered. The standard was approved about seven or eight years ago and has allowed the fax to become a universal way of communicating. Before we had standards, the fax was very frustrating to deal with because every company had different protocols. OSI has the potential for setting the standards for desktop to desktop communications throughout the world. And it is absolutely going to happen. A second protocol, Fiber Distributed Data Interface (FDDI), is a protocol for moving data around at about one hundred megabites per second. It is an open standard and should encourage real innovation on the part of entrepreneurs who can now design devices to operate at either end of the communication link.

ISDN stands for Integrated Systems Digital Network, although some people say it means, "I still don't know." ISDN is going to be important for a variety of reasons. A major one is that it is a network solution that can deliver fairly high-speed data to the home over existing copper wire; all that is required is for the consumer to buy a fairly inexpensive appliance to receive the data. There are many ways to get data to the home by various broadcast means, but they are very limited. With a network solution we have the flexibility of a telephone or the fax machine. So, while there are a lot of uncertainties with ISDN, no competing solution offers a network solution, delivery over existing copper wire, and the ability of a relatively inexpensive consumer appliance to receive the data.

This is a quick tour of a few of the important technologies that I think are going to influence not only retailing but all businesses. As such, my purpose has been to corroborate the comments of Drs. Achabal and McIntyre and reinforce issues regarding how these technologies can be used more effectively and efficiently.

The real challenge facing retailers is how can they harness the benefits of these technologies rapidly enough to beat their competitors. This is a much bigger challenge than the technologies themselves.

4

Mass Merchandising/ Traditional Retailing

Stanley C. Hollander and William W. Keep

The working title of this chapter was "mass market retailing/the department store," and it still deals primarily with those retail formats. Although these terms seem clear and familiar, there may be some incongruity between mass retailing and department stores. Actually, further discussion of terminology is necessary.

First, we are concentrating on *retailing* as defined by the Bureau of the Census, that is, businesses primarily engaged in the final sale of tangible goods to individual, ultimate consumers and households. In recent years, marketing professors have increasingly realized that some or most sectors of the service industries, those establishments engaged in selling intangibles, have many locational, operational, and promotional opportunities and problems analogous to those of merchandise retailers. In fact, many writers now speak of services retailing (Berry 1986; Berman and Evans 1989). In another sense, even merchandise retailing is itself a service industry as distinguished from processing and extractive domains. Of course, customer service is also an important component of merchandise retailing. Recognition of all of these relationships is important, but there are also strong advantages to consistency in the use of terms. Since the most commonly used macro statistics published by the U.S. government distinguish between tangible retail trades and intangible service businesses, we will do the same. Note that the U.S. Census, and consequently we, locate the borderline "eating and drinking places" industry within the retail census, a practice that is not followed by all other national censuses.

By "mass market" we simply envisage retailers who appeal to large sectors, the bulk of the American public. The toy market provides a good example. By definition, those customers who impose atypical requirements on either the ambiance or the assortment of the outlets they patronize, who desire unusual levels of intellectual stimulation, aesthetic development, environmental friendliness, lavish opulence and obsequious service, prestige-laden gift labels, avoidance of role stereotyping, or absence of militarism have excluded themselves from the mass market. But those who want to select from a fairly standard collection of dolls, traditional board games, military vehicles, model kits, and the like and who are willing to trade some of the (supposed) advantages of personal attention for the lower prices and greater flexibility of self-service constitute the main market. There are mass-market specialists and mass-market generalists. The distinction is based on differences in the merchandise assortment's width (variety of categories carried).

Department stores have been defined in various ways at various times. Historically, the line between large dry goods stores and department stores has been vague. In fact, until after World War II the department store trade association (now the National Retail Federation) was called the National Retail Dry Goods Association. Department stores were, and are, large establishments organized and merchandized on a departmental basis that has meant subordinate executives could be considered responsible for the profit performance of their respective product jurisdictions. Those stores had a base in apparel, especially female apparel, and other textile products but also sold many other types of goods. In fact, they probably carried their widest assortment in the 1920s (Hower 1943).

The U.S. Census did not distinguish between types of department stores until 1982. In that year it divided the category into three subgroups: the conventional or traditional department stores (terms that their proprietors thoroughly dislike); national mass merchants, which seems to mean such chains as Sears Roebuck & Co., Montgomery Ward & Co., and J. C. Penney; and discount department stores.

The traditional department stores, the businesses typically rooted in a family-owned, single, large, downtown emporium and more recently expanded through the opening of suburban branches, generally have an upscale image these days. There are historical justifications for, and contradictions to, that image. Some of the major pioneer 19th century stores were housed in "marble palaces" and exuded an air of opulence (Appel 1930; Resseguie 1965). Yet many writers claim that these stores "democratized consumption" (Zola 1886; Boorstin 1965). Their design, which provided free access, relatively easy circulation, much physical separation between customers and salespeople, and concomitant anonymity for the customer, was far less intimidating to the moderate-income or bashful customer than the competing specialty shops where staff or proprietors pounced upon every entrant.

In addition, until the post-World War II period, many traditional department stores were far removed from haute couture. The department stores in any city of substantial size ranged from "luxurious" to "promotional" (Sternlieb 1962). Also, over the years many of those stores established "bargain basements." Nevertheless, most traditional department store proprietors probably aimed at what they considered "mid-America" (more or less upper-middle class according to Susan Benson (1969)).

The national mass merchants were positioned a notch or two below the traditional department stores and, in the case of Sears and Montgomery Ward, developed more of a reputation in hard goods than in fashion apparel. In some ways, they have been stereotyped as "men's stores" in contrast to female-oriented traditional department stores. In recent years, they have experimented with upgrading their assortments but have obtained mixed results.

These mass marketers and discount department stores have eliminated most of the lower-end conventional department stores. Although the department store industry talks most about competition from specialists, the 1987 reported retail market share for the three types of department stores combined was 9.64 percent, not too greatly different from the 8.41 percent reported in 1963 and the 10.14 percent in 1933, when the traditional stores constituted almost the entire category (U.S. Census of Retail Trade). The difference is that, in 1987, the two new subgroups did 68 percent of all department store volume while the conventional did only 32 percent. Discount selling is not new (Hollander 1954 [1986]). The self-service discount department store is, however, a new format that emerged in the 1960s (Drew-Bear 1970; Bluestone 1981). Whenever the context requires it, we will identify the type of department store under discussion.

A Caveat

In preparing this paper, as noted, we have placed great reliance upon the *Censuses of Retail Trade* that have been conducted by the U.S. Department of Commerce, Bureau of the Census, at roughly five-year intervals since 1929. Anyone who has studied U.S. retail trade in any depth knows the enormous difficulty involved in trying to reduce the baffling complexity of American retail trade to a few volumes of rigid statistical tables. A certain degree of omission, undercount, overaggregation, and miscategorization is inevitable. Some misrepresentation is systemic. Business establishments are classified on the basis of the major source of their sales volume—it is difficult to think of any other practical way of classification—a fact that tends to underplay subsidiary and sideline activities. (This problem is partially offset by publication of supplementary "merchandise line" sales figures for each major Census business type. However, there are also problems with these figures because they are partially based on samples of firms. Consequently, we have used them infrequently.)

Practical considerations have also led the Census to use some nonparallel classifications. Most major Census "kinds of business" are based on type of merchandise handled, such as food, clothing, or motor vehicles. The type-of-business category "nonstore retailing" is based on method of operation. Thus any one Census will have its weaknesses. To make matters worse, but probably also unavoidable, the dynamic nature of the retail economy, the changing needs of Census users, and the desire of the Bureau to constantly improve its product cause changes in classifications, nomenclature, and definitions from one Census to another. Precise comparability may be lost. Yet, when all is said and done, there is no better source of data on the basic changes that have been underway in American retail distribution for the past fifty to sixty years.

The most fundamental problem in using the Census for our purposes is not one of precise calibration. The real difficulty is the rule that extrapolation of the past is a very good way to predict the immediate future, but it will miss the turning points. The latest Census, the one from which figures have just become available, was taken in 1987, the peak of an expansionary era. By 1989, many retail sectors were experiencing serious problems; and at the end of 1990, as this is being written, the specter of a retail recession is becoming clear (Wayne 1989; Barmash 1990; *New York Times* December 14, 1990). This will undoubtedly impose new strains, elicit new responses, and induce retail structure changes. We have tried to make judgmental adjustments for what we believe will be the new or changed forces that are likely to impact American retailing.

Let us remember that we are talking about the year 2000, which is not all that far away. A decade normally is not a very long period in retailing history and even in the lives of many individual companies. Retail formats rarely disappear. At various times since the mid-1800s independent retailers have thought that they were about to be exterminated by mail-order houses, department stores, and chain stores. That never happened. So what we are talking about are changes of degree, incremental change, not revolutionary change.

RETAIL GROWTH

We are impressed by the growth, the real growth, of retail business over the years. Retail sales have advanced substantially. Retail sales per capita, adjusted for inflation, in short the actual amount of goods purchased per ultimate consumer in the United States, have grown steadily since at least 1948 (see Figure 4.1). We will, however, note later that some of this growth, particularly recent credit based growth, rests upon a fairly shaky foundation.

Figure 4.1. Per-Capita Change in Retail Sales, 1948 to 1987

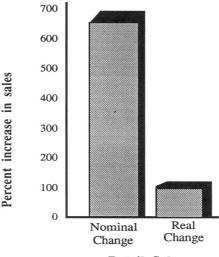

Source: U.S. Retail Census data from 1948 and 1987.

This growth came in spite of an increase in recent decades in the share of consumer income directed toward the purchase of services rather than goods. As noted, the Census defines retailing as the business of selling goods; any increase in the service share will have a negative effect on the Census retail sales figures. The government figure is in some respects a statistical abstraction that may be more suitable for macroeconomic accounting than for business planning—it includes such imputed nonexpenditures as the rental value of owner-occupied housing. Nevertheless, the fact is that both product and service purchases increased. There is a theory (the Clark-Fisher hypothesis) that advancing societies regularly shift expenditures toward the service (and also the luxury) sectors (Clark 1957). Merchants who believe that the United States is on the threshold of new prosperity may want to take this into account. As goods and services are interchangeable, however (e.g., private automobiles and public transport are substitutes for each other), and as businesspeople have to make decisions about specific offerings, looking at the potential demand for any particular service is more helpful to the executive than looking at or trying to predict the overall goods-to-service ratio.

IN-STORE VERSUS NONSTORE RETAILING

We have been struck by the remarkable tenacity of in-store retailing. About 97 percent of total retail sales (as reported by the Census) (i.e., the sale of tangible goods to consumers) takes place through stores (see Figure 4.2).

Figure 4.2.   Nonstore Share of Total Retail Sales, 1953-1988

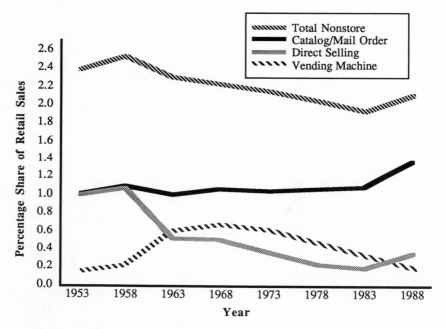

Source: U.S. Retail Census Data from 1954 to 1987 for selected retail categories.

This is true even though pundits have long predicted the demise or the sharp decline of in-store retailing. The Census figures do not give a completely accurate picture of total merchandise flow to consumers, through either stores or other channels. There undoubtedly is some "black market" or "off the books" activity that enters into neither the figure for all retail sales nor the subtotal for any type of distribution channel. Several attempts to measure the size of the nontaxed market were made several years ago, but none could be considered definitive (Houston 1987; McCrohan and Smith 1986).   Some of that activity includes consumer visits to business establishments (e.g., occasional, nonsystematic "back-door" sales at wholesale and manufacturing establishments); some takes place outside commercial channels (e.g., neighborhood garage sales). We also understand that sales by airport and shipboard duty-free shops and order-takers, who arrange to deliver tax-advantaged merchandise to American travelers when they have left the country, are not included in the Census figures, but that business is marginal both geographically and economically and much of it originates in shop visits.

Traditional department store mail-order (and telephone-order) sales are credited to the in-store sector, unless the company involved has set up a separate facility to handle the mail orders. This aspect of nonstore retailing is often mentioned in conversation as a contradiction of the Census in-store/non-store ratio. However, the total conventional department store group is responsible for only about 3 percent of total retail sales, and the mail order portion is only a small fraction of that. Some retail sales made in response to promotional material included with credit card monthly bills may also be omitted. Partially offsetting those undercountings of mail orders, some "over-the-counter" sales, particularly outlet clearance sales within mail order company distribution facilities, may slightly over-represent nonstore business, but really are not more important.

A conceptual problem is more interesting. If a customer encounters a stockout in a unit of a retail chain that has no mail order division and the salesperson undertakes to remedy the gap by ordering the merchandise from another branch store or from a central warehouse, even for direct shipment to the customer, the transaction is treated as in-store. If the company has a mail order division, however, and the clerk or the customer completes the purchase by requisition from the catalog division, even for ultimate pickup at the store, the sale is probably recorded as mail-order business. Yet both events are essentially similar and are store-based. All in all, while nonstore retailing may well be larger than the Census figures indicate, we think that it is substantially less and has grown less than generally believed. We believe that its total market share is well within the single-digit percentage range.

Another consideration is that catalog pricing is quite different from in-store pricing. Because of the time cycle involved in printing, distributing and utilizing catalogs, catalog prices are "sticky," that is, they lag substantially behind changes in the prices displayed on store shelves. This attracts mail-order volume (although it can create gross margin problems) during periods of rising prices, but it also discourages business during periods of falling prices. This exaggerated cyclical effect has manifested itself in the adverse 1990 pre-Christmas season according to Rosalind Wells, chief economist for the National Retail Federation (*New York Times*, November 29, 1990). The J. C. Penney Co. reported a substantially greater fall in its 1990 third-quarter catalog sales than in store sales because of this stickiness of catalog prices and the difficulty of taking markdowns. A company spokesperson said "We know that other catalog retailers have been pretty hard hit" (Gunin 1990).

We have just celebrated the centennial of the publication of Edward Bellamy's utopian novel *Looking Backward: 2000–1887,* in which Bellamy forecast consumers making many choices at home from catalogs for goods delivered by pneumatic tube and selecting other items at central warehouses for similar delivery (Bellamy 1888). Moving away from Jules Verne-like prophesy to supposedly hardheaded marketing wisdom, numerous experts such as E. B. Weiss in the 1950s insisted that we were soon to be in the age of mechanical or electronic in-home shopping. Conceptually there is no reason why one should have to go to the store for routine purchases such as toothpaste. But we continue to do it. That is good news for those whose income arises from in-store retailing and certainly those whose income flows either directly or through insurance companies and pension funds from retail property investments. We often hear that in-home shopping is, and will be, particularly suited to the harried and time-pressed overinvolved, overachieving consumer—the modern and future man and woman. Yet we defy anybody to watch one of the largest and best-known in-home shopping ventures, Home Shopping Network, and tell us that it is designed for time-poor people.

If we were forecasting developments of the next twenty, thirty, or forty years, we would not be quite so cavalier about in-home shopping. We have concentrated on the resistances. We note that even in countries such as France, where government-supported videotex has had extensive distribution, consumers mainly use the machines for nonshopping purposes (Mayer 1988). But probably there is an analogy with automated bank teller machines. As successive machine cohorts become more user friendly, receptivity will probably increase. The question is as much one of economics as of technology, and a large, computer-trained audience may be a key element.

SYSTEMIC COMPLEXITY

Not only has the American retailing system grown larger over the years, it seems to have grown more complex. It probably contains more formats, and perhaps more variations within formats, than ever before. Although two basic forces, one external and one internal to retailing, account for these changes, they probably have conflicting implications for the future.

The external factor is the level of the economy. A high-level economy will have a more elaborate pattern of goods and services than a low-level one (Clark 1957). Carson (1967) has commented that the casual traveler will be struck by the apparent variety of goods and inter-outlet variation in African upriver bush country *dukas* or rural stores, but the experienced patron will note the limitations, lack of choice, and austere homogeneity of the stocks. A pessimistic view of the economy, according to this line of reasoning, would imply an eventual simplification of the retail structure. The key word, however, is eventual. A short-term recession, even a year or two, would probably unleash an assortment of entrepreneurial innovations.

The other argument is that, while new retail formats emerge from time to time, old ones adjust but never disappear. This is consistent with views expressed by Goldman (1975). In fact, old ones may experience a renaissance, as has happened with street vendors in New York, Washington, D.C., and elsewhere (Greenberg et al. 1980). Actually, though, some formats do decline to levels of very limited commercial or economic importance. For example, the 1930s Censuses contained separate figures for two store types no longer distinguished in the reports: "public utility stores" and "industrial stores." The public utility stores were outlets the gas and electric companies established to sell home appliances to consumers at lower prices in a successful effort to build load factors (power consumption). Most public utility companies eventually discontinued these stores because (a) as they increasingly catered to a replacement market, they decreasingly stimulated new power volume, and (b) they increasingly roused the ire of the independent appliance dealers, who in turn could influence state regulatory commissions. The companies saw little point in continuing difficult marginal businesses that contributed less and less to the basic corporate objectives and endangered basic goodwill.

The industrial stores were employer-operated retail establishments at plantations, logging camps, mines, factories, and offices. Historically they existed to supply workers at remote locations without commercial facilities or to enable employers to recapture much of the wages they paid their workers. Post-World War I inflation led to a new type of industrial store in factories and even urban offices, where the employer used corporate buying power to obtain staples and even some luxuries for employees at advantageous prices. These stores were an employee benefit that gradually evaporated with the waning of inflation and the emergence of new low-cost commercial outlets, such as supermarkets (Hollander and Marple 1960). But, just as from time to time one encounters an old-fashioned drugstore with a soda fountain and wire-backed chairs at marble-topped tables, some vestiges of all types remain. And, to repeat, life sometimes is pumped back into them, just as Woolworth is now trying to revitalize the variety store concept with Woolworth Express.

SINGLE STORE INDEPENDENTS

The growth in retail volume has had important and beneficial implications for all types of retailers. Even the so-called single store "mom and pop" retailer has gained in actual volume over the years, although at a much lower rate than the multiunit chain store retailer. Consequently, single-unit enterprise market share has steadily declined but total business has grown. Stores of this type will have to find a special locational, merchandise, or service niche in which to prosper.

To include an optimistic note, we also need to point out that one of the ways (although it is only one of several) in which the single store category is reduced is by graduation. Some single unit businesses become multiunit.

MULTIUNIT RETAILING

In general, although the rate of increase has varied from time to time, multiunit (i.e., chain store) market share has expanded over the years. As can be seen in Figure 4.3, such businesses now account for half or close to half of all retail sales. (The ambiguity results from a desire to avoid arguing whether two- and three-store firms should be considered chains. The question is not important in the big picture).

There are several factors that suggest continuation of multiunit market share growth during the foreseeable future. Technological improvements facilitate the type of centralized management that characterizes these organizations. The economies of scale that result from increasing store count and the ability to divide tasks between store operations and central merchandising put them in very powerful positions vis-à-vis both their customers and their suppliers.

There is considerable danger that some chains will become so overly centralized they will not respond well to local market variations. There is also the danger that personnel policies and operating methods that consistently routinize store work and reserve analysis, planning, and strategy for headquarters will produce a collection of store people incapable of coping with the slightest deviation from anticipated routine transactions. The chains do have to watch out for the perils of becoming overly short-run efficient but long-run ineffective.

Our fear of overcentralization flows from several trends. The first and most important factor is the rate of improvement in data transfer and manipulation processes. Let us look at a very broad, long-run picture. Management of geographically separated units (a problem for the old international and colonial trading companies) had to be very decentralized in the days of the stagecoach and the sailing ship. The Hanseatic League, for example, put its potential trading-post managers through many years of arduous training, including severe corporal punishment for mistakes, to develop an elite corps that could handle local problems without recourse to central management. Business historians (e.g., Chandler 1977) pay much more attention to the invention of the telegraph than do marketing teachers because they, the historians, recognize that the introduction of virtually instantaneous information transmission permitted a new level of management control. Constant increases in management's technical ability to monitor store operations will increase centralization.

Figure 4.3. Multiunit Share of Retail Type, 1929-1987

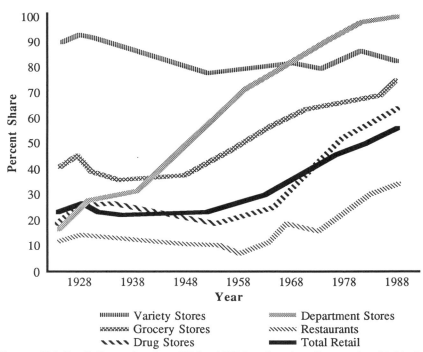

Source: U.S. Retail Census data from 1929 to 1987 for selected retail categories. Multiunit refers to firms having three or more outlets.

Of course, data can flow both ways, although many executives are not comfortable about sharing information with subordinates. Another major factor, the desire for short-term cost-control, will hamper decentralization. For example, many chains that sell packaged goods now send their stores "planograms," detailed drawings that show just how much shelf space at just which spot should be allocated to each brand, package size, and variety in the assortment. The amount of space allotted and its positioning is based upon potential sales, gross margins, management knowledge or belief about customer buying habits, and space allocation in return for "slotting allowances" (display payments) from vendors. The completion of those agreements, the acquisition of the necessary data, and the technical expertise to prepare the planogram are all processes or attributes that can most easily be located at central offices. The use of prototype stores, which increases intracompany, interstore homogeneity, the transfer of some logistical and supply decisions to vendors (functional shift), the existence and likely reinforcement of labor legislation that aims to reduce the role of individual caprice and prejudice in personnel decisions, and the desire of some retailers to present a uniform offering to mobile customers all argue for standardization. Many large retailers also believe in the "metro concept," a policy of always placing a number of stores in large communities to share advertising, supply, and supervision expenses and to make a substantial impact on each such community. This concept tends to involve a strong desire for uniformity among the units in any given metropolis and thus removes much decision-making from the store managers to at least the area supervisor.

Recent years have witnessed much such centralization in the department store business, partially because of increased competition from more centralized mass-market specialists and generalists. Once consisting of completely autonomous family businesses, in the 1920s and 1930s many of its leading firms amalgamated into loose agglomerations such as Federated, City Stores, Allied, and Associated Dry Goods (these were so loosely articulated that the Census set up a special category termed "buying groups" to distinguish them from conventional chains). In the 1960s the firms moved to a centralized flagship and suburban branch format for the individual geographic units. Finally, in the 1980s they began to consolidate those units (e.g., Foley's/Sanger Harris; Macy's/Bambergers home furnishings).

Several years ago, Sears Roebuck engaged a well-known consulting firm to advise it on "how to reduce duplication of decision making," unquestionably a euphemism for centralization. Such bellwether chains as Toys "R" Us insist on standardization (*Chain Store Age* 1980). Federated/ Allied described centralization of merchandising and nonmerchandising functions as one of its major objectives, while the Dayton-Hudson Company is working to integrate its Marshall Field acquisition into its now Minneapolis-based combined Dayton and Hudson department store operations (Barmash 1990).

There probably is some Hegelian dialectic tendency of action and reaction in corporate organization structure. Overcentralization may stimulate decentralization. Nordstroms has recently attracted much attention with a decentralized organization plan that locates at least some "buying" control in each branch or group of nearby branches. But all of the short-term forces appear likely to work in the opposite direction. Central management will thus have the challenge of keeping store-level jobs sufficiently stimulating and rewarding for the calibre, of unit management needed to cope with the pressure situations that cannot be referred to headquarters.

POLITICAL CLIMATE

We should remember that in the 1920s, a period of enormous chain store growth, and in the 1930s, a period of great economic stringency, the chain store enterprises encountered very serious political opposition. Chain store tax movements flowered throughout the country and resulted in oppressive or potentially oppressive progressive tax schedules in almost half of the then existing states. In the 1930s Congress passed the Robinson-Patman Act, a relatively ineffective law but something that was very much dreaded as the "anti A&P bill" by chain store interests. National resale price maintenance and state minimum markup laws were also adopted under the rubric of antichain activities. Is it possible that the downturn in economic activity that may well loom directly ahead will also produce antichain legislation? This is always a possibility. The chains have lost their surprising support from liberal, "New Deal" economists who were otherwise opposed to big business. That loss, however, has much less political significance today than it would have had in the 1930s.

Unless economic conditions become very much worse than most analysts believe likely, the appearance of restrictive retail legislation is very questionable. For one thing, there is no really organized antichain lobby of consequence today. The popular mood is still probably antiregulatory, although that could change under economic pressure. Further, chain store companies and their trade associations are more politically sophisticated today than they were in the 1920s, and the consumer movement—which tends to be prochain—is of course more strongly entrenched. Also, the chain sector may now have reached the critical mass at which thoughts of dislodging it appear futile.

Even so, chain-threatening clouds appear on the horizon. As Lewis (1990) notes, in the last five years or so state attorneys general have begun to move quite vigorously against *national and regional* mergers that they believe will adversely affect competition within their states. Lewis further notes, the state officials' "Guidelines on Horizontal Mergers" issued by the National Association of Attorneys General presume that large mergers have adverse consequences, a very different view from the current position of the relevant federal agencies (the Department of Justice and the Federal Trade Commission) that starts with the assumption that large mergers are likely to be efficiency-enhancing. The states may institute the equivalent of private antitrust action against proposed or consummated mergers, they may seek all civil remedies available to the federal government including injunctions, hold-separate orders, and divestiture and, provided they move with reasonable promptness, they can bring action even after a federal agency has approved the merger. Finally, although Lewis specifically notes that state government interest is not confined to retailing, three retailing cases are the leading ones in the burgeoning area of antitrust activity (Pennsylvania v. May Dept. Stores Co. 1986; Mass., Maine & New Hampshire v. Campeau Corp. 1988; and Calif. v. American Stores Co. 1988).

The political pressures for such action are easy to discern (Palamountain 1955). Yet a Minnesota experience in 1987 may be more indicative of at least the prerecession mood of the electorate. When the Dayton-Hudson Corporation was faced with an unwelcome takeover attempt, it was able to muster enough grassroots support in a few days to force a reluctant governor to convene an emergency session of the legislature for the sole purpose of passing an antitakeover bill (Bandow 1987). The Dayton-Hudson incident emits mixed signals. The corporation is closely identified with Minnesota, and part of its public relations message was, "We, and our jobs and our economy, against the outsiders," the same theme that fueled antichain sentiment in the 1930s. Dayton-Hudson is also very generous to certain key aspects of community life in the places where its stores and facilities are located, and it gives quite publicly. The most significant thing, however, is that a very large chain store company could muster support in a state where a populist government imposed antichain legislation fifty years ago.

Of course, size itself is no guarantee of continued success. Retail history demonstrates the intensity of the rivalries among the giants. For reasons discussed later, it appears that the market may become even more competitive and price promotional. If so, large scale retailers will have to continue to keep their buying and cost-control skills well-honed. They also will have to work hard to maintain credibility. Everyone knows retailers who are on television almost night-after-night, year-after-year, announcing how overstocked their warehouses are. The technique apparently continues to work, but disbelief is going to set in if more and more retailers try this approach. Consumers already seem quite skeptical of some markdown claims.

CONGLOMERATION

One very interesting and little-studied aspect of post World War II retailing has been the growth of conglomeration. We do not know whether this is good or bad news for retailers and/or consumers. We do suspect that it is probably bad news for shopping center developers and perhaps other suppliers. By conglomeration we mean the operation of two or more different types of retailing enterprises by the same parent corporation (Tillman 1971). It may also include the operation of retail businesses by essentially nonrelated, nonretailing enterprises. There probably has always been a certain amount of small-scale conglomeration in American communities. The successful dry goods store proprietor with a little extra time and some money to invest might have purchased a substantial interest in a local hardware store or a restaurant or a bookstore; several retail proprietors may have decided that the community needed a new bank or a new hotel and joined together to establish one and so on. But until the 1950s it was unusual for a major retailing company in one line of business to operate stores in another retail sector.

The record on conglomerate mergers has been spotty, and information is lacking about the nodes of commonality, that is, the extent to which a company operating dress shops can gain economies of scale by operating toy stores. Some such mergers seem to be purely financial-portfolio transactions with each division retaining operational autonomy and identity; in other instances there are some transfers of functions. Clearly participating in several different commodity sectors provides insurance against short-term style and taste risks in any one. Whether retailing ability is as easily transferred from one type of merchandise to another as it is from one set of stores in a given line to another in the same line is an open question.

Traditional department store management practices in recent years have assumed that buyers possess something called "merchandising skill" that is entirely independent of product and industry knowledge and that permits transfer from disparate department to disparate department. However, that belief may be one of the problems of the traditional department store business.

CONCENTRATION

One of the more interesting questions associated with chain store (multiunit company) growth is its impact on concentration—the share of business conducted by the largest firms in the industry. Because retailers operate in two markets—the supply market and the consumer market— concentration has two aspects. It can be assessed in terms of the market share that X number of retailers (grocers, pharmacists, clothiers, etc.) enjoy in a particular community. In some ways that may be the more important aspect from the individual consumer's standpoint—how many supermarkets or discount stores or building supply firms he or she can choose from. Measurement of such concentration is clearly beyond the scope of this paper.

National concentration is also important because it suggests access to resources and the availability of countervailing powers. Measurement again is very difficult. Economists use a number of technical tools, of which concentration ratios are the simplest. Such ratios as CR_4, CR_8, CR_{20}, and CR_{50} indicate the percentage of total sales volume obtained by the largest 4, 8, 20, or 50 firms in a specified line of business. Table 4.1 shows these ratios for retailing as a whole and for a number of typical businesses.

Table 4.1. Retail Concentration Ratios, 1972 and 1987

Category	Concentration Ratio			
	CR_4	CR_8	CR_{20}	CR_{50}
Total Retail				
1972	6.0	9.0	13.5	18.9
1987	5.2	8.8	14.3	20.3
Department Stores				
1972	38.8	51.4	68.4	82.1
1987	44.4	66.0	85.4	95.5
Grocery Stores				
1972	17.5	24.4	34.8	43.9
1987	17.4	26.8	37.2	47.7
Women's Clothing Stores				
1972	11.2	15.7	22.8	31.6
1987	22.1	30.0	39.8	50.4
Household Appliance Stores				
1972	8.8	10.9	14.3	19.4
1987	10.7	14.0	20.3	27.2
Drug and Proprietary Stores				
1972	10.9	17.0	27.7	35.1
1987	23.4	36.8	51.0	57.6
Shoe Stores				
1972	19.6	27.6	37.7	44.5
1987	33.3	44.2	56.2	63.8
Nonstore Retail				
1972	17.6	25.2	35.3	42.3
1987	10.4	16.5	29.3	42.8

Source: U.S. Retail Census data from 1972 and 1987 for selected retail cateogries.

These figures must be taken with some reservations. The results will almost always vary as a line of business is more widely or narrowly defined.

Moreover, these numbers pay no attention to scrambled merchandise—the extent to which nonmembers of a trade, say supermarket companies, provide competition to the members of the specified trade, say drugstore companies.

Yet the figures in Table 4.1 do point up some notable aspects of modern American retailing. In spite of the tendency toward conglomeration, concentration ratios for retailing as a whole have actually declined at the CR_4 and CR_8 levels and have increased only moderately at the CR_{20} and CR_{50} levels. Apparently, giants have not developed that can straddle all retailing successfully. Given the uncertain and uneven records of most conglomerates, such development seems unlikely.

The pattern is quite different in most of the "kinds of businesses" noted. Concentration has tended to increase, usually substantially, in the kinds of businesses studied with the exception of the biggest grocery store companies (a category that includes supermarkets, convenience stores, delicatessens, and quite a number of nonspecialized food outlets) and in nonstore retailing. The contrary pattern in the grocery business may be due to the rivalries of the giants, the adverse fortunes of some of the largest companies, and a tendency toward geographic consolidation. Concentration in nonstore retailing may have been deterred by the decline of mail order generalists and the decline of the importance of machine vending—a field dominated by a few big enterprises. Given the probable growth in chain market share, we expect some increase in concentration.

INTERNATIONALIZATION

Despite its presumed parochialism, retail enterprise has long had its international manifestations. The oldest retailing company in North America, the Hudson's Bay Company, was in a sense an international organization until it moved its official headquarters to Canada a short while ago. British, French, Dutch, German, and other trading companies followed agricultural and mining enterprises with expatriate retailing in Africa, Asia, and South America and elsewhere early in the century. Singer sponsored a worldwide sewing machine dealer network in the 19th century and F. W. Woolworth established a British subsidiary early in this century (Brandon 1977; Hollander 1970). Surprisingly, while much of the current literature notes the overseas efforts of some major fast-food and other franchisors (e.g., "Fast Food in Europe," *International Journal of Retail and Distribution Management* 1990), little or no discussion seems to be devoted to direct sellers' international programs, something that dates back to Singer in the mid-1800s and Fuller Brush and others in the early 20th century (Fuller 1960).

We should distinguish two types of international retailing: overt and discreet. Overt international retailers emphasize their very foreignness as a major selling point. Aside from stressing cosmopolitanism ("New York, Paris, London"), they often parade their origin in a country highly regarded for excellence in their product line. They are likely to operate very upscale stores. French perfumers are an excellent example (Caldwell 1989). Many internationally owned stores, particularly in the overt-luxury category, are associated with the sale of a particular product brand. They may be intended as the manufacturer's primary distribution in the host country or as one or a few demonstration stores to teach local retailers how to operate. These merchants are a highly conspicuous and a highly interesting group of relatively little economic significance, whatever their aesthetic and cultural influence may be.

We will be more concerned with the discreet international retailers, those who buy into or try to build large-scale enterprises. While they in no way keep their foreign origin secret from the financial and business communities or anyone else who wishes to inquire, they see no reason to advertise it to the shopping public. In essence we have a 2x2 matrix between brand-specific and nonspecific and overt/discreet. Our focus is on the nonspecific/discreet quadrant.

During the 1950s, 1960s, and early 1970s many leading American retailers expressed new interest in foreign operations. Those who previously had branches in Cuba received a lesson in the political hazards of crossing borders but apparently did not regard it as an ultimate deterrent. Inspired by messages from W. W. Rostow (1964) at the State Department and J. K. Galbraith (1964) at Harvard, the belief spread that what the developing countries and indeed the world needed was a good strong dose of American mass retailing.

There were some successes, but many major firms such as J. C. Penney, Safeway Stores, Federated Department Stores, F. W. Woolworth, and Sears Roebuck eventually sold off some or all of their foreign investments. It is now clear that an infusion of mass market retailing will not be enough to solve all the barriers to economic development in the less-developed countries, and that in many instances indigenous firms can outperform expatriates. Currently there are a number of U.S. retailers with overseas branches and American fast food franchising is rapidly expanding in many countries. (Although fast food franchising may not yet be very profitable, the world market appears fairly receptive.) As James Wood, chairman and CEO of A&P (1989), stated, "Although Americans are regarded as aggressive marketeers, it has not shown in any retail expansion outside that of North America."

More recently, however, entrepreneurship and particularly acquisitiveness have traveled in the opposite direction, with purchase money flowing from Canada, Europe, and Australia. For example, in 1985 Europeans invested $5.55 billion in American retailing, more than twice the amount invested by Americans in European retailing that same year (Salmon and Tordjman 1989).

The results have been very uneven. Some writers, such as Kacker (1990) and Treadgold (1990), conclude that, on balance, the overseas entries into U.S. merchandising have been both active (as distinguished from passive investments) and profitable. In contrast, Wood (1989), who is the operating head of a supermarket company that was revitalized under foreign ownership, claims that the successful east-west investments have been portfolio ones. Certainly, foreign ownership of such major (and in some instances now extinct) U.S. retailers as Orbach's, Korvettes, Kohl's, Gimbal Brothers, Saks Fifth Avenue, Marshall Field, Bonwit Teller, B. Altman, Sakowitz, Federated Department Stores, and Allied Stores Co. did not prove sustainable. Yet the German acquisition of A&P and Spiegel were very successful, and Vendex International's (Holland) purchase of a 49 percent nonvoting interest in Dillard Department Stores must be considered money well spent.

The most important question is whether the pattern will continue. Some forces that favor internationalization will remain or even be enhanced. The noneconomic motives that predispose some executives to be "world players" (and inhibit others from venturing outside home markets) will persist, but probably in a business and social climate that will consider globalization and internationalization as characteristics of industrial leadership. Technological advances that facilitate the international flow of information will also be a facilitating factor. Entry barriers and controls over profit repatriation should decline unless either (a) the world settles into tripartite blocs—North America, Pan-Europe and Pacific a distinct possibility, and/or (b) depression breeds new protectionism.

Other writers, such as Hamill and Crosbie (1990), note the uneven performance of British acquisitions in U.S. retailing and suggest that, at least for the post-1992 short term, British retailers would be well advised to redirect their internationalization strategies toward Europe. Robinson and Clarke-Hill (1990) conclude that the total international volume is very small compared to total domestic sales and that, like cheap wine, retailing concepts and management may not travel well.

The uneven record of past entries is an adverse factor. Without discussing individual companies, we note that a number of supposedly successful current foreign investments in U.S. retailing have been made in businesses selling very specific, almost faddish clothing styles and in luxury goods stores that may be recession-vulnerable. The record may look worse two or three years from now. The widespread view that the United States is currently overstored should be a deterrent. Alexander (1990) finds that U.K. retailers are now inclined to look more toward the European Community than toward the United States for expansion opportunities. Finally, there is the question of exchange rates. As this is being written, the

Federal Reserve Board is gradually lowering interest rates. Although highly leveraged acquisitions in the United States should no longer look as attractive to financial institutions as they once did, a cheaper dollar should make American retailers less costly for foreign participants. It will also make their short-term earnings less attractive. On balance, there will probably be some new internationalization, but given the managerial and other difficulties, a low rate of net increase.

MASS-MARKET GENERALISTS

"The Accordion Pattern" is a name now used to describe a belief or a hypothesis that the "dominant form" (a term not precisely defined) in American retailing alternates between stores with wide and stores with narrow assortments of goods (Hower 1943, Appendix A; Hollander 1966). Widespread acceptance also is given to the belief that traditional department stores have been overpowered by the growth of specialty stores. Yet, as we have already noted, the total business of discount department stores (a post-World War II development), so-called mass merchandising chains (the retail stores of the traditional large mail order companies plus J. C. Penney and probably a few others, a group that has expanded substantially since 1950), and conventional department stores still equals the department store market share of the 1940s. Although the actual picture is more complex, one could say statistically (and with some degree of descriptive power) that department store business has simply shifted among the three types of stores. One has to note the sharp decline in limited-price variety store market share to find the generalists in a poorer position now than they were forty or fifty years ago. Some of that variety store share may now be located in super drugstores, which are classified among pharmacies and proprietary goods stores but which sell much more than health and beauty aids. Some of these super drug units might properly be classified as general merchants.

This is not the place to discuss individual companies and their prospects. One of the major mass merchandisers seems to be going through quite troubled times; another two—although faced with real difficulties— may have found better formulas. The subgroup possesses substantial staying power and is well-entrenched. We would not simply dismiss it.

The discount department store business, which has gone through several shakeouts since the New England soft goods discounters emerged in the 1950s and 1960s (Drew-Bear 1970), may have turned into a battle between three more-or-less national leaders and some strong regional chains. Limits to growth may be or become a serious problem for this industry. In many key categories, such as toys, health and beauty aids, and hardware/construction goods, they face stiff competition from well-stocked specialists (Pereira 1990). In some markets they face intense price competition from warehouse clubs, a group to be discussed later. Yet they do offer the convenience of one-stop shopping, the freedom and flexibility of self-service, and attractive prices. *Chain Store Age Executive* sponsored a survey in which more respondents in every demographic group gave discount stores a higher rating than any other type of outlet as a source of "value for money." Respondents tended to report increased shopping trips to discount stores, fewer to other types than in the previous year (*Chain Store Age Executive* 1989). If a store type proves popular with all age groups, all income levels, all household sizes, and households with and without children, can we ask whether segmentation has not sometimes been overemphasized in marketing discussions? While the discount store category may have difficulty in increasing its total market share, it should remain an important competitor.

WAREHOUSE CLUBS

Discount stores in some markets do face competition from (and may be co-subsidiaries of companies that own) "wholesale warehouse" membership clubs, another form of low-priced generalists. These outlets carry large stocks of a wide and somewhat erratic assortment, concentrate on large packs and large sizes of packaged foods and other quick consumables, promise more continuity of category than of brand or specific SKU, aggressively seek bargain purchases, operate on about an 8 percent margin, and limit patronage to small business owners (reportedly responsible for about 60 percent of dollar value) and selected consumers, such as members of employee groups, who pay an annual membership fee of about $25 (Lev 1990).

In many ways, warehouse clubs resemble the "closed door" discount houses that also flourished on a membership basis in the United States in the 1950s and 1960s, but with much more attention to food and other nondurables than was characteristic of those electronics/appliance/camera/jewelry/luggage/gift closed-door stores. The closed-door (restricted membership) retailers felt a constant urge to expand the membership or customer base, and over time the same thing will probably happen to the warehouse clubs.

There is absolutely no legal advantage, such as enjoying greater freedom from minimum price legislation, in membership restriction. The membership system does provide a source of additional funds; it also provides a good list of names for inexpensive direct mail promotion, it facilitates check acceptance and, probably most importantly, it gives customers a sense of being the selected beneficiaries of special bargains not available to the general public.

The clubs are even closer to the cash-and-carry wholesalers who flourished in Germany in the 1960s and 1970s. These institutions have continued to be strong in that country, where they have the advantage of staying open two hours later than the mandatory 6:30 P.M. closing imposed on most other retailers. The wholesale membership club format has considerable appeal, and the present small number of units throughout the country leaves ample room for growth. But the present low margins (the customer's reward for the service and assortment deficiencies) require very skilled management. Many early entrants have failed. The "wheel of retailing" phenomenon is likely to occur here, if club warehouse retailing grows to the point where customers in most major markets can choose among competing outlets. Expenses and margins will probably rise as traffic is divided among the rivals and as those rivals begin to offer more amenities or more stable stocks. Many potential household customers will also continue to be unhappy with restaurant-sized food packs. This format has its inherent limitations.

MASS-MARKET SPECIALISTS

One of the implications of the expansion of retail sales, which of course refers to the growth of markets, has been an opportunity for the growth of large scale mass market specialists. This is the type of retailing that Burt McCammon has often referred to as including the "power retailers." The firms, such as Toys "R" Us or Home Depot, can dominate selection and price in a way that no multiline retailer can. Such "category killers" have developed in many fields, such as consumer electronics, pharmacy, and carpeting (Pereira 1990). The technique seems less suited to style or ego-intensive merchandise than to staples and common durables.

SUBURBAN MALLS

Population Census statistics from 1990 and the very spotty record to date for downtown retail rehabilitation (Frieden and Sagalyn 1989) suggest that purchasing power will remain concentrated in the suburbs. American suburbanization has provided a very congenial and nurturing environment for chain store retailing. Suburbanization is not a necessary condition, witness chain growth in the 1920s, but it is so encouraging one could almost call it a sufficient condition.

Suburbanization, we believe, means continuance of domination by shopping centers, malls, and clusters of the free-standing mass-market specialists just discussed. The malls, once jokingly defined as "fountains surrounded by four shoe stores," have settled into a pattern of apparel emphasis supported by convenient medleys of other retail and service establishments. They have remedied an original lack of in-house eating places. They also have fairly adequate parking, an absolute suburban necessity in this country. They thus seem quite comfortable for much suburban shopping. Those centers are also thoroughly diffused throughout suburban space to minimize driving distance and thus have a fairly high protection against any adverse effects of a gasoline price rise. This does not mean that individual centers are immune to depressed sales conditions, intensified competition, and adverse trends that may affect individual tenants or types of tenants. It does mean that we expect suburban malls to remain important. In contrast, we think "theme" and "mega amusement" super centers can easily lose their novelty and touristic appeal.

RETAIL LINE OF BUSINESS SHIFTS

Figure 4.4 reveals that general merchandise, drug and pharmacy, gasoline, automotive, and on-premise food retailers gained sales at an above-average rate from 1954 to 1987. Nonstore growth also was probably slightly above average. Building materials, apparel, off-premises food, and miscellaneous products displayed below-average sales growth, and the growth in home furnishings sales was about average.

Figure 4.4. Nominal Change in Retail Sales by Retail Category, 1954 to 1987

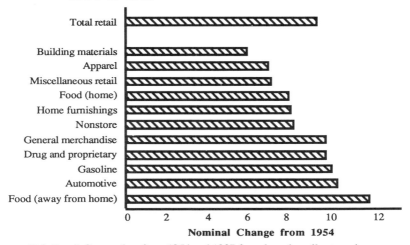

Source: U.S. Retail Census data from 1954 and 1987 for selected retail categories.

There are great difficulties in trying to measure what was really going on. Were the changes in those categories due to variations in the amount of merchandise sold or to differential impacts of inflation that brought in more nominal dollars per unit in some lines than in others? For the few trades where we have fairly specific price deflators, actual retail sales look rather different from nominal ones. (Of course, retailers must take nominal dollars to the bank.)

As Figure 4.5 indicates, apparel units apparently held up very well, but price tags stayed relatively low (at least for the items and grades included in the CPI). Foreign sourcing probably helped, but the falling value of the dollar in international money markets will now increase overseas costs. Home furnishings is an interesting case in doing well during a period of supposedly declining family values. The electronics sector must have helped, but it is now faced with a shortage of interesting new products.

Figure 4.5. Real Change in Retail Sales by Selected Retail Category, 1954 to 1987

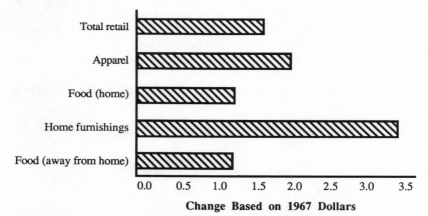

Change Based on 1967 Dollars

Source: U.S. Retail Census data from 1954 and 1987 for selected retail categories.

The food trade did not boom in spite of the sale of more prepared and semiprepared items with "built-in maid service," the inclusion of more gourmet foods, the proliferation of franchised restaurants, and the increased sale of nonfoods in food stores. This conforms to conventional wisdom that food is a noncyclical sector. The food store sector went through a consolidation and realignment process a few years ago and may now have a rather stable base. Some shifts in average store size may occur, but it is not as easy to develop hypermarkets in this country as it was in France and

Germany where legislation severely restricted the competition that they faced. The fast-food sector may have more overstoring problems.

LIMITS TO GROWTH

In general we are troubled by one or two other developments. The great growth in retail sales was accompanied by, and undoubtedly flowed from, a great growth in household real income. But in recent years, even before the current recession or near recession, earnings per worker had turned down. See Figures 4.6 and 4.7 for supporting data.

Figure 4.6. Per-Capita Disposable Income, 1949-1984

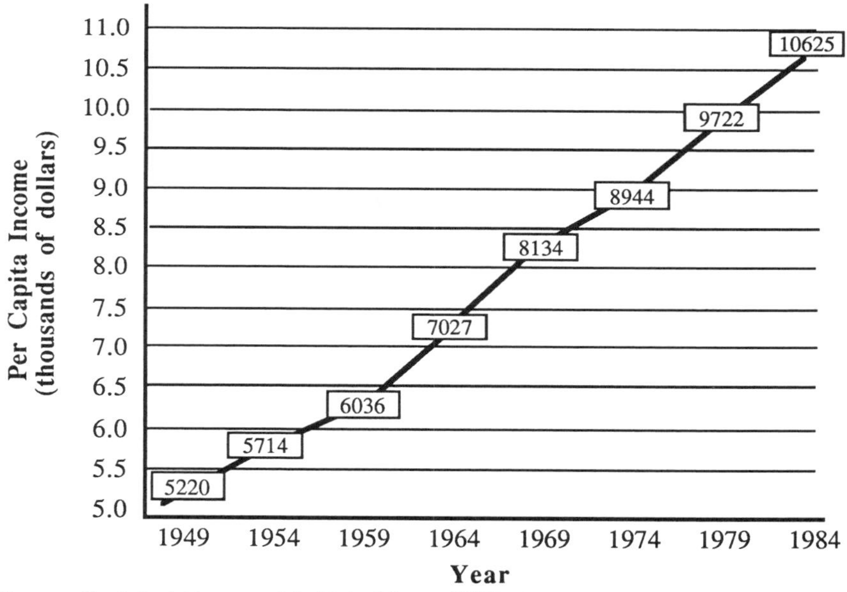

Source: *Statistical Abstract of the United States* (1989). Data represent per-capita disposable income held constant in 1982 dollars.

The causes of retail sales growth are the subject of some debate and may include deindustrialization, demographic changes, and changes in government policy. Household income continues to rise because of an increase in the number of workers per average household. The limits on that sort of growth are fairly obvious, particularly as we remain a monogamous and graying society. Households will not provide more workers, and unless worker income increases the retail market will become more circumscribed. The relative impact of this on mass and upscale markets is a matter of conjecture. We believe that the affluent market is likely to remain affluent while industrial workers are likely to be furloughed.

Figure 4.7. Person Hours Worked and Compensation Index (1967 = 100)

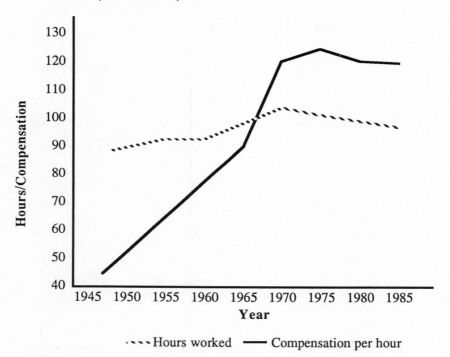

Source: *Historical Statistics of the United States: Colonial Times to 1970 and Statistical Abstract of the United States* (1989). Data are for production and related workers in mining, manufacturing, and nonsupervisory employees in other industries. Data exclude agriculture.

We believe that hopes for continuously expanding consumer spending (hopes that nurtured what the industry and analysts now consider an overexpansion of retail capacity) cannot continue to be based on the widespread assumption of increasing two-worker household income. The burden of private, corporate, and public debt is too well known to need repeating here. Moving into recession, consumers will not only have to repay their own installment and home equity debt under adverse conditions, they will also have to pay a good bit of public debt through increased taxation or inflation.

The 1990 election, which occurred while this paper was in progress, showed that American voters did not take kindly to new taxes or those who proposed them. Yet new federal excise taxes did emerge. Many states are now pressing close to, or even over, their own constitutional mandates for balanced budgets. Federal financial aid and provision of services to the states are likely to decline, and recession is very likely to increase demands on the states. Consequently, increases in state taxation that will further reduce consumer spending appear inevitable. All of this comes at a time when, to put it kindly, the financial sector (the banking, insurance, savings and loans, and brokerage industry) is not in a position to exercise strong leadership in stimulating the economy. Our decline in industrial leadership exacerbates the problem.

A second concern comes from the widespread belief in the retail trade that we have become overstored, a belief that seems justified. Specifically, sales per square foot have declined as the growth in retail square footage outpaced the growth of retail sales. The inevitable impact of this will be increased competitiveness, which in turn will mean more bargain promotion at the lower end and even probably upscale.

The apparent overstoring does not, however, appear to affect the future plans of retailers drastically. *Stores* magazine, the official organ of the National Retail Federation, discusses the store expansion plans of a number of apparel and other specialty chains (Schultz 1990). Although some of the indicated expansion involves the purchase of existing stores that are now, or have been, under other ownership, clearly a large amount of new retail space has come and will come in some sectors that are not now booming. Of the surveyed chains, pervasive downsizing was reported only in the home electronics group (not presented in the tabulation) and to some extent in the very troubled menswear industry. Other chains are slowing their growth ambitions, allegedly because of the lack of good new mall locations, and apparently some firms were more willing to talk about what they had done in 1990 rather than what they would do in 1991 and beyond.

Yet the result must be increased chain pressure on each other and on the independents. Similar expansion plans undoubtedly can be found in other sectors, because as one executive interviewed by *Stores* put it, "We plan to grow because we believe in our business." The dynamics of American business are oriented toward growth. Growth attracts the best resources, both human and capital, it solves many problems, and it provides the greatest rewards. Some or much of the short-term growth indicated here must result from decisions and commitments made in more prosperous times; some of the more ambitious ten-year developments may not materialize. But as long as retail executives see economies of scale and return to market dominance (in either supply and/or sales markets), and such advantages do exist, the pressure for growth will continue.

It may be noted that in addition to using Census and other government data, we rely to an unusual degree on very recent business and news media reports of 1990 developments in the retail trades. We are particularly attentive to reports and comments associated with the general economic recession that entered the country's consciousness during the second half of the year. So much attention to immediate phenomena is unusual and even questionable in what is supposed to be an intermediate (ten years) term analysis and forecast. Our justification is that we believe much of the expansion of the 1982-89 period (the period after the 1980-81 recession) was illusory and was grounded in imprudent financial practices.

We do not need to be entirely gloomy. The situation is not necessarily a repetition of 1929. There are some safety nets in the economy now that were not there then. And the central authorities, particularly the Federal Reserve Bank Board, may well be better prepared to anticipate and respond to financial problems than it was sixty years ago. But we do believe that the economy and particularly the retailing economy is currently going through a process that is not merely "fine-tuning." It is a substantial readjustment. One might say that it will be a readjustment toward reality.

That is not to say, and this should be emphasized, that we envisage a new world of permanently gray, humorless, ascetic consumers. Even during the Great Depression and its sluggish recovery period, such recreational fads as miniature golf and mahjongg swept the country and flippant magazines such as *College Humor* and *Ballyhoo* became popular. More importantly, the great majority of the labor force continued working and spending. But we do expect that consumer spending will decline, that there may be greater caution in the use and/or the extension of credit, and that some existing retail space will have to become dormant until population growth catches up with the supply of retail facilities.

OVERVIEW AND IMPLICATIONS

The picture we have painted so far suggests a world that is reasonably congenial to large-scale mass retailing. We have some difficulty in defining "traditional retailing." If that means mom and pop corner stores, the picture suggests a long-term general decline—nothing cataclysmic, but fairly steady long-term erosion of market share. If it means "the traditional department store retailer," the picture is not very good. It is only in the last decade that we have census figures for various types of department stores. They indicate that the historic "Big Store" business has declined from perhaps 8 to 10 percent of total retail volume at the start of World War II to about 3 percent. Although individual companies may well forge ahead (such names as Dillard, the May Company, and perhaps Dayton-Hudson, assuming the latter does not put more emphasis on mass operations, come immediately to mind), the industry as a whole suffers many problems. It was slow to move to the suburbs in the 1950s and 1960s when they became the bedroom communities of America. Department store proprietors perhaps intuitively recognized that even though they would become the anchors of the shopping malls, they were in a less advantageous position in the suburbs than they were in city center, where they were the epitome of "one-stop shopping." One problem that needs consideration is whether as department stores lose their pulling power, they will also lose their relative importance to mall developers and consequently lose their opportunity to obtain particularly favorable occupancy terms.

Changes in life-style have probably reduced the extent to which recreational shopping is a major component of American female time allotments. We see several factors operating here. One is the growth of two-career families and general increased female participation in the work force. Another is a good probability that recreational shopping may more often than not be a characteristic of restricted purchasing power. One argument is that one who can buy many toys wants to spend time playing with them; one who can only buy few may be much more willing to invest time in selecting them. Daniel Boorstin and others have said that "the department store democratized consumption." Michael Schudson (1984) says it "democratized envy." If, as we will suggest, limits on consumption could be in the offing, this argument could suggest a return to the traditional department store. But there are what physicists call irreversible processes. We suspect that wistful recreational shopping is for dreamers, not for those who remember the past. In any event, department stores do not make much money from those who are "just looking" and really mean it.

Folk wisdom tells us that there are always some people who do well, no matter how bad things get. There are many corporations listed on the New York Stock Exchange that never missed a dividend throughout the Great Depression of the 1930s. According to this view, the market for luxuries never disappears. But folk wisdom also says, "You always have to eat even though you can do without a new powerboat," or, in other words, the more basic retailers are more recession-proof. In some past recessions luxury retailers have remained relatively immune compared to the pressures on more popular priced outlets.

This may be changing. Problems in the financial, brokerage, and real estate community look disturbing to part of the upscale retail market for at least the short run. The 1990 budget/tax debate may be a harbinger of a more redistributive fiscal policy. Obviously the 1992 election will tell us more about the national mood. A trend toward more income disparity, however, unless eased, is likely to fuel political drives for redistribution.

While there are figures that say, in effect, "the wealthy are getting wealthier," and we see that as a potential long-term political problem for upscale retailing, there may be another paradoxical problem—not enough wealthy. In addition to the current difficulties of particular higher income groups mentioned above, we must ask just how much income is out there.

According to figures presented by Danzinger and Gottschalk (1988-89), the top 5 percent of American households had an average annual income of about $148,000. More specifically, the top 20 percent of American households, those who control about 45 percent of the nation's income, we find that average household income was about $98,000. Those are means, not medians, but the nature of the statistic is such that we can assume at least half of the households in those categories were below those means. By historic or world standards, that is still enormous affluence. Yet what does that mean in discretionary retail spending power after paying taxes, mortgage, and credit card finance charges and sending the kids to college? At a time when many retailers want to stress designer and bridge lines, we must ask how many four-digit dresses can a six-digit income family afford? Only 60,000 tax return filers reported income in excess of one million dollars last year. Are too many designer lines chasing too few wallets? (Admittedly some luxury-line display is primarily intended to help sell more moderately priced goods. But we still wonder whether there are enough carriages to accommodate everyone who wants to cater to the carriage trade.) The chairman of Montgomery Ward & Co., in explaining his firm's rebound, says, "There is an enormous market in middle-income America that has been abandoned by other retailers" (*New York Times,* December 11, 1990). At J. C. Penney Co., vice-chairman William Gill says, "Designer labels, upscaling and higher prices will be far less important" (Barmash 1990). Dayton-Hudson Company suggests that the Target discount store division will play the largest role in its expansion plans for the next five years and the mid-price Mervyn's division will be next. *Business Week* recently reported that many upscale retailers are now looking toward the great mass of lower-income consumers (December 3, 1990). Montgomery Ward may soon have considerable company in the middle market. In essence, we are suggesting a ratcheting down of American retailing.

There is also a follow-the-leader tendency in retailing. For a long time it was a question of trying to out-Bloomingdale Bloomingdales. Now attention focuses on Nordstroms. In a slow economy many retailers are attracted to the idea of vastly increased emphasis on sales incentives. One question, and it is a very serious question, is whether this will lead to an overemphasis on high pressure selling. Just as the researchers who tried to survey corporate policy on dealing with the problems of workaholics received many responses asking where workaholics could be found, many retailers would like to find salespeople who want to sell. But in the 1930s the pressure practices tended to alienate customers and led to internal rivalries that eventually were dysfunctional. The suggestion would be that one carefully examine corporate culture, to use a current buzzword, and management style before borrowing another firm's approach lock, stock, and barrel.

In short, we see some modification, possibly a hiatus, in the expansionary trend in American retailing. Large-scale mass retailing seems relatively well positioned. Many of the forces that fueled retail growth are now weakening or even reversing. We can talk about strategies, and the market will remain diverse and complex enough to support a variety of strategies. But attention to the tactics of having the right merchandise at the right price at the right time offered in the right manner, as platitudinous as that sounds, will be increasingly important. The period ahead will not be easy.

SUMMARY

The following points summarize our conclusions from reviewing trends in mass merchandising and traditional retailing.

- Real (adjusted for inflation) retail sales "in toto" and per capita have grown substantially since World War II. But retail sales growth is likely to slow in the years ahead. Per-capita real sales may actually decline.
- The variety and complexity of formats within the retail structure have increased and probably will continue to increase.
- The market share of the single-unit enterprise, still substantial, will probably continue to decline. Those businesses will generally need to find some special locational, operating, or merchandising niche in order to prosper. Conversely, multiunit market share growth is likely to continue.
- Some retail chains will face the danger of becoming overly centralized.
- The political climate probably will not be particularly hostile to multi-units even though there are one or two ominous signs on the horizon.
- Chain store price competition will probably increase.
- Large-scale conglomeration, that is, diversification at the major enterprise level, developed and grew in the American retail trade after 1960. It may continue to grow, but to date its managerial and economic implications have received little study.
- Retail concentration will probably increase, at least in some lines of business.
- Some new internationalization may be expected, but little net growth. Currently, foreign investment in U.S. retailing substantially exceeds U.S. investment in foreign retailing.

- Although the conventional department store industry seems most concerned about specialty store competition, it has lost much of its market share to mass market generalists. There are limits to the department store strategy of retreat into very heavy emphasis on upscale female apparel.
- Mass-market generalists, such as mass merchandisers and particularly discount department stores, should remain strong.
- Wholesale warehouse membership clubs will continue to grow. The format, however, does have its limitations.
- Mass-market specialists or category killers will take on increased importance in many nonfashion lines.
- Suburban malls and centers will remain important, especially for apparel-based shopping. Some shakeout is likely.
- The chain supermarket business looks quite stable, but the franchised fast-food industry may be facing severe problems.
- Although the volume of nonstore retailing has been growing in recent years, it still constitutes a very small percentage of total retail trade.
- In general, falling worker income and limits on the number of workers per household will limit retail growth.
- An overstoring problem has to be resolved.

REMARKS

Donald J. Stone

For years we have been reading and hearing about the demise of traditional retailing, especially department store retailing. Indeed, it has been predicted that by the year 2000 a majority of consumers will not be shopping in traditional stores. I, though, am skeptical of such overly broad, simplistic, and perhaps premature generalizations. Such generalizations are, if anything, greatly exaggerated. All one has to do is go to a shopping mall on any Saturday afternoon and notice how many young individuals, especially females, are in the mall. If young people still enjoy the experience of shopping, is there any reason to assume that, as they reach their 20s and 30s when they traditionally spend large portions of their income for apparel, they will not shop in the future much as they have in the past? After all, prior behavior still remains the best predictor of future behavior.

We have obviously seen a great increase in catalog sales, telephone selling, and other forms of direct selling, but the impact of that increase, coming as it does from an extremely low base, only accounts for a miniscule percentage of total retail sales. Even more interesting is the almost total lack of success that shopping by television has experienced. Ten years ago, we at Federated invested our corporation's money in a new shop-by-television company just so we would be in on the ground floor if this form of retailing had a future. We even had one of our corporate executives put on the board of this new company so we would not miss a trick. Five years later, with no success in sight, we sold our share of that company after making the decision that nothing was going to happen of importance in electronic shopping during our business lifetimes.

The fact of the matter is that department stores' share of apparel purchases has grown rather dramatically. Census Bureau data reveal that from 1980 to 1988 (which are the last figures I had), department stores' share of the apparel market (not the total market) grew from 15.9 to 18.9 percent while department stores' share of GAF sales remained relatively stable, going from 11 percent to 11.8 percent. As all observers are aware, the department store industry has rearranged itself to focus less on home furnishings and totally exiting businesses such as toys, books, garden equipment, and so forth. The change in Penney's strategy exemplifies the move into apparel with great visibility.

Further, it is perhaps not too surprising that for many lines of merchandise, including most categories of men's and women's apparel, accessories, cosmetics, and even the better-quality end of home furnishings, the traditional department store still remains the *preferred place* to shop. This preference is stronger among upper-income households (the top 50 percent) that control about three-quarters of the nation's purchasing power and form the bulk of department stores' business.

Finally, it is important to note that traditional department stores currently control the best retail locations in all of the nation's shopping malls. I do not see any way this can or will change in the foreseeable future. What all of the above says to me is that traditional forms of retailing, as we know them today, will be around in the year 2000 and most likely will be around for many more years after that.

There will obviously continue to be evolutionary changes. One must not be misled by what has happened to retailing in the past five years or so. In the long run these changes will probably be viewed as "blips" or perhaps even as aberrations in the history of retailing. Certainly great changes have taken place recently with great speed. These changes did not come about because of pressures from consumers, but because of pressures from LBO-created debt. Many department stores—like other major entities in this country in the 1980s—provided a mechanism for people to get instantly rich. Unfortunately, the people who got rich were not the retailers but the lawyers and the investment bankers. Many department store organizations simply got caught with too much debt. Consequently, they are having to do things differently.

Change—evolution—is inevitable and must be faced by all retailers. Weak companies will go out of business whereas strong companies will become stronger. There will continue to be "smaller" retail companies that become quite large. Dillard Department Stores is a wonderful example of that. Dillard was a tiny, one-store operation in Arkansas that gradually acquired other retailers that were not performing well. Eventually it became a dominating force in retailing. (As an aside, one of the secrets to Dillard's success, in addition to the fact that it has by far the best computerized information system in the industry, is the fact that it is the largest customer of almost all of its major suppliers. For example, Dillard's is Estee Lauder's largest customer.)

Similarly, look at what happened to Nordstrom in the past ten years. Nordstrom began as a family-owned shoe store in Seattle and until recently was only in the Pacific Northwest. When Nordstrom opened its first remote store in South Coast Plaza in Los Angeles, conventional wisdom was unanimous: it was inconceivable that a department store could be successful in a market like Los Angeles with only one unit. It made it very, very well. Nordstrom has a unique strategy that has worked well every place it has located. After moving into a center in Washington, D.C. (again, only one store), it did twice as much sales volume in the first year as a Bloomingdale store was doing in that center after ten years.

Not only do Dillard and Nordstrom illustrate the constant evolution traditional retailers are going through. They also illustrate that there are many different ways to succeed in retailing. Consider the following examples of well-known retailing companies. Each has achieved its success through a very different mechanism.

Penney's has evolved from being a traditional chain department store to being a fashion department store. Its strategy appears to be working, certainly a great deal better than Sears' strategy or lack of strategy.

It is possible that The Limited will become a new form of "department store" within the next ten years as it combines its various separate units into one shopping experience. The Limited started out as a niche marketer whose distinctive competency lay in its distribution system. Driven by technology, The Limited created the most efficient way of planning, buying, and distributing merchandise that has been done to my knowledge in the retail business. It has manufacturing facilities in the Far East and even bought its own airplane to transport merchandise from the Far East to a huge warehouse in Columbus. By doing so it has been able to reduce by 60 to 80 percent the time the rest of us in the business were experiencing when we were doing business overseas or when we were buying the product at the source instead of through a manufacturer or middleman.

The Dayton-Hudson Corporation may be the only large retailing organization that has positioned itself to cover the market from one end to the other with Target, Mervyn's, and its department stores. This is even more true now that it has acquired Marshall Field. One needs to applaud the May Company's performance as a very centrally driven department store aimed almost exclusively at the middle market.

As I have mentioned Federated's competitors, I want to hasten to add that I do believe Federated/Allied Department Stores will emerge from Chapter 11 and again become a successful publicly owned, traditional department store company. Even after losing Foley's and Filene's to the May Company and Bullock's and I. Magnin to Macy's, Federated/Allied still retains many of the top department store businesses in the country. Once it is able to get out from under the debt imposed on it by Campeau, it should again be a dominant competitor.

In brief, I have great confidence in the future of traditional retailing. It has changed and it will continue to change, but the change will be evolutionary, not revolutionary. One of the reasons I have always found the department store business to be so exciting is that a department store, by its very nature, can change itself rather quickly to represent the changing needs of its customers. It can become more upscale or more promotional. It can feature apparel or emphasize home furnishings. It can change in the future just as many times as it has changed in the past. For that reason and all of the others I have mentioned, I believe that traditional retailing, as we have known it, will be around in the year 2000. It will be pretty much the way it is today and it will still be the dominant form of retailing by a wide margin.

5

The Direct/Database Marketing Challenge to Fixed-Location Retailers

Don E. Schultz

Over the past twenty years, the growth of direct marketing in the United States (defined here as products sold through various media channels such as catalogs, direct mail, broadcast, telephone, magazines, newspapers, and the like, rather than fixed-location retailers) has been phenomenal. Although no exact figures are available, Fishman (1990) estimates that mail-order sales only now exceed $183.3 billion, up 11.5 percent in just the last year. If we were to include all forms of direct marketing, the figure would doubtless be double or perhaps triple that. Because sales have grown so dramatically, direct marketers have become household names and even major national brands such as Spiegel, L. L. Bean, Eddie Bauer, Time-Life Books, and so on.

While the value of products sold directly may appear small now, when compared to traditional fixed-location retailing, the trends of change are clear. There is also strong evidence that direct-marketing volume will increase dramatically in the next ten years. The growth, however, will come mainly from a new form of direct marketing, database marketing. Indeed, direct/database marketing could become the dominant form of retailing by the year 2010.

In this chapter, three topics will be covered. Initially a description and definition of present-day direct marketing and the newer forms of database marketing will be presented. Then, four major trends/factors that will create the growth of direct/database marketing and marketplace change will be discussed. Finally, specific predictions regarding the changes that can be expected to occur in the next ten years in direct/database marketing will be developed.

DIRECT AND DATABASE MARKETING DEFINED

Traditional, or what will be termed classical, direct marketing is defined by the Direct Marketing Association as "an interactive system of marketing which uses one or more advertising media to effect a measurable response and/or transaction at any location" (Stone 1988, p. 3). This definition is important in understanding the changes that are occurring in traditional direct marketing and the impact they will have on the future marketplace. It is also clear that the Direct Marketing Association (DMA) is attempting to move beyond the common understanding of direct marketing, which has been primarily catalog and mail-order selling, and into new areas of marketing and exchange between consumers and what are now called retailers, manufacturers, wholesalers, and the like.

While the Direct Marketing Association (DMA) definition is very broad, it allows us to differentiate direct marketing from what, in this chapter, will be called fixed-location retailing. Fixed-location retailing is defined as an establishment, store, or warehouse where goods are gathered, stored, and offered for sale. In most cases, customers come to the fixed location to select from the assortment and make purchases.

Database marketing, which will change the methods of retailing in the future, not only in the United States but around the world, is defined as a strategic and conceptional extension and refinement of traditional direct marketing. In database marketing, the marketer collects or purchases behavioral, demographic, psychological, sociological, attitudinal and other bits and pieces of information, background, and history on individual customers or households that it either already serves or would like to serve. This information is captured and stored in an electronic database that can be instantaneously updated and amended. This information can then be used by the marketer to develop more specific, effective, and efficient marketing programs. Generally, database information is used to help identify, classify, and profile individual customers. This enables the marketer to develop more effective product offerings, pricing strategies, and communication programs and improves its skill at product timing and delivery. With the database information, the marketer can develop forms of two-way communication with each individual customer. Thus, a buyer-seller relationship is created.

The database therefore becomes the backbone of the business. It is not only the framework around which the business plans, but also the basis for all ongoing and future activity. Perhaps the most important change database marketing creates is an opportunity to know and understand the customers who make up the business or the prospects who might be encouraged to become customers of the business. This is obviously a dramatic change from the merchant-driven approach that has traditionally dominated retailing. By having extensive information on each individual customer or prospect, the database marketer can avoid many of the pitfalls of traditional retailing such as overstock, out-of-stock, markdowns, inventory adjustments, poor customer service, and the like. It is this major change from merchant to marketer that will dominate the field of retailing in the 1990s and beyond.

Database marketing as defined can be used by traditional direct marketers, by fixed-location retailers, and by other newer retail marketing systems that will be discussed later. Although it might be possible for some present fixed-location retailers to move to direct/database marketing, most traditional direct marketers and fixed-location retailers are so wedded to their systems that they will have great difficulty, both physical and philosophical, in converting to database marketing systems. Therefore, direct/database marketers will largely replace traditional retailers and become the dominant force in the marketplace.

The differences between traditional or classical direct marketing and the new form of database marketing are important to understand, for they explain why direct/database marketing will supersede classical direct marketing and even fixed-location retailing in the years ahead. These differences are highlighted in Table 5.1.

Table 5.1. Differences between Classical Direct Marketing and Database Marketing

Classical Direct Marketing	Database Marketing
• Broad appeal products	• Specialized, niche, or personalized products
• Lists based on response or affinity	• Customer/prospect file
• Mass mailings or broadcasts	• Personalized communication
• Common offers	• Targeted offers
• Immediate response	• Relationships
• Single impressions	• Continuous communication

As can be seen, present-day or classical direct marketing is essentially just another media form for the practice of mass marketing. Currently most direct marketers use the same approaches as fixed-location retailers, that is, they attempt to have a fairly wide range of products, although the products may be in a specialized category. They then attempt to sell these products through catalog, direct mail, or telemarketing systems to a broad audience. They rely on common offers through catalogs or mailings and seek an essentially immediate response in the form of a purchase.

Alternatively, database marketers tend to offer a more specialized type of product selected on the database characteristics of the customers they hope to serve. The offers are more targeted, that is, they are personalized based on information that the marketer has collected or that the customer has provided. Although there is an interest in achieving an immediate sale, the database marketer is more interested in developing a lasting business relationship with the customer rather than simply achieving a one-time-only sale.

While database marketers can use direct marketing, classical direct marketers generally make very little use of database marketing. Database marketing, as the extension and replacement of traditional direct marketing, is the key element in the changes that are predicted to occur in the next ten years.

DISTRIBUTION AND RETAILING REVISITED

To understand how direct/database marketing will affect traditional fixed-location retailers, it is necessary to briefly review the basic principles of distribution and retailing. Traditionally, distribution channels have provided the functions of buying and assorting, bulk-breaking, warehousing, transporting, financing, risk bearing, market information gathering, selling, promoting, and various forms of management services. Often these channels have been populated by independent organizations that have provided these services to manufacturers and processors and finally to ultimate consumers (e.g., Kotler 1983, p. 420).

The functions of retailers in the channel have been to assemble merchandise, maintain an inventory, price, promote, advertise, sell, and account for the merchandise, again as a service to the manufacturer and the ultimate consumer. Further, retailers have also provided a place for consumers to shop and find other services that might assist them in obtaining or using the available goods (Duncan, Hollander, and Savitt 1983, p. 4).

The channel systems that have developed and, granted, have been improved over the years, have been built on some very basic beliefs about consumers, their needs and wants, and what they are willing to accept from channel members. It is these basic marketplace assumptions that are being challenged by direct and database marketers. If the assumptions on which our channel systems have been built are no longer valid, can the marketplace system we have devised over the past hundred years or so continue?

For the most part, it is technology that is changing and will change the marketplace, the channels, and the systems that have been developed. We now look at some of the marketplace assumptions that have created the system presently in place. We will then review some of the challenges to these assumptions that will result in the major predicted changes.

A basic tenet of fixed-location retailing has been the "wheel of retailing" as conceived by McNair in the 1950s. The "wheel" suggests that retailing is an evolutionary process. Retail formats emerge and evolve as a result of economies of scale, pricing, and margin adjustments, plus location and amenities offered. As competition increases, these retail formats evolve upward and more efficient forms develop. Thus, the cycle is repeated (Samli 1989, pp. 42-47). The basic assumptions of the wheel of retailing are that the merchant is king and that a mass market exists. Both of these assumptions perhaps appear flawed when we look at what will occur in the 1990s.

The "merchant is king" concept assumes that merchants know more about consumer likes and dislikes and needs and wants than do the consumers themselves. It at least implicitly assumes that merchants have more information and control over the marketplace than do consumers. If this was true in the past, it was because the manufacturer and then the retailer controlled the sources of product and market information. Information gave these institutions power over the consumer in the marketplace. Now that information system has changed. Marketplace information and thus control are now in the hands of the consumer. Today, because of technology, consumers have access to massive amounts of information that allow them to make their own decisions more effectively and efficiently than when they relied on the manufacturer or retailer. This change is illustrated in Figure 5.1.

Figure 5.1. The New Information Power Paradigm

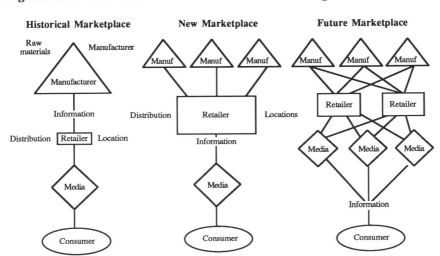

This change in the diffusion of information has much to do with the demise of the mass market. As consumers gain information, they become aware of more and more marketplace and product alternatives. The resultant demand for more specialized and personalized products erodes the traditional mass market. It is this change in information availability and access that is at the root of many of the changes that are coming in retailing.

The wheel of retailing has been recently challenged by May (1990) and others (e.g., Brown 1990). They argue that social and environmental changes in consumers drive the changes in retailing, rather than the activities and adaptations of the institutions. Certainly the information power shift just described would support their view. Technology is obviously part of the environment and will increasingly be so in the future. The more important question, however, is whether, if retailers do respond to consumers (and indeed they must), will the development of direct/database marketing as a separate activity will be an evolutionary or a revolutionary process. Fixed-location retailers might evolve into direct/database marketers, as Saks, Bloomingdale's, Nieman-Marcus, and others are attempting to do today. More likely, though, is that the changes in consumers, the environment, technology, and the marketplace will be so great that the impact of direct/database marketing on traditional fixed-location retailing will be more revolutionary than evolutionary. The argument that the consumer, rather than the institution, drives the retailing wheel is central to this position.

There are other arguments as well for the revolutionary perspective. Because of the massive investment in present retailing operations, particularly in real estate and fixtures, it will be particularly difficult for existing fixed-location retailers to give up their present operations. These assets, along with their inventory, are essentially the basic value of their businesses.

Thus, most fixed-location retailers will find it an almost devastating economic blow to close, reduce, or change their basic business form. Direct/database marketers will supersede fixed-location retailers because the assets of the direct/database marketers in the future will be based on the stream of income from their customer base. These expected and anticipated incomes, resulting from transactions, will be valued and managed tomorrow just as the fixed assets of retail locations and fixtures and inventory are today. Once this basic concept of customers as assets is adopted, it becomes apparent that, in the traditional economic sense, mass marketing and mass retailing will probably no longer be viable commercial enterprises. With these distinctions between present day fixed-location retailing, classical direct marketing, and the emerging direct/database approaches to retailing in mind, the case can then be built for the rather dramatic structural changes that will occur in retailing, first in the next ten years and more extensively in the next twenty.

FOUR WATERSHED CHANGES

In the past fifteen to twenty years there have been four major economic/social changes that have had, and will continue to have, a dramatic impact on the domestic U.S. marketplace. These changes, the principal driving forces that will cause the shift from fixed-location to direct/database marketing, include changes in consumers, changes in manufacturing, changes in manufacturer-retailer relationships, and changes in the economics of fixed-location and database marketing.

Consumers and Consumer Market Composition

Changes in the makeup of the consumer marketplace in the United States have been well documented. Major demographic, sociographic and psychographic changes that began in the 1960s are still being felt today. The dramatic sociological changes of the 1970s and 1980s are just now beginning to be understood. In essence, the U.S. marketplace has moved from one of growth to what might be called maturity. There is slower economic growth and an almost stagnant population. The economic system is reflecting the move from cash to credit. Major deficits are a way of life for the government and many commercial organizations. We still have an almost constantly changing and fluid social system. Six major consumer trends will likely fuel the drive toward direct/database marketing and away from fixed-location retailing.

Population Growth. The first trend is slow to no population growth. In the period from 1980 to 1990, the total U.S. population increased by 10.1 percent. Projections are that during the period 1990 to 2000 it will increase by only 7.1 percent. Thus, overall population growth is slowing; but perhaps more important, the growth of specific segments of the population that are critical to retailers will decline. For example, those 18 to 24 years olds will decline from 13 percent of the population in 1980 to only 9 percent by the year 2000. Those between the ages of 25 and 34 will decline by 15.5 percent compared to 1980 (Ambry 1989).

As retailers move from their traditional growth strategy to one based more on maintenance, holding on to present customers becomes one of the most important ingredients for success. For the most part, in a mass market situation, retailers have neither known who their customers were, nor did they need to. Retailers were driven by the need for volume brought about by self-service and nonpersonal merchandising. As in-depth knowledge of the customer becomes more important in product selection, merchandising, and customer retention, direct/database marketers, simply because of their supply of behavioral and attitudinal information on households and individuals, will be much better positioned to adapt and adjust to this new marketplace than will fixed-location retailers.

Time.   A second major trend is that time is becoming more important than money to many consumers.   For the most part, this trend is fueled by the increasing numbers of two-income households where both the man and wife work full time outside the home.   Currently, for example, 94 percent of the men and 76 percent of the women between the ages of 25 and 34 work full-time outside the home.   In the 35 to 44 age group, 96 percent of the men and 74 percent of the women hold full-time jobs (Ambry 1989).

As a result of this full-time employment situation, convenience, rather than price, will dominate consumer purchasing processes.   With the multitude of methods and ways in which direct/database marketers can serve the consumer, often at the convenience of the consumer, they will have major marketplace advantages over fixed-location retailers.

Age.   Third, an aging population will demand better access to the marketplace in ways that recognize their declining mobility.   From 1990 to the year 2000, the number of Americans aged 75 and up will increase by 27 percent.   This group will account for more than 6 percent of the total population by the year 2000 (Ambry 1989).

These individuals will increasingly seek and demand retailing systems that provide access to the marketplace.   Direct/database marketing, with its off-site product availability and in-home ordering and purchasing capability, will have greater appeal to this increasing number of older consumers than will traditional fixed-location retailers.

Crime.   Crime is on the rise.   This is of concern to almost all population segments but particularly to the elderly.   We have already seen the impact of this concern in the demise of evening shopping, not only in cities but in smaller towns as well.   As consumers become more concerned about their own safety and well-being, they will likely increasingly accept the lower-risk methods of shopping from their homes and offices through direct/database marketing rather than from fixed-location retailers operating in the open marketplace.

Income Polarization.   Traditionally, the income distribution in the United States has bulged in the middle with relatively few people at either the high or low ends.   Thus, we developed the great middle-American market, where movement up the social and economic ladder was not only possible but probable.   Presently, though, there are relatively more high-income and low-income households and fewer middle-income households than in the past (Ambry 1989).

The mid-range household has traditionally been the backbone of the mass market fixed-location retailers sought to serve. As the middle-income group shrinks, there is more and more emphasis on differentiated products and services that are demanded by upper-income consumers. Traditional fixed-location retailers such as department stores and mass merchandisers will find it increasingly difficult to serve this growing group. Simultaneously, there will likely be more opportunities for direct/database marketers because of their ability to identify, segment, and market to the various income groups. The more flexible operations of direct/database marketers allow them to shift not only product lines but market positions much easier than fixed-location retailers.

Ethnicity. Major ethnic population shifts are occurring. For example, the total U.S. population between the ages of 35 and 44 is expected to increase by 8.8 percent between 1990 and 2000. During this period, the number of whites in this age group will grow by only 3.2 percent, blacks will increase by 14.6 percent, Hispanics by 38.6 percent, and Asians by 40.1 percent (Ambry 1989). As this illustrates, the composition of the U.S. population is shifting markedly. While fixed-location retailers can respond to these ethnic changes, they are not nearly as flexible as direct/database marketers. Thus, the changing ethnic population will likely create opportunities for direct/database marketers and challenges for fixed-location retailers.

Manufacturers and Market Structure

There have been and will continue to be dramatic shifts in the manufacturing of products and the market structures used to bring these products to consumers in the United States. Increasingly U.S. manufacturers and marketers will be affected by the global marketplace. The changes this increased competition creates will be accelerated. What we will likely see in the global marketplace will be dramatically different in the year 2000 from what we know today. Most of these changes will work to the advantage of the direct/database marketer and against the fixed-location retailer. Four of these changes are briefly overviewed here.

Increased Global Marketing. Improved and enhanced distribution and communications systems have made global marketing not only possible but a reality. The possibility and potential for direct manufacturer-consumer communication, interaction, and exchange from anywhere in the world continues to grow. Global marketing will likely have two major impacts on fixed-location retailers. First, as markets diffuse, it will become more and more difficult for fixed-location retailers to compete on a global scale. Thus, the small-town merchant, unless it is connected to or has a relationship with very large product sources, will increasingly be at a selection and price disadvantage relative to larger and more sophisticated competitors. We already see this disadvantage occurring in small towns across the country in the form of store closings. Because direct/database marketers are able to source, sell, and compete wherever they choose, they will have a dramatic advantage over most fixed-location retailers.

Further, it may well be that direct/database marketing will be a more attractive form of retailing for third world and developing countries. For the most part, these countries do not have the investment capital necessary to establish market infrastructures needed to support fixed-location retailing. Thus, it may be that direct/database marketing, if only because of the lower capital requirements, may become the retailing form of choice for new businesses around the world.

Demise of the Mass Market. As was discussed earlier, technology and communication allow consumers to learn about and demand increasingly differentiated and even personalized products. As this occurs, the traditional economies of scale that have accrued to those manufacturers and retailers with extensive facilities and large sales volumes are no longer important in the marketplace. Smaller companies, using technology and direct and database marketing approaches, can compete not only effectively, but in many cases more efficiently than can large companies. As technology expands and CAD-CAM manufacturing and sales-driven inventorying become more prevalent, the balance will shift to direct/database marketers simply because of their ability to respond more quickly and more effectively to consumer demand.

Marketplace Surplus. In the United States, as in Europe and Japan, there is now a surplus of products, distribution systems, and retail space. This will likely continue into the foreseeable future. The natural result of this oversupply situation is increasing emphasis on price competition and discounting at all channel levels. Indeed, many marketplaces are reaching or will soon reach a stage of disarray; traditional retailers will find they can no longer compete and will simply close their doors. We see the beginnings of this today in the department store field where high debt ratios force reduced prices and margins to generate cash flow. Reduced prices and margins result in further demands for volume, which can be achieved only through lower prices and margins. So the spiral continues.

The marketplace in the 1990s will be the result of the chaotic system that developed in the past decade. The development of this "surplus marketplace" is illustrated in Figure 5.2.

Figure 5.2. The Surplus Marketplace

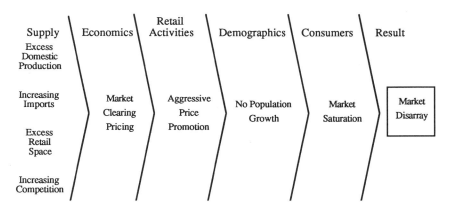

There is little question that declining margins will result in a major restructuring of present distribution systems and that it will have particular impact on fixed-location retailers. Because direct/database marketers are free to market wherever and whenever there is demand and to move with that demand, they will enjoy major advantages over fixed-location retailers in the coming years.

Marketplace Saturation. The oversupply situation illustrated above has resulted in almost saturation levels for many products and even product categories. Long-term economic prosperity in the United States, Western Europe, and the Asia-Pacific Rim, along with the prevailing discounting tendency of retailers, declining real costs of many products due to technological innovation, and the availability of easy credit have persuaded consumers to purchase almost up to their capacity. In fact, many consumers simply cannot consume more in some product categories. The traditional demand curve can even be questioned in certain instances.

An assumption of classical economics is that there will always be more consumer demand than supply. Thus, if the price of a product is lowered sufficiently, market demand should always clear the supply. The problem today is that manufacturers and marketers have built their businesses on the concept of mass production and economies of scale. Plants are constructed to maximize return by operating at full capacity. If they are operated at less than full capacity, the cost per unit produced rises. Many manufacturers and even fixed-location retailers operate on this concept. They must keep producing or selling or merchandising even if there is no demand simply to hold down unit costs and remain competitive.

In a saturated market, however, even reducing price to the point where margins disappear no longer generates sales volume. So the produce, discount, produce, discount spiral is built and continues. For many fixed-location retailers, the problem is compounded by the fact that in saturated categories, hefty price reductions and resulting margin declines do not generate sales. For the most part, it is the traditional retailer that is caught in this nonprofit spiral. Direct/database marketers, because of their flexibility, knowledge of consumers, and ability to move from market to market, have major advantages over fixed-location retailers in saturated situations.

The result of these four factors has been an increasing move to niching and market selectivity by retailers and manufacturers. This has put even more power in the hands of consumers. Thus, consumer demand truly is driving and will continue to drive the marketplace in the years ahead. Manufacturers and channel members will have less and less control over their businesses and will be forced to respond more effectively and quickly to consumer demands. Direct and database marketers will have major advantages over fixed-location retailers in this type of marketplace.

Manufacturer and Retailer Relationships

Three factors are changing the traditional methods of operation and relationships between manufacturers and retailers. These changes will have major impacts on the way all forms of retailing are conducted in the 21st century. These factors are reviewed here.

Retail Consolidation and Concentration. Powerful fixed-location retailers such as food and drug chains, mass merchandisers, department stores, building supplies, automobile dealerships, and the like are changing the relationship between the manufacturer and the channel members in the U.S. marketplace. The prime example of this change is the growth of what is called category killers. Organizations such as Toys "R" Us, Circuit City, and Office Depot are gaining control over their suppliers. Where once the manufacturer had control, today it is the powerful retailers with major market shares who are demanding and gaining concessions from the manufacturer. Because of the power of technology, logistics, and marketing expertise, we will likely see more and more of this domination of the manufacturer by the retailer.

In an effort to control their own futures, as retailers become more powerful and more demanding in the marketplace, manufacturers will form alliances or consolidate and concentrate to protect themselves in an attempt to develop some sort of market equilibrium. We have already seen indications of this by the actions of Philip Morris, Sara Lee, Pepsico, and others in their mergers and acquisitions.

The other alternative open to manufacturers to counter the power of retailers is to develop increasing expertise through various forms of direct/database marketing. Already we see these kinds of programs being developed by Kraft General Foods, Quaker Oats, R. J. Reynolds, and others. As manufacturers gain experience and expertise in direct/database marketing, there will be more and more emphasis on direct manufacturer-to-consumer marketing approaches.

Manufacturing Technology. Increased and improved manufacturing technology using robotics, new materials, CAD-CAM, and the like have made it possible for manufacturers to perfect just-in-time inventory and manufacturing-on-demand approaches to serve their markets. Although these technologies are currently being used primarily to improve the operation of current channels and distribution networks, there is little question that they have numerous applications in direct/database marketing.

Bicycle manufacturers traditionally made a fairly narrow range of bicycles, limiting themselves to a few styles and colors. They relied primarily on economies of scale to produce the bicycles at a low cost that provided the necessary channel margins. They then offered their production to bicycle dealers who stocked and sold the bicycles to consumers who came to their shop. If a dealer did not have the particular bicycle the consumer wanted, the consumer generally went to another store and continued the search until a suitable bicycle was found.

Today, however, it is possible, through CAD-CAM engineering and robotics, to custom-build bicycles in about two weeks using a series of basic units. An almost infinite variety of bicycles can be efficiently produced on demand. Rather than selling the bicycles to dealers who would then stock and display them, it is now possible for the manufacturer to deal directly with the final consumer. There is little reason for a dealer to be involved in the sale of a personalized bicycle. It is really a transaction between the manufacturer and the ultimate consumer. While this is a hypothetical example, all the necessary technology is already in place. It requires only that the manufacturer communicate with the consumer about the availability of the custom-made bicycle for the link to be complete.

This new ability by the manufacturer to build on demand will have major impacts on the relationships between the manufacturer, the retailer, and the consumer. It will reduce the value of economies of scale on which most manufacturers have relied for competitive advantage. It will reduce the experience curve to nothing more than an academic concept. It will allow quick and nimble manufacturers, particularly those having strong ties to their ultimate customer through direct marketing and databases, to distribute and retail directly. It will reduce the need for manufacturers to have complex channel associations and distribution patterns, as they will be integrating forward toward the ultimate customer.

Retail Inventory Changes. One of the major changes in retailing, particularly fixed-location retailing, has been for the retailer to attempt to reduce inventory continuously by pushing that responsibility back up the channel. Today, many retailers select suppliers on the basis of their willingness to accept the inventory responsibility and their capability in meeting tight and demanding deadlines for product delivery.

As manufacturers become more skilled at logistics and distribution systems in response to retailers' demands, they will soon be able to handle the entire process themselves. When that occurs, the manufacturer will likely ask the question: "Why am I doing all this for the benefit of the retailer? If I have the skills and abilities to handle inventory and orders, why not turn it to my advantage and deal directly with the final customer rather than through some type or form of retail outlet?"

These changes in logistics and distribution all signal the increasing capability of the manufacturer to handle more and more of the traditional functions of channel members themselves. As the manufacturer becomes more adept at channel functions, there will be a natural move to absorb these activities internally, thus further expanding the use of direct/database marketing activities by the manufacturer and, in some cases, the wholesaler as well.

Economics of Fixed-Location Retailing and Database Marketing

The sheer economic viability of fixed-location retailing is declining in most areas. In the United States, three factors will increasingly shift the competitive advantage from traditional fixed-location retailers to direct/database marketing: crossing cost patterns, cost of energy and transportation, and desire for added value.

Crossing Cost Patterns. The cost of fixed-location retailing with respect to factors such as real estate, personnel, improvements, taxes, and the like will continue to escalate. As communities lose their established manufacturing tax bases and as resident demand for services continues, the burden of cost will likely be increasingly shifted to real estate taxes. This will have a major impact on the cost and profit structure of fixed-location retailers. Other operating costs will also continue to escalate. For example, the minimum wage will likely increase as will the cost of employee benefits. Costs of security will rise, and there will be increasing losses to theft and shoplifting. The major cost increase to fixed-location retailers, however, will be that of customer service. As competition intensifies, the retail battle will likely be fought in the arenas of promotion and customer service. As these costs grow, the margins for fixed-location retailers will be adversely affected.

In such situations, fixed-location retailers have only two choices: reduce margins or increase prices. Neither will enhance the economic viability of the operation.

Alternatively, direct/database costs will likely continue to decline as data capture, storage technology, and distribution logistics are improved. In addition, enhanced database analysis will likely not only lower the cost of marketing but also improve the effectiveness and efficiency. By the year 2000, there is little question that there will be definite economic and operational advantages to the direct/database marketer over the traditional fixed-location retailer.

Cost of Energy and Transportation. As the costs of energy and transportation increase, one might think the advantage would lie with the fixed-location retailer. Such is not likely to be the case.

Fixed-location retailers have traditionally required the consumer to bear the cost of search and product delivery from their central location. This system worked well when the mobility of the consumer was constantly increasing and the costs of that mobility in terms of transportation and energy costs were quite low. Today, increased energy costs, the cost of an automobile and its related upkeep, and the declining quality of the nation's transportation infrastructure all argue for a change in the consumer's attitudes toward product search, acquisition, and transportation. If and when fuel costs increase dramatically, there will probably be a rapid shift in the consumer's interest in shopping, product search, and transportation. When that occurs, there will be a dramatic impact on fixed-location retailers, especially on regional shopping malls and centers.

Because direct/database marketers make use of more economical forms of search, acquisition, and product delivery through various electronic and common carrier distribution systems, there will be an inherent economic advantage to them in the years ahead. Customers will initially change their traditional search and acquisition activities for frequently purchased replacement items. As they become successful at that, the use of direct/database marketing will grow. We can expect consumers to quickly shift their shopping patterns for more valuable and high involvement products. We already have seen dramatic growth of direct purchasing of furniture, clothing, jewelry, and even computer equipment by telephone and interactive computer. By 2000, purchasing all types of products through direct/database marketing will be common.

Added Customer Value. Traditionally, the fixed-location retailer has had an advantage over the direct/database marketer in terms of shopping ambiance, ability for consumers to physically inspect products, existence of wider assortments, and so on. In the future, as fixed-location retailing becomes more expensive and retailers thus become more resistant to making changes in their physical property, there will be advantages to the database marketer in terms of inventory, pricing, and distribution. These advantages will come about primarily as a result of greatly enhanced communication systems.

High definition television is only moments away, and interactive audio and video are not far behind. Technology is moving consumers more and more towards the acceptance of off-site shopping, working, and even socializing (witness the growth of electronic mail and other communication devices). As these technologies become increasingly accepted, we will likely see a growth curve for direct/database marketing similar to the one experienced with ATM cards. At first there was resistance; then came acceptance. Now consumers appreciate the value and convenience of all forms of financial transactions in a nonpersonal way. The same will occur with shopping and product acquisition.

As fixed-location retailers become more alike because of the similarity of stores and products, consumer values will likely shift from decisions being made on purely physical attributes of products and retailers to those that are more perceptual. We already have evidence of catalog marketers such as L. L. Bean, Spiegel, Tweeds, Jackson & Perkins, and Norm Thompson creating perceptual value for their products and services, which allows them to maintain images that would not be possible for traditional fixed-location retailers. Database marketers, with their continuous, two-way flow of communications programs, will have a major advantage over the more limited contact that fixed-location retailers can achieve either through personal contact or through various forms of costly mass media.

SOME CLOUDS ON THE HORIZON

While a strong case has been made for the growth and shift of retailing from fixed-location to direct/database marketing, some factors are on the horizon that might slow the timetable. In no way can they prevent the inevitable shift, but they could delay the impact somewhat beyond that predicted here. Four of these factors are delineated here.

Slowly Developing Distribution Systems

Currently fixed-location retailers enjoy a distribution advantage over direct/database marketers. Consumers can visit the store, make a purchase and receive instant gratification. Traditional direct marketers and many database marketers as well rely on the U.S. Postal Service, with all of its inherent problems and costs, for distribution and delivery. Although the Postal Service is attempting to improve, it is unlikely that its bureaucratic and labor problems can be overcome by automation and technology. Service will likely continue to decline and costs rise.

At some point, consumers will demand or the federal government will recognize the fallacy of the postal privacy acts and the monopoly position that the Postal Service enjoys. This will open the way for new, alternative distribution and delivery systems to develop and emerge. The opening of these new, direct-to-consumer distribution channels in the United States will have a major impact on the diffusion of direct/database marketing in this country. At this point in time, however, direct/database marketers are largely constrained by the existing distribution and delivery system of the U.S. Postal Service.

Cheap Energy

Energy in the United States is still relatively inexpensive. As the costs of transportation increase, however, the shift by consumers to direct purchasing and delivery from database marketers will increase. The cost of energy and resulting transportation will have a direct impact on the diffusion of the direct/database innovation. Suffice it to say, as long as we have low-cost energy, fixed-location retailing will survive. As costs increase, there will be a direct parallel with increased consumer interest in and use of direct/database delivery.

Privacy

There is increasing concern over the rights of privacy for U.S. citizens. Legislation or restrictions on the use of names obtained by outside sources and/or solicitation either through the mail or by telephone of noncustomers could delay the development of database capability. The major question is still that of outside information gathering, accumulation, and manipulation that is unknown to the consumer. There seems to be little question that a company with which the consumer chooses to do business will continue to be able to gather information on purchase behavior and other factors that will allow it to serve the customer better.

It is also likely that marketing companies will be willing to pay consumers a fee to receive permission to obtain and use this shopping information. In those cases, a contract between the consumer and the data gatherer or marketer is not likely to run afoul of even the most stringent privacy laws that might be enacted. Privacy legislation is likely to have much more impact on classical or traditional direct mailers than on direct/database organizations.

My view is that in the future there will be sufficient benefits to the consumer that he or she will be willing to give up a major portion of what is today considered private information to receive the benefits that direct/database marketing will bring. As increasing levels of product shopping, selection, and customer service are provided by the direct/database marketer, consumer resistance or concern about privacy will diminish.

Control of Communications

The development of new communications technologies such as Integrated Systems Data Networks (ISDN) will have a major impact on how information and contact between marketer and consumer is exchanged in the future. There is some chance that our traditional "free-or-low-cost-to-the-consumer" systems of communication such as newspapers, magazines, and broadcasting may be co-opted by cost-to-consumer-or-user systems such as ISDN, pay-TV, 900 telephone numbers, cable, and fax. Should this occur, there may be delays in the development of database marketing.

An increase in the cost of information to the consumer could have as much or more impact on the fixed-location retailer as on the direct/database marketer. Fixed-location retailers are successful because they are able to disseminate information about their products and location through relatively low-cost forms of advertising and communication. Should the cost of sales message distribution increase substantially, it would impose as much of a threat to them as it would to the direct/database marketer.

Although the above factors all might have an impact on the time schedule of the shift from fixed-location retailing to database/direct marketing, they will require only time adjustments for the shift. The result is inevitable.

SUMMARY OF PREDICTIONS

The result of the major societal, environmental, and economic factors on fixed-location retailing and traditional direct marketing are summarized as follows. First, the advent of database marketing as the dominant retail channel in the United States will be a revolution, not an evolution. The technological capabilities and the social and environmental changes are all being driven by the consumer and communications. The change may well be as dramatic as was the "revolution of democracy in Eastern Europe" and the fall of the Berlin Wall. As marketplace power shifts from the manufacturer and retailer to the consumer, the rise of direct/database marketing will follow directly.

Second, direct/database marketing will become the dominant mode of manufacturer-consumer exchange in the United States early in the 21st century. Direct/database marketing may occur more rapidly in Europe and Japan. This will be the direct result of more enlightened views of electronic communications and the government's involvement with the development of such systems. For example, the Minitel program in France, in which the government is a major contributor to the development of the systems, has put that country in the forefront of direct/database marketing capability. The other factor that will likely drive the development of direct/database marketing is the nature of product distribution systems. The development of the economic community in Europe will do much to expand and enhance the distribution systems that are presently in place. These will probably be driven more by technology and logistics than those in the past have been. All these factors work to the benefit of direct/database marketing and against traditional fixed-location retailing.

Third, traditional market-seeking, mass-marketing retailing approaches will disappear. These will be replaced by more focused, targeted, database-driven marketing programs where there is a known need or want recognized by both the buyer and the seller. This change in communication systems will have a severe effect on the cost and availability of mass media systems. As marketers become more targeted and focused in their efforts, this will have a dramatic impact on the availability and cost of traditional mass media such as newspapers and television. Costs will go up, and some of the vehicles will disappear. This will create additional promotional problems for traditional fixed-location retailers that rely on these forms of media to deliver sales messages to prospective customers.

Fourth, new distribution systems will be developed to create and service the database-driven marketplace. Many entrepreneurial endeavors will evolve to provide the distribution systems needed for direct/database marketers. Those that can be envisioned now include product distribution centers, which will be central locations where direct-ordered products can be picked up by consumers at their convenience if home or office delivery is not possible. There may well be boxes attached to houses and apartments, similar to the traditional milk delivery box, where products can be delivered and stored when the customer is not at home. In short, new types of delivery and distribution programs will emerge, all of which will be designed to make the purchasing and delivery of products selected by direct/database means more convenient than the present-day search-and-carry system consumers use with fixed-location retailers.

Fifth, backward integration by retailers and forward integration by manufacturers will boom. Manufacturers will integrate forward to get closer to their customers. We already have begun to see this with the growth of outlet stores. In the process, many of the traditional distribution channels will be shortened or perhaps even disappear. The goal of the marketer will be to sell directly from the manufacturing plant to the ultimate consumer.

Alternatively, some fixed-location retailers will likely integrate backwards to assure themselves of an adequate source of product supply. The difference will be that, as fixed-location retailers integrate back up the distribution channel, they will discover that being able to reduce channel members will result in greater profit margins for them. Thus, they will be increasingly inclined to shift more and more of their operations to direct/database marketing simply because it increases their profitability. We will likely see major organizations that provide a seamless flow of products and services from the manufacturing facility to the consumer with fewer and fewer stops in between than has been the case in the past. In short, all types of businesses will move towards the concept of direct/database marketing in the future.

Finally, new forms of trading companies or what will be called pure marketing organizations will develop. These organizations will simply be intermediaries between the manufacturer and the consumer. They will operate somewhat like present-day catalog companies but be much more extensive and offer wider selections and better service. These organizations will be strictly marketing operations. They will sell from manufacturers' inventories or on-demand production. They will be highly skilled in communication and logistics. While many will be independent, they may well hold equity positions in their suppliers. They will rely primarily on their database of customers and communications for market success.

In summary, the day of the traditional fixed-location retailer is limited. The functions these traditional channel members have provided are either no longer needed or can be collapsed without loss of customer service. The emphasis in the future marketplace will be on information and communication rather than on location, ambiance, assortment, or the other physical properties traditional retailers have provided.

Retailing will become direct/database marketing, and direct/database marketing will become retailing. There will be a seamless flow from manufacturer to consumer. Perceptual value developed through communication will replace physical location value in consumer acquisition of products. The 1980s and early 1990s have provided the high water market for traditional fixed-location retailing. Tomorrow, it will be direct/database marketing.

REMARKS

David Shepard

Succinctly stated, Dr. Schultz's thesis is that in the not-too-distant future direct/database marketing will be the dominant form of retailing. Although I agree that retailing will be significantly influenced by database marketing methodologies in the 1990s and beyond, I do not believe that database marketing is going to completely dominate fixed-location retailing. Direct/database marketing is going to capture a lot of sales dollars, but it is primarily going to be at the upper end of the market. To purchase through direct marketing, you have to be fairly literate and have a fair amount of money. However, it is not going to be a revolution; it is going to be an evolution.

Admittedly, there are a good number of products and services currently sold and delivered through fixed-location retail channels that could just as easily be ordered and delivered through direct marketing channels, that is, ordered by telephone, mail, or computer and delivered through the mail. And, to the extent that this occurs, I would expect to see these more efficient ordering and delivery systems eventually replacing the current retail structure.

Even so, the bulk of retail sales will continue to be executed by consumers behaving according to established shopping patterns, if for no other reason that the shopping experience is much more than simply a way to replenish consumed goods and services. Therefore, database marketing programs should be designed not to replace the retail experience, but to enhance it.

Assume that direct/database marketing currently captures 9 percent of the retail sales dollar. Further assume that it is going to double in size to 18 percent. But this growth is not going to come from the middle-income group and it is not going to come from the lower-income group. It is going to come from the upper-income group. Hence, to reiterate, direct/database marketing will grow, but there are some natural limitations on how big it will get.

If direct marketers are to double their sales, they will have to communicate to build relationships with upper-income consumers. Successful direct/database marketing requires building relationships with customers at an individual level. However, there is a limit as to the number of direct marketing relationships each consumer is willing to enter into. Therefore, retailers expecting to develop meaningful customer retention programs should have a clear understanding of their customers' current shopping habits and retail relationships and should design their programs to preclude competitive inroads. Both retailers and manufacturers can influence shopping patterns by strengthening their ties with customers through loyalty and/or retention programs built on the data contained in a marketing database. There is already considerable evidence of the power of database marketing from the travel and hotel industry.

However, at the present time the vast majority of retailers are woefully unaware of the opportunities offered by database marketing. This, though, will change as innovative retailers begin to experiment with database-driven promotions.

What is going to happen is change. Direct marketers are getting better and better at database marketing. They are going to be serious competition, but that competition is not too important. What is really important is that sophisticated, perhaps new retailers with access to a great deal of information will be the ones that are going to make real strides forward in database marketing because they have the data and they can buy or develop the systems to capture all that information, either by themselves or through joint programs. I think change is going to come from such innovative retailers. And the reason the change is going to come is that retailers will have to move to direct/database marketing in order to survive.

Consumers are already demanding the ability to buy when they want to and in the mode they choose. The more information consumers have, the more power they have and the more they are going to demand. I think much of the impetus for direct/database marketing will come from consumers. I do not think change is going to come simply because institutions want to do direct/database marketing themselves. Institutions are reactionary, but they are going to have to move very quickly because consumers will reward those that provide the convenience and service that direct/database marketing does. To the extent that a retailer can be the first in its market segment to deliver a benefit-rich program, as opposed to a me-too, catch-up program, the better prepared it will be to compete in the next century.

6

Direct Selling in the Year 2000

Thomas R. Wotruba

Predicting the future is both challenging and hazardous, particularly when such predictions are the groundwork for planning the continued viability and success of a business. Predicting the future for direct selling is even more complex because direct selling is a unique business operation whose success depends heavily on providing an attractive and enduring work opportunity and then satisfying the collective desires of the multitude of its individual salespeople. These salespeople, in their independent agent status, seek a diversity of rewards including income, self-esteem, entrepreneurial success, friendship, and a flexible work situation that dovetails with their family responsibilities and other life-style interests. How well direct selling organizations prosper in the future will depend on how well the opportunities offered will match the various rewards sought by this legion of independent performers as their needs and life styles evolve.

Other factors affecting direct selling in the coming years are more commonly shared with other retailing and business operations. Marketplace changes in buying behavior, values, and accessibility will impact product lines offered and mechanisms for channeling them to buyers. New technologies will achieve more widespread public acceptance and offer new ways of communicating with prospects and customers. Competitors will proact, react, and in the aggregate produce a shifting matrix of marketing efforts aimed at capturing customer patronage. New markets in other parts of the world will beckon with tantalizing opportunities in unfamiliar and challenging cultural settings.

Before we can review these factors in more detail and speculate on their impact for direct selling, we need to establish the state of direct selling today and document some recent trends. Doing so will provide a departure point for our look into the future.

CURRENT STATUS OF, AND
RECENT TRENDS IN, DIRECT SELLING

Direct selling (hereafter noted as DS) can be defined as a method of distribution of consumer goods and services through personal contact (salesperson to buyer) away from a fixed business location. The emphasis is on personal contact at a nonstore location convenient to the customer either individually (one-on-one at the consumer's home) or at an in-home party hosted by a consumer, reinforced with a high degree of personal service.

An additional feature of some DS organizations is a multilevel organization wherein salespeople recruit others to become salespeople and benefit from the productivity of the latter. This chain can continue as a recruited salesperson becomes a recruiter of others. The recruited salespeople (and others further down the chain) become the "downline" of the recruiter, and various arrangements exist among multilevel firms to compensate the salesperson for sales by his or her downline.[1]

Direct Selling Industry

A few facts about the DS industry will clearly indicate its significance in the U.S. economy. The Direct Selling Association 1988 Industry Survey included data from one hundred seven firms that were association members as well as 67 nonmember firms. These one hundred seventy-four companies utilized a total of 3,996,067 salespeople, or an average of nearly twenty-three thousand salespeople per company. Total retail sales of these firms reached $9.7 billion, of which 79 percent occurred through a one-on-one sales approach and the remaining 21 percent were achieved via party plan or group sales methods (Direct Selling Association 1989). Recent estimates of worldwide DS activity by the World Federation of Direct Selling Associations show that 9.3 million salespeople produce sales of about $40.2 billion in thirty-two countries (World Federation of Direct Selling Associations 1990).[2]

Salespeople

The vast preponderance (98 percent) of DS salespeople are independent agents and thus their own boss. To them, DS offers a job opportunity with great flexibility. Of the nearly four million salespeople engaged in DS in the United States in 1988, about 80 percent were part-time workers (less than thirty hours per week), and many (perhaps the majority) of these held some other job. Among the 20 percent who worked thirty or more hours per week in DS, a sizable minority held some other employment as well (Direct Selling Association 1989).

The flexibility in hours and time commitment for this job has been especially appealing to women, many of whom seek a work opportunity that can be tailored around family responsibilities. DS also provides an entry into the business world for individuals without the formal work experience imposed for employment in other organizations. About 81 percent of direct salespeople are women and nearly two-thirds are married. The typical direct salesperson has some college education and is somewhat younger than the general public, although the age range is quite wide. In fact, direct salespeople are found in all education levels, occupational groups, ethnic groups, income levels, and household sizes. The age, marital status, and education patterns noted above are tendencies suggested from a handful of studies over the past few years (May n.d.; Harris 1977; Thistlethwaite et al. 1985; Wotruba, Sciglimpaglia, and Tyagi 1986). In terms of life-style or psychographic characteristics, those active in DS are more outgoing (vs. reserved), aggressive (vs. passive), enthusiastic (vs. mild mannered), and venturesome (vs. shy) than others in the population. In addition, more DS salespersons are desirous of being their own boss than are Americans in general (Thistlethwaite et al. 1985).

Recruiting new salespeople is a constant challenge for DS companies, especially in periods of low inflation when the need to supplement the household income is less pressing (McGuire 1984). Turnover rates among DS salespeople are much higher than in other selling jobs. Various rates have been cited, depending on the calculation method used, and range from a low of 47.3 percent to a high of 150 to 200 percent (Granfield and Nicols 1975; Wotruba, Sciglimpaglia, and Tyagi 1987). One problem in calculating turnover rates is in determining when a salesperson has actually quit. In most DS firms there is no formal quitting procedure by the salesperson or official notice of termination by the company. Further, a few months of inactivity does not always indicate quitting because many DS salespeople cycle periodically from low to high activity levels.

Product Lines

Four major categories of products and services are sold by DS firms (Direct Selling Association 1989). The largest category in sales volume is household products, which includes cookware, tableware, kitchen and decorative accessories, vacuum cleaners and other appliances, security alarms, household cleaning products, water filters, nutritional products, and foods and beverages. In 1988 this category accounted for nearly half of all DS retail sales.

The second-largest category involves personal care and beauty items, including primarily cosmetics, fragrances, skin care items, and jewelry, as well as clothing and shoes. This category comprised about one-third of all retail sales by direct sellers in 1988.

Leisure and educational products make up the third category, encompassing encyclopedias and other educational publications, toys, crafts and hobby items, computers and software, and various self-improvement or vocational training programs. About 8 percent of retail sales by direct sellers in 1988 occurred in this category.

The fourth category is comprised of services and other product lines varying widely in character. Included are buying club and travel club services as well as cemetery property, foliage plants, books and magazines, photographic supplies, baby shoe bronzing, livestock feed, copy machines, and medical equipment. In 1988 this highly diversified category accounted for just under 10 percent of all DS sales.

Products comprising a large percentage of sales are not necessarily bought by a large percentage of DS customers, however. For instance, more than 25 percent of all sales volume in 1988 occurred in cosmetics and related products, but a study in the Pacific Northwest showed that only 15 percent of households buying from direct sellers purchased cosmetics (Baranowe and McNabb 1988). While this discrepancy may be a geographical phenomenon, it may also occur because the average buyer of these products is a relatively heavy user. Conversely, 10 percent of DS buyers in the Northwest bought books or magazines even though only about 5 percent of total DS sales fell into that category. In comparison with cosmetics, the per-household purchase of books and magazines is relatively small on average.

Markets Served and Customer Characteristics

Studies comparing buyers from direct salespeople with nonbuyers suggest that the typical buyer is somewhat younger, more likely to be female, higher educated, comes from a larger household, and has higher income (Baranowe and McNabb 1988; Peterson, Albaum, and Ridgway 1989). No major differences have been found between buyers and nonbuyers with regard to ethnicity, marital status, home ownership, occupation, or employment status. Some evidence has been found that DS buyers differ from nonbuyers on selected personality traits. Buyers are less talkative, sensitive, sociable, outgoing, and religious than nondirect sales buyers (Baranowe and McNabb 1988).

It should be made clear, however, that there are buyers and nonbuyers with all shades of personality characteristics and in all demographic categories. A remarkable statistic is that only 8 percent of a national sample of households had never purchased from a DS company (Peterson, Albaum, and Ridgway 1989). Studies generally confirm that a DS purchase has been made in the majority of American households within the past one to three years, and nearly one-quarter of all households have bought from direct sellers within the previous six months (Lumpkin, Caballero, and Chonko 1989).

Purchases from DS companies take place through different modes. In the national sample noted above, 36 percent of all households had purchased from a one-on-one meeting with a direct salesperson in the buyer's home during the prior twelve months. A one-on-one meeting at the workplace was the place of purchase for customers in 27 percent of these households, whereas 27 percent also purchased at a party at someone's home. Parties held at other locations, such as a clubroom, meeting hall, or church attracted purchasers from 10 percent of these households.

These results represent various buying segments for direct sellers, but probably do not reflect the popularity of these four modes among buyers as much as the degree to which DS companies emphasize these approaches in the marketplace. Given a choice, many consumers express a preference for the party approach over a one-on-one encounter at their doorstep (Lumpkin, Caballero, and Chonko 1989), although whether they would all put forth the effort to attend such parties is open to question. Party methods are especially favored by consumers in larger families whereas the one-on-one mode is seen as slightly more favorable to people who are younger, non-Caucasian, and possess less formal education. Parties offer the buyer opportunities not only to buy desirable products, but also to enjoy desirable social relationships with those hosting and attending the parties (Frenzen and Davis 1990). Parties at nonhome locations are being increasingly encouraged by DS companies in order to find new customers among today's working women. The need for tapping this new market was aptly summed up by one long-time Tupperware party-goer who stated that she and her friends were becoming "all Tuppered out" (Daily and Vamos 1985).

Advantages and disadvantages attributed to buying via DS have been investigated in a few studies of consumers (Albaum and Peterson 1987; Baranowe and McNabb 1988; Jolson 1972; Lumpkin, Caballero, and Chonko 1989; Nowland 1982). The main advantages, in descending order, include convenience, personal attention, and ability to examine the product and/or talk with the seller. Major disadvantages, again in order, involve pushy or high-pressure salespeople, inconvenient or bothersome interruption, and problems with salespeople's reliability, service, or accessibility after the sale. Price is seen as an advantage by some and as a disadvantage by an equal number of others, whereas product variety or selection is seen more as a disadvantage. While there are some changes in the order of these rankings depending on which DS mode is being evaluated, the patterns from one mode to the next and also from one demographic category of customers to the next are much more similar than different. As these studies have typically used open-end questions, however, many of the results have depended on the researchers' interpretations of respondents' statements. Some DS companies may have more definitive proprietary data on consumer attitudes towards DS as well as preferences for various purchasing modes, but the lack of accessible data on these topics suggests that they may be areas for more definitive research (Enis 1986).

Recent Trends and Issues

Use of New Channels and Channel Integration. Changes in consumer demographics, life-styles, and work patterns have brought about some pointed shifts in retail buying behavior. Direct mail, catalogs, telemarketing coupled with the use of toll-free 800 numbers, and electronic media such as computer and cable TV shopping have grown in popularity. Supermarket chains are again experimenting with home delivery service. The effect of these changes is to make shopping more convenient for the buyer, both in time and location. DS fits this pattern very well, as the time and location of the meeting between salesperson and buyer can be arranged to fit the buyer's convenience.

Some DS firms have incorporated these increasingly popular channels of communication into their selling network. While the independent salesperson is still their primary marketing effort, these firms have expanded their use of advertising and direct mail to maintain consumer awareness and interest and to support the salespeople's efforts. Some DS firms have even begun printing 800 numbers in their literature as well as on their product packages to assist customers in reordering company products or making contacts regarding problems or questions. These firms are quick to point out, however, that customer orders generated by the toll-free numbers or direct mail pieces are steered to their salespeople to fulfill. This maintains the preeminence of the independent salesperson, the sine qua non of success for DS firms. A personal service relationship is preserved between customer and salesperson, and salespeople view the 800 numbers and direct mail efforts as truly support methods rather than ways of competing with them and cannibalizing their market.

Of course, the major portion of total U.S. retail sales is still made through fixed location retail stores, and some DS firms have ventured into this mode as an adjunct distribution channel. Avon moved into the retail store channel when it acquired Georgio, Inc., a widely recognized brand available in many prestige department stores (Dunkin 1987). Earlier, Avon had purchased Tiffany's, a posh Manhattan jewelry store, but sold it shortly thereafter (Mintz 1982; "Avon Tries a New Formula . . ." 1984). Bose, Hanover Shoe, Fuller Brush, and Encyclopaedia Britannica have all used fixed location stores, although under a variety of circumstances. In some cases, stores are used in areas where no independent salespeople have been recruited. In other cases, the stores are temporarily established at high-traffic locations, such as kiosks at state fairs. In these latter instances, the stores are staffed by the DS sales force in that geographic area. Some stores are primarily prospecting mechanisms where potential customers come in, obtain information, and arrange appointments with salespeople to call at their homes. Mixed success has occurred with fixed-location stores. Fuller Brush eliminated its shopping mall stores. Tandy, on the other hand, eliminated a direct selling operation in order to concentrate on fixed-location stores for its computer product line.

Opportunities in Global Markets. As already noted, DS occurs around the world, with thirty-two countries belonging to the World Federation of Direct Selling Associations. Japan, in particular, has 1.5 million direct salespeople. Gakken, a large catalog sales firm in Japan selling books to school children, has about eighty thousand direct salespeople, while Mutow, Japan's largest publicly owned mail-order house, is using its growing direct sales force to sell complex services such as tour holidays (Sanghavi 1989).

Many U.S. DS companies have overseas operations—Avon, for example, is sold in a hundred countries today and earns a substantial portion of its profit from these international operations. Amway has more than one hundred thousand salespeople in Japan, who have been lured by the prospect of pay for performance rather than the traditional practice of pay for seniority (Ono 1990). With the development of the Pacific Rim and the opening of Eastern Europe, many DS firms are entering these markets or making plans to establish operations there.

Evolution of Company Product Lines. Although a firm's product line should evolve to match the needs and interests of its target markets, there is a scarcity of information on DS markets and market segments. Product line changes have taken place in many DS firms, however, but not necessarily in direct response to changing consumer needs.

Some firms have recognized the need for a more systematic product management approach. This can occur, for example, when a DS firm is acquired by a non-DS parent company with experience in the consumer package goods field. Many consumer package goods companies have a strong product management orientation, which can then be applied to the new subsidiary. The resulting impact may be more in organizational structure, product groupings, and filling in holes than in substantive responses to consumer needs.

Product line adjustments in other firms have been dictated by the actions of their sales organizations. For instance, the number of alternative colors, styles, and sizes possible in personal care products (e.g., cosmetics, fragrances) is very large and can become unwieldy and confusing to the sales force. One solution is to reduce the line, allowing for greater focus and stronger promotions on fewer items. Whether the items cut back are those with strong appeal to newly emerging markets may not be given strong consideration.

New technology also gives rise to product line additions and changes. Encyclopaedia Britannica has introduced its Compton's Multimedia Encyclopedia: all twenty-six volumes on one compact disk, which operates on a PC with a CD-ROM drive. It not only provides the traditional text but also includes animation (the joints of the human skeleton are seen moving), sound (speeches by Churchill, Roosevelt, and Kennedy), and high-resolution graphics. Targeted currently for libraries and schools, the system will become available to households in the future as they acquire the hardware to operate it.

DIRECT SELLING IN THE FUTURE: PROJECTIONS AND IMPLICATIONS

DS companies, like any other organization, must prepare for the future by identifying likely changes, determining the impact of those changes on company goals and operations, and planning effective responses. Some types of companies may entertain dramatic changes in all parts of their marketing strategy as possible responses to anticipated future events. Product lines, pricing and credit policies, promotional methods including advertising and selling, and distribution channels might all be candidates for major overhaul.

DS companies, however, are limited because the cornerstone of their marketing strategy is the independent salesperson. If this element were changed, the direct selling company would no longer be a direct selling organization, thus losing the quintessential character which has earned this business its viability in the economy and society. By downplaying the role of the salesperson and shifting its major marketing thrust to retail stores, mail order, or some other strategy element, a (former) DS company would no longer truly fit within the definition of the direct selling industry. So one element in the future marketing strategy of DS companies that will not change is the fundamental role of the independent salesperson.

The implications of this reasoning are clear. Future success of DS companies will depend on how well they can simultaneously satisfy their markets and their sales force and facilitate the successful bonding of these two groups. Thus, we begin with projections about these two groups and the circumstances affecting how they will link in the future.

Projections Regarding Markets

Some demographic changes in the population can be anticipated with considerable reliability (Kern 1986). One involves age patterns—the "aging" of America. According to the U.S. Census Bureau, the median age of the U.S. population is expected to increase from 33 in 1990 to 36 in 2000 and then to 41 in 2020. The bulk of the population growth is expected in persons aged 35 and above, whereas a decline in absolute numbers is expected in the age group from 20 to 34. The ethnic mix will also evolve, with greater proportions of Asians and Hispanics. Some employment patterns are also quite predictable. Women are expected to be 50 percent of the total employed in the year 2000, with a large proportion shifting from part- to full-time positions. Already the majority of women today with children under age 6 are in the labor force. Increased employment of women will not occur entirely in jobs involving traditional work hours and locations, however, as upcoming comments will indicate.

Overall population growth is lessening, and in the year 2000 it will be one-half of its average annual 1 percent increase today. Average household size will drop from slightly above 2.6 people today to slightly below 2.5 in 2000, reflecting substantial growth in the proportions of single-adult, single-parent, and nonfamily households. Geographic mobility will increase, with many households changing residence every one or two years. Mobility may become even more prevalent as home ownership becomes more difficult to attain financially. Average household income has been estimated to grow about 40 percent over the next five years, however, although the impact of this growth on real buying power is subject to future levels of inflation and taxes.

Concurrent with these demographic shifts will be some major changes in life styles, values, and behaviors. While such changes are more speculative than the demographic developments, many who study the future have identified nine such changes with some consistency (Lazer et al. 1990; "Trends and Predictions ..." 1989). The *first* is the increasing importance of convenience, the desire for easy and immediate gratification. Consumers will become more impatient, less willing to wait or to travel long distances to shop or obtain services they need. Embedded in this convenience orientation is the desire for "user friendly" modes of shopping, recreation, transportation, and other activities. The *second* involves a growing emphasis on self-identity and self-expression. Consumers will balk at being part of a mass market and instead will look for ways to boost their individualization through customization or unique varieties of possessions. Accompanying this is a *third* trend toward a greater importance of value, which typically translates into quality and service. The quality of a product depends on its features and appearance and the apparent care with which it was made. Brand names will continue to be one guide to quality. Service is seen more as what a particular seller adds to the transaction. As some retail stores cut service to control costs, transactions in these stores will be perceived as having lower value. Value sensitivity will grow as consumers become more proactive in the purchasing process. Price alone will lose its significance as a value measure as people gain information and pay greater attention to what they buy. This leads to a *fourth* development, which is a greater desire for information in order to become knowledgeable and participate more actively in the acquisition process. People are becoming more concerned about making themselves heard and will utilize communication methods that are convenient in bringing them information and passing on their own opinions. New technology such as teletext (broadcasting messages over standard television programming to special TV set computers in the consumer's home) and interactive cable TV may play an increasing role here. The general population will become more knowledgeable about this technology and attuned to its use because, if occupational projections are accurate, the majority of all employed persons will earn their living in some segment of the information industry by the year 2000.

A *fifth* aspect of changing life style involves the increasing availability of leisure or discretionary time. At the same time, opportunities for its use will proliferate and many leisure-time activities may become contracted and programmed (e.g., aerobics classes, tennis club programs). In a sense, spending our leisure time may become hard work. Some futures scanners suggest a *sixth* major dimension of life-style change—a greater dependence on products and services in our everyday lives and especially in our home environment. Appliances and devices of various sorts will be our assistants in cooking, cleaning, communication, entertainment, and recreation. Our growing service economy will uncover new ways (in addition to supplying leisure activities) to benefit our personal lives as well as our business operations. Some of the services will be needed to maintain and repair the products that surround us, of course. Coupled with this trend is a *seventh* development, a greater desire for new products and for replacing our possessions more frequently to achieve the self-expression and the improved convenience, quality, and service noted previously. Consumers will attribute less and less value to permanence, although the desire to discard and replace might be countered by environmental concerns such as pollution and recycling. Some futurists single out a conservation orientation as a distinct life-style change, although here it is treated as a counterpoint to the desire for new things, which is basically a nonconservation orientation.

The *eighth* part of this emerging life-style pattern is the continuing trend toward flexibility in employment, involving such aspects as flextime, job sharing, and telecommuting. Traditional workplaces and work schedules will give way to new approaches, especially with the assistance of computers and other facilitating technologies. Urban congestion, environmental pollution, and high energy costs will also reinforce this change.

Accompanying this, or perhaps hurrying it along, is the *ninth* trend, which can be termed a return to the family ethic (as opposed to the "me" ethic). This trend will materialize as more women leave traditional jobs, set up a business at home, and have children. Others will keep their jobs but perform them more at home via telecommuting. A shrinking of job advancement opportunities in corporations caused by the cost-cutting elimination of middle management positions will foster these changes.

These life-style developments will affect some market groups more than others, of course. Less impact may be seen in the older groups, who have more entrenched attitudes and behaviors. Studies of mature consumers point out that shopping has been a major part of their life-style, more a pleasure than a burden, and they are more desirous of maintaining than changing that behavior (Lumpkin, Caballero, and Chonko 1989). The greatest changes are likely in the generations born in the 1960s and beyond, a smaller number by comparison with the baby boomers born beginning in the mid-1940s and through the 1950s, but in demographic terms the more likely target market for direct selling.

Projections Regarding Direct Salespeople

Changes forecast for the population in general will also, of course, affect the pool from which DS salespeople are drawn. Thus, the demographic and life-style projections just discussed will apply to DS sales forces as well. In fact, it is important that they do in order to have a breadth of demographic and life-style characteristics in the sales force that corresponds with those characteristics in the market. Such matching is conducive, if not absolutely necessary, to building close seller-buyer relationships.

DS companies might face some difficult challenges over the next decade in attracting the quantity and quality of salespeople desired, however. For instance, as job opportunities become more available for women, greater competition will occur in the labor market. More members of the younger generation, especially those with strong motivation and achievement orientations, are obtaining college degrees and searching for positions with traditional career paths and fringe benefits. As telecommuting expands, entrepreneurial types in the labor pool might find increased opportunities to pursue careers with many firms but with a time and location flexibility that fosters a semi-independent status.

As the proportion of single-adult households grows, the preference for jobs with security, full-time earnings opportunities, and fringe benefits will also grow. The independent status of DS salespeople coupled with the perceived high turnover rates in these positions and, to some extent, the undesirable image of selling held by many people might make such positions unattractive. The single-parent adult might find the flexibility of a DS position attractive, but the lack of benefits, uncertain job stability, and impact on self-image might be perceived negatively.

As people take DS jobs for a variety of reasons, any one development posed here might discourage some but encourage others to become direct sellers. There are at least four different types of motivations for taking on a DS position (Wotruba and Tyagi 1990). One involves dollar income. Another focuses on more intrinsic rewards such as feelings of accomplishment, self-fulfillment, and skill development. A third consists of interpersonal relations or sociability needs such as gaining attention and respect, getting recognition, making friends, and working on a team. A fourth relates to enjoying an association with a well-known company and identifying with its products, which are seen as highly regarded. Perhaps there is even a fifth type, which is the desire to prove that one can succeed in a position requiring an abundance of initiative and effort and laden with potential rejection.

Differences in motivation can produce quite different results. While management encourages its salespeople to set high goals for sales volume and recruiting, such goals are not set by many and do not boost the sales and earnings of most of those who do set them (Wotruba 1989). Salespeople with the first three types of motivation might all make an active effort to recruit additional salespeople for their downlines, but their reasons for doing so and the types of recruits they seek could be totally dissimilar. The money-oriented salesperson might seek someone who is aggressive, persuasive, and had many prospect contacts. The salesperson seeking intrinsic rewards might recruit just the opposite type with the hope of making her (or him) into someone more "successful." The third or sociable type might look for someone like herself or himself, perhaps a friend or neighbor with whom the DS job could become a regular topic of conversation, a source of anecdotes and amusement. None of these types is inherently undesirable, since all can add to the DS company's success as well as make the salesperson's own life better through this job. These various motivations are not unknown to many DS company executives, but a clearer recognition of them and tailoring job opportunities and conditions to nurture them might become more important in the future as labor market challenges increase.

Other Projections

Traditional retailing through fixed-location stores is facing a perplexing future. Slowing sales growth signifies a maturing industry, whereas intense price competition and expanded retail space have brought on a situation of overcapacity with insipid (or no) profit margins. To today's shopper, retailing is becoming a less exciting and enjoyable pursuit. In the words of one informed observer (Wortzel 1987, p. 45), "Retailing, like many other industries, is becoming 'commoditized.' Retail stores (and products) are becoming more and more alike—so much so that retailing looks more like a commodity industry every day."

Few national brand names are the exclusive province of any one store, as consumers can find branded appliances, clothing, and other items in many types of stores, including discounters. After-sale service such as delivery and repair, which was once an important factor in choosing a retail store, has been relegated to independent service companies. Use of store credit cards, which formerly fostered store loyalty, has given way in large part to the use of bank credit cards that place few limits on where one can charge a purchase.

Demographic and life style changes have affected the enticement of retail store shopping as well. Single-person or single-parent household members lack the time to shop, as do those in two-career families. Poorly trained, overworked, and under-motivated store clerks compound the problem. Many who have viewed shopping as a pleasant social experience for a number of years are bothered by new electronic devices and procedures such as scanners and their in-store impact such as unclear pricing (e.g., "the sale price or discount will automatically be recorded when the clerk rings up your purchase"). Their devotion to shopping may wane.

These developments have given rise to an enormous increase in direct marketing via catalogs with toll-free 800 numbers, unconditional return policies, and home delivery via UPS or other carriers. If direct marketing continues to flourish, the U.S. Postal Service will undoubtedly mandate larger residential mailboxes to hold the onslaught of catalogs. Printed media may accede to electronics, however. By the year 2001, 70 percent of U.S. households are projected to have computers ("Trends and Projections . . ." 1989). Many futurists have been predicting that there will be steady if not dramatic increases in retail shopping via electronic catalogs transmitted via teletext, interactive cable TV, or systems patterned after the Prodigy videotex service (e.g., Hiller 1983).

Implications for Direct Selling

Table 6.1 summarizes the preceding projections and offers some corresponding implications for DS companies. The demographic projections suggest that recruiting efforts must be directed to obtain a sales force that mirrors the evolving age and ethnic makeup of the population. Product lines and promotional programs must also be devised to match these demographic changes. Increasing employment among women expands the already-existing challenge to find efficient methods of approaching this market and also offers an opportunity to recruit among those whose job has brought them a new set of contacts as possible customers. Growing mobility rates call for more efforts on how to facilitate the continued patronage of these movers and acquaint them with a new salesperson at their destination. Declining household size but increasing household income suggest the objective of increasing individual orders, either from a broader product line or higher-priced (and also higher value) items. The general slowdown in overall U.S. population growth reinforces the need to look to other markets, such as the newly opening Eastern Europe countries as well as the Pacific Rim.

Table 6.1. Implications for Direct Selling Firms of Market, Sales Force, and Other Projections

Projection	Implications for Direct Selling Firms
Market Demographics	
• Older average age	• Increase efforts to recruit in older age categories; consider product-line expansion and promotional programs to appeal to older market segments.
• Greater ethnic mix	• Increase efforts to recruit members of growing ethnic groups; adjust product offerings and promotions to appeal to these groups.
• Greater employment among women	• Consider ways of communicating more efficiently with these households (e.g., direct mail, workplace meetings); explore recruiting opportunities with customers who may have access to new sets of contacts.
• Slowdown in overall population growth	• Look at other market possibilities, such as Pacific Rim, Eastern Europe.
• Declining average household size	• Broaden product line to maintain average order size; improve efforts to help salespeople recruit and build downlines.

- Increase in geographic mobility

- Develop convenient reorder systems and efficient ways to acquaint customers with new salespersons at new geographic locations.

- Increasing household income

- Downplay price appeals; strengthen quality and value appeals; consider promotions involving expanded packages of products and/or larger models that deliver more quality or convenience.

Life-Styles

- Desire for convenience

- Since these changes are somewhat speculative, a basic implication is to initiate a careful market research program to learn about customer values and to monitor how they are changing.

- Emphasis on self-identity

- Importance of value (quality and service)

- Some of these projections complement the strengths of direct selling—DS is convenient, can help customers build self-identity through personalized service and product choice, can provide value and facilitate communication and information exchange, is flexible to adjust meeting to times that do not conflict with a customer's work or programmed leisure.

- Desire for more information and communication

- More (but programmed) leisure time

- Dependence on products and services

- Desire for new products

- The essence of this pattern is a greater desire for service, individual attention, and information, but less time available to receive these things.

- Flexibility in employment

- Return to family ethic

- Programs to make the buyer-seller relationship more efficient (i.e., communications, ordering, reordering) must be developed for the upcoming generation while maintaining the approaches traditionally effective for long-term customers.

Direct Salespeople

- Demographics and life-style of the general population

- Recruit to parallel these changes; if an imbalance exists in the sales force, it is unlikely that the existing salespeople will correct it through their own recruiting efforts.

- Increased competition in labor market for women

- Entice those with full-time jobs elsewhere to take on a DS position as a part-time "moonlighting" position and help focus their efforts on recruiting as well as selling; then attempt to convince them to switch to their DS position full-time.

- Higher priority on full-time, secure jobs

- Devise ways of making DS job more stable and secure, but also emphasize the security of working for oneself.

- Greater realization of diversity of reasons for taking direct selling jobs

- Offer a variety of rewards that will satisfy the various motives to take a DS job.

Other

- Maturing of in-store retailing

- Train salespeople and inform customers that these problems of in-store retailers are strongholds of direct selling.

- Lessening of retailing services

- Direct selling firms can take advantage of the success of direct marketing by using similar methods as support to their salespeople.

- Increased incidence of computers in the home

- Future plans for electronic communications should be made based on research to determine the desirability of these methods and the best approaches to take in the eyes of customers and salespeople.

Life-style projections suggest that the convenience, personal service, and individual attention that are the hallmarks of direct selling will fit nicely within the developing life-styles in the coming decade. The personal contact approach of DS offers great potential to satisfy the desire by consumers for more information and communication. Properly trained, and with the right support materials, the DS salesperson can become a storehouse of environmental, nutritional, fashion, or any other kind of information important to a DS firm's buyers and will be able to discuss these issues with a contemporary perspective. Many DS products play a central role in the life-style of consumers, contributing significantly to their self-identity and individualization. Those returning to the "family" ethic and/or telecommuting or otherwise working at home may present a resurgence of opportunity to the DS salesperson with a "one-on-one at home" approach. To confirm these expectations and fine tune their strategies, DS firms must commit to a strong research program that maps out the value and attitude profiles of its markets and monitors those changes as life-styles transform and diverge over time.

Projections regarding the availability of persons as prospective DS salespeople present some particular challenges beyond simply adjusting the demographic mix via recruiting efforts. A broader spectrum of work opportunities will be open to many, especially women, who might previously have found DS as their chief occupational choice. The appeal of non-DS jobs will be strong because of a variety of factors, including greater apparent stability, wider range of fringe benefits, and clearer career paths, as well as being less problematical (i.e., "Can I really sell?" and "What will people think if I turned down an office job at XYZ Company to sell widgets door-to-door?"). The entrepreneurial types in the labor market may still opt for, and flourish in, direct selling, but even they will find attractive opportunities elsewhere.

To keep DS jobs attractive may require adjustments in the job, especially with respect to how the salesperson is supported in finding prospects, communicating with customers, and establishing longer-term relationships with buyers whose access time becomes increasingly scarce. Well-organized programs expounding the benefits of part-time commitment to DS may be very effective in attracting individuals who choose other full-time positions (Wotruba 1990b). Recognizing and catering to a wide variety of motivations to become a DS salesperson will also loom as important, as many of those who now quit soon after starting would find their expectations better fulfilled and remain a contributor to the company longer.

Projections about traditional in-store retailing suggest that problems in this economic sector are, if anything, boosting the desirability of DS to larger groups of consumers. Such problems have already been noted and have led to an explosion of direct marketing activity by these same retailers as well as by some newly established competitors. DS companies will continue to benefit by learning from the trials of direct marketing companies and should be able to borrow some direct marketing tactics to support their salespeople's efforts.

Projections regarding various applications of electronic technology come in all shapes and sizes, from those who feel we will be literally controlled by technology in the 21st century, to those who are skeptical about any widespread impact on consumer marketing for many years. In fact, such predictions have been with us for more than a decade (Rosenberg and Hirschman 1980). Based on a retrospective assessment of these predictions, it seems unlikely that any swift epidemic of technological change will inundate consumer buying unless such change is supportive of evolving life-style patterns. While much technology is available that may be applied to communicating, shopping, and buying, the mass adoption of any specific technological system or device will ensue only if it complements life style patterns that are clearly in place ("Retailing in the Year 2000" 1987).

DS firms might want to experiment on a small scale with the capabilities of videotex for electronic catalogs and computer-related devices for customer inquiries and orders. Past studies have suggested that DS firms commit seriously to providing hardware, software, and training for their sales representatives' personal computers (Enis 1986). However, given that many people take DS jobs for reasons other than pursuing strictly monetary goals, their willingness to use any such analytical capabilities might be doubtful. To the extent that this is true, such an investment by DS firms seems unwarranted. Some research might be done to shed light on the potential payoff from assistance to salespeople in this technology, but the bulk of the firm's research budget is probably better spent learning about values, attitudes, and general life-style patterns of its customers and prospects as well as its salespeople.

PRESCRIPTIONS FOR DIRECT SELLING COMPANIES

Prescribing what DS companies should do in the future is somewhat presumptuous, if not altogether arrogant. The prescriptions offered here are not delivered in that spirit, but rather in the hope that they will spark a discussion from which will come fresh and viable ideas that are likely to survive into implementation. Some of the projections and implications reviewed earlier do suggest plausible and even imaginative actions, however, and these are presented below.

Pursue New Markets

As total population growth tapers off in the United States, future sales expansion opportunities will require more careful targeting. Three such targets are:

Older Age Groups. The typical DS customer has been young relative to the population median, but the bulk of population growth will be occurring in older age categories. Appealing to older customers will require possible product line additions, a broadening or repositioning of some promotional programs, greater recruiting within these customer age categories, and some additional training of salespeople to highlight the distinct attitudes and needs of this group.

Expanding Ethnic Groups. Many DS firms will find that expanding growth within various ethnic groups, especially Hispanics and Asians, will offer substantial new sales opportunities if approached with salespeople, products, and promotions tailored to these markets.

Global Markets. More than thirty countries now have an active direct selling industry, and some DS firms sell in more than a hundred countries. As Western Europe evolves into a single market in 1992, DS firms such as Tupperware are gearing up to broaden their marketing as well as manufacturing operations there (Ryans and Rau 1990, p. 149). The recent democratization of Eastern Europe offers still more global opportunities. Most Eastern European countries suffer from a sparse and inefficient retailing infrastructure. Although income in these countries is relatively low, the desire for products that represent the "American life-style" appears to be great, and the entrepreneurial desire of many citizens in these countries seems strong. These conditions bode well for the success of DS, as low entry cost makes DS selling jobs very attractive.

Entry into global markets does not automatically assure success, however, because cultural influences and legal constraints might be vastly different from what a firm has experienced in this country. For example, the establishment or change of a price might have to receive government approval in many countries. Moreover, because the opportunities are so vast, very successful DS salespeople in these countries might decide to strike out for themselves, entering into competition with the firm that initially nurtured their success.

Increase Support for the DS Salesperson

The sales force is the DS industry's paramount resource. Further, most industry executives firmly believe in the superiority of independent agents over company-employed salespeople to preserve that entrepreneurial feeling deemed essential for success. The challenge to keep these salespeople strong in numbers and motivation in light of the upcoming demographic and life style changes can be met by some or all of the following.

Assist in Lead Generation.   Many salespeople who become inactive might be tempted to remain at work if they had names of prospects with some interest in their products (Beltramini and Evans 1988). Of course, one of the values of an independent sales organization, especially a multilevel type, is its lead-generation ability through networking. But as time becomes an increasingly scarce commodity, both for salespeople (especially the part-time moonlighters) and for customers, help in initiating the salesperson-customer contact can pay off with a well-designed program. Some DS firms are already experimenting with Yellow Pages listings containing toll-free 800 numbers that prospects can call. Names and addresses of these callers can be passed along to company salespeople for follow-up and order taking. Once such an inbound telemarketing operation is successfully established, the firm might wish to experiment with an outbound effort to initiate calls and learn if those called have any interest in receiving literature or even attending a party. Such interest can be followed up by one of the firm's salespeople. Direct mail incorporating an 800 number can be used similarly to the Yellow Pages, as can advertising in many other media. The danger with 800 numbers is the temptation to use this channel as an order-filling device, thereby alienating the salesperson. Any such conflict with the sales force could portend the downfall of a DS firm.

Another aspect of lead generation occurs with customers of DS salespeople who become inactive. Some DS firms have devised ways of obtaining customer names and addresses from the departing salespeople. These names then become leads for new or remaining salespeople. Such lead-generation programs benefit customers as well, for they help alleviate the frustration occurring because one's source of supply has gone out of business.

Adjust Product and Service Offerings.   The expansion of product lines and promotional programs to match changing population trends has been noted earlier, and the use of telemarketing as a sales support service has been discussed. There are other product and service packages that might be devised to correspond with consumer life-style and shopping behavior changes. Such packages would clearly support the sales force, but they are of sufficient importance to warrant a separate category of actions and are discussed in more detail below.

Promotional Support for the Concept of Direct Selling.   A few DS firms have devised advertising campaigns in major media to emphasize their product lines and serve as lead generators. Very little has been done, however, to promote the concept of direct selling itself and the benefits it offers to buyers relative to purchasing via other distribution methods. As already noted here, DS can be positioned to complement the evolving life-styles of the 1990s, and DS sales jobs can satisfy a variety of needs and motivations within its incumbents. This story might make good copy.

Studies noted earlier show that the public perceives some disadvantages in buying from a DS firm. Evidence also exists that image questions still haunt the perceived legitimacy (e.g., pyramids) and ethical propriety of direct selling, as well of selling in general. Major negative factors attributed to DS by a cross section of consumers are high-pressure selling, unreliable salespeople, and loss of contact after the sale. While some instances of these behaviors undoubtedly exist, they are far from endemic to the industry. These image problems should be addressed and alleviated using effective promotional programs aimed at both the public and DS salespeople. Even within a firm's sales force there are individuals harboring these problems that may affect their job satisfaction, commitment, and productivity and eventually hasten their termination (Wotruba 1990a).

Provide a Way for DS Salespeople to Obtain Fringe Benefits if Desired. The value of fringe benefits in attracting and retaining good employees is not in doubt, and these benefits may become even more critical as the labor market tightens. The key issue is how to provide such benefits while maintaining the independent status of the sales force and minimizing the administrative time and cost associated with such programs. A few DS firms have found ways to provide some fringe benefits to their salespeople or to upper levels in their sales organization (e.g., district directors). Some have suggested the Direct Selling Association as a logical agency to initiate and coordinate fringe benefit programs for its member companies, although others object to use of the association's resources in this manner. A separate organization could be set up and funded by those industry members wishing this service, of course, or individual firms could devise programs in cooperation with agencies that are now fringe benefit providers, such as health insurance organizations. Details on eligibility, salesperson payment, company contribution (if any), and so on must then be worked out. Many companies who employ part-time workers in nonselling positions now offer them some level of fringe benefits. Providers of these benefits surely have enough experience in these matters to be able to create some program options for consideration.

Develop New Product and Service Packages

Beyond simply adjusting the product line and promotional efforts to reflect changing demographics and new market opportunities, there is room for new programs or packages. These should encompass a variety of product-service components that would appeal to the consumer of the next decade by reflecting new life-styles and the developing competitive situation with in-store and direct marketing and by retaining a strong focus on the DS salesperson as the continuing key to industry success. Two such programs respectively involve convenience and education.

Convenience Package. The bond between salesperson and customer must be maintained, but perhaps in less time than in the past. A "convenience package" of products and services involves periodic meetings between customer and DS salesperson but provides a mechanism for ordering and delivering products between those meeting times based on the establishment of a standing order. This program would be implemented with a customer after one or a few meetings deemed necessary to establish trust and to diagnose what types of products, delivered with what frequency, will be most suitable for this customer. For instance, one customer might be interested in an unchanging order every four weeks. Another might want part of each order to include one or more new items based on his or her strong interest in creative self-expression and his or her desire to be recognized as an early adopter. Payment can be arranged via credit cards, and direct mail updates on new products and promotions can be supplied to members of this program. A change in the standing order can be made at any time via an 800 number or by contacting the salesperson directly.

If such a program were successful, the dollar sales per hour spent by a DS salesperson with each customer in this program would increase. The firm's administrative costs might increase as well. Shipping costs might also go up, as a greater number of smaller shipments would be necessary. Inventory control might improve, however, and sales fluctuations might level out. A variation in salesperson compensation rate might have to be introduced under these circumstances, with greater amounts paid at the initiation of a standing order and smaller amounts paid for unchanged follow-up shipments. If a salesperson quits with customers in such a program, those customers' purchases are less likely to end, and the account can be reassigned.

Educational Package. An "educational package" is based on the life-style trends involving desire for more information, emphasis on self-identity, and more programmed leisure. It fits best into a party-plan approach to DS, but could also be used with one-time high-ticket items or even with frequently purchased low-ticket items. The essence of this package involves coupling parties (or other group sales demonstrations) with theme discussions about issues important to the target market. Such issues might include conservation, pollution, nutrition, travel, gardening, fashion, or even entrepreneurship. These discussions can be arranged in a series with specific times and dates so that participants can program them into their leisure time schedule.

The DS salesperson becomes responsible for coordinating the educational portion as well as the sales efforts. Thus, one DS salesperson might invite a local expert on nutrition to lead a discussion on cholesterol-reducing diets. If the discussion topic relates to the DS salesperson's product line (e.g., discussion of fashion at a cosmetics party), the salesperson might take on the role of discussion leader or provide printed materials or even a videotape supplied by the DS firm that serves to generate discussion. Videos of experts on various topics could be devised by the DS firm and supplied to its salespeople for use in these sessions as well. The genesis of such materials might already be found in the consumer newsletters published periodically by the Direct Selling Education Foundation, which explore pros and cons of current and controversial issues. Eventually, perhaps, this program might be expanded to incorporate teleconferencing or other electronic communication mechanisms. Such discussions are similar to short-course programs offered by university extension divisions on current events. The difference, of course, is that the discussion group also becomes a marketplace for selling efforts.

Establish a Program of Marketing Research

The projections discussed earlier and their implications for DS firms as outlined in Table 6.1, as well as the prescriptions offered in the preceding paragraphs, are based on ideas, opinions, and judgments from many sources.[3] Whether one agrees or disagrees with these individual forecasts and prescriptions, they do touch on critical aspects of future business success in direct selling. Thus, it is only prudent to improve management's understanding of these aspects with an investment in research, particularly research on a firm's specific target markets. Of near-equal importance is research on a firm's sales force members, their expectations, motivations, and realistic suggestions for improving their job and cementing their loyalty. These points have been made a number of times in this chapter, and no further elaboration is needed.

IMPACT OF DIRECT SELLING ON RETAILING

Direct selling is probably not viewed by the rest of the retailing industry as a strong threat, as DS sales account for less than 1 percent of total U.S. retail sales. But in light of the declining compatibility between fixed-location retailing and evolving consumer life-styles and work patterns, it might be useful for retailers of all types to consider whether they could benefit from borrowing some DS strategy for their own use. Consumers in the coming decade will favor those suppliers who can provide convenience, service, personal attention, and quality merchandise. Direct selling has succeeded by offering these same benefits. Many retailers have taken a step in this direction with a rapidly expanding direct marketing program. Well-designed catalogs and brochures have enticed many purchase decisions made in the comfort of the buyer's home. Can these same retailers augment their success by sending salespeople to customers' homes in addition to, or perhaps along with, those catalogs?

Astute observers of retailing believe that "storeless shopping" will grow rapidly over the next decade (e.g., Hyde 1990). For products that require demonstration, explanation, or advice on use, personal selling at a time and place convenient to the customer offers a differentiating opportunity to many retailers. Some, such as Nordstrom, are dabbling in it today. To the extent that retailers are looking at Eastern Europe and other developing markets, direct selling might be a way to establish a presence while waiting for the infrastructure to develop that could support eventual fixed-location operations.

Three factors seem critical for effective direct selling by non-DS retailers. One involves appropriate products—those benefitting from some aspect of personal service as well as those with well-known and respected brand names that connote quality. The second is a customer willing to place quality, convenience, and service above price as reasons for buying. Evolving life-style patterns indicate that such customers will be increasing in numbers. The third is an effective person to carry out the selling task. Successful direct sellers are independent agents, entrepreneurs with self-motivation who respond to incentives. If other retailers employ salespeople with different characteristics, such efforts might not succeed. For instance, an attempt by Dayton-Hudson to pay its salespeople with an incentive compensation plan brought about great dissatisfaction among them as well as a vote favoring unionization (Schwadel 1990). It is unlikely that these employees would fit into the desired entrepreneurial model.

Some direct selling experimentation by retailers with suitable product lines seems warranted on a limited scale. These efforts might be coupled with a telemarketing operation to book individual appointments as well as "parties" with service or social clubs that have regularly scheduled meetings. If such a program proved successful and the rewards to the salesperson were lucrative, these sales positions might be used as an advanced career-stage step to reward enterprising salespeople working in the store.

CONCLUSION

As direct selling approaches the year 2000, it faces some major challenges in its customer market and its labor market. DS seems well poised, however, to capitalize on emerging consumer life-style changes and to compete more effectively with traditional in-store retailing.   By borrowing from the experiences of direct marketers and by reshaping the DS job to remain attractive to the millions of independent sales representatives who are its missionaries, this industry should find that the decade of the 1990s offers great potential for prosperity.   Other retailers might also find value in employing selected direct selling ideas to differentiate their market offerings and meet their customers' needs and priorities.

NOTES

1. This definition and discussion are drawn from Bernstein (1984), Biggart (1989), Direct Selling Education Foundation (1984), and Granfield and Nicols (1975).
2. Excluded from these statistics are many salespeople engaged in some type of direct selling but whose firms have not traditionally been members of the Direct Selling Association. Examples include life insurance companies whose salespeople visit prospects in their homes, and retail store and service firms whose salespeople make house calls on their customers (e.g., decorators, financial planners).
3. In addition to sources implied by the references, telephone interviews were held with Richard C. Bartlett, president, Mary Kay Cosmetics, Inc.; Charles A. Collis, owner, Heart and Home, Inc.; Jay Hescock, executive vice president, Direct Selling Association; Robin H. Kirkland, president, Jafra Cosmetics, Inc.; James E. Preston, CEO, Avon Products, Inc.; and Patricia A. Wier, president, Encyclopaedia Britannica, USA.

REMARKS

James E. Preston

The direct selling industry has been in a state of transition for the past six or seven years. Successful as they have been for so many years, traditional door-to-door selling, party plans, and other familiar variations no longer guarantee success. Too many consumers are not at home when we call. Too many consumers are too busy to participate in parties. And virtually all consumers are demanding more product choices and—because they have less and less time—more convenient ways to buy. In the case of beauty products, the typical consumer wants something that works for her—just for her—and she is not interested in whether it works for anyone else.

Direct selling is changing because the consumer is changing. But the industry was slow to recognize these changes—or at least slow to react to them. Then, beginning in the early 1980s, the industry scrambled hard and fast to adapt. Amway dramatically expanded its product line. Mary Kay upgraded and expanded its product line and moved aggressively into direct mail. At Avon, we endorsed and emphasized something that many of our more adventurous and successful representatives were already doing, selling in the workplace. Presently sales in the workplace account for almost 40 percent of Avon's $1.4 billion in U.S. sales.

These and other innovations met with varying degrees of success. Avon is continuing to refine and hone its new ways of doing business and is conducting a wide variety of tests.

In short, the direct selling industry is in a period of transition, and I suspect that this transition will last another five years or more. The end result—by the late 1990s or early in the next century—will be what we might term a hybrid. Selling will still take place in the traditional ways, but we will also be providing customers with direct access by telephone, by mail, perhaps by fax, perhaps by home computer, perhaps through media we are not even aware of yet. Today, for example, 40 percent of Avon's orders in Taiwan arrive by fax.

Each consumer will decide how she wants to buy. It will be her choice, not ours, and she will have more choices than ever before.

We live in a world of segmentation, even personalization. We segment our product lines, segment our sales forces, and segment our delivery systems. If that sounds like a complicated and costly overhaul of our industry, it is. But that is exactly what we must do. We must offer the consumer choices, and we have no choice about doing so. The company that fails to make the required investment today in developing the systems, procedures, and skills needed to implement and maintain the changes I have outlined will either slow down to a crawl or simply disappear.

Dr. Wotruba pointed out the considerable economic impact that direct selling has in the United States. But he also pointed out how tiny the industry is compared to its gargantuan competition, the retail industry. These are two ways of looking at that. Recall the old story of the two salesmen who were sent out to a new territory. One wired back, "Terrible prospects. Only half the people use our products." The other saw things differently: "Great prospects. We can double our business." That is how direct selling stacks up at present against retail, except that our market share is much smaller and thus our opportunities are much greater, especially now that retail stores have become less-than-pleasant places in which to shop.

The question might be asked, "Why then has direct selling not done better over the years?" In fact, direct selling was fairly stagnant in the

1980s. Most direct sellers could probably go back and see where their sales were at the beginning and at the end of the 1980s. They were probably flat, and some firms actually lost sales. There were two key reasons for that condition. The first was access. Turnover in direct selling is high; Avon's is over 100 percent. As long as we have that high turnover, we will continue to generate new customers, but if a sales representative or distributor leaves and there is no replacement, which happens often, we have lost customers. We know at Avon, through our research, that this rate has been consistent for the past six or seven years. At any given time we have ten or eleven million households that would buy our product if only they could access us. They do not buy from us, not because they dislike our products but because they can no longer reach us.

The question then becomes, "Why can't you fill these needs differently?" Not so easy, as anyone in this industry can tell you. If, for example, you try to compensate for the loss of representatives by going into a fixed-location retail environment or by direct mail, you kill the goose that lays the golden egg. Now, Avon thinks there are ways around this dilemma and is undertaking a major test of a modified direct mail program to retain customers, but the problem remains very real.

The second reason that the industry has not grown is that it has not kept pace with consumer demands. If you are going to be in the cosmetics industry as we are, you cannot expect a woman to wait three weeks to look good. If she is out of a cosmetic, she is out of it. And unless your representative happens to stock a few products that she knows her customers want and use in her market, if that customer wants to get a lipstick or skin cream product she will have to wait a week or perhaps even two or three.

Avon has the most efficient distribution system in the world for us, but not for the customer. So what we are doing today is looking at how we have to change and telling our representatives and customers that if you run out of our product today, call us at this number and we will get it to you in twenty-four hours. Our cost, not yours, by the way. Costly? Yes! But we have to find ways to reallocate resources to become more consumer-responsive as opposed to being distribution-driven. This is one of the things that has killed direct selling companies over the past decade. Companies, Avon included, have paid too much attention to their sales force at the expense of their customers.

I am not suggesting that we should ignore the sales force. But we have to understand that we need to be better consumer marketers. There is not a direct selling company in this country, including Avon, that has the consumer marketing skills that are required if it is to successfully compete in the next decade.

As an aside, there are two other requirements for successful direct selling companies in the years ahead. Many direct selling companies are multilevel. Avon has one level. There are advantages and disadvantages to each. Multilevel companies have virtually no fixed costs in their sales organization. We have a high fixed cost in maintaining our sales management organization. Even so, one reason Avon is so big and why most multilevel firms will not get to our size is that they do not control their markets. The success of a multilevel company to a great extent depends on how successful its distributors are in penetrating a market. But distributors come and go. At Avon we control the market. We have zoned the United States into eight hundred thousand 100-home territories. In some cases we know more about the markets than the Census Bureau does. We know where our sales come from and where they do not on a very micro basis.

The other thing that has hampered direct selling in the past is that many of these companies have been started by very charismatic entrepreneurs. What happens when that individual leaves the company? Some companies have done pretty well. Amway, I think, has made a good transition from the days of Devoss and does quite well. Mary Kay is working at the transition, but transitions are difficult. Because so many of these companies focus all of their efforts on the charisma of the leader, it will be interesting to see what happens when that person ultimately leaves the company.

Analogous to direct selling, retailing has undergone an enormous transition. Sophisticated technology allows retailers to know at any given time exactly what product is selling to whom, how fast, and in many instances on a store-by-store basis.

With knowledge comes power. In negotiations for promotions, firms with the knowledge hold all the cards, and some of them dictate shelf space. Retail margins are being painfully squeezed. Stores have had to tighten their belts, and the result is that the helpful retail clerk is a vanishing species. Sometimes it seems impossible to find even a surly one!

And yet, there are some real winners in retailing today. There are organizations that have overcome the obstacles. Look at The Limited, Toys "R" Us, Wal-Mart, The Gap, Dillard Department Stores, and Nordstrom. Some, like Dillard, have superior technology of their own. At Nordstrom, the culture is that the customer is *always* right—no questions asked. But virtually all of these leaders have somehow managed to offer product segments that match consumer segments. They are efficient. They are effective. And they are profitable.

We in direct selling can learn from these favored few retailers. It may sound ironic, but one of the best ways to make gains against retailers is to do what the best of them do: offer segmented products to segmented consumers. Doing so calls for local decisions on sales and marketing strategy. In a company such as Avon, certain operations should be centralized—global information, sourcing, and so on. But the local businesses, from Pasadena, California, to Paris, France, and Lima, Peru, must be empowered to identify spot changes—and act directly. They cannot spend three months preparing a presentation for headquarters and another three months waiting for a decision.

The new way of direct selling, a hybrid, will be very different from the world we know. Difficult to organize? Certainly. Costly? Undoubtedly. But we must make these changes in the way we do business, and we must make them fast. The world is spinning faster than ever. Time is compressed. The United States went from sweatshop to Silicon Valley in forty years. But Thailand went from rice bowl to satellite in just ten years. And in Taiwan, wages rose from $30 a month ten years ago to $500 a month today.

These are just random examples of the exponential changes every business faces. All over the world, we are attempting to attract and please consumers who simply are not going to wait two years or more while we research a trend to death to figure out if it is enduring or faddish. But these same consumers will respond to the nimble marketer, the fleet of foot. Particularly in mature markets such as the United States, the female consumer of the 1990s and beyond will be increasingly demanding. Our research paints this picture of the typical U.S. customer:

- She will want to buy from companies she trusts. She wants a "trusted" company to help her sift through the clutter of the marketplace and help her make brand selections without having to invest a lot of time.
- She will insist on products that seem designed for her as an individual. That means we must stop trying to appeal to the broadest possible audience. As one expert stated, "It's okay if 80 percent of your market hates you, as long as the other 20 percent loves you. But they need to love you a lot."
- She will be increasingly skeptical of claims. Products that promise to magically change her life will earn her scorn.
- She will want to know the nuts and bolts of the products. By no accident, we at Avon have found that our consumer information services reach an increasingly broad audience. Last year we distributed, at consumer request, almost four million pamphlets on ingredients and skin care products alone. This is a service we offer to all our customers, and one they enthusiastically welcome.
- Finally, women will spend more to get more. But they will not spend carelessly.

On the other hand, today's marketplace is a global one, and firms of all ilk, retailers and direct sellers alike, must be prepared to take advantage of this fact. Avon's sales today are almost 60 percent international; 63 percent of its earnings are internationally derived. Our international markets are growing twice as fast as our domestic markets, and our developing markets are growing at an even faster rate. By developing markets, I mean the third world markets—Mexico, Brazil, Venezuela, Chile, Peru, Taiwan, Thailand, East Germany, and so forth. Eastern Europe has enormous opportunities. As the Wall came down a year ago, our district sales managers were there with tens of thousands of gift packages. Guess what they contained. That's right, Avon products. We started by putting our first Avon sales representative in the eastern part of Germany in March of 1990; eight months later there are over ten thousand. In 1990 we will do over $10 million in sales, and we will make $2 million in pretax profit in the eastern part of Germany in less than eight months. In November 1990, Avon had the grand opening of its first direct selling business in China. In ten days, seven hundred sales representatives were appointed; our challenge there is simply to meet demand.

The future is internationalization, not only for direct sellers but for retailers in general. Firms that do not internationalize are missing the boat because there are enormous opportunities off-shore. People need the work, the quality of local products is often shabby, and American companies that come in can fill an incredible void. We have to stop talking about globalization and start acting globally, because that is where the action is.

The United Sates is a mature market. Companies can grow by taking share from others, but taking share is difficult and costly. I would much rather make the heavy investment required elsewhere where I know the operating margins are likely larger and profits easier to come by.

Finally, in addition to internationalizing, firms that hope to compete in the year 2000 must position themselves to anticipate change and react quickly. Those that do not anticipate change will cease to exist. Those that do anticipate change will not only survive; they will prevail.

7

Multiple Channels of Distribution and Their Impact on Retailing

Gary L. Frazier and Tasadduq A. Shervani

Manufacturers and retailers of consumer products are separated from their customers and prospective customers in many ways. Products are produced and displayed before they need to be consumed, and production and retail locations are geographically removed from where consumers reside. The channel of distribution, which refers to the set of people and institutions that performs the functions necessary to move a product from its producer to prospective customers, provides a mechanism through which separation can be overcome. Time, place, possession, and form utilities can be facilitated for consumers through the performance of necessary functions or job activities in the channel of distribution. Bucklin (1966, p. xi) underscores the critical importance of distribution channels when he states, "Study of the distribution channel is basic to the understanding of the marketing process. It is basic because it focuses upon the essential nature of marketing: the interaction among commercial institutions and between these institutions and the consumer."

The view that a single channel of distribution (e.g., manufacturer to specialty retailer to consumer) is sufficient for any line of consumer products has been dramatically challenged over the past two decades (cf., Weigand 1977). More and more, multiple channels of distribution are being utilized by manufacturers as well as retailers to market their product lines, whether personal computers, running shoes, or food products. The potential benefits for the initiator are many, including increased exposure and sales. However, certain problems can accompany the use of multiple channels. For example, intrabrand competition can become intense and within-channel conflicts can rapidly accelerate. At this point, there is a paucity of knowledge regarding the trade-offs involved in the use of multiple channels.

The purpose of this chapter is to provide a series of insights (predictions) regarding the impact that multiple channels will have on the nature and structure of retailing in the 1990s and beyond. Toward this end, we will first define "multiple channels" and examine the underlying rationale for all channel-related activities undertaken by firms, including the use of multiple channels to bring products to market. Next, we will provide some examples of manufacturers and retailers currently making use of multiple channels of distribution. The motivations behind the establishment of multiple channels will then be considered, followed by a discussion of the problems that can accompany their use. We will highlight that, for many products, the key question appears to be not whether a multiple channel approach should be utilized, but rather how many and what type of channels should be established by the firm. Finally, based on the earlier material, seven predictions will be made concerning how multiple channels are likely to influence the face of retailing in the future.

It is important to note that our intent is to be provocative and to stimulate thinking about retailing in the future, not to provide a comprehensive review or a detailed examination of either multiple distribution channels or retailing distribution channels. Hence, the relative abstractness and sometimes sweeping generalizations should be considered in the context of our intended contribution.

DEFINITION AND OBJECTIVES

A separate channel for a product line is in place whenever a distinct process exists through which a product can be selected, purchased, ordered, and received by the firm's customers. The process could be varied based on ownership (i.e., a company-owned or independent channel), type of intermediary (e.g., mass merchandiser or discount store), location (e.g., in-store or at-home) or technology (mail-order or electronic-order). Accordingly, multiple channels exist for a product line whenever more than one process or mechanism is used in moving it from its producer to prospective customers. For example, a manufacturer could distribute a product line through company-owned stores as well as through independent specialty stores, department stores, and a TV shopping channel. Retailers can also use multiple channels in serving their various customer groups. Stores could be used to facilitate and serve walk-in customers in shopping malls and stand-alone locations, whereas telemarketing efforts and catalogs in conjunction with a delivery service could be used to sell and distribute merchandise to other customers.

The rationale for developing dual or multiple distribution for certain products and services is firmly rooted in a firm's overall channel strategy objective. Broadly speaking, there are three sets of considerations that guide a firm's channel strategy and the resulting mix of channels, commonly classified under three headings as economic, control, and adaptability considerations (Kotler 1988).

Economic Considerations

It is difficult to imagine a situation in which economic considerations would not be important to a firm in determining channel strategy. Although there are several instances in which economic considerations might be relegated to a secondary position relative to other factors, they almost always play a major role in determining channel strategy. Firms look at the economics of their distribution channel(s) vis-à-vis their competitors as well as their own past performance. Unless a channel can meet certain basic economic goals, it is likely to be jettisoned in favor of more efficient alternatives.

The economic objectives of the firm with respect to a distribution channel can be divided into two parts—the cost efficiency and the revenue generation capabilities of the distribution channel. The critical question is the extent to which the channel is able to deliver required outputs while staying cost competitive. However, focusing solely on cost efficiency is dangerous because it ignores the second important economic goal, the revenue (sales) generation performance of the channel. Sales performance refers to the market coverage and penetration the channel is able to achieve. Often a high level of cost efficiency comes at the expense of revenue performance. This may be undesirable and, if so, firms must constantly try to balance cost efficiency and market coverage objectives. The overall economic assessment of a distribution channel is usually represented as a ratio of revenue to costs.

Control Considerations

In addition to economic goals, firms also establish control objectives for their distribution channels. They attempt to exercise control over their distribution channel to enhance their ability to guarantee channel outputs such as service, channel support for the product, and acceptance of the firm's pricing and promotion approach, as well as future product line offerings. In some instances, the firm may relegate economic considerations to a secondary role to achieve control objectives. For example, backward and forward channel integration is often undertaken for control considerations even though the firm may experience certain cost inefficiencies and reduced market coverage.

Control considerations also have at least two dimensions—channel competence and channel compliance. The competence of the distribution channel is its ability to provide the level of support (e.g., selling) required by the firm. Channel compliance is the extent to which the distribution channel in question has the willingness to provide necessary support. Together, the ability and willingness of the distribution channel determine the extent to which the firm has control over its distribution channel. If a channel has the ability but not the willingness, or vice versa, the firm must take corrective action (possibly integration) to ensure support for its products.

Adaptability Considerations

Adaptability considerations are the third set of considerations a firm must take into account when developing channel strategy. At times, the cost efficiency of the channel or the level of control achieved is secondary to the ability of the channel to evolve as future customer, competitive, and market conditions change. In such situations the adaptability of the distribution channel is likely be an important consideration in the process of developing distribution strategy.

Channel adaptability has at least two dimensions—growth and flexibility. Channel growth refers to the extent to which various entities in the distribution channel are open to the idea of growth. In some instances, divergent expectations and goals with respect to growth are major causes of channel conflict between suppliers and other channel members. In addition to growth, flexibility is a second dimension of channel adaptability. Flexibility refers to the ability of the distribution channel to adapt to changes in the channel environment. In a rapidly changing environment, a firm may give precedence to flexibility over costs and control as the major channel objective. Consequently, the firm is likely to trade increased flexibility for perhaps higher costs and/or lower control over the activities of its distribution channel(s).

Trade-offs

Clearly, any firm faces several trade offs as it develops channel strategy, in particular, the decision on whether to use a single channel or dual or multiple channels to bring products to market. Further complicating the situation is that additional channels may be in-house or third party. For example, if a firm utilizes an in-house distribution channel, and the additional channel is also in-house, the firm is likely to achieve greater market coverage and lower costs (as customer segments are better matched to the "right" channel) but may also experience loss of flexibility as the development of in-house channels requires further investment and greater asset exposure. As the firm invests in additional in-house channels, it reduces its ability to react to future changes in market, customer and competitive conditions. On the other hand, if a firm moves from a single in-house channel to additional third-party channels, it maintains flexibility (lower asset exposure) while gaining market coverage and lowering costs. Simultaneously, though, the firm is likely to sacrifice some degree of control over its distribution channel to obtain these benefits.

If the firm's existing channel is third party, the decision to add an additional in-house channel is likely to lead to higher levels of control overall, even though existing channel members will perceive the additional channel to be a threat. At the same time, the firm gives up future flexibility because of greater asset exposure while getting the usual benefits of better market coverage and perhaps lower costs. Finally, if the firm has a third party channel and adds an additional third-party channel, it can expect to achieve the usual expanded coverage and lower costs while losing some degree of control. Flexibility, of course, is maintained as the firm does not increase asset exposure.

Table 7.1 summarizes the trade-offs involved in the multiple channel decision. Although the trade-off analysis is only indicative (i.e., trade-offs may differ in some instances), it does provide insight into the complex nature of the multiple-channel decision.

Table 7.1.   Trade-offs in Going from Single to Dual or Multiple Channels

Existing Channel	Additional Channel	
	In-house	Third-party
In-house	Economic (+) Control (0) Adaptability (-)	Economic (+) Control (-) Adaptability (+)
Third-party	Economic (+) Control (+) Adaptability (-)	Economic (+) Control (-) Adaptability (0)

THE INCREASING USE OF MULTIPLE CHANNELS

In spite of the complex nature of the trade-offs involved, the use of multiple channels by both retailers and suppliers is increasing rapidly. This section looks at the phenomenon of multiple channels from the perspectives of both retailers and suppliers and presents examples of the use of multiple distribution channels. Next, the trade-offs involved in using multiple channels are identified and discussed.

Manufacturers

Numerous examples exist of manufacturers that make use of multiple distribution channels. Carnation relies on a variety of retail stores to sell its pet foods (e.g., supermarkets, discount stores). Recently, it began promoting and selling a brand of pet food directly to consumers through the mail. Rubbermaid acquired Little Tikes a couple of years ago, a toy company that originally made its mark by selling through specialty stores. After the acquisition, Rubbermaid made a decision to expand distribution by selling the toy lines to discount stores (e.g., Wal-Mart) as well. The existing relationships that Rubbermaid had with discount stores played a key role in the decision.

Apple Computer's primary channel to the consumer market is from the company through a group of independent distributors to an array of different types of independent retailers. At the same time, Apple uses a company sales force to sell to university bookstores that, in turn, sell to college students, staff, and faculty at special educational discounts. Dell Computers started out selling its low-end personal computers through mail-order. It has opened up another channel in the past year by agreeing to sell its computers through a chain of independently owned retail stores. IBM is selling its PS/1 line of personal computers through mass merchandisers (e.g., Sears) as well as its own dealer network.

A majority of manufacturers of hearing aids use multiple channels of distribution. Physicians specializing in hearing problems, audiologists, hospitals, and specialty dealers can all be used in their channels of distribution. Likewise, fashion trend setters like Laura Ashley, Ralph Lauren, and Esprit make a majority of their sales through independent retailers (e.g., department stores) while at the same time they own retail outlets that sell their own fashions exclusively. Levi-Strauss sells its jeans through specialty stores, department stores, and mass merchandisers (e.g., Sears, J. C. Penney).

Other examples of the use of multiple channels by manufacturers include factory outlets. Dansk (a manufacturer of fine china), American Tourister Luggage, and Walden Books make use of factory outlets in addition to their traditional retail channels. Increasingly, manufacturers are using "special event marketing" as a means to promote and distribute their products. Special events, such as a 10K race or a home show, provide opportunities to appeal to a specialized segment of potential buyers in a relatively uncluttered environment. Such events can be exclusively sponsored by a firm and matched with a product that is sold at the event. For example, Anheuser-Busch has sponsored surfing competitions on the West Coast where it sets up booths to sell its various brands of beer. Nike has sponsored running races where it has sold its running shoes. Weyerhaeuser has sponsored home shows where some of its building materials could be viewed and ordered.

Retailers

Many examples also exist of retailers using multiple channels to reach their customers. Customers of Vons, a supermarket chain in Southern California, can place orders over the phone. Vons employees fill each order, which customers then pick up. Other supermarkets, such as Jorgenson's in Beverly Hills and Pasadena, and D'Agostino Supermarkets in New York, not only will fill orders but will also deliver them to their customers' homes. Kroger Supermarkets is experimenting with a PC-based ordering and home delivery system. Such a system has been used with success in England. Several supermarket chains are now placing convenience stores within the same buildings as their supermarkets.

First Interstate Bank is using supermarkets in another way. It has established branches in certain Ralph's supermarket locations in California. Customers can carry out simple banking transactions in these branches. Moreover, First Interstate has salespeople at each branch who contact people while they shop for groceries. If the individual is currently a First Interstate customer, the salesperson asks whether he or she can be of service. If the shopper is not a customer, the salesperson will attempt to sell him or her on the merits of joining the First Interstate family.

Many domestic department stores (e.g., Nordstrom) have set up mail-order operations. Their main offering to customers is the convenience, time savings, and broader selections available through mail order. In one particular instance, the Nordstrom store in Alaska sells special cold-weather merchandise not normally carried at other Nordstrom locations by mail order to customers nationwide. Harrods of London has taken this a step further by developing an international direct-response campaign. Concerned by a falloff in tourism (foreign tourists account for a significant proportion of sales), Harrods has used newspaper advertising and an international 800 number in implementing its multiple channel approach in other countries. J. C. Penney has started its own home shopping channel on television.

In other examples, Paul Harris, a retailer of fashion products, sells through both regular specialty stores and discount stores. Merchandise that remains unsold after reasonable markdowns in its regular stores is shipped to its discount stores. Florsheim's primary sales-distribution channel rests on customers walking into its retail stores and finding shoes they desire. However, frequently individual stores are out of particular styles or sizes demanded by customers. In an attempt to solve this problem and better serve its customers, Florsheim has established a distinct and separate channel based on a videotex system. Customers can use the videotex system to locate and order shoes directly from central warehouse locations. The shoes are then delivered through a private parcel service.

Discussion and Conclusions

Both manufacturers and retailers are experiencing greater use of multiple channels than ever before. Clearly, many have felt that there is a positive net benefit from using multiple channels. In the case of Little Tikes, Rubbermaid traded off lessened control for higher cost efficiency and greater market coverage. On the other hand, Dahlberg, a major supplier of hearing aids, opted for greater control over market coverage by moving towards substantially fewer franchisees instead of a large number of independent dealers. The same logic prevails in decisions by retailers to add additional channels. J. C. Penney opted for greater market coverage and cost efficiency by moving into home shopping on television. However, these benefits were offset to some extent by the loss of future flexibility as investment levels and asset exposure also rose.

Although we have developed an approach that explains the logic behind the use of multiple channels, we still need to understand the reasons behind their increasing use in most advanced economies. What are the underlying conditions that are driving both suppliers and retailers to develop a portfolio of channels to bring products to market? In the next section we present some of the trends that have led to the increased use of multiple channels in recent years.

MOTIVATIONS FOR THE USE OF MULTIPLE CHANNELS

Three trends have contributed to the increased use of multiple distribution channels in recent years. These trends are, respectively, demographic trends, technology trends, and competitive trends. Each is briefly overviewed below.

Demographic Trends

A number of significant demographic trends are evident in our country in recent years. Income and wealth-holding patterns are evolving rapidly. The middle class is shrinking, whereas both the upper and lower classes are growing. As a result, the financial resources available to American households are very different now than in the past. A much larger percentage of households than ever before is now considered wealthy and possesses the buying power to satisfy a great many desires. The sale of high-end products (e.g., $3500 television sets) has been facilitated by this trend. On the other hand, a large percentage of households is considered poor in an economic sense. These households are constrained in the merchandise that they can afford; even the purchase of bare necessities can be problematical.

The numerical increase at the high end of the income distribution is due, in part, to the increase of dual income households. As more and more women enter the workforce, this tendency is likely to continue over the next decade. Along with a high level of financial resources, these households face major time constraints because both adults are working. Consequently, less time is available for traditional shopping activities, and members of such households should be willing (and able) to pay for value-added services within channels of distribution that conserve their time. The number of families headed by a single adult has also increased significantly, leading to major time pressures here as well, although their ability to pay for convenience will be less than that of dual-income households.

The increased time constraint means that increasingly consumers are seeking value not only from goods, but also from the transaction itself. Hence retailers need to be aware that consumers are likely to consider the price of the goods plus transaction and acquisition costs when deciding what and where to buy.

Another major demographic trend has been the aging of the U.S. population. Aside from making certain product categories more germane (e.g., pharmaceuticals), this trend has resulted in greater demand for hassle-free, convenient shopping. Mobility is the primary constraint in shopping for the aged, not the amount of time available during the day or week to shop. While a good deal of the wealth in this nation is held by households headed by elderly individuals, a large percentage of elderly households face serious financial difficulties.

These and other demographic trends have led to an extreme fragmentation of the consumer market. A larger number of meaningful population segments exists now than in years past, each with different wealth, life-styles, attitudes, brand preferences, and shopping patterns (cf. Bates 1989). The utility of each segment to a particular retailer should reflect such factors as the importance of convenience and product quality as well as the desire for augmented products and services.

This increased fragmentation of the U.S. market is a primary reason for the increased use of multiple channels by manufacturers and retailers. Distribution channels provide the means by which merchandise is made available to consumers. What functions are performed in the channel and at what level are largely dependent on the value that particular groups of consumers place on them. If a firm sells a product line to one very homogeneous segment of customers placing similar value on convenience, price, and all other product and channel attributes, a single channel of distribution may be sufficient. However, in the more likely case where a firm is attempting to sell a product line to each of several distinct segments that vary in the product-channel attributes they are seeking, a single channel will be insufficient. As Wasson (1983, pp. 233, 234) states:

> Because the same or similar offerings often are bought by quite diverse kinds of buyers, many producers must sell through multiple channels to reach their full potential. . . . The segments served, the assortments desired, and the appropriate channel contacts of most . . . segments usually differ too widely for any line to be sold through a single channel, even for physically identical offerings.

Therefore, the increased fragmentation of the consumer market in the United States has led many manufacturers and retailers to develop a portfolio of distribution channels that provides varying levels of value-added services to varying segments. Without the use of multiple channels, market coverage will likely be inadequate, with sales and competitive position weakened as a result. The use of multiple channels is consistent with consumer expectations that merchandise be available when and where desired to satisfy and complement varied life-styles. However, the use of multiple channels leads to lower levels of control if the additional channels are third party, and loss of flexibility if the additional channels are in-house channels. Trade-offs involving economic, control, and adaptability objectives are inherent in the development and use of multiple channels.

Technology Trends

Rapid advances in technology have also been taking place over the past few years. New technologies include 800 and 900 telephone services, interactive television, computer bulletin boards, cellular telephones, various manifestations of personal computers, on-line information services, shopping networks, videocassette recorders, and fax machines. Moreover, new methods have been developed to conduct business in conjunction with these new technologies. For example, increasing proportions of catalog orders are placed by phone on 800 numbers, and a majority of the deliveries are made through private parcel services. Services such as Compuserve and Prodigy not only provide information and entertainment but also provide opportunities to shop for and order a wide variety of products and services ranging from groceries to travel services to fashion products.

These advances in technology and methods have helped to promote the use of multiple channels in two distinct ways. First, they provide firms with additional distribution options. No longer must traditional means of distribution be utilized, as customers can now shop by telephone, mail, television, computer, fax, and surrogate. These new technologies and methods have helped to make in-home shopping feasible.

Second, they can provide firms with cost-efficient means to contact prospective customers. For example, manufacturers who were primarily communicating with customers through nonintegrated channels are now finding it is possible to reach them also through telemarketing efforts at a substantially lower cost than other integrated channel alternatives. In this case, manufacturers increase their channel control by adding an additional in-house channel (telemarketing) while keeping cost efficiency high through the application of information technology. At the same time, firms must move with caution as the increase in integration is likely to result in less flexibility. However, the net result is that new technologies allow firms to enter customer segments much more easily than before. In other words, market entry barriers are no longer so high, as new technologies enable firms to enhance market coverage while containing costs.

Competitive Trends

While the fragmentation of the consumer market and advances in technology appear to be the two primary drivers behind the increasing use of multiple channels, at least two additional factors also appear to contribute. First, competition at each level of the channel for consumer products is becoming more and more intense. Firms cannot afford to stand by while major competitors make inroads into important market segments through nontraditional distribution channels. The use of multiple channels is a natural response to the issue of market coverage.

Second, firms that are highly dependent on any one distribution channel are competitively vulnerable. In such situations, the firm could possess a serious power disadvantage relative to associated channel members and/or major competitors. As a result, control is likely to be low if the single channel is nonintegrated. Moreover, should the channel become mature or start declining in its performance relative to other channels, the firm's own performance will suffer as well. If the channel in question is integrated, the firm has low flexibility because of sunk costs. The use of multiple channels provides a means of reducing its dependency on the idiosyncrasies of one specific channel while simultaneously insulating itself from environmental volatility. With enhanced control and greater adaptability, the firm's risk may be lowered.

POTENTIAL PROBLEMS WITH MULTIPLE CHANNELS

Despite their benefits, the use of multiple distribution channels has several potential limitations. Although certain of these limitations are common across firms, many are unique to manufacturers and to retailers.

Potential Problems Faced by the Manufacturer

While multiple channels offer a good deal of promise, manufacturers of consumer products must think carefully before adopting a multiple channel strategy. Such caution is based, in part, on the fact that considerable intrabrand competition can accompany the use of multiple channels to the extent members of the manufacturer's various channels compete vigorously with one another. If intrabrand competition gets out of hand, lower channel control is likely to result.

Intrabrand competition in a multiple channel context is based in large part on the ability of consumers to shop for the product through a variety of means. For example, if a brand of personal computer is sold through specialty stores, mass merchandisers, and mail-order houses, consumers can collect information from and shop each channel. A certain proportion of customers will identify the store-channel that offers the personal computer and associated services at the lowest price. Other channel members selling the brand will become aware of such behavior and develop and/or adjust their behavior to promote their own success. The greater the degree of cross-shopping by consumers, the more intense the intrabrand competition will be.

Only if the customer groups served by a firm's multiple channels were perfectly distinguishable from one another with no cross-shopping occurring would intrabrand competition not be an issue. However, the likelihood of such a scenario appears very low. Experience indicates it is extremely difficult to keep multiple channels completely independent from one another.

High intrabrand competition in a multiple channel context is likely to lead to tremendous pressure on the retail price of the brand, as members of any one channel will be sensitive to the prices offered by members of other channels. In order to effectively compete and win business from others, prices will tend to be lowered. Such pressure on the retail price can seriously reduce the gross margins attained by members of the various channels from selling the brand.

Channel members that provide significant value-added services are especially vulnerable in this context. Providing value-added services (e.g., advice on the best camera for a particular use) takes considerable resources (e.g., hiring, training, and retaining experts on cameras). Value-added resellers normally have a disadvantage in cost structure compared to channel members that compete mainly on the basis of price or convenience, such as discount stores or mail-order firms. This means that the value-added reseller in a diverse multiple channel context must either (1) charge a higher price than other channel members based on the provision of valued services or (2) live with a relatively small gross margin.

If the value-added reseller does charge a higher price, the problem of "free ridership" can become critical. A free rider is someone that relies on other channel members to provide essential services or information for the consumer and then gains a portion of these consumers as customers by charging a lower price for the core product. For example, a customer may go to a specialty camera store and gain knowledge about cameras from a salesperson. Given this knowledge, the customer may then buy a preferred brand of camera from a discount store, which is a free rider in this situation, knowingly or not.

When the use of multiple channels by the manufacturer leads to intense intrabrand competition and greatly lowered prices and gross margins among members of its various channels, at least two other negative effects can occur. First, considerable ill will can arise among channel members toward the manufacturer. The manufacturer may be seen as possessing no loyalty and little concern about the welfare of its channel members. Conflict and disharmony among channel members are also likely to arise (Weigand 1977).

Second, members of the various channels may begin to reduce the support and attention they give to the manufacturer's product line. They may add additional suppliers who are major competitors of the focal manufacturer. They may switch resources (e.g., shelf-space, salesperson time) to other lines. Customers may be directed away from the manufacturer's product line. Value-added resellers appear to be especially prone to perform such actions.

While a lessening dependence on any one channel member or channel can represent an attractive outcome of using multiple channels from the manufacturer's point of view, it also has its potential disadvantages. Key among them is that the manufacturer is likely to be less important to any single channel member under a multiple channel approach, as sales and profit dollars are spread across many channel members. This means that the manufacturer's power may be relatively low in many of its channel relationships. Ultimately, the control of the manufacturer over associated channel members may be in jeopardy.

Another common multiple distribution problem can arise when the manufacturer uses an integrated channel or channels in conjunction with a nonintegrated channel or channels. Independent channel members often perceive that the manufacturer's integrated channels receive preferential treatment, even when this is not the case. For example, independent retailers may accuse the manufacturer of structuring product line sales quotas and terms of sale in such a way they are placed at a competitive disadvantage vis-à-vis the integrated channel. Such perceptions become especially acute during difficult economic times and are a further source of conflict in multiple channel systems.

Two other potential weaknesses with the use of multiple channels need to be considered by the manufacturer. First, some channels may be better matches with the image of the product line and manufacturer than others, whereas other channels can hamper the image of the manufacturer in the marketplace. For example, a manufacturer of top-of-the-line stereo equipment may hurt its brand identity by using discount stores in one of its channels. Manufacturers must be very careful in deciding which channels make sense for a given product line.

Second, a good deal of complexity is inherent in the use of multiple channels. The manufacturer must contend with channel members having widely varying capabilities, profit structures, and servicing requirements. Idiosyncratic differences in cultures and policies across channel members also must be addressed. Distinct market strategies and investment and performance criteria may need to be developed for each channel type. At the same time, comparative assessments of performance across channels will be necessary. If the manufacturer does not have the resources and capability to deal with such complexities, use of multiple channels may impede rather than promote its performance.

Potential Problems Faced by the Retailer

If the retailer restricts itself to company-owned multiple channels (e.g., stores, catalogs), which is the typical case, it is not circumventing other members of associated channels in implementing a multiple channel approach. In such cases, the major challenge is to ensure that each of the channels makes sense on economic grounds. A major problem could arise if certain of the retailer's suppliers become upset by the mechanisms or means through which the retailer is selling their products. For example, a supplier could become irritated if one of its prestige product lines (e.g., gourmet cheese) were being sold through a retailer's catalog that primarily emphasized basic, nonprestige items. This could interfere with the supplier's marketing plans and harm the image of the its entire product line. In general, however, suppliers may be very supportive of retailer attempts to develop multiple channels, as the retailer is attempting to sell their products through as many means as possible.

However, if the retailer links with independent channel members in one or several of its multiple channels (e.g., it uses independent sales representatives), the same basic challenges faced by the manufacturer in utilizing multiple channels could be faced by the retailer as well. Intrabrand or intratype competition could be heightened in the territories served by the retailer's multiple channels, prices and margins could be reduced, conflicts and alienation could arise, and support and control could wane (at least in the independent channels). Increased complexity may not be handled well by the retailing firm, and its image could be diffused and hampered in the marketplace. While the use of independent intermediaries by retailers in a multiple channel approach does not appear to be all that common, this could change in the future.

As evident, utilization of a multiple channel approach has its potential strengths as well as its potential weaknesses. In some situations, the former dominate the latter, in which case the emergence of multiple channels is to be expected. When changes in demographics, needs, wants, and preferences at the consumer level dictate that multiple channels be used in a wide variety of circumstances by manufacturers and retailers, this trend is reinforced. Adequate market coverage and the satisfaction of customers must take precedence over everything else. In such instances, the main question is not whether multiple channels should be used, but rather how many and what type of channels should be utilized.

MULTICHANNEL PREDICTIONS

How the use of multiple distribution channels will influence the nature and structure of retailing in the 1990s and beyond is the question to which we now turn. Specifically, seven predictions are made regarding the use of multiple channels in retailing in the future. These predictions are summarized in Table 7.2 and discussed below in detail.

Prediction One

The first prediction is that all firms, from manufacturers to retailers, will increasingly emphasize resource analysis and an understanding of power-dependence relationships with their suppliers/channel members. This is only logical given the increasing sophistication of management and the heightened competition likely to exist in the future.

Table 7.2.   Predictions About Multiple Channels in Retailing

Prediction One

Firms will increasingly emphasize resource analysis and an understanding of power-dependence relationships with their suppliers/channel members.

Prediction Two

Firms attempting to serve multiple and diverse groups of customers will increasingly establish multiple channels.

Prediction Three

Retailers that emphasize width rather than depth of product lines in their stores will need to develop multiple channels to enhance their performance; suppliers that emphasize depth rather than width of product lines will need to develop multiple channels to enhance their performance.

Prediction Four

Firms catering to the high-end market will increasingly establish multiple channels.

Prediction Five

Firms possessing significant resources and aspiring to market dominance will tend to establish multiple channels.

Prediction Six

In cases where multiple channels are needed, retailers will increasingly establish nonintegrated channels by means of independent intermediaries.

Prediction Seven

Firms will consider distribution channels among the alternative media for use in communicating with consumers about their merchandise.

With the use of multiple channels by manufacturers becoming the rule rather than the exception, it is more critical than ever that a firm understand its business position relative to each of its suppliers/channel members currently and in the future.   Because business positions can change very quickly when based on the use of multiple channels, it is necessary for the firm to perform a thorough resource analysis.   A resource analysis is essentially a supplier/channel member portfolio analysis that recognizes the need to monitor channel trading relations and develop strategic plans for future distribution needs.   Development of an effective resource strategy is dependent on the firm's knowing its relative power or bargaining position with its suppliers/channel members.   Only then can it make commitments and plan for change with any degree of confidence.

To understand its business position vis-à-vis the manufacturer (hereafter referred to as the "supplier" in this discussion), the retailer must consider (1) What is the current and future importance of the channel in which the retailer (supplier) is a part to the supplier (retailer)? and (2) What is the current and future importance of the retailer (supplier) within its channel to the supplier (retailer)? If other channels are much more important to the supplier and the retailer represents a relatively unimportant player in its own channel to the supplier, and these conditions are expected to continue or even be strengthened in the future, the bargaining power of the retailer would be relatively low. This bargaining power would be even more precarious if, at the same time, the retailer depended on the supplier a great deal to achieve its performance goals.

Based on such an analysis, the retailer has a number of strategic options available. It may need to lessen its dependence on certain suppliers. This may mean adding more suppliers for the product lines in question or reallocating resources (e.g., shelf-space, promotional money) to other areas of the business or product lines. Establishing multiple channels of its own represents another possibility. Abandoning certain suppliers is another option. On the other hand, the retailer may decide to increase its dependence on other suppliers and develop stronger relational exchanges with them. A reallocation of more resources (e.g., retailer time) to these suppliers may be necessary.

It has always been true that, at any point in time, a firm may be investing, entrenching, and retreating in its channel activities (Dickson 1983). However, with the increased reliance on multiple channels, both the need for such activities and the rapidity with which they occur are increasing.

Prediction Two

Firms attempting to serve multiple and diverse groups of customers will increasingly establish multiple channels. This prediction is nearly a tautology.

When a firm is attempting to serve a large number of customer groups that are highly diverse in nature in terms of their demographic characteristics, shopping patterns, preferences, and the like, both the incentive and the pressure to use multiple channels will be great. The value each group places on quality, services, convenience, and price will likely vary. By establishing multiple channels the firm can make available different bundles of product-channel attributes and benefits to each of these diverse customer groups. Sales and customer satisfaction will likely be promoted as a result.

The viability of a multiple channel approach by the firm will be enhanced if the level of consumer cross-shopping across alternative channels is relatively low. In such cases, the integrity of each channel can be more easily maintained, with low cannibalization occurring across channels. For example, Cort and Dominquez (1977) found the level of cross-shopping to be low across specialty stores and budget stores for women's fashion products.

Prediction Three

Retailers that emphasize width rather than depth of product lines in their stores will need to develop multiple channels to enhance their performance; suppliers that emphasize depth rather than width of product lines will need to develop multiple channels to enhance performance. Retailers that emphasize the width rather than the depth of product lines in their stores (e.g., department stores) currently tend to be at a competitive disadvantage, because consumers increasingly seem to prefer to shop in stores carrying a wide array of brands within any particular product category (e.g., VCRs) rather than shopping in stores carrying more limited arrays (the exception being convenience stores). The success of many specialty store operations (e.g., Circuit City) in today's marketplace can be attributed, at least in part, to the depth of their product lines.

The use of multiple channels offers a possible way out of this dilemma for retailers committed to a "width" concept in their stores. By developing multiple channels based on the use of new technologies such as videotex and 800 numbers and adding additional suppliers for these channels, these retailers can offer product depth through other means. The benefits of having wide product lines within their stores would be supplemented by the benefits of having deep product lines in nontraditional channels. A competitive weakness could be at least partially alleviated in the process.

On the other hand, suppliers that emphasize depth rather than width will need to develop multiple channels to enhance market coverage for their product lines. As a deep product line results in the existence of an array of price-performance combinations, the use of multiple channels is needed to reach as many customers as possible for each price-performance combination (within reason). A single channel may lack the market coverage needed to make a strategy based on product-line depth successful.

The match between the needs of suppliers that emphasize product line depth and retailers that emphasize product-line width is fortuitous because it facilitates their cooperation. If customers like to choose from a broad array of brands and product configurations at a single location (because of convenience, etc.), the pressure on suppliers to offer many brands and features and the pressure on retailers to carry multiple brands and feature combinations enables them to work together profitably.

Prediction Four

Firms catering to the high-end market will increasingly establish multiple channels. Key among the benefits sought by a large portion of upscale consumers are convenience and saving time in their shopping efforts. For such benefits, these consumers are willing and able to pay a higher price. The traditional shopping trip is often perceived as inconvenient and time-consuming for many products, especially frequently purchased consumer package goods (e.g., detergents, beverages).

Firms catering to these upscale consumers need to find better ways to provide more convenience and save them shopping time. The development of multiple channels represents the clearest and surest way to do just this. Channels that allow up-scale consumers to shop from home appear especially attractive. Based on the usage trends of catalogs, 800 numbers, computer viewing and ordering systems, and television shopping channels, there is no question that in-home sales will increase substantially in the future.

Firms failing to take advantage of the multiple channel approach to serving the upscale market could see their performance decline severely. For example, supermarkets with a high proportion of upscale consumers in their trade area may need to offer electronic ordering and home delivery to maintain their competitive position. Because the high end of the market possesses the resources to pay for many of the additional services desired, it is attractive for firms to develop their own distribution channels to serve this market and appropriate the resultant higher margins.

Prediction Five

Firms possessing significant resources and aspiring to market dominance will tend to establish multiple channels. The successful development and management of multiple channels is extremely challenging. It takes resources, both financial and managerial, to plan and implement a multiple channel approach in an efficient and effective manner. Furthermore, the complexity the firm will confront when utilizing multiple channels cannot be underestimated. Therefore, firms with significant resources, especially managerial resources, will be in a better position to make use of this channel approach.

However, simply possessing the resources to efficiently and effectively make use of multiple channels is not sufficient to establish competitive superiority. High aspirations are also necessary, as only firms striving for market dominance may be open enough to innovation and daring enough to make use of multiple channels. A proactive approach to management most often occurs when the firm is threatened or is striving to improve its position. Firms that are content to rest on their current market position are not as likely to develop and implement a multiple channel approach as are these attempting to change the status quo.

Prediction Six

The sixth prediction primarily pertains to retailers, although it possesses implications for suppliers as well. In cases where multiple channels are needed, retailers will increasingly establish non-integrated channels by means of independent intermediaries.

Retailers making use of multiple channels until now have generally utilized a high level of integration within them. In other words, company-owned multiple channels have been the rule at the retail level. It is expected that this will change in the future. For example, a retailer could use independent sales representatives to call directly on consumers in their office or home. An agreement with an independent firm could be fashioned whereby it would operate discount or off-price stores that would be supplied by the retailer's regular stores, or a joint venture could be established with an independent telemarketing firm. The possibilities go on and on.

The rationale for this prediction is rather obvious. No retailer has unlimited resources, yet when potential opportunities arise they should not be dismissed. Linking with independent organizations allows the retailer to take advantage of an opportunity without committing either financial or managerial resources it does not have or needs to employ elsewhere. As pointed out earlier, the risks associated with the use of multiple channels are reduced as the retailer employs nonintegrated channels. Further, Lilien and Kotler (1983, p. 435) make a telling point:

> The important thing about a distribution channel is not the institutions that make it up but the functions they perform. These functions can be performed in different ways by different distribution channels, operating at different levels of cost and generating different levels of sales. The major reason for a channel change is a discovery of more effective or efficient ways to accomplish the same work.

Prediction Seven

The final prediction is that firms will increasingly consider the communication value of alternative distribution channels when judging their performance. Traditionally the value of a channel of distribution has been determined primarily by the sales it generates versus its costs of operation. The use of multiple channels has made this valuation practice outdated. In the future, the communication or promotion value of a distribution channel will also be considered in the valuation process.

It was previously mentioned that consumers can obtain information from one channel at one point in time that leads them to purchase from another channel at a later date. For example, Victoria's Secret is a specialty retailer dealing primarily in lingerie and sleepwear. It sends out a catalog to customers once every few weeks. Although the catalogs generate sizable sales, they also generate top-of-mind awareness of the company. This awareness may in turn entice customers passing by a Victoria's Secret store in a shopping mall to see what is currently being offered there. The "bottom line," so to speak, is that the communication or promotional value of a channel must be considered in addition to the sales and profits it directly generates.

CONCLUSION

Multiple channels of distribution are being established with increasing frequency by manufacturers and retailers alike. This chapter has attempted to provide a brief (albeit somewhat simplified) perspective on the selection, development, use, and evaluation of multiple channels in retailing. We began by introducing some fundamental concepts and terminology relating to multiple distribution channels. Trade-offs involved in developing multiple channels were next discussed, followed by a description of the motivations leading to their use. Potential weaknesses of multiple channels were then explored for manufacturers and retailers respectively. Finally, predictions were made concerning how the use of multiple channels is likely to impact the nature and structure of retailing in the 1990s.

Not every consumer-goods firm or retailer should establish multiple distribution channels. However, all consumer-goods firms and retailers will be influenced in some fashion by multiple distribution channels. It is difficult to think of a more important distribution strategy decision that firms will be faced with in the coming decade.

REMARKS

William R. Davidson

I would like to begin my comments on "Multiple Channels of Distribution and Their Impact on Retailing" with a rhetorical question: Do we have the subject backwards? Would we not be better off if we were to focus on the impact of retailing on channels of distribution rather than on the impact of distribution channels on retailing? The perspective of Professors Frazier and Shervani is certainly the more prevalent and traditional one, especially among academics. It is clearly a manufacturing point of view of channels and their determination. Indeed, most marketing textbooks, and consequently many marketing instructors, start with a product that is being made or is going to be made. The "marketing manager" must decide how to get it to the right place through something called the channel of distribution, a chaotic maze of distribution organizations or institutions.

Another view is that channels of distribution and their multiplicity are brought about basically by the interaction between consumers and the options that they have among store and nonstore retailers. Unfortunately, this viewpoint has not been very well reflected in the marketing literature, although I personally believe it better reflects reality than the traditional perspective. For example, Procter & Gamble, no matter what kind of power it may have as a manufacturer, has no choice whatsoever but to make Crest toothpaste available wherever people want to buy toothpaste. Likewise, consumers can go to a Sam's Club or almost any wholesale club and purchase from a discount broker a new Lincoln or a new Chevrolet without any channel decision whatsoever by the Ford Motor Company or General Motors. Or, if consumers want to buy Izod Shirts or Arrow shirts from T. J. Maxx or Marshalls, they are going to find them there. These are not isolated examples; they could be multiplied numerous times.

In general, the vast majority of channel options are determined by consumers. Notable exceptions include prescription pharmaceuticals, which must be purchased from a registered pharmacist, alcoholic beverages in some states, and firearms in some localities.

Consumers, the real base of power, have made a massive shift in distribution in recent years by bringing about a multiplicity of channel arrangements. Wal-Mart reassessed its supply structure and found many of its suppliers used a channel of distribution that involved agents and brokers. Wal-Mart decided that it would not accept in its cost of goods sold the expense of a manufacturer using such agents and brokers. Agents and brokers were not seen as a value-added service to Wal-Mart, as it already had within its multistate organization all of the facilities it believed it needed to get its products to all of its stores when needed.

The Limited is primarily an overseas resourcing company that has been able to use a remarkably high degree of vertical integration to ensure that the whole cycle from product concept to finished product to availability in stores occurs in a small fraction of the total number of weeks it normally takes in the nonintegrated channel traditionally used by the department store apparel industry. But for reasons that involve international monetary exchange as well as uncertainty in world political conditions, The Limited recently decided it would like to do more domestic sourcing of the products it sold. It invited about three hundred domestic manufacturers of apparel to its Columbus, Ohio, headquarters to explain how The Limited operated and how much it would like to do business with more of them. One might expect that not everybody was happy with the meeting because a great part of it was dedicated to explaining how any suppliers that wanted to do business with The Limited would have to accommodate its cycle. Some manufacturers said they would not have a retailer telling them how they were going to do business. At the same time, though, others looked at The Limited's proposition as a dramatically new opportunity in which they would be forced to make changes in distribution that they probably should have been making a long time ago anyway.

At Kmart, not long ago, there was an increasing realization that there were quite a number of situations in which the firm was doing business with several companies that were owned by a single holding company. There are a fair number of these in the housewares division, where one company owns four or five distinct companies, each of which has a separate sales force charged with the responsibility of generating its own sales. Kmart reviewed a number of these companies and decided that rather than having five sales forces from one company calling on it, there should be a single company-to-company relationship. The result has been both increased effectiveness and efficiency.

Dillard Department Stores became very impatient with the lack of electronic data information (EDI) progress by its manufacturing suppliers. The company held a meeting with some three hundred preferred suppliers to let them know that, within a very short period of time, they would have to comply with Dillard's specifications for EDI exchange.

In brief, marketing thinkers have too often addressed channel issues from the perspective of a manufacturer or a "forward decision-making process." This has led to the retailer being considered primarily a channel captive. Furthermore, this traditional treatment results inevitably in a lack of attention to the multiplicity of intermediary channel relationships. Hopefully, the above examples have pointed out that retailers are not all reactive; many are proactive and often provide channel leadership.

Many specialists have evolved that are not the conventional middle-men of the marketing literature. Today the physical flow of the product and the ownership of it through channels of distribution is likely to be quite separate from the flow of product information. Order processing and order fulfillment may be quite separate functions and be accomplished by entities who are not dealers or title takers and who have no influence on marketing decisions. Rather, they handle many of the physical aspects of the distribution process. The flow of payments is likely to be quite different from the flow of product ownership. The processing of transactions is going to take place somewhere other than at the retailer's place of business; and if the retailer gives coupons, someone else is likely to do the processing of them. The entire intermediary level of distribution channels today is quite different from what existed in the past and what will likely exist in the future.

At Management Horizons, we have recently published our own view of retailing in the year 2000. In this publication (Hyde, Steidtmann, and Sweeney 1990), we identify a number of characteristics of retailing today, all of which clamor for channel of distribution changes:

- Too many stores
- "Sameness" among stores in the same general kind of business
- Excessive price promotions
- Poor customer service
- Inadequate equity capital
- A widening gap between the performance of the few high performance retailers and the many marginal or submarginal performers

In particular, there are too many stores in the United States today, with a tremendous amount of sameness among them, especially those in the same general lines of business. Drugstores are drugstores, and typically you cannot tell which one you are in unless you go outside and look at the store sign. There are excessive price promotions that are, at least in my opinion, not as much of a consumer-motivating factor as retailers seem to believe they are. Poor customer service is endemic. Retailers exist, especially large-scale retailers, that possess very inadequate capital positions, let alone inadequate sales growth rates.

Finally, there is a widening gap between high performance retailers and the many marginal or submarginal retailers. For about the last six years, Management Horizons has made an annual study of high performance retailers. These are retailing firms that have demonstrated upper quartile performance in sales growth, in profit growth, and in rate of return on total assets employed in the business (not on equity, because doing so eliminates the aspect of leverage). There are about three hundred public companies in the United States in retailing, excluding automobiles and restaurants. Only about thirty of these have been in the upper performance quartile on all three of these factors for five consecutive years. Seventy-five percent of the public retail corporations in the United States today do not possess what could probably be termed long-range profit survival potential. This is a much more dramatic fact than is generally understood.

The Management Horizons assessment of the forces of change considered predictable "outside" factors that will bring about new dimensions for retailing and distribution channels as we move towards the next century. These include our assessment of the impact on channels that will result from the interaction of the forces of

- Geographic trends and changes in the trading world
- Most probable economic scenarios
- Consumer market changes
- Technological developments
- Availability and distribution channel access to resources
- Longer run profitability survival requirements

Many of these forces have been adequately explored elsewhere and do not require discussion here. For the most part, our views are consistent with those of others. Consider, though, technological developments. Retailing companies that today are the most advanced in information technology are the ones that are the most concerned about inadequate preparation for the future. They are also the ones making massive investments in information technology for the year 2000 that will further separate them from the average competitor in their lines of business, accentuating the tendency toward greater concentration.

There is also a large variation in the availability of and channel distribution access to resources, both human resources and capital resources. Retailers today do not have the capital resources available to them for the kind of expansion that occurred in the 1970s and 1980s.

Retailing in the 1990s is going to have a much smaller playing field. There are going to be fewer stores, less store space, many store closings, and a lot fewer retailing companies than there are today. One reason for these changes is that there will be more storeless shopping. For a variety of reasons, in every aspect of procurement by the consumer, there will be a role played by some form of nonstore retailing. A rise in relationship marketing will be dramatic in its impact on individual consumers and small groups of them. The demise of the contemporary discount department store, those like the Kmart type, can be expected. On one hand, it is vulnerable to the highly specialized retailer—the mass merchandising types that have been called commodity killers—or various other types of specialists. On the other hand, it is vulnerable to commodity megastores of the hypermarket type.

This decade will witness a slower pace of retail innovations because of the trend toward conservation by those companies that will be more and more dominating in their respective categories. There will be a decrease in middle management positions because information technology will enable lower-level employees to make better decisions than middle managers. There will be changes in the attitudes of consumers about value. Attitudes will focus less on low price and more on what something is really worth. These attitude changes will be accompanied by a great deal of environmental concern and social consciousness about wastefulness of resources. There will also be a much wider range of retailers, suppliers, and alliances trying to capitalize on the opportunities presented by these concerns.

Management Horizons' expectations regarding the increasing use of multiple channels in the year 2000 are quite consistent with those of Frazier and Shervani. However, I have two final observations about their propositions. The first is that their propositions deal with a single consideration affecting channel choice or development. A single-consideration approach is logical and perhaps unavoidable, but it is superficial. Channel choices by manufacturers or retailers are based on many factors, distinct yet interacting, that somehow have to be pulled together in a short time period. While single-factor discussions are useful pedagogically, they do not help in understanding, within an individual company, the decisions that need to be made.

My second observation is about the sixth proposition, which I think has more to do with the concept of what a channel of distribution is rather than what it does. Specifically, I do not consider the provision of consumer options by a retail entity as comprising "multiple channels of distribution," whether integrated or nonintegrated. For example, department stores have long provided optional arrangements for cash or credit, take-with or home delivery (by the store or a third party), in-store or at-home retailing by mail, telephone, personal selling, and main store or branch store purchasing. I do not believe either suppliers or customers of department stores would view these options as different channels. Hence, what constitutes multiple channels of distribution network merits serious consideration.

8

A Retailing Agenda
for the Year 2000

Richard C. Bartlett and Robert A. Peterson

This final chapter synthesizes the facts, opinions, knowledge, and predictions contained in the previous chapters and the symposium's discussion sessions and combines them into a comprehensive agenda for retailing leadership into the next millennium. We have purposefully decided not to encumber readers by referencing specific materials presented herein or attempting to attribute properly any and all insights. Similarly, we have purposely not provided detailed commentaries on either our predictions or the consequences of the predictions we make.

Our objective was to develop and present an action agenda for anyone marketing goods and services to consumers wishing to become or remain competitive in this decade and the next century. Because this objective is pragmatic, we have organized the agenda into twenty-five issues and two hundred eighty-two questions, questions that all retailers need to ask themselves and answer to their benefit, if they can! All of the questions are designed to stimulate retailing practitioners to explore new approaches to what often might seem intractable problems. Academicians will find many hours of spirited classroom dialogue in these same questions. By proactively addressing the issues raised by the questions, practitioners may well obtain retailing leadership in the 1990s. The book concludes as it began, by emphasizing that the value of looking into the future is not to predict events therein with certainty, but to prepare for those events by continuously asking "what if."

COMPELLING REASONS TO CONSIDER
A NEW RETAILING AGENDA

In 1990, in-store retailing demonstrated a remarkable tenacity to retain the lion's share of the more than $2 trillion dollars in U.S. retail sales including automobiles and food. This share was estimated to be 94 to 97 percent of the total; the exact figure depends on the definition of a retail establishment. The sheer size of in-store retailing, decades of tradition, and the fact that consumers show a strong resistance to giving up shopping would seem to argue that the present agenda is fine for the year 2000.

"If it ain't broke, don't fix it," is heard from many entrenched senior retailing executives. The next millennium is just around the corner, retailing formats "rarely disappear," and the mass merchandiser's share of total sales "should" increase. Why then in late 1990 did R. H. Macy & Company place a full-page advertisement in *Women's Wear Daily* saying it could survive the Christmas season without "Miracles on 34th Street"? Or why did Federated and Allied Department Stores lose $24 million in October 1990? Why then are Campeau and Hooker bankrupt? If your answer is LBO debt, you are only partly correct. In addition to LBO debt, blame can be laid on managers who failed to provide the leadership needed to survive into the next century.

Retailing leadership will be seized by those executives who understand the consumer and have a clear vision expressed as a concise and explicit mission. But above all, successful retailers of the next century will be those able to develop healthier, psychologically mature, and efficient organizations capable of coping with increasing uncertainty and rapid change.

Too Many Stores

Many of the retailers that prospered in the 1960s and 1970s did so despite a "seat-of-the-pants" or "we are merchants, not marketers" management mentality. The 1980s brought new forces and an increased competitive turbulence that continues today. The fact remains that there is a surplus of retail store space beyond that required for population growth and consumer spending. The United States is overstored and overmalled, with too much unprofitable retail space.

By the end of this decade, 50 percent of today's fixed-location retailers may be out of business, reflecting in part a concentration into fewer, leaner, marketing-directed "power" retailers. Future expansion will be in large companies with good marketing and financing and especially good return on investment (ROI). As few as thirty or forty retailers may be setting the competitive agenda by the year 2000.

There was much consolidating and downscaling of conventional retail outlets in the 1980s. Of the top twenty discount department stores in 1980, only half were in existence at the end of the decade. In the current decade some of the survivors will evolve into commodity retailers, such as Wal-Mart and Sam's Club, with sophisticated and powerful purchasing ability, low prices, and a unique type of "convenience." Others will evolve into merchandise specialists or into category killers; still others will become downscaled versions of hypermarts. (Wal-Mart is already retreating from 200,000 square-foot to 150,000 square-foot hypermarts). Many will fail. More than 20 percent of the regional shopping centers are forecast to close by the year 2000. By then some product categories may be controlled by as few as five organizations, each with its own discrete concept appealing to specific consumer segments.

Price Competition

During the 1980s competition for market share was primarily through price competition. Consequently, consumers began to distrust the word "sale." What is a "real" price? What is a "regular" price? Heavy emphasis on price has replaced the time-worn "location, location, location" prescriptive as the leading determinant of consumer preference. The financial realities facing most consumers have created a preoccupation with price and an emphasis on value. Retailers who, night after night, year after year, advertised how overstocked their warehouses were contributed to consumer disbelief. However, even blatant price misstatement seems to work, at least for some consumer segments for some period of time, and many retailers will not see a need for change until the day they advertise yet another "price reduction" and no one shows up—with the possible exception of a consumer group or regulatory agency. Already, the National Association of Consumer Agency Administration's newsletter reports increased monitoring of such possibly questionable marketing practices by local and state government agencies.

Today, the upscale consumer is discerning, critical, perceptive, inquiring, tasteful, demanding, sophisticated, and streetwise on price. In essence, a new consumer paradigm has emerged for the 1990s. Within this paradigm, consumers will pay more for quality, but they will also demand a fair price.

Specialty Marketing

During the 1990s upscale consumers are going to demand more customization. Boutiques specializing in consumer indulgences, particularly in services and "ideas" retailing, will entice some customers away from power centers and even category killers. The boutique future is basically untapped, although success is not guaranteed. According to Dun and Bradstreet, more than ninety-three hundred stores, most small, closed in the first nine months of 1990, not a good start for the decade. Boutiques have to be wary of specialty powers such as The Gap, Pier 1, and discounters such as Wal-Mart.

The success of The Gap would seem to prove that fashion apparel is in decline, style on the ascent. "Fashion free, and proud of it" is the shopping mantra of many. The Gap sells classic, style-oriented apparel that can, if necessary, survive a recession or the criticism of the antirich. The Gap now has more than a thousand stores, and annual sales have tripled since 1983 to $1.6 billion. Another success story in the "got to be me" category is Pier 1, the largest retailer of imported home furnishings. Estimated sales are projected to reach $1 billion by 1995, with one thousand stores the target by the year 2000. Pier 1, the nation's fastest-growing home furnishings retailer, allows consumers to be themselves in controlling their home environment and emphasizes value consciousness over price. But Pier 1, selling "wants, not needs," could be impacted by recessionary trends in the 1990s.

One trend would seem certain and ominous for small boutiques. Those with nondescript offerings, tied by vendors to "fashion" introductions, or those that cannot or will not offer stylish merchandise, great service, and good price/value ratios, will be in trouble. Restricted cash flow, tightening credit, and less tolerance by creditors in repayment of debt will put a real squeeze on middle ground retail stores without a healthy financial foundation and a strong consumer franchise.

More Services

More specialty stores and department stores will add services as contrasted with products. Food, insurance, financial services, travel services, legal services, accounting services, catering, personal shopping, and tailoring are all targeted as standard additions to department stores' offerings. By targeting such services, department stores can acquire a larger share of actual spending rather than just a larger share of product expenditures.

In brief, per capita spending on tangibles and durable goods will be down, services up. A larger percentage of consumer expenditures will be on medical services, education, and travel, especially by the maturing segment of the market. A lower proportion of discretionary income will be allocated to retail-oriented tangible products. Although a higher percentage of income will be spent on housing in the 1990s than in the 1980s, this does not reflect an increase in new home formations, which is not forecast. It is simply that more of the household budget will be paid out for basic shelter needs. Sales of other durables such as furniture, appliances, and new automobiles will be on the downtrend. Minorities and immigrants, the only segments of the U.S. population that will grow significantly in the 1990s, are less able to afford new homes, furnishings, and automobiles but rather will be renting and using public transportation.

In addition to increased services marketing, in-store retailers will intensify and expand their efforts at relationship marketing. A great deal of relationship marketing already takes place in the form of personal customer contact during the purchase of cosmetics and apparel, plus outside decorative and home improvement products such as drapes and carpets. Direct sellers and direct marketers will continue to step up their relationship marketing, because it gives them an edge in a highly fragmented market environment.

Suburban Malls

Surburban malls, although marginally on the wane, remained centers of social life, leisure, recreation, and even entertainment in the 1980s. The number of shopping centers grew from three thousand in 1960 to twenty thousand in 1980, reflecting an annual growth rate of 10 percent. The continued movement from rural to urban areas and the growth of suburbs, combined with the generally inept performances of downtown rehabilitation programs, favored suburban malls in the 1980s. Simultaneously, though, "close to home or work" strip shopping centers with easy access parking are nibbling away at the suburban malls when their hours of operation are more convenient than those of the malls. Further, the sheer size of megamalls is intimidating to many consumers. Indeed, in response to an early 1991 *Dallas Morning News* consumer survey, 75 percent of the individuals interviewed stated they were "turned off" by shopping and "tired of being mauled by malls."

Consumers persist in the pursuit of experiences, including entertainment. The "entertainment" factor is seen by many retailers as a key to success in the 1990s since the "now" generation is entertainment-oriented. Many shoppers speed-scan images, absorbing only fragments of presentations, and so advanced communication techniques are required to break through the clutter of modern malls' multiple messages.

Declining Service

Increased customer service remained an illusive concept in the 1980s despite an overwhelming barrage of "service quality" messages, books, and mission statements. There are a few brilliant exceptions, such as Stew Leonard's, Nordstrom, L. L. Bean, Mary Kay, and Wal-Mart (yes, Wal-Mart, which asks no questions on returns). Very few in-store retailers learned to use service as a competitive weapon along with price, value, selection, access, and convenience. The external forces of the 1990s discussed below may worsen already-sorry service to the point of customer revolt, even by those customers "born to shop." Poor service quality, including unreturned phone calls, missed messages, and processing errors, is responsible for the loss of millions of retail customers annually. A common complaint is the absence of a salesclerk "when you need one," not to mention inadequate product knowledge, loitering, and a general lack of professionalism. Reducing the number of dissatisfied customers by just 5 percent can increase profitability in most retail businesses by 25 percent or more. Nine out of ten customers who have had a bad experience with a retailer will not purchase from it again, and 13 percent of those dissatisfied customers will each spread the word to twenty or more people. What is worse, twenty-six out of twenty-seven customers who have had a bad experience will not tell the retailer, so the problem is hidden unless there eixst good customer-service monitoring, measurement, controls, and research.

Kenneth A. Macke, chairman of the Dayton-Hudson Corporation, went on record in early 1991 as stating: "It is a time to execute better all that we do rather than a time for uniqueness. The consumer is restless and has expectations of us that we can't afford to ignore in terms of service, being in stock on desirable goods and offering fair prices."

Store Sameness

Look-alike store layouts, cookie-cutter products and packaging, forced fashion trends, and copycat presentations are making the individualistic consumer wonder if it's worth the trip to many retail outlets. Parity proliferates! Frequently the salespeople in such retail outlets are uneducated about the products they are supposed to sell and more often than not appear to be bored. No wonder consumers increasingly pick up the phone and place a catalog order, or invite a direct seller to their home (or talk to one at the next desk over), or go to a new commodity discounter and buy just as inexpensively and quickly as they can. At least the pallets are piled high and the crowds are not boring. Specialized mass merchandisers, such as Toys "R" Us and the Home Depot, and superstores gained market share during the 1980s from both general merchandise retailers and unwary "boutique" operations.

Institutions Resistant to Change

Just as many of the world's centrally controlled *gosplan* governments imploded in the 1980s, so did many large, hierarchically organized retailers. These institutions, which like Sears, Montgomery Ward, and Avon took years to build, can take years to change. Ingrained cultures, which are in large part responsible for the previous successes of such organizations, are tremendously resistant to change. Avon estimates it took a year to penetrate each level of management with major change concepts. Remember when Woolworth believed that if it charged more than 25 cents it was doomed? Today, following major restructuring and cultural changes, Woolworth's has learned to adapt and is projected to be one of the fastest-growing companies in retailing. By focusing on specific merchandise such as VCRs, Montgomery Ward generated record profits in 1990.

Through 1990, Sears continued to lose money in its retailing operation. Sears, Carter Hawley Hale, J. C. Penney, and the May Company all reported sales declines in late 1990. Sears' 1990 profit was estimated to be reduced as much as 66 percent from 1989. Significantly, on Pearl Harbor Day, 1990, Sears announced it was beginning its "after Christmas" sale! Some confused consumers remember the announcement in 1988 of the widely touted "everyday low price" strategy that implied no more sales—not a graceful pirouette for Sears. In early 1991, Sears eliminated twenty-one thousand jobs to "cut expenses."

Examples of "retailing elephants" that are adapting include Albertson's. With management less wedded to and constrained by "the way it's always been," Albertson's, with $8.2 billion in sales, is the most profitable food and drug chain in the country. Such retailers literally take control of their channel despite the presence of powerful multibillion-dollar packaged goods manufacturers in the channel. Store brands are a primary weapon increasingly being used to neutralize the impact of major national brands. Many supermarket chains, though, appear to have lost their customer focus in recent years as they concentrate on controlling their channel and focus on the profitability of coupons, slotting allowances, trade deals, and the like.

"You don't create. You don't innovate. You implement." This is the May Company's top management credo. Consequently, a middle management executive has to be very strong to even suggest change. As a result, this elephant didn't learn the two-step, much less the waltz or tango, and was in trouble as the 1990s began. In late 1990 the May Company announced a management reorganization in a search for new dance steps.

An apparent contradiction to the May Company is Dillard Department Stores, a strongly centralized organization. But Dillard has an excellent computerized information system that facilitates its centralized management and has achieved great economies of scale. It is the largest customer of many of its vendors, including Estee Lauder.

In general, multiunit chains now account for approximately 50 percent of all retail sales, and most chains are centrally controlled. Warehouse clubs—part department store, part discounter, part supermarket—are retailing's hottest growth concept.

Simultaneously, mass-market specialists sprang up in the 1980s and include "power" retailers such as Circuit City, Toys "R" Us, and the Home

Depot. In early 1991, Circuit City announced plans to open "many more" of its small Impulse stores that sell smaller size electronic items. These retailers dominate selection and price as no multiline retailer can. Electronics, music, pharmacies, carpeting—all experienced the impact of category killers in the 1980s.

Multichannel Marketing

Marketing through a single channel may not yield the sales and profits needed for survival in the 1990s. If a manufacturer is too dependent on one channel and it becomes clogged by the sandbars of increasing competition, fragmented markets, and other demographic shifts, the firm's future will be in jeopardy. For many products, multiple channels are a given, the only question being which channel mix will generate the most profit.

Channel competition can be fierce from powerful channel captains such as Wal-Mart, Kmart, and Dillard. Wal-Mart, aiming at $100 billion in sales by 2000, is such a large customer that it can discourage vendor use of agents and brokers. It will likely pass Sears to become the number one retailer in sales volume during 1991. Kmart refuses to be contacted by several sales divisions of the same company. Dillard enforced electronic data interchange (EDI) compliance on over three hundred vendors, assuring instant, accurate data exchange and just-in-time (JIT) service. Retailers such as these can suck much of the consumer buying power out of a channel.

Multiple channel retailing became much more prevalent in the 1980s but assessing the resultant advantages and disadvantages proved difficult. For example, using multiple channels can heat up intrabrand competition and cause channel conflict and debilitating price competition. When a full-service retailer competes against a channel that emphasizes price, such as a discount store, the full-service retailer either has to continue to offer the higher price and risk a free ride by the discounter or has to lower price and decrease margins. From a manufacturer's perspective, using multiple channels risks creating ill will among members of an existing channel and subsequent loss of resource support such as shelf space. Manufacturer-integrated channels can create the perception of preferential treatment; moreover, some channels might not be a good match for a brand image or might dilute the image.

Despite these factors, both manufacturers and retailers with significant resources and high aspirations began to establish multiple channels in the 1980s. This was particularly true for those manufacturers serving multiple and diverse customer groups, because different groups vary in their need for quality, service, and price. The answer was to adjust channels for each customer group. Many retailers began to establish integrated channels and learned to use alternative channels for their communication value. For instance, customers can gain information from one channel and purchase from another, as illustrated by Mary Kay's direct mail support of its independent sales organization; all sales are consummated by the independent salesperson, none by the company. Avon has discovered that fully 75 percent of its direct sales customers also order from its catalogs. Sears, Apple, Levi Strauss, Carnation, Florsheim, and Victoria's Secret are powerful examples of vendors using multiple channels because of their sales and communication value. Victoria's Secret uses catalogs as its primary distribution channel but supplements them with mall stores. Florsheim solves an incredible SKU count by utilizing videotex to help customers find the best-fitting shoes.

Multiple channels are particularly important to vendors with deep product lines. Depth usually requires an array of price and performance combinations plus a need for adequate market coverage that a single channel usually cannot provide. Finally, the need for multiple channels of distribution results from the choice alternatives consumers have among store and nonstore retailers. For example, General Mills has no choice but to make Cheerios available where people buy breakfast cereal. If the consumer wants to buy Cannon bath towels at T. J. Maxx or Marshall's, that is where they will be sold.

The agenda considerations noted earlier in this section—sorry service, too much unprofitable store space, excessive sale/price merchandising and boring sameness—all exert pressure on retailers to add or change channels. Other compelling economic and demographic forces of the 1990s (some of which are discussed in the following section) will exert tremendous pressure to further explore alternative channels. Technological advances and globalization of markets and suppliers will also push retailers toward multiple channels of distribution.

Multiple-channel decisions have dimensions beyond immediate profitability, including channel control and loyalty and adaptability. Adaptability of the channel to future consumer needs and wants may well be more important than near-term cost and control considerations.

The New Computer Technologies

During the 1980s many of the long-awaited breakthroughs in computers and analytic technologies took place, yet few retailers jumped on the bandwagon. Wal-Mart did, and literally blew away all of its small town competition; its success demonstrates how wise use of new technologies can help create true conglomerates. Data capturing, processing, and analysis technologies as well as other new technologies will continue to advance— often exponentially—in the 1990s. Moreover, these technologies will be available to everyone, from the toughest competitors to new entrants and adventuresome manufacturers. By the end of the 1980s, Dillard, Wal-Mart, J. C. Penney, and The Limited, among others, increased their competitiveness through basic computer technologies. For example, The Limited cut 60 to 70 percent of its new product cycle time, in part by integrating its computers with those of its suppliers.

The real competitive advantage will go to retailers that mix and blend different techniques to solve their financial and marketplace realities. In the future, competition may well come from such unexpected sources as Intel or AT&T. Even so, many major retailers have stated they are "not terribly worried about technology companies taking over." Most CEOs don't even want to think about data processing, let alone invest in the new technologies. Many have abdicated their responsibilities to the "MIS gurus" with (at this time) unknown consequences.

In the 1980s farsighted retailers enhanced their computer capabilities and technologies, transforming them into the basic building blocks of increased efficiencies. One of their most promising technologies is the relational database. Such databases organize data in less space, reduce redundancies, improve flexibility, and permit two-way communications with individual customers. Even so, the 1980s saw very few retailers deploying advanced communications technologies such as teletex and fewer still using neural network technologies, decision support systems, or expert systems.

In most U.S. retailers, buyers still control the operation; purchasing and warehousing are still the drivers. Marketing functions, merchandising, and selling are subordinated. Thus, electronic data capture, storage, and retrieval still tend to be considered "mechanical" or backroom functions rather than being used in proactive marketing programs. A notable exception is checkout system scanner technology. Scanners are also being used as data capture devices for frequent buyer/shopper programs to better understand purchasing patterns. The customer's bar code is scanned at the beginning of the transaction stream, then all products purchased are recorded for future reference, cross-ruffs, and alternative brand promotions. The greatest limitation to the growth of marketing-related retail activities rests in the corporate structure that believes it is merchant first, marketer second.

Nonstore Marketing

In the United States, both direct selling, at $10 billion, and direct marketing, at $180 billion, should continue to capture larger shares of the consumer's dollar, principally because of convenience. Nonstore buying is a major consumer trend of the 1990s. If all forms of direct marketing were included, some sales estimates range over $400 billion. There is evidence that direct marketing volume will increase significantly by the year 2000.

Consumers like direct selling for reasons that include personal service, convenience at both home and work, representatives' knowledge of the products, guarantees, value-added features including buyer/seller and quality/price relationships, and product demonstrations. Direct mail customers' buying reasons include ability to obtain items not available where they shop, buying convenience, nonpressured and leisurely buying decisions, less costly purchases (taking travel time into account), locational convenience, guarantees, the chance to comparison shop without leaving home, less knowledgeable service from fixed-location retailers, and the ability to find the exact item they want.

Both direct selling and direct marketing make wide use of telemarketing techniques. Telemarketing itself is a rapidly growing form of retailing and is used both in support of traditional retailers and as a freestanding channel.

Direct marketing also makes use of technological innovations including electronic kiosks, ATMs, videotex, audiotex, and cable interactive systems such as home shopping networks. TV shopping alone has increased more than tenfold since 1985, to over $1 billion annually.

The "plasticizing" of the purchase process and the expansion of U.S. communications and distribution systems has made the entire country, indeed, much of the world, the "store" for millions of consumers. WATS lines, 800 numbers, UPS, and Federal Express have virtually eliminated geographical shopping boundaries.

Traditional direct marketing, as contrasted with database marketing, is a form of targeted mass media marketing commonly using forms of print media distributed through the postal system. It relies on a broad appeal of the merchandise or offer, lists based mainly on prior responses, and mass mailings (or broadcasts) of common offers, and requires an immediate response from a single impression. Many retail outlets as well as direct-selling organizations have been using direct-mail marketing for decades, relying on names and addresses, list affinities, and other basic demographic and segmenting information for targeting customers. A 2 percent response rate is considered excellent.

Database Marketing. Today the capability exists to build databases on customers and prospects to an extent never before imagined. This capability is one of the major factors that will enhance direct marketing in all retailing through the 1990s and explosively into the 21st century. In database marketing, a great deal is known about an individual consumer's purchasing behavior, geodemographic, psychological, sociological, and attitudinal characteristics, and life style. This information, derived internally or obtained from outside marketing sources, permits the development and presentation of a unique offering to each consumer. Further, it allows the establishment of an ongoing relationship between the consumer and the firm.

Database marketing can be used to reach a specialized niche or to personalize a product or service. It is used to help identify, classify and profile individual customers. It allows highly personalized communications, finely targeted offers, and the building of a two-way flow of communications. Importantly, this resource is available to everyone; in-store retailer, manufacturer, and direct marketer alike can utilize it. Database marketing enables the marketer to develop more targeted products, more refined pricing, clearer communications, and more precise timing of activities.

As retailers find differentiation more difficult, database marketing will increase. Airlines, food stores, and drug chains are increasingly using database marketing. Database marketing emphasizes competition through promotion rather than price. Most importantly, value can be added to the transaction through it.

Retail organizations in specialized fields and marketing to niches were among the first to embrace database marketing, as were retailers who required capital intensive inventories such as home furnishings. In the short term, retailers obtaining the most value from database marketing are those who have already identified their customers. This is particularly true of direct sellers who know exactly who their best customers are and in some organizations, such as Mary Kay, can direct support materials and communications at those buyers with the highest purchasing potentials. Mary Kay's direct support program has achieved a 30 percent purchase response rate from customers receiving targeted mailings.

Retailers of the last century—and even into this one—knew their customers by name, needs, and wants as individuals. Such retailers were vital to the growth of the nation. The "massification" of the marketplace destroyed this. Database marketing and direct selling, with their emphasis on detailed customer information, will allow retailing to once again become person-to-person with resulting gains in customer service and the entire concept of quality retailing.

Leading-Edge Communications Technologies

Applying new technologies to perceived new customer needs is a high risk proposition with a considerable cost that could sap resources from other critical areas. Technologies such as interactive TV, computer bulletin boards, cellular telephones, 800 and 900 telephone services, PCs, on-line interaction services, home shopping networks, and fax services were readily adapted by more progressive retailers. But many retailers who ventured into newer forms of media or technology, such as videotex, audiotex, or various forms of electronic shopping, were burned and have retreated.

Recently J. C. Penney shut down Telaction, a bleeding-edge system that allowed customers to access and browse through video information and purchase products and services viewed on their television set. In the meantime, Sears and IBM continue their national rollout of the Prodigy consumer shopping and retail information service. CompuServe's electronic mail uses games to entice viewers to browse through product selections. Electronic Yellow Pages allow the caller to obtain information from a recorded message and have the option to be connected to a retailer.

Innovative retailers and manufacturers continue their aggressive attempts to "talk" to consumers via new technology. Buick is using an electronic brochure that lets "readers" take a "free disk drive." On the very leading edge is the Interactive Television project, a joint effort of AT&T, General Motors, McCann-Erickson, Coca-Cola, and ACTV. ACTV provides the interactive TV technology. In the Springfield, Massachusetts, test market, viewers can actually "direct" TV coverage of sports events. Implications for marketers are immense, including marketing research and product knowledge applications.

Media advertising will undergo a dramatic technological revolution in the 1990s. Advances such as digital radio, personalized magazines distributed by computer, and video billboards will provide new creative opportunities for retail advertising. Concepts such as passive people-meters, drive-in shopping, and holographic media will test the resources of the most imaginative creative director. Advances in satellite transmission will open new programming options.

These advanced technologies, when added to advances in direct marketing, database marketing, and personal selling, will further meld so-called mass marketing with personal marketing, and reinforce the need to tightly target and build relationships with particulates and individual consumers.

Store-based technology will lead to satellite broadcasts right into retail outlets such as supermarkets, drive-in shopping to avoid checkout lines, and enhanced communication of product information, including more interactive systems, expert systems, and even "robotic" clerks. Some futurists even see computer chip "wristwatch" technology that will connect consumers to cash registers and media usage-measuring devices to allow collaboration of media exposure and consumer consumption. Others forecast faxed newspapers, with interesting opportunities for "real time" retail advertising.

One of the high-tech lessons of the 1980s would seem to be that a large computer literate (or at least computer-comfortable) audience is necessary for major success for several technologies in retailing. Some of the attempts, such as cable television home shopping, did not really deliver convenience, time savings, or even exceptional value to the consumer. Fiber optics, high definition television (HDTV), and interactive computer software can give customers the excitement they seek in shopping with control and customization. As the 1990s began, there were 140 million PCs worldwide; as PC ownership accelerates like TV ownership in the 1960s and VCRs in the 1980s, electronic marketing will become a prime force in retailing.

COMPELLING EXTERNAL FORCES THAT WILL SHAPE THE NEW RETAILING AGENDA

The Economy

Numerous external and essentially uncontrollable forces will shape retailing in the next millennium. The first is a fickle consumer, especially when the consumer lacks confidence. All economies are built on people, and consumer confidence in the economy is a major influence on consumer spending. The consumer's purchasing environment is bounded by disposable income and credit availability.

The 1990s began with confidence trending downward, with people unsure about the future. Consumer confidence was further impacted by calamitous news such as Desert Storm and by uncertainty reflected in increases in the "misery" index, the sum of the unemployment and inflation rates.

The last decade of the 20th century will witness a relatively stable economy despite a shaky start that includes a recession. The country's ability to withstand an oil shock has been enhanced by the fact that there has been a fundamental restructuring of the world order. During 1991 Deng Xiaoping, Fidel Castro, and Saddam Hussein could be removed from power, followed by other third world dictators.

With the iron curtain down, Eastern Europe and the Soviet Union can act together with the United States, Western Europe, and Japan on trade issues; the world should begin to receive a peace dividend in the late 1990s. Even China has liberalized its economic policies, and major middle-class markets are emerging in South America and India as well as in other third world nations. It would appear that the world is beginning to realize there is no freedom without free enterprise. But the "creative destruction" of the communist world will create a misery index of chaos-producing proportions. Consumers in much of Eastern Europe and especially Russia will experience despair.

The focus of the future will be on economic competition, not war machines. America, post-Iraq, should be able to reduce its foreign debt and budget deficits. International relations will address economics and trade instead of mutual defense treaties and nuclear warheads.

World conditions favor an American rebirth because business can and will respond to economic competition. The United States will remain the single world superpower; this should mean a continuation of the decrease in defense spending from the 10 percent of GNP in Eisenhower's presidency to the 6 percent under Reagan to perhaps as low as 4 percent by 1995. There are signs that U.S. economic growth will be "slightly stronger" on average in the 1990s than in the 1980s. The United States ended 1990 with a population of 252.7 million and a GNP per capita of more than $17,000. Canada increased 1.0 percent to 26.7 million, with a GNP per capita in excess of $20,000 in U.S. dollars. Although labor force growth will be down, productivity will increase significantly, creating real economic growth in the 1990s in the 2.5 to 3.0 percent range. Manufacturing productivity increased by 3.5 percent per year in the 1980s; absolute productivity remained above that of Japan and Germany. Leading the way to real growth are demographic shifts, technology, and service industries. Inflation should be low and relatively stable, mainly because the Federal Reserve has demonstrated its inflation-fighting capabilities and resolve. Also helping keep inflation under control will be global surpluses (there is great excess capacity in the global economy) and intense international competitiveness. Rising wage rates could fuel inflation, but not excessively.

LBOs, S&Ls, and M&As

Consumer confidence is also affected by the great financial debacles of the 1980s, led by the savings and loan crisis and fostered by the mania for debt to finance leveraged-buyouts (LBOs) and merger and acquisition (M&A) transactions. There still remains a risk of financial institution and business failures due to the excesses of S&L executives and greed-driven investment bankers, some of whom were also convicted felons in the Milken mode. Junk bonds will continue to create problems for the corporations that used them to finance LBOs and for the institutions and individuals that own them. Management's focus on short-term goals and operating cash flow will likely continue to lead to lower R&D and capital investment, layoffs, and ultimately lower personal income, which obviously would diminish retail revenues.

Erosion of financial institutions would cause consumers to be more risk averse and reduce their expenditures for tangible and durable goods. This would obviously impact retailing. The household savings rate dropped to only 5 percent in the 1980s, from 8 percent in the 1970s. As the decade began, consumers were borrowing less because they wanted to reduce their personal debt. Banks had money to lend for consumer purchasing, but the urge to borrow waned as consumers perceived a coming credit crunch and experienced the effects of a recession. Commercial banks and life insurance companies are experiencing rising delinquencies and foreclosures; real estate values are declining in most areas. Bank failures will continue in the 1990s. Government dissaving created by the fiscal deficit continues unabated in the

1990s. Consumer confidence can be sustained only to the extent the United States can cope with and pay for the excesses of the 1970s and 1980s.

As 1991 began, weaker retailers with high debt loads were at risk. These retailers badly need new operating concepts and new ways of motivating employees.

Demographics

Unlike economic forecasts, demographic trends have a high degree of certainty. Between 1990 and 2000 the U.S. population will increase 8 percent or 22 million, to 275 million. Retailing uncertainty comes in the interpretation of accurately projected demographic facts. Much of the 1960s and 1970s market research was quantitative and assumed that behavior could be accounted for by age, ethnicity, gender, and income differences. In the 1980s, attitude surveys were the rage in consumer research.

Marketers in the 1990s realize that individuals group themselves according to interests, values, and concerns regardless of other characteristics. They could group as opera goers or goat ropers, fitness nuts or gourmets, or, to confound the researchers, all of the above. Every person with similar demographic characteristics does not behave the same way.

Of one fact retailers can be certain: the more they focus on their customers and understand them, the better will be their chances for survival in the 1990s. The remainder of this section will summarize major demographic forces and related consumer trends that will shape the 1990s and beyond.

America Is Aging. No wonder that the largest association in the United States is the American Association of Retired Persons (AARP). By 2020 one in three Americans will be age 50 or more and eligible for AARP membership. The oldest baby boomers were born in 1946, which means that during the 1990s more families will be entering prime earning and buying years. By the year 2000, the median age will be 36; by 2020, it will be 41. Marketing to maturing segments will be increasingly rewarding yet competitive.

However, marketing to the boomers will not be easy as they will be saving more, spending more discreetly, and shopping less frequently. They have learned from painful personal experience not to shop for status, as in their yuppie heyday, but rather to shop to enhance their quality of life. These trends will affect home purchases, automobiles, and many other durables such as big-ticket furniture and appliances. Exceptions include the automobile aftermarket and escalation of the home entertainment boom, with continuing growth in VCR ownership as well as other advanced music and entertainment durables. Interest in the performing arts will surge in the 1990s.

By 2020 the number of men in their 60s will increase by 75 percent to seventeen million and women by 68 percent to nineteen million. The age cohorts of the next century will be very different from those of today. The whole concept and definition of aging will continue to undergo radical redefinition. Retailers must reexamine what "old age" means. The elderly generally consume fewer goods and services and spend a higher proportion of their budgets on essentials. Their greatest fear is that a debilitating illness will cause them physical and financial dependency.

Many older Americans will have the motivation, resources, and energy to become entrepreneurs and run their own businesses. They are much more somber today about their own economic prospects and feel sharply the need to protect themselves from the encroachment of the outside world, whether real (such as crime) or imagined (such as being poisoned by Alar). They will have a desire to perpetuate their heritages, and the ethics and cultural patterns of the 1940s and 1950s will reemerge, ethics of moderation versus excess, of morality versus hedonism, of meaningful and satisfying work versus mammon worship. They will have a great concern for wellness and a strong desire for good health to enhance their longevity and create a new way of life. Boomer bodies are not what they used to be, and so nutritional concerns and label reading will be *de rigueur*. "Fat free" is the war cry; walking and biking, not jogging, are the exercises of the 1990s.

The boomer group is ready and willing to stand up and be counted. Many are disillusioned. Some do not trust government, and their trust in retailers and manufacturers of consumer goods has eroded. Boomer activists express this distrust as members of highly vocal groups and are a major force behind the rise of environmental concern in the United States and Europe.

The boomers want to age attractively. They will accomplish this in part by their retail choices; it will be more comfortable to be older in the coming decades than in the past. They believe that it is important to look good and to revel in their maturity. Many of the boomers are dropping out of their corporate careers for a simpler, higher-quality life, and many have started giving back to society through volunteerism.

The aging of the boomers will enhance U.S. productivity. As workers become more experienced, they typically become more productive. Retailers and low ticket service sector employers will face a declining percentage of workers in the 16-to-24 age group, as well as a decline in the absolute numbers of the 20-to-34 age group, and therefore will be staffing from AARP-qualified individuals, the new waves of immigrants, ethnic groups, and the handicapped.

A major consequence of demographic changes will be the distinct bifurcation of consumer markets. There is, and will continue to be, a growing distance between high-priced, upmarket goods and low-priced, mass-market ones. This bifurcation will be driven by changes in the distributions of both age and income.

Ethnic Diversity.   There will be an increase in the number of people who will be immigrating to the United States in the 1990s, helping to more firmly establish the country as a pluralistic "world nation" with direct links to virtually every part of the globe. This trend, added to the already established ethnic diversity of the United States, has important implications for retailing, especially with respect to further market fragmentation. Many of these immigrants and most other ethnic groups will use retailing as an economic building block, either as employees of retailers or as retailers in their own right, often as direct sellers. One implication, only dimly seen by in-store retailers, is that newer immigrants in the retailing sector will not only facilitate reaching U.S. ethnic and immigrant markets but also facilitate globalism of retailing by carrying it back to their homelands. Franchised retailers and direct sellers have already taken major advantage of this potential.

Market fragmentation will be not solely by ethnicity, but by stronger ethnic identification and the desire to maintain cultural heritages. This will change the fabric of American society in many ways. Many immigrants came to the United States a hundred years ago to leave behind their cultural heritage. Although there are many examples of pockets of ethnicity, such as the German communities in the Texas Hill Country, most individuals purposefully have become diluted in their ethnic identification and cultural heritage. But in the last decade immigrants began to arrive who wanted to retain their culture, particularly those who settled in the coastal areas. Immigration—especially after the recent changes in immigration laws—will bring badly needed new talent and youth to our country's aging population. This has the potential to provide a competitive advantage over xenophobic countries such as Japan that have little or no immigration and relatively low birth rates. Many immigrants are true entrepreneurs, and it takes only one generation to spin off new, highly motivated capitalists. Retailers who act early on immigration trends and the "new internationalism" will be the survivors of the 1990s.

Mobility.   Strong regional population shifts dominated the United States in the 1980s and will continue to do so through the 1990s. Over the decade the West grew by 21 percent to fifty-two million and the South grew by 15 percent to eighty-seven million. In all, the Sunbelt captured 90 percent of the nation's growth. The Northeast grew by 10 percent to fifty-two million. The Midwest grew by only 2 percent to sixty million.

Vast areas of mid-America are returning to a near natural state, with small towns and small farmers becoming endangered species. By the year 2000, it is estimated that 80 percent of the U.S. population will live within a hundred miles of a coastline. This coastal concentration has tremendous implications for retailers.

During the 1980s some demographers were predicting a shift in the century-old population drift from farm to city, citing movement back from cities to rural and exurban areas. They were wrong. The glacial shift from rural to urban areas continues, with both inner-city ghettos and suburbs growing as a result.

The ratio of one out of six Americans moving annually held firm in the 1980s and is expected to hold through the 1990s. Although the median moving distance is only six miles, it is still enough to alter shopping and consumption patterns. The "location, location, location" adage, which lost much of its credibility in the 1980s because of seat-of-the-pants location strategies, will gain fresh meaning in the 1990s as retailers cope with a moving target.

Smaller Households. Remarkably enough, only 7 percent of U.S. households consist of the traditional two married adults and two children. One person in four lives alone, up 26 percent since 1980, with the trend toward smaller households likely to continue through 2000. Between 1980 and 1990 the average household size shrank from 2.8 to 2.6 and will continue to shrink. The fastest growing household segment consists of women with children and no husband. During the 1980s its size increased 36 percent.

Still, retailers should be aware that the family is back, at least in boomlet proportions. The boomers are now in the family-forming and child-raising years, giving welcome new vitality to the family structure.

Income Polarization. A tremendous polarization is taking place in income and wealth accumulation, and history shows that when this happens, next follows revolution. A U.S. revolution, while not a shooting one, is already in progress as Congress agreed to tax the wealthy and millions of Americans voted against conspicuously wealthy politicians in the first major election of the decade. In Texas, oilman Clayton Williams attempted to "buy" the governorship with $8 million of his own, plus another $12 million. He lost. In Minnesota, millionaire Rudy Boschwitz was defeated by Paul Wellstone, who hammered at Boschwitz's wealth.

Growing resentment of the conspicuously wealthy, such as Leona Helmsley and Donald Trump, can easily be noted by the media attention given their life-styles—a mirror of the increasing number of Americans who say the country would be better off if there were no millionaires and that the rich are not paying anywhere near their fair share of taxes. Recent surveys indicate the United States is not the only country with widening income differences; Canadian, German, Swedish, and Australian survey results show similar trends.

The income gap has become a chasm. Sales of Rolls Royces reached a peak in the 1980s, at the same time the number of homeless peaked. The number of private security guards in the United States is now greater than public police forces. Seventy-seven percent of the nation's wealth is held by the oldest 20 percent, so many "have nots" will become "haves" through inheritance in the 1990s. But there is polarization within the elderly segment. The median income of older persons living alone was $12,500 for men but only $7,000 for women in 1989.

Between 1980 and 1990, the national median household income, adjusted for inflation, increased a mere 3 percent to $30,000. Yet, tax returns for incomes of $1 million or more grew from 8,408 in 1982 to 65,303 in 1988, and the estimated share of U.S. after-tax income for the top 1 percent of families grew more than 50 percent, from 8.3 percent to 12.6 percent between 1980 and 1990. The top 5 percent of U.S. households averaged $140,000 annual income at the end of the decade. The top decile had 22.8 percent of household earnings. The top fifth had 46.8 percent. In 1990, the top 20 percent of working Americans had more income than the remaining 80 percent. In contrast, the lowest decile earned 3.4 percent of household income. This polarization would seem to call for a "first class" versus "classless" strategic choice: Nordstrom versus Sam's. Many of the United States urban areas are really two distinctly different cities, the wealthy city clearly isolated from the city of service and sales people, clerks, and transportation and garbage collection workers. Consequently, there are growing inequities in the quality of social, educational, and community services.

Just over thirty million Americans are below the government-defined poverty line of $12,675 for a family of four. The poverty rate has been declining since its recent high in 1983 of 15.2 percent, and in 1990 reached 12.8 percent. Unfortunately, Desert Storm and the 1991 recession will delay further decline in this rate.

Although there is obviously a strong upscale market, and upscale retailers are gearing up to grab first, the true size of the upscale market may be greatly exaggerated. Even multimillionaires are hearing the populist message and de-glitzing their life-styles. The boomers are switching to the "things money can't buy" to demonstrate their concern for quality of life—theirs and others. Life has become more serious for many, and for many the excesses of the 1970s and 1980s now appear anathema.

However, for the department store retailers there is a ray of hope. Upscale merchants such as Neiman Marcus are expanding their sales forces, planning to open new stores, and exerting their healthy financial muscle to dominate their channels, based in part on the knowledge that the upper 50 percent of American families control 75 percent of the disposable income—a healthy target for the retailer of the 1990s with the right merchandise and marketing mix.

Educational Decline. A paradox exists in education in that there was a record percentage of high school graduates, 77 percent of those eligible in 1990, but at the same time more of these graduates were functionally illiterate. Reading is becoming a lost skill.

Although 20 percent of all high school graduates complete at least four years of college, minorities, with the exception of Asians, are dropping out of high school at an increasing rate and not attending college. The federal government's share of the cost of grade and high school education has dropped to 6 percent; cities and states with wealthy residents spend more on education, creating an imbalance. The lower income groups, white, black or Hispanic, receive lower-quality education. In Texas, the richest school district spends over $19,000 per year per student, the poorest about $2,000.

Many American students cannot compete at the graduate school level because they have not been well taught or well motivated through more than 16 years of mediocre schooling. Since the 1970s, the absolute number of American students granted doctorates has diminished. Foreign-student admissions are on a dramatic increase, more than doubling in recent years.

The United States has slipped precipitously in skill levels in technology, mathematics and hard sciences. The citizenry has become impoverished in science and technology, severely handicapping the country's economic competitiveness. The United States is losing ground to the world in building intellectual talent.

Time Poverty

Time impoverishment among upscale and middle-scale consumers will continue to plague them in the 1990s. There will continue to be a decrease in the time people will have to shop. Work demands will increase, just to keep even with basic material needs. Most consumers will likewise face ever-expanding domestic obligations, including parenting (both for children and parents) and the need for leisure-related experiences, all of which will be constrained by increasing financial needs.

Although retirees will have more time, they too will be caught up in experiential and informational activities, will have medical and other financial pressures, and will demand convenience. Many retirees will also be returning to work, either out of necessity or sheer boredom.

The 1980s showed growth in "turnkey" retailing operations that did everything for a price. Convenience thus takes on a new meaning, because values now reshape expectations about how much time is to be allocated to certain activities, including shopping. The shopper of the 1990s will be a shortcut shopper. Convenience in access, product selection, hours of operation, and terms of purchase will become more important than at any time in the past. Location, parking, and the costs and hassles of operating an automobile will be major determinants of the success or failure of fixed-location retailers.

The logjam at traditional retail store checkout counters helped create the "convenience store." Now, as such outlets add gasoline, fast food services, and even financial services to their offering, their checkout counters are clogged. Inconvenienced customers may turn in frustration to other retail sources, some yet undefined. Today, many consumers make quick buying decisions without leaving their homes, from a direct salesperson, a mail order catalog, or even a modem attached to a phone line.

Working Women

The recent election of Ann Richards as Governor of Texas continues the 1980s trend of women achieving both political and economic success. Women entering the workplace was one of the most important trends to retailers of the 1970s and 1980s and will continue to be so. This change has been almost revolutionary. Between 1986 and 1990, 64 percent of workplace entrants were women, 42 percent United States-born and white. In the year 2000 nearly 90 percent of new workplace entrants will be women and minorities. In contrast, white males, long considered the prime working group, will make up less than 10 percent of the twenty million people expected to be added to the labor force by the year 2000. However, males will still comprise 52 percent of the work force.

In 1990, fifty-five million women, 60 percent of all women 16 years of age and older, were employed outside the home. More than 3.2 million women had selected careers in direct selling, while millions of others found jobs that allowed them to work at home, often through computers. Two-income families, the rapid increase in single households headed by females, and the rapid increase in the number of businesses owned by women are trends that will continue in the 1990s.

Increases in women in the work force obviously reduce the time available for purchasing and shopping. One implication of this is that the shopping habits of the sexes will start to converge and the typical retail shopping ratio of 70 female to 30 male may move closer to 60:40 by the end of the decade.

Working women, as the main shoppers, are really driving the culture of convenience, seeking out services and products that give them more time for themselves. Businesses that provide home delivery services for such items as dry cleaning, groceries, and personal care products will be sought out by many working women. "Easy to buy; easy to use; easy to dispose of" (providing disposal doesn't pollute) is the consumption cry of working women. These same women have a rising frustration level with poor service and represent a large potential for home shopping services.

Working women and their changing retail habits are also having a profound, double impact on media in America, helping to create a fragmentation of media markets. Time constraints coupled with four decades of explosive growth in network and cable television programming have heightened the importance of visual impact over the written word. Visual recall is a key, as the challenge is to make messages seen, not just heard, amidst commercial "zapping" and VCR use (while away from home). Media costs have increased, viewership and listenership have declined, and newspaper readership is down from an average of thirty minutes a day to fifteen minutes (per newspaper). Mass magazines gave way to niche magazines and special-interest books and magazines to reach these women. Retail marketing communications departments are focusing more on other channels: direct mail, inserts, community newspapers, telemarketing, radio, and cable television. These channel switches will have a major impact on retailing and the mass media in the 1990s.

Unless they repackage their editorial appeal and attract new sources of ad revenue, newspapers will find they may have to operate with reduced budgets and less space as retailers decrease advertising expenditures. At the end of 1990, an *Advertising Age* poll showed that 74 percent of the respondents were allocating the same or less advertising dollars to newspaper run-of-press than previously. This could have a significant effect on the quality of U.S. print journalism, which, despite having been the world's bastion of freedom of speech, is already on the decline. Newspapers rely on retailing for about 50 percent of their advertising revenues. Profit is the true protector of freedom of the press, not objectivity. News accuracy and integrity have given way to shallowly researched sensationalism in all but the finest newspapers and periodicals.

Two-income families will put pressure on employers to modify current benefit programs, as will the increasing size of the self-employed, independent contractor female work force. There will be increasing demand for flexible work hours and schedules and part-time jobs. Nearly 60 percent of working women who bore children during the years 1981 to 1985 returned to their jobs within six months. Job-sharing programs will become increasingly important. In addition to the purchasing impact these factors bring, retailers must be alert to their own personnel needs. Both in-store retailers and direct sellers have large turnovers of part-time personnel. But most women leave jobs for other than personal reasons. Businesses are still not retaining women as successfully as men; gender issues are still not being addressed by a majority of retailers.

Families in which both spouses are employed have major challenges in balancing the competing demands of work and home. Especially among younger families, there are trends to experience the new and different, to indulge with little luxuries, to take life with an almost "sound bite" approach of sampling here and there in quest of information, direction and self-satisfaction. Many working women have also hit a "glass ceiling" in the corporate world and are frustrated by the constraints and inequities and tired of being paid 70 cents on the dollar vis-à-vis males. These women are ready to explore new ventures, new adventures, and motherhood in the 1990s. They represent real opportunities for retailers.

The Environmental Movement

Although the "Big Green" referendum failed in California, the environment is a permanent and important concern for the majority of household decision makers. Consumer environmental values are changing at a rapid rate that will have a major impact on American retailing in this decade.

There is strong and growing support for recycled and recyclable packaging. Some firms, such as Mary Kay, are switching their entire packaging to recycled or recyclable material. Beware of generalized "environmentally friendly" claims—they will come under increasing fire from state agencies. Burger King uses only recyclable packaging, and this example has been followed by McDonald's commitment to recyclable packaging material. Star Kist has a sixty-second commercial in prime time on dolphins and places a sticker on each can of tuna to demonstrate to consumers that it not only is conscious of changing values but also is committing resources to ensure that the change is reflected in the product the company produces. DuPont has announced it will suspend all production of chlorofluorocarbons (CFCS) by 2000 or sooner.

Environmental activism is very much on the increase as reflected by membership growth in organizations such as the Sierra Club, Wilderness Society, and Environmental Defense Fund. The efforts of such groups are often aimed at punishing those companies that continue to ignore the environment. More than 40 percent of Americans were critical of Exxon for its handling of the Valdez oil spill; there was even a declaration of "Valdez Principles" drawn up asking companies to reduce waste, market "prudent products," and take responsibility for past harm.

Other environmental groups, such as Ducks Unlimited and the Nature Conservancy, are at the vanguard of a quieter but potentially stronger conservation movement that seeks nonconfrontational solutions to environmental concerns. The Nature Conservancy is the fastest growing of all environmentally oriented organizations.

The green trend will not go away. Consumers will seek to modify the ancient cycle of consumption-destruction-consumption, but slowly and not at great sacrifice to themselves. The reality of scarce resources will increasingly be translated into higher prices for those resources and will affect consumer buying behavior.

Recycling is an easy way for consumers, manufacturers, and retailers alike to assuage guilt and "do something." Consumers have recourse to penalizing those producers or retailers who are perceived to be uncaring of the environment and reward those perceived to be "green." Direct mail has come under fire for the waste of paper through unwanted mail. But U.S. consumers are still among the world's largest per-capita energy consumers. This consumption is the greatest source, by far, of pollution and the greenhouse effect.

Social Concerns

Although the environment is a major consumer concern, it ranks behind concerns for medical costs, education, chemical substance abuse, and crime (of course, in early 1991, concern about Operation Desert Storm overshadowed all others). But even the lowest level of concern, animal testing, has the power to influence large numbers of consumers and to affect product sales from cosmetics to furs. The Body Shop emphasizes a wide range of social and environmental causes and issues in its consumer marketing and market products that are consistent with its expressed philosophies including "cruelty free," non-animal-tested products.

During 1990, thirty-five states had major financial shortfalls, mirroring the federal government's deficit. These financial pressures will create a flood of revenue-enhancing legislation at all levels of government. The Internal Revenue Service will continue to seek new enforcement power and will especially target independent contractors.

There is great consumer pressure, both directly and through politicians, for all manner of reforms, with special focus on but not limited to food and drug regulation, consumer scams, and crime issues. Downtown retailers and shopping malls are especially vulnerable to crime, which could cost customer traffic. Direct mail and telephone solicitation firms raise privacy and other consumer issues. Negative option direct mail, 900 telephone sex conversations, and phony award scams are particularly irksome to consumers. The unprincipled use of multilevel marketing hype generates a backlash of concern for legitimate direct sellers. All this means that there will be more and wider-ranging consumer pressures for tighter safeguards and for stricter standards. The regulatory environment will become more restrictive in the 1990s than it was during the Reagan era.

The greatest threat to the financial security of low- to middle-income Americans is the cost of health care, including long-term care and insurance premiums. This alone will influence the purchasing behaviors of an increasingly large number of consumers.

INTERNATIONAL AGENDA FORCES

Resistance to International Marketing

U.S. retailers appear to suffer from an "Ugly American" complex when assessing the potential impact of internationalization. The entry of foreign organizations into American retailing is viewed with some alarm despite the fact that most such entry is by acquisition (versus startup), such as the Japanese acquisition of the Southland Corporation, owner of 7-Eleven stores, and foreign investments in department stores, specialty retailing such as clothing, and entertainment organizations. U.S. retailers seem to fear they cannot compete internationally because they do not know the territory, the language, or the culture. If they venture internationally, retailers seem to believe they will be viewed as "ugly Americans."

In fact, the original ugly American in William J. Lederer and Eugene Burdick's book by that name was a physically unattractive (i.e., ugly) American whose substantial practical skills were used to enhance the life-styles of third world nations. He was a "good guy!" American retailing is in a remarkable position to capitalize on the rapid growth and changes in retailing in Asia, Europe, and South America. American retailers, especially since the 1980s, are experienced in working with constant change, with experimentation, and in marketing fundamentals and should be able to transmit these hard-won skills to any international venue. The "ugly American" retailer can be beautiful indeed!

The sweep of democracy across the world was influenced by American media, by jazz and rock 'n' roll, hamburgers, fried chicken and jeans, to mention just a few American cultural ideograms. U.S. retailing expertise has had its impact far abroad. An important message hammered home by journalists is the freedom of speech in America. An important message hammered home by American retailers is the wide variety and availability of consumer goods. This message has not been lost on the would-be consumers of totalitarian states. The world traveller of 1990 was astounded by the openness of consumer comment in China even after Tiananmen Square and the outspokenness of the average Soviet citizen, especially about the dearth of Russian consumer goods.

However, there is relatively little movement yet by U.S. retailers to other countries. Instead, the large investment is from overseas, with approximately 10 percent of U.S. retail sales now under substantial control of foreign companies. U.S. retailers still tend to react as if they compete in an insulated, island economy and are content with their own geographic and cultural ethnocentricity. Sadly, most retailers do not have the leadership to meet the challenges and opportunities of the international marketplace.

Internationalization is not likely to cause displacement by foreign competitors in the United States, but rather will create new opportunities for growth and profits abroad. American retailers have greater opportunities for penetrating retail markets abroad than do retailers from any other country. Whether they realize it or not, American retailers probably have major advantages compared to foreign competitors, probably more than at any time in history.

The major problem facing U.S. companies trying to enter foreign markets is almost always the difficulty of breaking into long-established distribution systems. This is well illustrated by the structural impediments faced in Japan. However, with creativity, such impediments can be overcome. For example, by utilizing direct selling, traditional distribution systems closed to Americans can be bypassed. For almost thirty years, U.S. direct-selling companies have been successfully competing in international markets, literally exporting this basic form of retailing to some fifty countries. Today, more than ten million individuals worldwide are involved in direct selling. Pioneers were Tupperware and Avon, followed by companies such as Shaklee and Amway. Amway is presently one of the largest exporters of American goods to Japan.

The 1992 European Community

As Table 8.1 suggests, the European Community (EC) will effectively become, at the end of 1992, a new market of 350 million consumers. These countries, along with eastern Europe and the Soviet Union, will effectively trilateralize world trade. But many of the necessary "rules" and agreements are still undecided. The European Community currently consists of twelve countries: Belgium, Denmark, France, Greece, Ireland, Italy, Luxembourg, Netherlands, Portugal, Spain, United Kingdom, and a unified Germany. But an exclusive club may no longer be feasible. Austria, Norway, Sweden, and Switzerland will be knocking on the door. Other countries in Eastern Europe will be slow to become a factor, but they ultimately will, despite a painful transition period. They, too, will be clamoring for EC membership.

The West's success, especially in the marketing of consumer goods, has had much to do with inspiring the people of Eastern Europe and the Soviet Union to topple totalitarian governments and move towards their own free markets and thus freedom itself. Unfortunately, the world capital markets, and especially those of the United States, are not positioned to supply the funding necessary to accomplish the economic restructuring that is needed. It will be well past 2000 before Eastern European living standards approach those of Western Europe. Adding to the difficulties is the chaos currently present and likely to continue in the Soviet Union. Because the USSR used to be the major trading partner of the Eastern bloc, its internal economic and political disabilities will impede the progress of Eastern European countries for the remainder of the decade.

Table 8.1. Population and Per-Capita Gross National Product of European Countries

Country	Population (millions)	1988 GNP per Capita (U.S. dollars)
Austria	7.6	$15,500
Belgium	9.9	14,500
Denmark	5.1	18,400
Finland	5.0	18,600
France	56.6	16,100
Germany	79.0	18,500
Greece	10.1	4,800
Ireland	3.6	7,700
Italy	57.8	13,300
Netherlands	14.9	14,500
Norway	4.3	20,000
Portugal	10.5	3,700
Spain	39.5	7,700
Sweden	8.5	19,500
Switzerland	6.6	27,600
Turkey	56.5	1,300
United Kingdom	57.6	12,800
EAST EUROPE		
Hungary	10.5	$2,500
Poland	38.1	1,900
Soviet Union	291.0	n/a

Source: *World Tables 1989-90 Edition.* World Bank, Baltimore: Johns Hopkins University Press, 1990.

The Pacific Rim and Australia

The economies of Japan and the western Pacific rim were ablaze in the 1980s and collectively grew at an annual rate that reached 7 percent in 1990. As shown in Table 8.2, counting mainland China, there was a total market of 1.7 billion consumers in Pacific rim countries in 1990. As target markets, major cities in these countries are expected to increase in size, on average, by 50 percent by the year 2000.

Table 8.2. Population and Per-Capita Gross National Product of Selected Pacific Rim Countries

Country	Population (millions)	1988 GNP per Capita (U.S. dollars)
Australia	16.5	$12,400
China	1140.0	300
Hong Kong	5.9	9,200
Indonesia	185.0	400
Japan	125.0	21,000
Malaysia	18.0	1,900
New Zealand	3.4	10,000
Philippines	63.0	600
Singapore	2.7	9,100
South Korea	43.0	3,600
Taiwan	20.6	6,000
Thailand	54.7	1,000

Source: *World Tables 1989-90 Edition.* World Bank, Baltimore: Johns Hopkins University Press, 1990.

India, Latin America, and the Third World

By 2020 India will be the most populous nation, surpassing China as the latter's birth control edicts take effect. India will have the largest middle-class market, at 250 million strong. Like the Pacific Rim, markets will be concentrated in cities and can be targeted.

Progressive new trade agreements between Canada and the United States, Mexico and the United States, and most likely for the entire Western Hemisphere, will have a profound effect on U.S. retailing. Mexico's middle-class market has already greatly expanded, as have those of Brazil and Argentina; their middle classes already have consumption patterns similar to those of the U.S. middle class (see Table 8.3).

SETTING THE RETAILING 2000 AGENDA

Too often retailers, be they discount, specialty, category killer, wholesale club, mall, direct seller, direct mail, telemarketer, or lemonade

272 The Future of U.S. Retailing

stand, think of themselves in a narrow, channelized sense. They are all retailers with customers who are real people with real wants, needs, and desires. The 1980s proved that many traditional forms of retailing simply could not survive without evolving. Many did not survive. The wheel of retailing began to spin like Vanna White's Wheel of Fortune.

Table 8.3. Population and Per-Capita Gross National Product of Selected Latin American and Third World Countries

Country	Population (millions)	1988 GNP per Capita (U.S. dollars)
India	837.0	$300
LATIN AMERICA		
Argentina	33.0	$2,500
Brazil	153.0	$2,200
Chile	13.3	$1,500
Mexico	90.5	$1,800
Venezuela	20.2	$3,300
AFRICA		
Kenya	23.0	$400
Nigeria	114.0	$300
South Africa	36.8	$2,300
Zimbabwe	9.8	$700

Source: *World Tables 1989-90 Edition.* World Bank, Baltimore: Johns Hopkins University Press, 1990.

If even the most enlightened retailers were to select from the available options, they could spin like Vanna's wheel, too. The key is to study options available for retailing in the year 2000, verify through research whether they apply to a particular form of retailing and, if so, test market them and only then attempt to implement them.

Change is costly. It often is very risky. And yet, change in the 1990s is imperative for all retailers, because they are in the midst of consumer revolution, not just evolution.

No outsider can pretend to set any one company's agenda. No one can predict the future with certainty or even with consistency. Even so, to survive into the next century let alone become or remain a leader, retailers must be prepared not only to react to the inevitable changes that will occur but to preempt those that will prove deleterious and inhibiting and embrace those that will be beneficial.

RELATIONSHIPS, THE MOST IMPORTANT AGENDA ITEM

As an industry, retailing has failed to develop the people management skills and consumer focus that characterize the most successful business organizations of the 1980s and 1990s. Personnel policies and operating methods often rely on highly routine and perfunctory policies that dehumanize the sales organization and stifle its interaction with customers. Creativity, planning, and strategy development are reserved for "top management." Management Information Systems (MISs) tend to focus on control of business components such as purchasing, inventory, accounting, and order entry rather than systems that enable the sales organization to build relationships with customers. Even store managers often cannot make customer decisions on the floor. The shift in emphasis from top-down, hierarchical, totally controlled management cultures to those that encourage leadership at all levels and especially at the customer interface is expressed by the following path for the evolution of information systems: MIS —> CIS (Customer Information Systems) —> HRS (Human Resource Systems).

A Systems Perspective

Management Information Systems were developed in the 1960s as the emerging computer sciences focused on the problems of dealing with masses of data somewhat unrelated to people issues other than routine accounting functions such as payroll and order entry. MIS executives became very powerful because they controlled the information needed for essential business decisions. Mass retailing was viewed by top managers as a chess game, every move of which could, in theory, be reduced to a computer model. Oversimplifying a bit, advertising, pricing, merchandise mix, store location, and design decisions were all reduced to computer-based models. No CEO moved without his MIS guru's total support.

In the future, firms that are successful will be those that treat retailing as a hockey game rather than a chess game. Powerful and unanticipated attacks, as yet unknown tactics, executed at blinding speed, unimagined strategic alliances, and the unpredictable behavior of 275 million consumers are in store for retailers in the 1990s and beyond.

Conventional wisdom aside, there never really was a mass market. Instead, the randomness of hockey has always existed. Retailers, manufacturers, and advertising agencies simply never recognized this fact. It is much more comfortable to rely on brand management forecasts that relate advertising expenditures to an eventual "harvest" of profits or to utilize surveys that show all the "right" demographics to be in place around a new store location or that certain levels of local newspaper ads will generate store traffic and that store traffic will in turn create store sales. In the 1950s and 1960s such "mass" strategies usually paid off because per capita disposable income plus population gains virtually guaranteed the success of nearly any reasonable strategy. It was hard to go wrong and easy to take credit for the "genius" of the merchant's product selection and the "success" of a mass advertising campaign. The few proven failures were viewed as anomalies. No one tracked mass advertising. expenditures to a specific consumer sales result, no one sought to repair the "leaky bucket" of customers out of stores (or out of specific brands), and "direct response marketing" and "direct selling" were viewed as very poor stepchildren.

The Emergence of CIS.   Almost unnoticed by manufacturers, retailers, and their advertising agencies, direct response marketing began to emerge in the 1970s and 1980s.   Direct response marketers fought for miniscule budgets, always promising "proven, measurable" results before asking for more funding. By and large, they were successful, carving out a $180 billion slice of retailing in less than two decades. As they did this, they creating Customer Information Systems (CISs) to improve both effectiveness and efficiency. Nothing was taken for granted;   everything was proved empirically.

The most progressive direct response practitioners eagerly grasped the next advance in information systems and research because no one had to tell them there was no such thing as a mass market. They knew customers were unpredictable and that no segmentation scheme was anywhere near perfect. The answer was—and is—to test continually to ensure a profitable response. The very bold introduced database marketing and began to talk of the lifetime value of customers and of establishing lasting relationships with customers. To mass market thinkers and ensconced merchants this was heresy. Few really believed in Stew Leonard's famous credo: "Rule #1. The customer is always right.   Rule #2. If the customer is wrong, reread Rule #1."

Relationship marketing relies on successful interactions between two individuals who enjoy what they are doing, even having fun, and who care about one another. The key to relationship marketing is culture, which starts with leaders, not merchants, who view total control of a many-tiered hierarchy as the appropriate managerial style of retailing. At the absolute bottom of such hierarchies are found customers and, almost unnoticed (by management), salespeople. Many "top managements" believe that people are primarily motivated by fear and greed and that salespeople can be "manipulated" to provide service.

Of course, customers and salespeople notice one another, usually without much enthusiasm, often as necessary evils to be coped with while shopping and clerking. Even enlightened managers, such as those at J. C. Penney, admit that until just a few years ago they had no way of identifying an individual's sales performance and therefore no way to recognize the exceptional salespeople, nor to motivate others to be exceptional. Until fairly recently, many large retailers possessed little knowledge of the turnover of salespeople or indeed, much about them as people at all.

Human Resource Systems—A Culture for 2000. The evolution has been from Management Information Systems to Customer Information Systems to Human Resource Systems (HRSs). Human resource system leadership can be vested in a superpower human resources department such as the one Marriott uses, but it should be the responsibility of every leader/manager, in every organization small or large. However HRS is implemented, the goal is the same—to achieve a culture that acknowledges both customers and employees as human beings. It should also utilize advanced technologies to ensure that employees are recognized as individuals, are motivated as both individuals and team members, and that a caring competence is developed within the organization. The "caring" is expressed in a smile, a handwritten note of thanks, a call, a brief touch, or even a personal delivery. The "competence" is demonstrated in product and service knowledge that enhances the shopping experience.

Retailing cultures must be created that celebrate, even idolize, the sales organizations, sales associates, and customer service representatives— whoever is in direct contact with the customer. Motivation is created by a blend of compensation, special incentives, and recognition. There is little doubt that a high level of cash compensation (with variable components) is the strongest motivator of all. However, with a large part-time sales force, retailers often cannot afford to motivate through cash compensation. In Texas, average annual retailing wages in 1989, at $12,126, were the lowest of all major industries. Government was at $21,593, construction at $22,792, and transportation was at $28,432. Low salaries are compounded by the need to recruit from ethnic groups, immigrants, and now older segments and from less-educated groups. Motivation, therefore, takes a high degree of skill, but it can be done. One need only walk through Disneyworld, staffed by minimum-wage earners, to see firsthand what the right motivation and culture can do for employee attitudes.

The reality of 1990 retailing is that most salespeople are thought of, if they are thought of at all, as sales clerks or order takers definitely not to be trusted with customer decisions. Retailers with this perspective ignore the fact that customers value polite, friendly treatment above price, especially when prices are near parity.

Common among the cultures which do seek to put the decision-making process close to the customer, in the hands of store managers and even salespeople, is a decentralized decision-making process, a free flow of two-way communications, and constant employee recognition supported by adequate compensation and targeted incentives. Incentives may include cash as Nordstrom does, or prize and travel incentives, or just recognition. Granting employees the freedom to experiment and take risks is a powerful motivator that will help attract and keep the best individuals.

Strong customer-oriented cultures start with a strong new-employee orientation program and progress through constant training, feedback and promotion from within. They view the sales organization as customers of all the corporation's services and near the top of an "upside-down" organizational structure with the customer at the very top. Functional cross-training and cultural education are important in "flat" organizations with strong cultures. Strong cultures stress tradition and teamwork. At companies such as Mary Kay and L. L. Bean, the culture is founded on the Golden Rule.

The culture will require leaders who can "coach"—those who can motivate and persuade a team that constantly must improve. Such employee forces must, of necessity, be more independent, more self-confident, truly interested in their work, and satisfied with their achievements. Learning by both individuals and groups must be constant in such organizations and must be viewed as enjoyable. A fundamental principle of psychology is that happiness is a byproduct of effort and is achieved with self-sufficiency. The goal of every organization should be to create a self-sufficient, empowered work force surrounded by a culture that encourages and rewards learning new job skills, leadership techniques, and personal self-improvement. Performance development will replace performance appraisal.

The Organizational World Is Flat. Where MIS has evolved into CIS, the middle manager has become a thing of the past and management hierarchies have flattened dramatically. The ratio of managers to workers has increased significantly from 1:7 in the 1970s and 1:12 in the 1980s to 1:20 today. By 2010, the typical large organization will have fewer than 50 percent of the levels of comparable firms in 1990. The successful organization of the future, regardless of industry, even including governments (the last to be debureaucracized), will look more like a molecular structure, neural map, or spider web than a pyramid.

Electronic information systems will do the connecting, often ad hoc, and not with artificial lines connecting boxes on a meaningless chart. Distributed information systems will push many retail decisions right out to the customer interface and will seek to empower as many employees as possible. At the same time, these new organizational structures will encourage close interpersonal contact, a free flow of information across all artificial lines—up, down, and sideways. The function of so-called top management should be viewed as providing support for those who serve the ultimate customer. In fact, a good place for such support executives is on the sales floor itself, listening and learning from the sales-customer interface, maybe even trying a little selling just to stay in touch with reality.

It is important to note that evolving into a networking culture such as described above has many pitfalls, and attempts will be made to thwart it at every level, including by the sales organization itself. Early pioneers such as Nordstrom encountered resistance to programs that provided incentives for extra effort, and there is always the possibility of dysfunctional consequences—disgruntled sales people and customers who feel pressured, not served, and so forth.

Often, the information systems to support such new organizations are designed by MIS wolves in sheep's clothing, and major attention is given to system architecture, not to developing an infrastructure that promotes creative and profitable performance. This is the point where CIS becomes HRS—where the networking technologies and the organizational structure encourage creative, action-oriented relationships, not just outstanding individual performance.

The old MBO (Management By Objectives) programs so highly touted in the 1970s failed when MBOs were individually set, measured, and rewarded. MBOs could discourage the evolution of a relationship-driven organization wherein individuals work together to achieve a common mission with common vision, expressed as a common strategy and implemented by teams composed of empowered individuals who are simultaneously caring and competent.

Faces versus Forces. External economic and even competitive forces cannot be controlled, whereas relationships with people in the "outside" environment can be at least influenced. Successful retailers in the year 2000 will have developed relationships with everyone who has any control of any aspect of their future, including vendors, the media, government, and related strategic fields. It is imperative that retailers establish a network of strategic organizational alliances that control those aspects of the external environment that can be controlled or at least influenced. One way to accomplish this is to think "faces," not "forces." A force can be viewed as inevitable, such as women entering the workplace and creating a "hopeless" scenario for in-home sales. No one at home, no sale. When Avon and Mary Kay began to think "faces," they began to control and even exploit this phenomenon by recruiting working women to sell Avon and Mary Kay in their workplaces.

Many U.S. organizations need a "revolution" to react to such phenomena as the environmental movement. By thinking "faces," managers can bring consumer advocates into the organizational network to advise them and help think through potential problems before they become burning activist issues or governmental regulation.

Tender Power.   Much management effort is being expended on the effects of women in the workplace, especially in positions of leadership. Women in the work force is a demographic fact. It would appear that women may in fact have an advantage in achieving leadership roles in an HRS-driven organization, one focused more on people than abstractions. However, the ability to lead, to conceptualize, and to think strategically is not gender based; power can be obtained and wielded regardless of gender. Although women are usually more adept at executing "tender power," men commonly use this tool, also. The fact is that gender leadership styles are more alike than different.

The real issue for retailers approaching the next century may well be that a substantial majority of customers are women buying goods and services designed for women and that by far the largest number of employees within this classification are women. The retailing giants of 2000 must and will have more women in leadership roles. The work force-diversing program at Corning Co. in New York has become a national model for recruiting and retaining women, a Catalyst Award-winner. Such programs recognize that there are special challenges for women in firms traditionally managed by and dominated by white males. The playing field is not yet level.

But, regardless of gender, the leadership of truly successful organizations will have, and display for all to see, values that underpin a caring and sharing relationship-driven company. These values include integrity, accountability, honesty, discipline, fairness, and a strong ethical sense that displays a social conscience.

The Next Steps to 2000

To succeed in the year 2000, retailers must recognize that the rate of change will increase geometrically—fast-forward ice hockey. Leaders will achieve constancy of purpose by developing a simple, clearly articulated mission statement that imparts an overarching vision. This statement must be written to stand the test of time and change and must reflect real and proper values.

The organization's structure must be redesigned to empower front-line employees, focus on the ultimate customer, and celebrate the sales force. It must reinforce that people really are human, have strong needs for self-esteem, need a sense of accomplishment, and have a sense of achievement that can be enhanced through motivation and recognition.

While retailers are redoing their mission statements and organizational structures, they must decide on the information systems that will allow them to grow profitably. Too often decisions are reached on mission and structure that cannot be supported by the existing information system, so nothing ever really gets done. This is a terrible scenario because big, bold, daring mission declarations and enormous organizational shifts can result in a totally demoralized organization if relationship-oriented information systems are not in place.

Finally, retail leaders in the year 2000 will have learned to respect the lifetime value of both employees and customers. Without such a philosophy, everything else will be for naught.

THE AGENDA

In the remainder of this chapter we present, in a question format, twenty-five issues that every retailer needs to address to be successful into the next century. The two hundred eighty-two questions listed below are not intended to be exhaustive. Nor are the questions completely independent; life is not that simple. Furthermore, each question is not necessarily germane to each and every retailer, although most should be thought-providing for the retailer with foresight. More importantly, we do not pretend to have the answers to the questions. Collectively, though, the questions constitute an agenda that must be faced by anyone aspiring to successfully compete in the retail arena, either now or in the future. Hopefully, the agenda will stimulate strategic thinking and foster creativity and innovation in retailing.

1. Hypersaturated Markets
1. Should you consolidate—become a power retailer?
2. Is downscaling for you?
3. Should you lease or sell your excess space?
4. Should you become a commodity retailer?
5. Should you become a category killer?
6. Should you become a specialty retailer?
7. Is shutting down centers or stores a viable option?
8. Have you discovered your "niche"?

2. Sales vs. Sales Margins
9. Have you become a "commodity pricer"?
10. Is your MIS/CIS powerful enough to provide constant, item-by-item review of price and pricing effects?
11. Should you consider a "price club" approach?

12. Do you understand the basic shopping habits of your customer base?
13. How can you best provide value to your customers?
14. How can you simultaneously offer new, interesting, and high-quality merchandise?
15. Are you overestimating the importance of price?
16. What role does quality play versus price?
17. How do you accurately test price variations?
18. How can you increase the effectiveness of your buyers?
19. How can you control your markdowns?
20. Should you include more high-margin goods in your offering?
21. How can you make inventory management more effective for your business?
22. How do your company policies, mission statement, and culture demonstrate your commitment to quality and value?
23. Does your store signage ensure transaction enhancement to help achieve the best margin mix?
24. Have you consolidated your suppliers to make your purchasing more effective?
25. Can you utilize "cost of service" pricing, such as optional delivery?
26. Can you calculate the effect of each price change on volume and gross margin?
27. Are you effectively marketing the concept behind your merchandise and organization?
28. Do you have effective shrinkage controls in place?
29. Can you increase prices on nonprice-sensitive items?

3. Customer Orientation

30. Are you using qualitative and quantitative research to better understand your customers?
31. Do you need to provide more convenient access for your customers?
32. Is a wider product/service array compatible with customers' needs?
33. Is a deeper product/service array compatible with customers' needs?
34. Are your selling hours convenient for your customers?
35. Should you modify the terms of purchase and/or credit?
36. Do your location/parking facilities measure up to those of competitors?
37. Do you facilitate purchasing through quick checkouts, including no lines, helpful salespeople, and high-tech computer and credit card processing for instant transactions?

38. Do you translate your customers' quality and service requirements into plans and actions?
39. How do you set and consistently measure customer-service standards?
40. Should alternative channels of distribution and communication, such as direct selling and direct marketing, be added or given more emphasis?
41. Should you offer "turnkey" packages of products and services?
42. How well do you and your employees listen?
43. Does your store have a "face" or personality to which your customers can relate?
44. Are your antishoplifting devices insulting to your customers?
45. Do security systems make it harder for customers to get interested in merchandise or actively insult them?
46. Do you provide special security services to customers in need of same?
47. Are you a tightly focused retailer, presenting a clear picture of products and services to your customers?
48. Are you a destination, or do you rely on "chance-encounter" impulse buyers?
49. Does your store appeal to "shortcut shoppers?"
50. Do you consciously seek ways to give your customers more value-added services?

4. Show-Biz Shopping

51. How can you make shopping more fun?
52. How can you add entertainment and education to the shopping experience?
53. Should you incorporate in-store demonstrations, video presentations, or music? If currently offered, should they be eliminated?

5. Sorry Service

54. How can you most profitably attain total customer satisfaction?
55. How can you more effectively ask customers what they want and gain a customer point of view?
56. What is the most convenient means of customer feedback?
57. Is the employee/customer ratio appropriate for the level of service desired?
58. Are employees easy for customers to identify in your store(s)?
59. What is the most appropriate way for employees to satisfy customers within appropriate controls?

60. How can you most effectively stop customer hemorrhaging caused by sorry service?
61. How do you educate employees that retaining customers can impact the profit line even more than gaining customers?
62. What procedures should be used to recognize employees for good service and make them feel a part of making things work?
63. How do you enhance job satisfaction and a sense of self-fulfillment to make your employees feel important?
64. How do you motivate employees?
65. Are telephone calls and letters from customers given priority attention and quick response?
66. How do you measure and reinforce service training on the job?
67. How do you assure continuous improvements in service?
68. How do you instill among all employees a love-your-customer approach—that adopting a "Can I serve you?" versus "Can I sell you?" attitude is the only way to survive?
69. Should you modify or strengthen the terms of your "satisfaction guarantee?"
70. Are the terms of your customer-return policy perceived as being better than those of your competitors?
71. Is your customer-return procedure accessible to your customers?
72. Is your return policy flexible enough to allow for unusual circumstances—can employees "bend the rules?"
73. How do customers know they are "the most important person in the transaction?"
74. How well have employees internalized customer-service concepts, and how well are these being used? How do you verify this?
75. Do you know your customers?
76. Do you imbue new employees with your culture and heritage of service?
77. Do you employ the Golden Rule in all dealings with customers?
78. Do you offer commissions or other incentives to your employees?
79. Do you teach your employees to treat mistakes as an opportunity to build customer relationships?

6. Boring Retailers

80. Should you change your store layouts more frequently?

81. How frequently should you change product displays? Do customers look forward to window and wall displays?
82. How can you increase your awareness of marketing trends, not just merchandise trends?
83. What is the best avenue for forming alliances with manufacturers to evolve new product and packaging forms?
84. How do you communicate your quality expectations to your suppliers?
85. To what extent can you add exciting new services?
86. Should you attempt to decorate for all holidays (including small ones) to give your store a festive feeling year-round?
87. What features should you add that will make you more user friendly so that the customer is considered as a friend, not someone to be manipulated through your layout?
88. What display vehicles can be used to facilitate impulse purchases?
89. What differentiates you from your competitors?
90. Should you utilize vendor "coordinators" or other product experts to help train and excite your sales force?
91. To what extent can you use CAD systems to design new stores and store layouts?
92. Can you develop product/service evenness?
93. Should you change your positioning to make yourself more distinctive?
94. How can you create interactive ways to demonstrate products better?
95. How can you minimize store confusion to allow customers to find what they want, quickly?
96. Have you given your business a special identity?

7. Strategic Changes

97. Do you have a corporate quality statement?
98. What is the role of your senior management in setting quality and service goals and rewarding results?
99. Is it possible to reduce middle management tiers?
100. Can you change "the way it's always been done"?
101. Can you dominate your current category or "establish" a new category and then dominate it?
102. Can you establish a clear identity in the consumer's mind?
103. How can you consolidate your power?
104. How can you improve your supplier relationships?
105. Should you initiate a "vendor day" in which vendors spend time with your sales force and customers?

106. How can you ensure that your vendors are paid on time and that your commitments are honored?
107. Are you aware of your target markets?
108. How willing are you to change your target markets?
109. Do you have a detailed plan for pursuing market leadership through providing superior quality products and service?
110. Has your mission statement or strategic plan been communicated to all employees and suppliers?
111. How is performance measured relative to your plan?

8. Channel Options

112. Have you established non-integrated channels by third-party intermediaries? Should you do so?
113. Is it possible to adjust or add channels for different customer groups?
114. Should you integrate channels?
115. Do you communicate differently in different channels?
116. To what extent do you give customers different options?
117. Can you broaden your reach through direct mail, telemarketing, direct selling, and the like?
118. How can you leapfrog to the next generation of technologies?
119. Do you know the power/dependence relationships of your supplier/channel members?

9. Technology

120. How can you form strategic alliances and partnerships with high-tech vendors?
121. What is the best way to integrate computer technologies such as EIM?
122. How can you take advantage of relational database technologies at all organizational levels?
123. How should you incorporate new communications technologies into your organization?
124. How can you use technology to touch your customers?
125. Who in your organization should be using technologies of intelligence, symbolic response, and neural networks to create expert systems and "what if" scenario analyses?
126. How can you minimize the negative effects of technology on your employees and customers, such as computer down-time, register noise, billing errors, and the like?
127. Are you using programmable video-disk technology to present maps of stores within malls, departments within stores, and merchandise in departments?

128. Does the adage "anything you can imagine, you can do—if you can afford it" apply to you?
129. Should you focus on ways to do things entirely differently?
130. Should you employ new technologies, from kiosks to cable TV, to interface directly with your customers?
131. What emerging technologies can you use so that sales take place as they "ought to?"
132. Who in your organization should be responsible for investigating what leading-edge technology(ies) will be the beginning of a new retail form for 2000?
133. How can you master the science and the gurus of MIS, not the other way around?
134. To what extent should you empower everyone in your organization, through the new technologies, to focus on the customer?
135. Who is responsible in your organization for mixing and blending different technologies to solve your marketplace and financial problems?

10. Nonstore Retailing

136. Have you considered fixed-location retailing? Should you?
137. Should you establish or acquire a direct-marketing operation?
138. Should you establish or acquire a telemarketing operation?
139. Should you establish or acquire a direct-selling operation?
140. Should you take a global view of your market via WATS, UPS, FedX, or 800 or 900 telephone programs?
141. Should you establish or acquire interactive systems such as kiosks or cable TV?
142. How can you best establish ongoing, two-way communications with your customers?
143. How do you measure the accuracy and timeliness of, and customer satisfaction with, these communications?
144. Should relationship marketing be in your future?

11. Database Marketing

145. Should you be marketing to one or more specialized niches or particulates?
146. How can you best personalize your products, services, and communications?
147. Should you compete through promotion or price, both, or neither?
148. How can you build favorable consumer perceptions?
149. How can you retain your most loyal customers?

150. How can you attract more loyal customers than the ones you lose?
151. How do you emphasize that the focus should be on the differences among customers rather than on customers?
152. Are you capturing and using all of the available information about your customer?
153. Would a consumer newsletter or other mailings pay off?
154. Do you have a well-planned and researched advertising strategy—one consistent with your other marketing efforts?
155. What are your customers' perceptions of your product quality and service versus their perceptions of your competitors' product quality and service?
156. How can you use perceptions to attract customers?

12. Economic Scenarios
157. How will future oil shocks affect you?
158. Are your recession strategies in place?
159. Does your strategy contain maximum flexibility?
160. Have you developed an organizational structure that can adapt to change and allow discrete units to be distinct?
161. What fundamental changes in the economy are you prepared for?
162. Have you maximized your internal resources?
163. Do you have a plan for exploring alternative product sources and cultivating a wide range of vendors?
164. Have you established strategic alliances with vendors?
165. Are you capable of more carefully timing your entries and exits from markets?
166. Have you developed a "real world" management team that can manage technological change, diversity, and globalization?
167. Have you built loyalty in employees to provide a "team environment?"

13. High Debt Levels
168. Do your customers really come first, before employees and stakeholders?
169. Are you able to think past your short-term pressures?
170. Are you investing sufficiently in research and capital development?
171. Have you developed a plan if employee layoffs are inevitable?
172. Are you still dedicating enough resources to building and maintaining a quality store or brand name?

173. Do you have a formal approach for instilling cost consciousness and cost control in the organization without sacrificing service/quality?
174. How will you reduce organization waste and remakes?
175. Who is responsible for improving response quickness in every function from accounting to inventory location?
176. Have you built just-in-time internal distribution systems?
177. Have you built just-in-time relationships with vendors?
178. Have you established the best possible vendor relationships?
179. Who is working at improving banking and financial institution relationships?
180. Have advanced technologies been used to streamline middle management?
181. Have improvements been made in all employee communications?
182. Do you have JIT communications with all employees?

14. The Aging of America

183. How do you determine the expectations of your older customers?
184. Do you measure changes in customer expectations over time?
185. Has your organization appropriately adjusted to the needs of older-population life-styles?
186. Do you offer older customers products and services to age attractively and enhance the quality of their lives?
187. Have you made shopping convenient and safe?
188. What is the role of specialized products and services for the older population in your organization, especially the disenfranchised?
189. To what extent will it be necessary to replace disappearing youth with mature workers?
190. Have you made in-store signage, sales slips, and so forth large enough to be read by those with failing eyesight?
191. Have you remodeled to market to mature consumers on the basis of psychological rather than chronological age?
192. Does your customer service adjust to the special demands of older customers?
193. Have you considered "feet-friendly" flooring, more and better rest rooms, better lighting, and the like?

15. Ethnic Diversity

194. Are you prepared to market to the new wave of immigrants?
195. Are you prepared to hire and train immigrants?

196. Are you prepared to use micro marketing to reach specific ethnic identifications and cultural heritages?
197. What opportunities are available because of differences in ethnicity and languages?
198. To what extent are specialized advertising and communication programs required for ethnic and immigrant groups?
199. Have you built ethnic and cultural diversity into your employee staff, especially management, and into your way of thinking?
200. Are you proactively recruiting younger employees from a diversity of ethnic backgrounds?
201. Are you providing special educational opportunities for employees from diverse ethnic backgrounds or for those who are new immigrants?
202. Are you providing leadership training for ethnic and immigrant employees?
203. Do your ads, in-store displays, windows, even mannequin designs, reflect the ethnic diversity of your customers?

16. Population Shifts

204. Are you in front of or behind the flow of population west and south?
205. Are you using database marketing to identify and hold customers moving only a few miles?
206. Is suburban movement taking place in your markets?
207. Are you taking advantage of the coastal concentration of the population?
208. Are you protected from the movement out of America's heartland?

17. Smaller Households

209. Have you considered the special needs of the customer living alone (smaller units, more store niceties, etc.)?
210. Do you monitor these customers apart from your total customer base?
211. Is an in-store play area, weekly "story hour," or some such device feasible to allow mothers more time to shop?
212. Are you providing special attention to single mothers?
213. Do you formally review your merchandise selection for smaller households (decorative accessories, cookware, appliances, etc.)?
214. Are you giving appropriate attention to individual motives versus family-consumption motivation?

18. Income Polarization

215. Are you considering the impact and/or possibilities of factory outlets?
216. Do you have a plan for marketing to upscale consumers?
217. Are you using database marketing to isolate income targets?
218. Can you capitalize on the trend toward "de-glitzing" when upper-income consumers downplay or do not display their wealth?
219. Are you prepared for the formula "more discrimination plus sophistication in purchasing equals tougher consumers?"
220. Will income polarization emphasize differences between those willing to pay for quality versus the lowest possible price?

19. Working Women

221. Are you prepared to meet working women's increasing demand for convenience?
222. How do you plan to react to there being more male shoppers?
223. Do you have easy-to-buy, easy-to-use, easy-to-find merchandise/service selections?
224. Are you prepared to respond to working women with better, faster, more accurate service and store hours that make sense?
225. Are you prepared to meet demands for value-added services, such as product information, and training by means of classes and clinics?
226. Have you considered channel alternatives so that working women can shop at home, at work, by mail, by phone, by fax, by TV, by computer, and through direct sales?
227. Do your women's alterations cost more than men's and take longer?
228. How do you determine the product quality and service expectations of your working-women customers?
229. Have you reviewed your organization's benefit plans for the impact of more working women?
230. Has the personnel department developed flex-time, part-time, or job-sharing employment programs?
231. How will you better control employee turnover through working conditions, recognition, incentives, pay, and benefits?
232. How can you more accurately, reliably, and quickly identify your best employees, especially in your sales force?
233. How can you better recognize and motivate employees, especially in your sales force?
234. Do you have retirement-planning, tuition-refund, educational-leave, and fitness programs?

235. Are you proactive with regard to providing child-care and child-wellness programs?
236. Do your female customers know about these benefit plans?
237. What is the appropriate level of parental leave and child-care leave that you should provide?
238. Do you recognize the need for care of parents as well as children?
239. Do you offer ways for working-women customers to experience the "new and different" within a tight time frame, such as lunch time and after work?
240. Have you considered offering "little luxuries" in merchandising to your working-women customers?
241. To what extent has your planning taken into account the fact that female employees and managers are the keys to your organization's future and that you need to recruit, train, motivate, and pay them accordingly?
242. Have you equalized operational hours and pay rates for male and female employees?
243. Have you considered setting up retail appointments to facilitate purchasing?

20. Customization
244. Have you considered establishing boutiques—perhaps in-store—or positioning yourself as a specialty power?
245. How do you propose to stand out with stylish merchandise, great service, and great value?
246. Have you analyzed your financial resources and staying power to establish highly specialized outlets?
247. Have you considered nonstore techniques, such as direct selling and direct marketing, to provide customization at a lower investment cost?

21. Building Relationships
248. Should you add services such as food, insurance, financial, travel, legal, accounting, catering, tailoring, dry cleaning, shoe repair, manicure, parcel mailing, or personal shoppers to improve your competitive position?
249. Do you have on-premises ATMs, postage stamps, notary public, copy, and fax services, or the like?
250. Are you targeting a higher percentage of spending per customer rather than sheer number of customers?
251. Are you building customer relationships through better in-store training, service, and attitudes?

252. Does your organization focus on and exploit the lifetime value of your customers?
253. Do you reward customer loyalty (frequent-buyer clubs, perks, etc.)?

22.   The Environment

254. Have you initiated employee recycling programs?
255. Do you sell environmentally appropriate merchandise where possible?
256. Are you using recycled/recyclable-friendly wrapping, shopping bags, packaging, and the like?
257. Do you contribute to and support appropriate environmental causes?
258. Does your organization welcome input from environmental groups?
259. To what extent do you support recycling by your customers?
260. Have you eliminated unnecessary packaging?
261. Are your store's lighting, heating, ventilation, air conditioning, plumbing, and waste disposal systems efficient and environmentally friendly?

23.   Concerned Customers

262. Are you aware that, fundamentally, many consumers do not trust business?
263. Do you quickly take the high ground in all consumer interactions by acting with integrity?
264. What steps have you taken to control your product liability costs (legal, medical)?
265. Have you established fair pricing and accurate advertising policies?
266. Does your organization contribute to and support local efforts at crime control and efforts to control local scam operations?
267. Does everyone in your organization respect consumer concerns for privacy, especially with regard to telemarketing activities and direct mail?
268. Are you a good neighbor by supporting cultural, civic, educational, and other community activities?
269. Do you consciously select and sell merchandise that does not create consumer concern?
270. Do you have a policy against phony or overhyped gift or award promotions?

24. Educational Issues

271. Are you contributing to the improvement of education in your area(s), from volunteer speakers to cash contributions, at the elementary level to the college level?
272. Are you prepared to educate your customers?
273. Are you prepared to use the most advanced training methods for your employees and to empower them through access to customer information systems?
274. Do you have programs in place for employees to go back to school?

25.   International Considerations

275. Have you considered taking your organization international?
276. Are you developing internal sources of international management experience?
277. Are you seeking out international strategic alliances?
278. Do you hire key nationals of countries you enter to cope with different cultures?
279. Have you developed a worldwide sourcing program for products and services?
280. Are you creative when considering alternative channels of distribution overseas?
281. Do you have a source for international marketing research?
282. Do you have a source for obtaining international personnel?

Only by thoughtfully considering and proactively addressing the implications of these questions or options—perhaps through management "brainstorming" or "retreat" sessions—will retailers be able to control a capricious environment. Only by preparing for the future today will retailers be competitive tomorrow.

References

Abramson, Bernard. "Retail Information Systems—What's Next?" *Touche Ross Retail Topics* (July 1989): 1–4.

Adams, Joe. "POS Systems." *Retail Systems Alert* (July 1990): 1–2.

Albaum, Gerald, and Robert A. Peterson. "Consumer Preferences for Buying from Direct Selling Companies." Working Paper, Washington, D.C.: Direct Selling Education Foundation, 1987.

Alexander, Nicholas. "Retailing Post-1992." *Service Industries Journal* 10 (Jan. 1990): 172–87.

Ambry, Margaret K. *1990–1991 Almanac of Consumer Markets.* Ithaca, NY: American Demographics Press, 1989.

Amsterdam, Lee Roberts, and Harvey Amsterdam. *The Complete Prophecies of Nostradamus,* 3rd ed. New York: Nostradamus Co., 1983.

Anderson, Wilton Thomas, and Linda L. Golden. "Timestyles and Time Trials: Patterns in the Days of Our Lives." *Basic and Applied Social Psychology,* forthcoming.

Appel, Joseph H. *The Business Biography of John Wanamaker, Founder and Builder.* New York: The Macmillan Company, 1930.

Armstrong, Larry. "900 Numbers Are Being Born Again." *Business Week* 3178 (Sept. 17, 1990): 144, 149.

——————————. "How Sony Became a Home-Movie Superstar." *Business Week* 3163 (June 11, 1990): 72.

Ashley, Richard. "On the Relative Worth of Recent Macroeconomic Forecasts." *International Journal of Forecasting* 4, 3 (1988): 363–76.

"Avon Tries a New Formula to Restore Its Glow." *Business Week* 2849 (July 2, 1984): 46–7.

Bandow, Doug. "Are Hostile Takeovers Good for the Economy?" *Business and Society Review* 63 (Fall 1987): 54–5.

Baranowe, Thad, and David E. McNabb. "The In-Home Shopper: Segmenting the Direct Selling Market." Working Paper, Washington, D.C.: Direct Selling Education Foundation, 1988.

Barmash, Isadore. "Disquieting Times in 1991." *Stores* 72 (Dec. 1990): 14–15.

——————. "Sales Softened in September at the Nation's Largest Retailers." *The New York Times*, 139, Oct. 12, 1990, p. C3.

Barringer, Felicity. "Population Tops 29 Million As California Widens Gap." *The New York Times*, 139, Aug. 28, 1990, p. A16.

Bartimo, Jim. "At These Shouting Matches, No One Says a Word." *Business Week* 3163 (June 11, 1990): 78.

Bates, Albert. "The Extended Specialty Store: A Strategic Opportunity for the 1990s." *Journal of Retailing* 65 (Fall 1989): 379–88.

——————. "Ahead—The Retrenchment Era." *Journal of Retailing* 53 (Fall 1977): 29–46.

Batra, Ravi. *The Great Depression of 1990*. Dallas, TX: Venus Books, 1985.

Beale, Calvin L. "Americans Heading for the Cities, Once Again." *Rural Development Perspectives* 4 (June 1988): 2–6.

Bellamy, Edward. *Looking Backward, 2000–1887*. Boston, MA: Ticknor and Company, 1888.

Beltramini, Richard F., and Kenneth R. Evans. "Salesperson Motivation to Perform and Job Satisfaction: A Sales Contest Participant Perspective." *Journal of Personal Selling & Sales Management* 8 (Aug. 1988): 35–42.

Beniger, James R. *The Control Revolution*. Cambridge, MA: Harvard University Press, 1986.

Benson, Susan Porter. *Counter Cultures*. Urbana, IL: University of Illinois Press, 1986.

Berman, Barry, and Joel R. Evans. *Retail Management*, 4th ed. New York: Macmillan Publishing Company, 1989.

Bernstein, Ronald A., and associates. *Successful Direct Selling*. Englewood Cliffs, NJ: Prentice-Hall, Inc., 1984.

Berry, Leonard L. "Retail Businesses Are Service Businesses." *Journal of Marketing* 50 (Spring 1986): 3–6.

Berry Leonard L., and Ian H. Wilson. "Retailing: The Next Ten Years." *Journal of Retailing* 53 (Fall 1977): 5–28.

Biggart, Nicole W. *Charismatic Capitalism*. Chicago, IL: University of Chicago Press, 1989.

Bluestone, Barry. *The Retail Revolution*. Boston, MA: Auburn House Publishing Company, 1981.

Boorstin, Daniel J. *The Americans: The National Experience*. New York: Random House, 1965.

Brandon, Ruth. *A Capitalist Romance*. Philadelphia, PA: J. B. Lippincott Company, 1977.

Brown, Stephen. "Retailing Change: Cycles and Strategy." *The Quarterly Review of Marketing* 13 (Spring 1988): 8–12.

——————. "The Wheel of Retailing: Past and Present." *Journal of Retailing* 66 (Summer 1990): 143–9.

——————. "Innovation and Evolution in UK Retailing: The Retail Warehouse." *European Journal of Marketing* 24 (Sep. 1990): 39–54.

Bucklin, Louis. *A Theory of Distribution Channel Structure*. Berkeley, CA: University of California Institute of Business and Economic Research, 1966.

Buderi, Robert. "Don't Miss HDTV'S Coming Out Party, at a Hotel Near You." *Business Week* 3163 (June 11, 1990): 75.

Buell, Barbara, and Richard Brandt. "The Pen: Computing's Next Big Leap." *Business Week* 3159 (May 14, 1990): 128–9.

Business Week. "Reshaping Europe: 1992 and Beyond." 3083 (Dec. 12, 1988): 48–51.

——————. "America's New Rush to Europe." 3151 (Mar. 26, 1990): 48–9.

——————. "Retailing: Who Will Survive." 3189 (Nov. 26, 1990): 134–44.

——————. "'Tis The Season to Be Worried." 3190 (Dec. 3, 1990): 33.

Caldwell, Helen M. "1920–1929: The Decade of the French Mystique in the American Perfume Market." *Proceedings* of the Fourth Conference on Historical Research in Marketing and Marketing Thought. East Lansing, MI: Michigan State University, 1989, pp. 259–72.

Carson, David. *International Marketing: A Comparative Systems Approach*. New York: Wiley, 1967.

Chain Store Age. "Toy Dominance Is Transportable." 56 (June 23, 1980): 23.

Chain Store Age Executive. "Entertainment Anchors: New Mall Headliners." 65 (Aug. 1989): 54, 63, 65.

——————. "Where America Shops." 65 (July 1989): 17–19.

——————. "Strategies for the New Century: High Performance Retailers Plan for the Year 2000." 66 (Jan. 1990): 27–9.

Chandler, Alfred D., Jr. *The Visible Hand*. Cambridge, MA: The Belknap Press, 1977.

Cheetham, Erika. *The Man Who Saw Tomorrow*. New York: Berkley Books, 1973.

Clark, Colin. *The Conditions of Economic Progress*, 3rd ed. London: Macmillan & Company Ltd., 1957.

Clark, Don. "Intel in Venture with East Coast Firm." *San Francisco Chronicle*, 126 1990, p. B3.

Coates, Joseph. "The Triple Revolution: Retailing in the 90's." *Retail Control* 57 (Mar. 1989): 2–9.

Connell, Evan S. *Son of the Morning Star*. San Francisco: North Point Press, 1984, pp. 138–9.

Cort, Stanton, and Luis Dominquez. "Cross-Shopping and Retail Growth." *Journal of Marketing Research* 14 (May 1977): 187–92.

Cox, David. "The Shape of Shopping to Come." *Accountancy* 104 (Nov. 1989): 158, 160.

Crossen, Cynthia. "The Future Is Ours to See; and Clearly, We're at Crossroads." *Wall Street Journal*, 86, Jan. 11, 1990, pp. A1, A4.

Daily, Jo Ellen, and Mark N. Vamos. "How Tupperware Hopes to Liven Up the Party." *Business Week* 2882 (Feb. 25, 1985): 108–9.

Danzinger, Sheldon, and Peter Gottschalk. "Increasing Inequality in the United States: What We Know and What We Don't." *Journal of Post Keynesian Economics* 11 (Winter 1988–89): 174–94.

Davidson, William R., Albert D. Bates, and Stephen J. Bass. "The Retail Life Cycle." *Harvard Business Review* 54 (Nov./Dec. 1976): 89–96.

Davidson, William R., and Alice L. Rodgers. "Changes and Challenges in Retailing." *Business Horizons* 24 (July/Aug. 1981): 82–7.

Dawson, John. "Review of Retailing." *Management International Forum* 7 (Sep./Oct. 1989): 30–6.

Deloitte & Touche. "Expert Systems in Retailing--Survey Results." Deloitte & Touche Retail Services and Artificial Intelligence Expert Systems Development Groups (Jan. 15, 1990): 1–12.

Depke, Diedre A. "IBM's New Bid to Be at Home." *Business Week* 3165 (June 18, 1990): 33.

Dickson, Peter. "Distributor Portfolio Analysis and the Channel Dependence Matrix." *Journal of Marketing* 47 (Summer 1983): 35–44.

"Direct Selling Glossary." Washington, D.C.: Direct Selling Education Foundation. 1984.

"Direct Selling Industry Survey." Washington, D.C.: Direct Selling Association, 1989.

Discount Store News. "New Ethnics Offer New Opportunities." 29 (May 7, 1990): 110, 113.

Doody, Alton F., and William R. Davidson. "Next Revolution in Retailing." *Harvard Business Review* 45 (May/June 1967): 4–16, 20, 188.

Drew-Bear, Robert. *Mass Merchandising; Revolution & Evolution*. New York: Fairchild Publications, 1970.

Drum-Beninati, Marie. "Trends in Retailing." *Retail Control* 57 (Nov. 1989): 3–7.

Duncan, Delbert J., Stanley C. Hollander, and Ronald Savitt. *Modern Retailing Management*, 10th ed. Homewood, IL: Richard D. Irwin, Inc., 1983.

Dunkin, Amy. "Big Names Are Opening Doors for Avon." *Business Week* 3001 (June 1, 1987): 96–7.

Dychtwald, Ken, and Greg Gable. "Portrait of a Changing Consumer." *Business Horizons* 33 (Jan./Feb. 1990): 62–73.

Dychtwald, Ken, and Greg Gable. *The Shifting American Marketplace.* Emeryville, CA: Age Wave, Inc., 1990.

Ellis, Joseph. "New Opportunities in the Retail Marketplace." *Retail Control* 58 (Mar. 1990): 3–8.

English, Wilke D. "The Impact of Electronic Technology upon the Marketing Channel." *Journal of the Academy of Marketing Science* 13 (Summer 1985): 57–71.

Enis, Ben M. "The Direct Selling Industry: A Systematic Appraisal of Future Managerial Issues." Working Paper, Washington, D.C.: Direct Selling Education Foundation, 1986.

Etgar, Michael. "The Retail Ecology Model: A Comprehensive Model of Retail Change." In *Research in Marketing,* Jagdish Sheth, ed. Hartford, CT: JAI Press, Inc., 1984, pp. 41–62.

Exter, Thomas. "Feathering the Empty Nest." *American Demographics* 12 (June 1990), 8.

Fierman, Jaclyn. "The Bosses See a Recession Soon." *Fortune* 121 (Oct. 8, 1990): 73, 76, 80–1.

Fishman, Arnold. "Guide to Mail Order Sales." *Direct Marketing* 53 (July 1990): 27–46.

Flatley, Bill. "Reshaping Retailing for the '90s." *Women's Wear Daily,* 159, March 1, 1990, pp. R6–7.

Forrester, Jay. *The Futurist* 25 (Jan./Feb. 1991): 61.

Fox, Bruce. "Why We Need Technology." *Chain Store Age Executive* 65 (Nov. 1989): 211.

_____. "Winning at Leapfrog." *Chain Store Age Executive* 66 (Feb. 1990): 101.

Francett, Barbara. "How Grocers Bag Shoppers." *Computer Decisions* 21 (Apr. 1989): 44, 48.

Frenzen, Jonathan K., and Harry L. Davis. "Consumer Motivations to Attend and Buy at Home Parties." Working Paper, Washington, D.C.: Direct Selling Education Foundation, 1989.

Frenzen, Jonathan K., and Harry L. Davis. "Purchasing Behavior in Embedded Markets." *Journal of Consumer Research* 17 (June 1990): 1–12.

Frieden, Bernard J., and Lynne B. Sagalyn. *Downtown, Inc.* Cambridge: MIT Press, 1989.

Friedman, Thomas H. "Creating the New Merchandising Advantage." *Retail Systems Alert* (May 1990): 1.

Fruendlich, Naomi. "Just Send the Funnies, Please." *Business Week* 3158 (May 7 1990): 125.

Fuller, Alfred Carl. *A Foot in the Door.* New York: McGraw-Hill, 1960.

Galbraith, John Kenneth. *Economic Development.* Boston, MA: Houghton Mifflin, 1964.

Gertler, Jane Felsen. "Designing for a New Decade: The Function and Feel of Power Centers." *Shopping Center World* 19 (June 1990): 36–7.

Gill, Penny. "What's a Department Store in the 1990s?" *Stores* 72 (Feb. 1990): 8–10, 15.

Glenn, Norval. "Duration of Marriage, Family Composition and Marital Happiness." *National Journal of Sociology* 3 (Spring 1989): 3–24.

Goldman, Ariel. "The Role of Trading-Up in the Development of the Retailing System." *Journal of Marketing* 39 (Jan. 1975): 54–62.

Granfield, Michael, and Alfred Nicols. "Economic and Marketing Aspects of the Direct Selling Industry." *Journal of Retailing* 51 (Spring 1975): 33–50, 113.

Greenberg, Jerome, Martin T. Topol, Elaine Sherman, and Kenneth Cooperman. "The Itinerant Street Vendor: A Form of Nonstore Retailing." *Journal of Retailing* 56 (Summer 1980): 66–80.

Gross, Leonard. "America's Mood Today." *Look* 29 (June 29, 1965): 15–21.

Guin, John. "Penney Suffers Third-Quarter Drop in Catalog Sales, Inventory Down." *DM News* (Dec. 15, 1990): 4.

Haber, Holly. "Automatic Restocking KOs Stockout at CHH." *Retailing Technology & Operations* (Dec. 5, 1988): 6.

——————————. "Getting Papers off Desks and into Computers." *Women's Wear Daily,* 157, March 6, 1989, p. 23.

——————————. "On Line at Dillard's." *Retailing Technology and Operations* (Apr. 24, 1989): 5.

Hadas, Moses. *Imperial Rome.* Alexandria, VA: Time-Life Books, 1965.

Haggin, Jeff, and Bjorn Kartomten. "Predictions for the 1990s." *Catalog Age* 7 (March 1990): 95–6.

Hallett, Jeffrey J. "Present Future for Retailing." *Retail Control* 57 (Sep. 1989): 4–8.

Halverson, Richard C. "Leisure in the '90s." *Discount Store News* 29 (May 7, 1990): 195.

Hamel, Ruth. "Raging against Aging." *American Demographics* 12 (Mar. 1990): 42, 44–5.

Hamill, Jim, and John Crosbie. "British Retail Acquisition in the U.S." *International Journal of Retail and Distribution Management* 18 (Sep./Oct. 1990): 15–20.

Hammer, Michael. "Reengineering Work: Don't Automate, Obliterate." *Harvard Business Review* 68 (July/Aug. 1990): 104–12.

Hammond, Keith. "High-Tech Gamble: Xerox Tries To Change Its Has-Been Image." *Wall Street Journal,* 86, Sep. 20, 1990, p. A8.

Hammond, Keith, Deirdre Depke, and Richard Brant. "Software: It's a New Game." *Business Week* 3162 (June 4, 1990): 102–6.

Harris, Louis, and associates. "Highlights of a Comprehensive Survey of the Direct Selling Industry." Washington, D.C.: Direct Selling Association, 1977.

Helfand, Mitch. "Retailing Goes Back to Basics: The Customer Is King in the 90s." *Deloitte & Touche Retail Topics* (Apr. 1990): 1–4.

Hilder, David B. "Do Downbeat Corporate Forecasts Foretell a Recession?" *Wall Street Journal*, 86, July 27, 1990, pp. C1, C2.

Hiller, Terry R. "Going Shopping in the 1990s." *The Futurist* 17 (Dec. 1983): 13–19.

Hirsch, James S. "Kodak to Unveil Photo Compact Disks That Show Images on Television Screen." *Wall Street Journal*, 86, Sep. 18, 1990, p. 10.

Hisey, Pete. "Future Shopping Echoes the Past." *Discount Store News* 29 (May 7, 1990): 178, 180.

——————. "House of the '90s." *Discount Store News* 29 (May 7, 1990): 188.

——————. "More Meaningful Values Replacing '80s Greed." *Discount Store News* 29 (May 7, 1990): 110, 117.

——————. "Stores to Be More Efficient, Flexible." *Discount Store News* 29 (May 7, 1990): 178–80.

Hogsett, Don. "Retail Must Brace for a Decade of Major Changes." *Home Textiles Today* 11 (July 2, 1990): 42–3.

Hollander, Stanley C. Discount Retailing 1900–1950, unpublished Ph.D. dissertation, University of Pennsylvania, 1954.

——————. "The Wheel of Retailing." *Journal of Marketing* 24 (July 1960): 37–42.

——————. "Notes on the Retail Accordion." *Journal of Retailing* 42 (Summer 1966): 29–42, 56.

——————. *Multinational Retailing*. East Lansing, MI: Michigan State University, 1970.

Hollander, Stanley, C., and Gary Marple. *Henry Ford: Inventor of the Supermarket?* East Lansing, MI: Bureau of Business and Economic Research, Michigan State University, 1960.

Home Textiles Today. "Exploration Age for Inner Space." 11 (July 2, 1990): 42.

——————. "Principles of Evolution Overtaking Discounters." 11 (July 2, 1990): 42.

——————. "Retailers Will Need to Improve Their Aim." 11 (July 2, 1990): 43, 45.

"Home Video." *Industry Surveys*. New York: Standard and Poor Corporation, 1990.

Houston, Joel F. "The Underground Economy: Trouble Issues for Policymakers." *University of Michigan Business Review,* 3 9 (Sep./Oct. 1987): 3–12.

Hower, Ralph Merle. *History of Macy's of New York, 1858–1919.* Cambridge, MA: Harvard University Press, 1943.

Hyde, Linda L. "IBM Unveils an Advance for Note-Pad Computers." *Wall Street Journal,* 86 June 19, 1990, p. 8.

Hyde, Linda L., Carl E. Steidtmann, and Daniel J. Sweeney. *Retailing 2000.* Columbus, OH: Management Horizons, 1990.

International Journal of Retail and Distribution Management. "Fast Food in Europe." Review of a report by the Economist Intelligence Unit 18 (Sep./Oct. 1990): i.

Jolson, Marvin A. "Direct Selling: Consumer vs. Salesman," *Business Horizons* 15 (Oct. 1972): 87–95.

Johnson, Jay L. "The Future of Retailing." *Discount Merchandiser* 30 (Jan. 1990): 70–2.

Juvenile Merchandising. "Detailing Retailing 2000." 43 (July 1990): 22–6.

Karaar, Louis. "The Rising Power of the Pacific." *Fortune* 121 (Fall 1990): 8–9, 12.

Kacker, Madhav. "The Lure of U.S. Retailing to the Foreign Acquirer." *Mergers & Acquisitions* 25 (July/Aug. 1990): 63–8.

Kahn, Herman, and Anthony J. Wiener. *The Year 2000.* New York: The Macmillan Company, 1967.

Kaplan, James. "The Changing Face of Small-space Users." *Shopping Center World* 19 (1990): 95–6.

Kardon, Brian E. "Consumer Schizophrenia." *Touche Ross Retail Topics* (Apr. 1990): 1–4.

———————————. "The Problem with Demographics: Disparities in the Coming Decade." *Deloitte & Touche Retail Topics* (Feb. 1990): 1–4.

Katayama, Frederick H. "Innovation." *Fortune* 121 (May 21, 1990): 138.

Keen, Peter G. W. *Competing in Time, Using Telecommunications for Competitive Advantage.* Cambridge, MA: Ballinger Publishing Company, 1986.

Keller, John J. "Fun and Facts Fly across Phone Lines as the Market for 'Audiotext' Explodes." *Wall Street Journal,* 86, May 25, 1990, p. B1.

———————————. "Technology." *Wall Street Journal,* 86, Sep. 28, 1990, p. B1.

Kelly, John R. "Recreation Trends." *Business* 38 (Apr./June 1988): 54–7.

Kelly, Mary Ellen. "Europe Receptive; Japan Stays Aloof." *Discount Store News* 29 (May 7, 1990): 149–62.

Kern, Richard. "USA 2000." *Sales & Marketing Management* 137 (Oct. 27, 1986): 8–30.

Klopfenstein, Bruce C. "Forecasting Consumer Adoption of Information Technology and Services—Lessons from Home Video Forecasting."

Journal of the American Society for Information Science 40 (Jan. 1989): 17–26.

Kotler, Philip. *Principles of Marketing,* 2nd ed. Englewood Cliffs, NJ: Prentice-Hall, 1973.

Kraar, Louis. "The Rising Power of the Pacific." *Fortune* 122 (Fall 1990): 8–9, 12.

Lazarus, Emma. "The New Colossus." In *The Poems of Ezra Lazaras*, vol. 1. Boston: Houghton, Mifflin and Co., 1889, pp. 202–3.

Lazer, William, Priscilla LaBarbera, Allen E. Smith, and James MacLachlan. *Marketing 2000 and Beyond.* Chicago, IL: American Marketing Association, 1990.

Lettich, Jill. "Consumer of '90s: Smarter and Wiser, But with Less Time." *Discount Store News* 29 (May 7, 1990): 110, 191–2.

Lev, Michael. "Hard Times? Not for These Stores." *The New York Times*, 140, Dec. 13, 1990, p. C1, C6.

Leventhal, Larry. "Retail Reality Is Placing a Wakeup Call." *Home Textiles Today* 11 (July 2, 1990): 16, 18.

Levy, Walter K. "The End of an Era: A Time for Retail Perestroika." *Journal of Retailing* 65 (Fall 1989): 389–95.

Lewis, Stephen D. "Why States Are Stepping Up Attacks on Large Mergers." *Mergers and Acquisitions* 25 (July/Aug. 1990): 37–40.

Liebeck, Laura. "Retailers Target MTV Generation." *Discount Store News* 29 (May 7, 1990): 125–6.

Lilien, Gary, and Philip Kotler. *Marketing Decision Making: A Model Building Approach.* New York, NY: Harper & Row, 1983.

Long, Kim. *The American Forecaster Almanac.* Boulder, CO: Johnson Books, 1990.

Long, Larry. "America on the Move." *American Demographics* 12 (June 1990): 46–9.

Lopez, Julie, and Mary Lu Carnevale. "Fiber Optics Promises a Revolution of Sorts, If The Sharks Don't Bite It." *Wall Street Journal*, 86, July 10, 1990, pp. A1, A4.

Lumpkin, James R., Marjorie Caballero, and Lawrence B. Chonko. *Direct Marketing, Direct Selling and the Mature Consumer.* Westport, CT: Quorum Books, 1989.

Magrath, Allan J. "What Marketing Can Learn from Manufacturing." *Across the Board* 27 (Apr. 1990): 37–42.

Mahajan, Vijay, and Jerry Wind. "Market Discontinuities and Strategic Planning: A Research Agenda." *Technological Forecasting and Social Change* 36 (Aug. 1989): 185–99.

Mallen, Bruce. "Functional Spin-off: A Key to Accepting Change in Distribution Structure." *Journal of Marketing* 37 (July 1973): 18–25.

Marcus, Stanley. "Merchandising for the 1990s." *Arthur Andersen Retailing Issues Letter.* Texas A&M University: Center for Retailing Studies, 1990.

Martino, Joseph P. "On Charles P. Steinmetz as a Prophet." In *1999 The World of Tomorrow,* Edward Cornish, ed. Washington, D.C.: World Future Society, 1978, p. 24.

Maslow, A. H. *Motivation and Personality.* New York: Harper & Row, 1954.

Mason, J. Barry, and Morris L. Mayer. *Modern Retailing,* 5th ed. Homewood, IL: BPI/Irwin, 1990.

May, Eleanor G. "Direct Selling—A Unique Channel of Distribution." Working Paper, Washington, D.C.: Direct Selling Education Foundation.

_____. "A Retail Odyssey." *Journal of Retailing* 65 (Fall 1989): 356–367.

Mayer, Robert. "The Growth of the French Videotex System and Its Implications for Consumers." *Journal of Consumer Policy* 11 (Mar. 1988): 55–84.

McCloud, John. "Powering Their Way to the Top." *Shopping Center World* 19 (June 1990): 32, 34–6, 39.

McCrohan, Kevin F., and James D. Smith. "A Consumer Expenditure Approach to Estimating the Size of the Underground Economy." *Journal of Marketing* 50 (Apr. 1986): 48–60.

McGuire, Jane. "Opening the Door to Door-to-Door Selling." *Chemical Business* 225 (Feb. 1984): 27–33.

McLuhan, Marshall. *Understanding Media.* New York: McGraw-Hill, 1964.

_____. *The Medium Is the Message.* New York: Random House, 1967.

McNair, Malcolm P. "Significant Trends and Developments in the Postwar Period." In *Competitive Distribution in a Free High-Level Economy and Its Implications for the University,* Albert B. Smith, ed. Pittsburgh, PA: University of Pittsburgh Press, 1958, pp. 1–25.

McNair, Malcolm P., and Eleanor G. May. "The Next Revolution of the Retailing Wheel." *Harvard Business Review* 56 (Sep./Oct. 1978): 81–91.

"Media and Measurement Technology Predictions for the Coming Decade." *BSB Projections 2000.* New York: Backer Spielvogel Bates, 1991.

Miller, Michael W. "Lotus Is Likely to Abandon Consumer-data Project," *Wall Street Journal,* 87, Jan. 23, 1991, p. B1.

Millett, Stephen M. "How Scenarios Trigger Strategic Thinking." *Long Range Planning* 21 (Oct. 1988): 61–8.

Mintz, Steven. "Avon, You've Looked Better." *Sales & Marketing Management* 128 (Apr. 5, 1982): 52–7.

Monitor. "Shopping the Big Centers," 20, June 1990, pp. 13–14, 18, 20–23.

Mount, Richard. "Economy to Pick Up Steam in Mid-'90s." *Discount Store News* 29 (May 7, 1990): 138, 140, 42.

Naisbitt, John. *Megatrends.* New York: Warner Books, 1982.

Naisbitt, John, and Patricia Aburdene. *Megatrends 2000.* New York: William Morrow and Company, 1990.

"1989 State of the Convenience Store Industry." Falls Church, VA: National Association of Convenience Stores, 1989.

Nisberg, Jay N. *Handbook of Business Terms.* New York: Random House, 1988.

Nowland Organization, Inc. "Consumer Experiences and Attitudes with Respect to Direct Selling." Washington, D.C.: Direct Selling Education Foundation, 1982.

O'Hare, William. "What's It Take to Get Along?" *American Demographics* 12 (May 1990): 37–9.

O'Neill, Robert E. "Consumers Rate the Retailers." *Monitor* 20 (June 1990): 26–30.

——————————. "You Can Do Business in the Inner City." *Monitor* 20 (May 1990): 221–7.

Ono, Yumiko. "Amway Translates with Ease into Japanese." *Wall Street Journal,* 86, Sep. 21, 1990, p. B1.

Palamountain, Joseph Cornwall, Jr. *The Politics of Distribution.* Cambridge: Harvard University Press, 1955.

Pancari, Denise, and Ann Senn. "Retailers Are Looking to Expert Systems to Improve Productivity." *Touche Ross Retail Topics* (Sep. 1989): 1–4.

Papandrew, Jackie M. "New Age of Europe." *Monitor* 20 (May 1990): 100–13.

——————————. "Shadows in the Sunshine State." *Monitor* 19 (July/Aug. 1989): FL–1, 3–14.

Parrish, Michael. "Focus on Books." *Business Horizons* 29 (Jan./Feb 1988): 79–80.

Pereira, Joseph. "Discount Department Stores Struggle against Rivals That Strike Aisle by Aisle." *Wall Street Journal* 86, June 19, 1990, p. B1.

Peterson, Eric C. "The 1990s: What's Ahead." *Stores* 72 (Feb. 1990): 73–6.

Peterson, Robert A., Gerald Albaum, and Nancy M. Ridgway. "Consumers Who Buy from Direct Sales Companies." *Journal of Retailing* 65 (Summer 1989): 273–86.

Peterson, Robert A., Gerald Albaum, and George Kozmetsky. *Modern American Capitalism.* Westport, CT: Quorum Books, 1990.

Pollack, Andrew. "A Credit Card Offshoot Blossoms." *The New York Times,* 140, Aug. 3, 1990, p. B10.

Porter, Michael E. *Competitive Advantage.* New York: The Free Press, 1985.

Prestowitz, Clyde V., Jr. *Trading Places.* New York: Basic Books, 1988.

Rapoport, Carla. "How the Japanese Are Changing." *Fortune* 121 (Fall 1990): 15–22.

Redd, Thomas A. "Power Retailers in the 1990's." *Retail Control* 57 (July/Aug. 1989): 24–33.

Reilly, Patrick M. "Newsweek Personalizes Magazines." *Wall Street Journal*, 86, May 25, 1990, p. B1.

Resseguie, Harry F. "Alexander Turney Stewart and the Development of the Department Store." *Business History Review* 39 (1965): 301–22.

"Retailing in the Year 2000." *Chain Store Age Executive* 63 (May 1987): 6–28.

Riche, Martha Farnsworth. "Boomerang Age." *American Demographics* 12 (May 1990): 24–27, 30, 52–3.

Richman, Tom. " Mrs. Fields' Secret Ingredients." *Inc.* 9 (Oct. 1987): 65, 70, 72.

Robins, Gary. "Wide-Area Networks." *Stores* 72 (Nov. 1990): 57–9.

Robinson, John P. "The Time Squeeze." *American Demographics* 12 (Feb. 1990): 30–3.

Robinson, T. M., and C. M. Clarke-Hill. "Directional Growth of European Retailers." *International Journal of Retail and Distribution Management* 18 (Sep./Oct. 1990): 3–14.

Rosenberg, Jerry M. *Dictionary of Business and Management.* New York: John Wiley and Sons, 1983.

Rosenberg, Larry J., and Elizabeth C. Hirschman. "Retailing without Stores." *Harvard Business Review* 58 (July/Aug. 1980): 103–12.

Rostow, Walt W. *View from the Seventh Floor.* New York: Harper & Row, 1964.

Rothfeder, Jeffrey. "School Cafeteria Takes 'Credit Cards'." *San Francisco Chronicle,* Sep. 30, 1990, p. 1.

Rothfeder, Jeffrey and Mark Lewyn. "Home Computers." *Business Week* 3177 (Sep. 10, 1990): 64–70.

Russell, Bertrand. *Icarus or the Future of Science.* New York: E. P. Dutton and Company, 1924.

Russell, Cheryl. *100 Predictions for the Baby Boom: The Next 50 Years.* New York: Plenum Press, 1987.

Ryans, John K., Jr., and Pradeep A. Rau. *Marketing Strategies for the New Europe.* Chicago, IL: American Marketing Association, 1990.

Salmon, Walter J., and Andre Tordjman. "The Internationalisation of Retailing." *International Journal of Retailing* 4 (1989): 3–12.

Samli, A. Coskun. *Retail Marketing Strategy: Planning, Implementation and Control.* New York: Quorum Books, 1989.

Sanghavi, Nitin. "The Japanese Yen for Non-Store Retailing." *Direct Marketing* 52 (Apr. 1989): 24–8.

Sarkissian, Richard V. "Retailing Trends in the 1990s." *Journal of Accountancy* 168 (Dec. 1989): 44–55.

Savitt, Ronald. "Looking Back to See Ahead: Writing the History of American Retailing." *Journal of Retailing* 65 (Fall 1989): 326–55.

Scarupa, Henry. "In 1990, the Crystal Balls of Top U.S. Psychics Were Clouded." *Austin American-Statesman,* 120, Dec. 31, 1990, p. A4.

Schewe, Charles D. "Get in Position for the Older Market." *American Demographics* 12 (June 1990): 38–63.

Schewe, Charles D., and Anne L. Balazs. "Playing Roles." *American Demographics* 12 (Apr. 1990): 24, 26–27, 30.

Schiro, Thomas J., and Amy M. Skolnik. "Europe 1992—Impact on Retail Sector." *Retail Control* 58 (May/June 1990): 3–9.

Schlosberg, Jeremy. "Grandparent." *American Demographics* 12 (July 1990): 32–5, 51.

Schlossstein, Steven. *Trade War.* New York: Congdon & Weed, 1984.

Schnaars, Steven P., and Conrad Berenson. "Growth Market Forecasting Revisited: A Look Back at a Look Forward." *California Management Review* 28 (Summer 1986): 71–88.

Schudson, Michael. *Advertising: The Uneasy Persuasion.* New York: Basic Books, 1984.

Schultz, David P. "Specialty Expansion Slowing." *Stores* 72 (Dec. 1990): 35–8.

Schwadel, Francine. "Chain Finds Incentives a Hard Sell." *Wall Street Journal,* 86, July 6, 1990, p. B1, B4.

Sheth, Jagdish N. "Emerging Trends for the Retailing Industry." *Journal of Retailing* 59 (Fall 1983): 6–18.

Sidey, Hugh. "Where the Buffalo Roamed." *Time* 135 (Sep. 24, 1990): 53–4, 56.

Siegman, Ken. "New Home Computer Blitz under Way." *San Francisco Chronicle,* 126, Sep. 24, 1990, pp. C1, C6.

――――――――. "Stanley Marcus on Technology in Retailing." *Stores* 69 (Sep. 1987): 72–4.

Smarr, Susan L. "Looking at the Big Picture." *Bobbin* 31 (Feb. 1990): 60–4.

Standard Industrial Classification Manual. Washington, D.C.: U.S. Government Printing Office, 1987.

Steidtmann, Carl. "Global Economy of the 90's." *Retail Control* 58 (Feb. 1990): 3–13.

Stern, Louis, and Adel El-Ansary. *Marketing Channels,* 3rd ed. Englewood Cliffs, NJ: Prentice Hall, 1988.

Sternlieb, George. *The Future of the Downtown Department Store.* Cambridge, MA: Joint Center for Urban Studies of the Massachusetts Institute of Technology and Harvard University, 1962.

Stone, Bob. *Successful Direct Marketing Methods,* 4th ed. Lincolnwood, IL: NTC Books, 1987.

Sutton, Sandra M. "Value-Oriented Retailing: Healthy, Wealthy and Wiser." *Monitor* 20 (June 1990): 35–6, 38, 41–2, 45–50.

Szabo, Joan C., and Nancy Croft Baker. "Hot New Markets of the 1990's." *Retail Control* 57 (Jan. 1989): 23–34.

Tahmincioglu, Eve. "Technology: Moving into a Basic Mode." *Women's Wear Daily,* 159, Jan. 4, 1990, pp. 7–10.

――――――――. "Penney's to Offer Satellite Service." *Women's Wear Daily,* 159, June 14, 1990, p. 8.

――――――――. "Technology in 2000: It May Already Be Here." *Chain Store Age Executive* 65 (May 1989): 175–6.

The New York Times. "Talking Business with Brennan of Montgomery Ward," 140, Dec. 11, 1990, p. C2.

――――――――. "Retail Sales Fell 0.1 Percent Last Month," 140, Dec. 14, 1990, pp. C1, C6.

――――――――. "Catalog Sales Lag," 140, Nov. 29, 1990, p. C8.

Thistlethwaite, Paul, et al. *Direct Selling in MidAmerica.* Macomb, IL: Center for Business and Economic Research, Western Illinois University, 1985.

Thompson, Tracie L. "Fremont Hopes to Stop Bad Checks with Prints." *San Francisco Chronicle,* 126, Sep. 30, 1990, p. A4.

Tillman, Rollie. "Rise of the Conglomerchant." *Harvard Business Review* 49 (Nov./Dec. 1971): 44–51.

Toffler, Alvin. *Future Shock.* New York: Random House, 1970.

Treadgold, Alan D. "The Developing Internationalization of Retailing." *International Journal of Retail & Distribution Management* 18 (Mar./Apr. 1990): 4–11.

"Trends and Predictions for the Year 2000 and Beyond," Special Anniversary Issue. *Omni* 12 (Oct. 1989).

Tuchman, Barbara W. *The March of Folly.* New York: Alfred A. Knopf, 1984.

Turchiano, Francesca. "Demalling of America." *American Demographics* 12 (Apr. 1990): 37–9.

U.S. Department of Commerce Bureau of the Census. *Census of Retail Trade* (note in some early years this was titled *Retail Distribution*), Washington, D.C.: U.S. Government Printing Office, 1929, 1935, 1948, 1954, 1963, 1967, 1972, 1977, 1982.

――――――――. *Historical Statistics of the United States, Colonial Times to 1970,* Bicentennial ed. Washington, D.C.: U.S. Government Printing Office, 1975.

_____. *Statistical Abstract of the United States*, 110th ed. Washington, D.C.: U.S. Government Printing Office, 1989.

Verity, John W. "Hypertext: A World of Information in the Blink of an Eye." *Business Week* 3165 (June 18, 1990): 180.

Walash, Eileen R. "Holograms Beam into Fashion." *Women's Wear Daily*, 160, Dec. 5, 1990, pp. 16,19.

Waldrop, Judith. "Spending by Degree." *American Demographics* 12 (Feb. 1990): 23–6.

_____. "Up & Down the Income Scale." *American Demographics* 12 (July 1990): 24, 26–7, 30.

Waldrop, Judith, and Thomas Exter. "What the 1990 Census Will Show." *American Demographics* 12 (Jan. 1990): 20–30.

Wall Street Journal. "Company-Owned Arby's to Accept Credit Cards." 86, Sep. 11, 1990, p 8.

Wallechinsky, David, Amy Wallace, and Irving Wallace. *The Book of Predictions*. New York: William Morrow and Company, 1981.

Ward, Fred. "Images for the Computer Age." *National Geographic* 175 (June 1989): 718–51.

_____. "What's Next: Hot Techno-opportunities." *Electronics USA* (Spring 1990): 10.

Wasson, Chester. *Marketing Management*. Charlotte, NC: ECR Associates, 1983.

Wayne, Leslie. "Rewriting the Rules of Retailing." *The New York Times*, 138, Oct. 15, 1989, pp. F3, F6.

Weigand, Robert. "Fit Products and Channels to Your Markets." *Harvard Business Review* 54 (Jan./Feb. 1977): 95–105.

Weinstein, Steve. "Pinning Down the Hispanic Market." *Progressive Grocer* 69 (June 1990): 69–72.

Wood, James. "The World Stage in Retailing." *Retail & Distribution Management* 17 (Nov./Dec. 1989): 14–16.

"Worldwide Direct Sales Data." Washington, D.C.: World Federation of Direct Selling Associations, 1990.

Worthy, Ford S. "A New Mass Market Emerges." *Fortune* 122 (Fall 1990): 51, 54–7.

_____. "Getting in on the Ground Floor." *Fortune* 122 (Fall 1990): 61–4, 66–7.

Wortzel, Lawrence H. "Retailing Strategies for Today's Mature Marketplace." *Journal of Business Strategy* 7 (Spring 1987): 45–56.

Wotruba, Thomas R. "The Effect of Goal-Setting on the Performance of Independent Sales Agents in Direct Selling." *Journal of Personal Selling & Sales Management* 9 (Spring 1989): 22–9.

_____. "The Relationship of Job Image, Performance and Job Satisfaction to Inactivity-Proneness of Direct Salespeople." *Journal of the Academy of Marketing Science* 18 (Spring 1990): 113–21.

_____. "A Comparison of Full-Time and Part-Time Salespeople on Job Satisfaction, Performance and Turnover." *International Journal of Research in Marketing,* forthcoming.

Wotruba, Thomas R., and Donald Sciglimpaglia.   "Turnover in Direct Selling: A Comparison of Active and Inactive Salespeople: Phase Two of a Longitudinal Study."   Washington, D.C.:   Direct Selling Education Foundation, 1988.

Wotruba, Thomas R., Donald Sciglimpaglia, and Pradeep K. Tyagi. "Turnover in Direct Selling: A Comparison of Active and Inactive Salespersons." Working Paper, Washington, D.C.: Direct Selling Education Foundation, 1986.

_____. "Toward A Model of Turnover in Direct Selling Organizations." *Proceedings*, Winter Educators' Conference, American Marketing Association, 1987, pp. 348–53.

Wotruba, Thomas R., and Pradeep K. Tyagi.   "Met Expectations and Turnover in Direct Selling." *Journal of Marketing* 55 (July 1991): 24–35.

Zola, Emile. *The Ladies' Paradise* (translation of *Au Bonheur des Dames,* 50th French ed.). London: Vizetelly, 1986.

Index

About the Contributors

Dale Achabal is director of the Retail Management Institute and the L. J. Skaggs Distinguished Professor at Santa Clara University. He received his Ph.D. in marketing and regional economics from The University of Texas at Austin. He has taught in the undergraduate, graduate, and executive development programs at the University of California-Berkeley, Ohio State University, The University of Texas at Austin, and Santa Clara University.

Dr. Achabal's research focuses on decision support and knowledge systems, productivity analysis, and retail patronage. He has published numerous articles in various journals including the *Journal of Marketing, Journal of Retailing, Decision Sciences, Geographical Analysis,* and *Social Science & Medicine.* He also has presented papers at industry and professional conferences throughout the United States and Europe and is active in the American Marketing Association and the National Retail Merchants Association. He is a member of the editorial board of the *Journal of Retailing* and the recipient of two national research awards.

Dr. Achabal is a lecturer and consultant to a variety of organizations in the areas of strategic marketing planning, retail information systems, and marketing research. His current and former clients include AT&T, ComputerLand, IBM, The Limited, Mervyn's, NCR Corporation, J. C. Penney, Safeway, Tandem Computers, and Thrift Drug.

Wilton Thomas Anderson is associate professor at The University of Texas at Austin. He received his Ph.D. degree from Michigan State University in 1969 and has been a member of the marketing faculty at The University of Texas at Austin since 1970, where he specializes in teaching and research in marketing management and communication. Professor Anderson is a recipient of numerous teaching awards and has published articles in journals including the *Journal of Marketing Research, Journal of*

Advertising Research, and the *Journal of Marketing.* A critical observer of the retail sector, Dr. Anderson spends part of every summer as an unpaid worker in a small family-owned rural retail chain to experience every facet of retailing from the bottom up.

Richard C. Bartlett is president and chief operating officer, Mary Kay Cosmetics, Inc. Mr. Bartlett joined the company in 1973 to guide the company's sales and marketing strategies and became an officer in 1976 and a member of the board in 1979. He became president and chief operating officer in 1987.

Mr. Bartlett's career has centered on more than thirty years of experience in direct marketing management, including at Tupperware, where he pioneered that company's international operations in Europe. He currently serves the direct selling industry as vice chairman of the board of the U.S. Direct Selling Association and as a member of the board of the Direct Selling Education Foundation. Presently, he is writing a book about the direct selling industry titled *The Direct Option,* proceeds of which will go to the Direct Selling Education Foundation. Mr. Bartlett serves on the Advisory Board of the Center for Professional Selling, Baylor University, and the Center for Retailing Studies, Texas A&M University.

Mr. Bartlett is a board member of several civic and arts organizations, including the Dallas Opera and the Santa Fe Opera. An active conservationist, he is vice chairman and a trustee of the Texas Nature Conservancy and vice president of the Corporate Recycling Alliance of Texas. He is coauthor of *The Sportsman's Guide to Texas.* Mr. Bartlett received his B.S. degree cum laude in communications from the University of Florida in Gainesville.

John C. Beyer is president of Nathan Associates Inc. Dr. Beyer received his B.A. degree from the University of the Pacific, a Master of Arts degree and a Master of Arts in Law and Diplomacy, both from the Fletcher School at Tufts University, and a Ph.D. from the Fletcher School.

Dr. Beyer has served in his present position since 1978 and has been with Nathan Associates since 1973. He has been a guest scholar at The Brookings Institute and a development economist with the Ford Foundation, where he was a consultant to the Indian Planning Commission and an advisor to the Nepalese Ministry of Finance. He has also been a state planning officer in Sarawak, Malaysia.

Dr. Beyer is a former president of the Washington chapter of the Society for International Development and an adjunct professor at American University. He is the author of two books, *Budget Innovations in Developing Countries* and *Cost Benefit Analysis*, and numerous articles.

William R. Davidson is chairman emeritus, Management Horizons Division of Price Waterhouse, and director of Management Horizons Holding Ltd. (United Kingdom). Before cofounding Management Horizons, Dr. Davidson was chairman of the Marketing Faculty at Ohio State University. He has also been a visiting professor at Harvard University and Stanford University. He possesses extensive retail management experience.

Coauthor of *Marketing* (ninth edition) and *Retailing Management* (sixth edition), Dr. Davidson has written many articles for national and international publications. He frequently addresses major business and professional groups, including the AMA, NRMA, and IMRA on topics such as strategic marketing planning, channels of distribution planning, and the implementation of marketing programs in the retail environment.

A member of the "Hall of Fame in Distribution," Dr. Davidson has been awarded the Central Ohio American Marketing Association's "Marketing Man of the Year" award. He was named 1970's "Marketing Man of the Year" by *Hardline Wholesaling* magazine. He is a past president of the American Marketing Association.

Dr. Davidson holds a bachelor's degree in business administration from the College of Emporia and a master's degree in business administration from Washington University. He earned his Ph.D. in marketing and finance from Ohio State University.

David V. Evans is vice president and director of Information Systems at J. C. Penney Company, Inc. Mr. Evans joined J. C. Penney in 1965 as a systems analyst and moved through a series of systems positions of increasing responsibility. In 1977 he was named manager of Systems and EDP for Sarma-Penney in Belguim. In 1980 Mr. Evans was appointed manager of telephone sales centers in the catalog division; his responsibilities were later expanded to include J. C. Penney Telemarketing, Inc., where he served as president. Appointed to his current position in August 1987, Mr. Evans was elected a vice president in October of that year.

Mr. Evans is a member of the Board of Directors of NRF Information Systems Division, a member of the Voluntary Inter-Industry Communications Standards (VICS) Technical Committee, a member of the EDI Advisory Committee of the Uniform Code Council, and a member of the Conference Board Council of N.A. Information Management Executives. Mr. Evans attended the University of Wisconsin.

Gary L. Frazier is professor of marketing and chair of the Department of Marketing, University of Southern California. Dr. Frazier received his B.S. in business administration and B.A. in history and social studies, magna cum laude, from Bemidji State University. His M.B.A. and D.B.A. are from Indiana University. He was an assistant professor at the University of Illinois before moving to his present university in 1984.

Dr. Frazier's research and teaching interests include distribution channel management, marketing strategy, sales force management, industrial marketing, business firm performance, and strategic marketing planning. He is the editor of a forthcoming book, *Advances in Distribution Channels Research,* and is a contributor to or editor of numerous other books and articles. He has received many professional honors for teaching and research. Dr. Frazier is a member of the editorial review board of several journals, including the *Journal of Marketing,* the *Journal of Marketing Research,* and the *Journal of Retailing.* Dr. Frazier has broad consulting experience with industry including General Motors, Hewlett-Packard, Carnation, 3M, TRW, Merck Pharmaceutical, and Southern California Edison.

Stanley C. Hollander is a professor in the Department of Marketing and Transportation Administration, Michigan State University. Dr. Hollander received his B.S. from New York University, his M.A. from American University, and his Ph.D. from the University of Pennsylvania. He has served as an instructor or professorial faculty member at the Universities of Buffalo, Pennsylvania (Wharton), and Minnesota; he has been at Michigan State since 1958. He was also a visiting faculty member at the Universities of Colorado and California (Los Angeles and Berkeley). Dr. Hollander has also had experience in retail business and government.

His research interests include marketing and consumer behavior history, macromarketing, and retailing. He has papers and presentations in all three fields currently in preparation. He is the author, coauthor, editor, or coeditor of several books and articles and is the coeditor of a marketing history issue of the *Journal of the Academy of Marketing Science.*

Dr. Hollander is currently on the Board of Governors of the Academy of Marketing Science and is past president of the American Collegiate Retailing Association. He has been cochair of the Conference on Historical Research in Marketing five times and cochair of the 1988 National Conference on Retailing. He has received several awards for teaching and research; he was named the 1991 Distinguished Marketing Educator by the Academy of Marketing Science. The Stanley and Selma Hollander New Traditions in Music series was established in 1990 by members, alumni and friends of the MSU Department of Marketing and Transportation Administration.

William W. Keep is instructor of marketing at the University of Kentucky. His professional interests include retail competition, competitive strategies, and marketing theory. He has presented papers at the Academy of Marketing Annual Science Conference and the UIC Symposium on Marketing and Entrepreneurship.

Mr. Keep's prior experience includes working in a trade association for retailers and wholesalers, working for a private wholesale firm, and working in the public sector.

Shelby McIntyre is chairman of the Marketing Department, Santa Clara University. He received a B.S. in Industrial Engineering from Stanford University. He also earned a Master of Business Administration and Doctorate from Stanford University. He teaches marketing research, marketing management, marketing information systems, and brand/product management.

Dr. McIntyre concentrates his academic research in the areas of retail promotions, marketing information systems, marketing research methodology, and decision support systems. He has published over forty articles in refereed academic journals including the *Journal of Marketing Research,* the *Journal of Retailing,* the *Harvard Business Review, Management Science, Organizational Behavior* and *Human Performance,* and the *International Journal of Forecasting.* He is an active member of the American Marketing Association, the Association for Decision and Information Sciences, the Institute of Management Science, and the Association for Consumer Research. He is a frequent session chairman and presenter of papers at the meetings of these organizations.

Dr. McIntyre is also an active business consultant and expert witness in cases of business litigation. He has worked on major research projects for Syntex, Oroweat, AT&T, IBM, Intel, Smith-Kline, Mervyn's Department Stores, and the California Strawberry Advisory Board, among others.

Robert A. Peterson holds the John T. Stuart III Centennial Chair in Business Administration and the Charles C. Hurwitz Fellowship at The University of Texas at Austin. Dr. Peterson is a past chairman of the Department of Marketing Administration at the University of Texas and past editor of the *Journal of Marketing Research.* Presently he serves on five editorial boards and is the editor of the *Journal of the Academy of Marketing Science.* He received his doctorate from the University of Minnesota.

Dr. Peterson has authored or co-authored in excess of 120 articles and books. His publications have appeared in more than three dozen journals, including *Management Science, Journal of Business, Journal of Marketing Research,* and the *Journal of Marketing.* His books and monographs include *Marketing Research, Strategic Marketing Problems* (with Roger A. Kerin), *The Role of Affect in Consumer Behavior* (with Wayne Hoyer and William Wilson), *Models for Innovation Diffusion* (with Vijay Mahajan), and *Modern American Capitalism* (with Gerald Albaum and George Kozmetsky).

Dr. Peterson has received numerous awards and honors. He is a past president of the Southwestern Marketing Association, a former vice president of the American Marketing Association, and has served on the governing boards of the Academy of Marketing Science and the Decision Sciences Institute. He is listed in such standard references as *Who's Who in America*. In 1988 he received the Outstanding Marketing Educator Award from the Academy of Marketing Science. He presently serves on the Direct Selling Education Foundation Board of Directors. Dr. Peterson has extensive consulting experience, having worked with such firms as Emerson Electric, Ford Motor Company, Pactel, and Pillsbury; he frequently testifies as an expert witness in litigation matters.

James E. Preston is chairman of the board and chief executive officer, Avon Products, Inc. He is a 1955 graduate of Northwestern University in Evanston, Illinois. Mr. Preston joined Avon in 1964 as a management trainee in the company's distribution center in Rye, New York. Between 1965 and 1970, he served in varying supervisory and management positions in the marketing and operations areas at the world headquarters in New York City. In 1971, he was elected vice president of corporate personnel, and the following year, group vice president of marketing. He was named group vice president of Field Operations-Worldwide in 1976, and later that year was elected senior vice president of Field Operations-Worldwide.

In 1977, he assumed the responsibilities of corporate executive vice president and was elected to the Board of Directors. In November of 1981, Mr. Preston assumed the additional position of president and chief executive officer of the Avon Division and was named to the corporate management committee. In May of 1988 he was elected president and chief operating officer of the corporation and in September was named chief executive officer. He assumed the additional responsibility of chairman of the board in January, 1989.

Mr. Preston serves on the board of the Cosmetic, Toiletry and Fragrance Association, is a member of the board and treasurer of the Fragrance Foundation, is a director of F. W. Woolworth Co., and serves on the board of the American Institute for Managing Diversity. Mr. Preston also serves on the boards of the Business Council of New York State and the American Women's Economic Development Council. He is a past chairman of the Direct Selling Association and the Direct Selling Education Foundation and served as chairman of the Cosmetic, Toiletry and Fragrance Association. Mr. Preston received the highest honor the direct selling industry can confer when he was inducted into the industry's Hall of Fame.

Don E. Schultz is a professor of advertising and direct marketing and chairman, Strategic Planning Committee, Medill School of Journalism, Northwestern University. Following his graduation from the University of

Oklahoma with a degree in marketing/journalism, Dr. Schultz began his career as a sales promotion writer for trade magazine publishers in Dallas. From there, he moved into publication sales and management, and was advertising director of a daily newspaper in Texas. In 1965, he joined Tracy-Locke Advertising and Public Relations in Dallas. He was with the agency for almost ten years in its Dallas, New York, and Columbus, Ohio, offices as branch manger. He was management supervisor for a number of national consumer product, service, and industrial accounts.

In 1974, Dr. Schultz resigned as senior vice president of Tracy-Locke to launch a career in academia. He obtained his master's degree in advertising and his Ph.D. in mass media from Michigan State University while also teaching in the MSU Department of Advertising. He joined Northwestern in 1977.

Dr. Schultz has consulted, lectured, and held seminars on marketing, sales promotion, advertising management, marketing strategy, and integrated marketing communications in Europe, South America, Asia, and the United States. His articles have appeared in numerous refereed journals and he is the author or coauthor of six books. He is currently working on texts in the field of marketing communications, advertising research, and marketing strategy. He is a regular columnist in the *Journal of Direct Marketing, Marketing News,* and *Outlook,* the publication of the PMAA.

Dr. Schultz is the first editor of the *Journal of Direct Marketing* and *Academic Research in Sales Promotion.* He was selected the first Direct Marketing Educator of the Year by the Direct Marketing Education Foundation. He is chairman of the U.S. Educational Committee of the International Advertising Association. In addition, Dr. Schultz is president of his own marketing, advertising, and consulting firm, Agora, Inc., in Evanston, Illinois.

David Shepard is president of David Shepard Associates, Inc. Mr. Shepard founded David Shepard Associates, Inc., in 1976. Since its inception the company has provided direct marketing and database consulting services to nearly one hundred direct marketing firms, advertising agencies, and Fortune 500 firms. In 1989 the firm won the coveted Gold Mail Box award for its innovative use of direct mail.

The company's list of clients includes such notable firms as American Express, Alcas Cutlery, Avon, the Book-of-the-Month Club, Children's Television Workshop, Grolier Enterprises, General Foods, Philip Morris, Random House Mail Order, Sotheby's, Simon & Schuster, Time-Life Books, US News Video, and WNET. In 1990 Dow Jones-Irwin published *The New Direct Marketing,* the firm's major text on database marketing and statistical analysis. Before starting DSA, Mr. Shepard held senior management positions at Doubleday & Co., Throckmorton & Satin Associates, and the Maxwell Sroge Company. He was chairman of the DMA's Marketing

Council and has spoken on database marketing at the Direct Marketing Symposium in Montreal and at the Bicentennial Direct Marketing Convention in Australia. Mr. Shepard is the 1991 General Chairman of Direct Marketing Day in New York. He is a graduate of CCNY and has an M.B.A. from Columbia University.

Tasadduq A. Shervani is assistant professor at the University of Texas. He received his Bachelor of Commerce degree with honors from Aligarh University in India and his PGDBM degree (equivalent to the M.B.A.) from the Xavier Labor Relations Institute in Jamshedpur, India. His doctorate is from the University of Southern California.

Donald J. Stone recently retired as vice chairman of Federated Department Stores. At Federated he had direct operating responsibility for most of the Department Stores Division (including Bloomingdale's and Foley's) plus Ralph's Groceries and Filene's Basement from 1980 to 1988. From 1975 to 1980 he was chairman and CEO of Sanger Harris in Dallas and before that held various positions in merchandising with Foley's in Houston, including that of vice president and general merchandise manager.

Mr. Stone is a member of the boards of directors of MCorp Bank Holding Company in Dallas, Bloom Companies Advertising Agency, Dallas, XTEK, Inc., Machine Tool Company in Cincinnati, the Dallas Symphony, the Aspen Institute, University of Texas College of Business Administration Advisory Council, Dallas World Salute, and Hebrew Union College in Cincinnati and New York.

Thomas R. Wotruba is professor of marketing at San Diego State University. He received his Ph.D. from the University of Wisconsin and has authored numerous textbooks, professional journal articles, monographs, and other publications. He has been the editor of the *Journal of Personal Selling & Sales Management* and is presently a member of its editorial board. He has served as a consultant to many businesses and government organizations on problems involving sales management, marketing planning, and market research. He has worked with direct selling organizations in consulting assignments, as an expert witness, and as a researcher. He has addressed a meeting of the World Federation of Direct Selling Associations as well as the Direct Selling Association in the United States and has attended and participated in many academic seminars sponsored by the Direct Selling Education Foundation. He recently completed a major study of turnover in direct sales forces under a grant from the Direct Selling Education Foundation.